HENRY HOLT & CO. For the poem "Fire and Ice" by Robert Frost. Copyright © 1923 by Holt, Rinehart & Winston and renewed 1951 by Robert Frost. Reprinted from *The Poetry of Robert Frost,* edited by Edward Connery Lathem, by permission of Henry, Holt & Company, Inc.

NEW YORK TIMES For the entry from the *New York Times Index.* Copyright © 1986 by The New York Times Company. Reprinted by permission.

RANDOM HOUSE For the dictionary entries *empty* and *empty-handed:* reprinted by permission from the *Random House College Dictionary,* Revised Edition, copyright © 1988 by Random House, Inc. For the thesaurus entry *empty:* reprinted by permission from the *Random House Thesaurus,* College Edition, copyright © 1984 by Random House.

SUSAN SUEHRING For the essay "Themes in *Frankenstein.*"

P. RUTH VANDERHOEK For the essay "Hazardous Drivers."

THE H. W. WILSON COMPANY For entries from the *Readers' Guide to Periodical Literature:* March 1985–February 1986, Volume 45, copyright © 1985, 1986 by The H. W. Wilson Company. All material reproduced by permission of the publisher.

In Memory of
MARY E. WHITTEN

PREFACE

The *Harbrace College Handbook* is a compact yet comprehensive guide for writers. Its approach is practical, its advice is clearly and concisely stated, and its purpose is to help students become more effective writers. Abundant, specific examples throughout the book demonstrate the principles of writing that are applicable to both coursework and professional tasks.

The Eleventh Edition is a complete revision of the Tenth Edition. Sections **1–30** have been thoroughly reviewed with current linguistic and rhetorical practice in mind: exposition has been clarified, examples have been set in rhetorical context where possible, and exercises have been rewritten where necessary. Sections **31–35** now give more attention to thinking and writing as a process. For example, the addition of the Toulmin model enhances the treatment of inductive and deductive reasoning in section **31**, and the replacement of many sample paragraphs helps to highlight the strategies of paragraph development in the expanded section **32**. Section **33** features more detailed coverage of the composition process, including the addition of an editing checklist. Section **34** contains greater coverage of both MLA and APA styles of documentation and includes student research papers that illustrate each form. Documentation styles of other disciplines are also discussed in this section. Section **35** has been greatly expanded: in addition to giving students guidance in writing letters and memos and preparing résumés, it now addresses analysis of and writing about literature and provides student essays on works of fiction, poetry, and drama. The glossary also reflects the greater attention given to thinking and writing as a process by now including rhetorical terms.

A four-color design displays the rules and the main structural elements of each section in red; the notes, cautions, and exceptions in yellow to alert the student; and the exercise directions in green. This color format allows the reader to locate the needed information quickly and to differentiate key points from finer points.

These additions to the Eleventh Edition of the Handbook do not overshadow the solid, proven coverage of the previous editions. The time-tested organization of the Handbook, which allows instructors the greatest flexibility in teaching the sections in any order they may choose, is still the same. Overall, however, the revisions demonstrate that the *Harbrace College Handbook* responds to the changing needs of instructors by reflecting the best of current research in rhetoric and composition.

Ancillaries

- Instructor's Manual by Robert K. Miller
- *The Resourceful Writer,* Second Edition (and its Instructor's Manual) by Suzanne S. Webb
- *Harbrace College Workbooks* (and their accompanying Instructor's Editions): Form 11A, "Exploring the Cosmos" by Larry G. Mapp; Form 11B (available in 1991) by Larry G. Mapp; Form 11C, "Writing for the World of Work" by Melissa E. Barth; and *Harbrace ESL Workbook* by Sheila Graham and Wynn J. Curtis
- *The Harbrace Tutor: Self-Correcting Lessons* by J. N. Hook, William H. Evans, and Sally B. Reagan
- Correction Chart
- Transparency Masters

- Test Package (also available on disk) by Alice T. Gasque
- *The Caret Patch* (a study disk) by Sheila Graham and Eileen Evans
- *The Writing Tutor* (word-processing software) by Laurence G. Avery, Erika C. Lindemann, and Joseph S. Wittig
- *PC-Write Lite* (word-processing software)
- *GramPop* and *DocuPop* (online reference software) by T. David Cowart
- Harbrace Grade Calculation Template by Reinhold Schlieper

Acknowledgments We wish to express gratitude to our colleagues who assisted in the development of the Eleventh Edition: Mary K. Allen, *Cameron University;* Anne C. Armstrong, *Walters State Community College;* Christopher Baker, *Lamar University;* Dorothy Bankston, *Louisiana State University;* A. D. Barnes, *Louisiana State University;* Donald E. Barnett, *University of Georgia, Athens;* Conrad S. Bayley, *Glendale Community College;* Lynne Beene, *University of New Mexico;* Art Bervin, *Linn Benton Community College;* Marlene S. Bosanko, *Tacoma Community College;* Allen C. Brock, Jr., *Eastern Kentucky University;* Elaine Brookshire, *Northeast Alabama State Junior College;* Harry M. Brown, *Midwestern State University;* Sara Brown, *Tulsa Junior College;* Therese Brychta, *Truckee Meadows Community College;* Ron Buchanan, *Auburn University, Montgomery;* Mary Buckalew, *University of North Texas;* Ellen A. Burke, *Casper College;* Robert E. Burkhart, *Eastern Kentucky University;* Christopher C. Burnham, *New Mexico State University;* Joan Karner Bush, *University of Michigan, Dearborn;* Sonja H. Cashdan, *East Tennessee State University;* T. A. Chandler, *Dekalb College;* David W. Chapman, *Texas Tech University;* Caro Church, *Tacoma Community Colege;* Paul Cohen, *Southwest Texas State University;* Walter Coppedge, *Virginia Commonwealth University;* Deborah Core, *Eastern Kentucky University;* David M. Cratty, *Cuyahoga Community College;* O. L. Crawford, *Cuyahoga Community College;* Bill Crider, *Alvin Community College;* Charlotte C. Crittenden, *Georgia Southern College;* Martha B. Crowe, *East Tennessee State University;* Alexandra d'Aste-Surcouf, *Clark County Community College;* George Diamond, *Moravian College;* William C. Duckworth, *Memphis State University;* Donald Duffy, *Central State University;* Donald J. Fay, *Kennesaw State College;* Michael Feehan, *University of Texas, Arlington;* Fred H. Fischer, *Imperial Valley College;* Kathy G. Fish, *Cumberland College;* Thomas E. Fish, *Cumberland College;* Frank M. Flack, *Los Angeles Pierce College;* Tom Frazier, *Cumberland College;* Loris D. Galford, *McNeese State University;* Marvin Garrett, *University of Cincinnati;* Pat Ingle Gillis, *Georgia Southern*

College; Jennifer M. Ginn, *North Carolina State University;* Myrna Goldenberg, *Montgomery College;* Donna Gorell, *St. Cloud State University;* Virginia Lowell Grabill, *University of Evansville;* Patricia Graves, *Georgia State University;* L. M. Grow, *Broward Community College;* Dorothy Margaret Guinn, *Florida Atlantic University;* Andrew Harnack, *Eastern Kentucky University;* Elree Harris, *Westminster College of Salt Lake City;* Louise E. Harris, *Northeast Louisiana University;* Richard Harrison, *Kilgore College;* Roberta T. Herrin, *East Tennessee State University;* Donald R. Hettinga, *Calvin College;* Vicki L. Hill, *Southern Methodist University;* Maureen Hoag, *Wichita State University;* Keith Hull, *University of Wyoming;* Robert Inkster, *St. Cloud State University;* Marette Jackson, *University of Central Arkansas;* Peggy Jolly, *University of Alabama, Birmingham;* Douglas Jones, *Jefferson State Community College;* Shirley L. Jones, *Indiana State University;* Francis E. Kearns, *City University of New York;* Sue B. Kelley, *Snead State Junior College;* Marilyn King, *Northeast Alabama State Junior College;* Douglas Kriencke, *Sam Houston State University;* David M. Kvernes, *Southern Illinois University, Carbondale;* Mervin Lane, *Santa Barbara City College;* David Latane, *Virginia Commonwealth University;* Jonathan T. Launt, *Central Piedmont Community College;* Anne LeCroy, *East Tennessee State University;* Nancy M. LeeRiffe, *Eastern Kentucky University;* Ulle Lewes, *Ohio Wesleyan University;* John Lowe, *Louisiana State University;* Robin Magnuson, *Washington State University;* Larry G. Mapp, *Middle Tennessee State University;* Mike Matthews, *Tarrant County Junior College;* Timothy May, *Yuba College;* Charles John McGeever, *Shepherd College;* Joe Medina, *San Diego City College;* Linda H. Meeker, *Ball State University;* Judith L. Merrell, *Community College of Allegheny County, Boyce;* Harry Moore, *John C. Calhoun State Community College;* Lyle W. Morgan, *Pittsburgh State University;* Harriot Murton, *Imperial Valley College;* Paula Nosett, *Vincennes University;* Frank G. Novak, Jr., *Pepperdine University;* Jeremiah O'Dwyer, *Allan Hancock College;* James F. O'Neil, *Edison Community College;* Roger Osterholm, *Embry-Riddle Aeronautical University;* Willene Perkins, *Gadsden State Community College;* Robert C. Petersen, *Middle Tennessee State University;* Linda H. Peterson, *Yale University;* Mary Ellen Pitts, *Memphis State University;* Helmuth C. Poggemiller, *Liberty University;* Joseph Powell, *Central Washington University;* Ruby Jean Powell, *State Technical Institute at Memphis;* James Preston, *Miami Dade Community College South;* James D. Pruitt, *Lewis and Clark Community College;* Joan Reeves, *Northeast State Junior College;* Peter P. Remaley, *Eastern Kentucky University;* Duane H. Roen, *University of Arizona;* B. Alice Rogers, *Nashville State Technical Institute;* Judith Rose, *Los Angeles Trade Technical College;* Paula Ross, *Gadsden State Junior College;* Timothy G. Roufs, *University of Minnesota, Duluth;*

Scott P. Sanders, *University of New Mexico;* Lewis P. Sego, *Indiana State University;* Frances A. Shirley, *Wheaton College;* Margaret Simpson, *San Jacinto College, South;* Rita A. Goodson Singleton, *Southern University;* Jacquie Skrzypiec, *University of Akron;* Sally K. Slocum, *University of Akron;* Hurst Sloniker, *University of Cincinnati;* Carolyn H. Smith, *University of Florida;* Malinda Snow, *Georgia State University;* Herb Stappenbeck, *Gadsden State Community College;* Barbara Stout, *Montgomery College;* Mary Lee Strode, *State Technical Institute at Memphis;* Mary Clare Sweeney, *Arizona State University;* Charles A. Sweet, Jr., *Eastern Kentucky University;* Shirley D. Sykes, *Mesa College;* Margaret W. Taylor, *Cuyahoga Community College;* Robbie Townson, *Snead State Junior College;* John Trimbur, *Worcester Polytechnic Institute;* Carolyn Vaught, *University of Nevada, Reno;* June Verbillion, *Northeastern Illinois University;* Richard Wakefield, *Tacoma Community College;* Irwin Weiser, *Purdue University;* John O. White, *California State University, Fullerton;* Julia Whitsitt, *Texas Tech University;* Frank Wiehs, *Tacoma Community College;* Nancy G. Wilds, *Armed Forces Staff College;* Thomas Willard, *University of Arizona;* Laura Weiss Zlogar, *University of Wisconsin, River Falls*

Our very special thanks go to Robert K. Miller, who worked closely with us in the preparation of the Eleventh Edition. Although he reviewed all stages of the manuscript, he contributed most heavily to section **34**, the revision of which was primarily his responsibility. We also wish to thank Kerri Barton and Don Cox (University of Tennessee, Knoxville), Elaine Lawless (University of Missouri, Columbia), Hugh MacDonald (Texas Christian University), and Larry G. Mapp (Middle Tennessee State University) for their many helpful suggestions. Our work was greatly eased by the help of Mara Battle, Meta Carstarphen, Anne Gervasi, Susie Guymon, Eleanor Ligman, and Betty Kay Seibt (and her daughter, Elizabeth, who tested many of our new ideas).

No set of acknowledgments would be complete without recognition of the staff of Harcourt Brace Jovanovich, who contributed to the quality of the Eleventh Edition: Bill M. Barnett, Marc Boggs, Lynne Bush, Jamie Fidler, Don Fujimoto, Eleanor Garner, Sam Gore, Tom Hall, Stuart Miller, Sarah Helyar Smith, Sandy Steiner, Lisa L. Werries, and Ellen C. Wynn.

Winifred B. Horner
Suzanne S. Webb

CONTENTS

Preface   v

GRAMMAR   1

1   SENTENCE SENSE   2
a Recognizing verbs   3
b Recognizing subjects, objects, complements   5
c Recognizing all parts of speech   10
d Recognizing phrases and subordinate clauses   17
    (1) Phrases used as nouns   18
    (2) Phrases used as modifiers   20
    (3) Subordinate clauses used as nouns   21
    (4) Subordinate clauses used as modifiers   23
e Recognizing main clauses and types of sentences   24

2   SENTENCE FRAGMENTS   28
a Phrases   30
b Subordinate clauses   31

3   COMMA SPLICE AND FUSED SENTENCE   34
a Without coordinating conjunction   35
b Without conjunctive adverb or transitional phrase   38
c In divided quotations   40

4 ADJECTIVES AND ADVERBS 42

a Adverbs 43
b Adjectives as subject or object complements 44
c Comparative and superlative forms 46
  (1) Comparative to denote degree or comparison 46
  (2) Superlative to denote degree or comparison 47
  (3) Avoid double comparatives and superlatives 47
d Awkward use of a noun as an adjective 48
e The double negative 49

5 CASE 51

a Pronouns in compound constructions 53
b Use of a pronoun in its own clause 55
  (1) *Who* or *whoever* as the subject 55
  (2) *Who* or *whom* before *I think, he says* 55
  (3) Pronoun after *than* or *as* 55
c *Whom* for all objects 57
d Possessive case before a gerund 58
e Objective case with an infinitive 59
f Subjective case for the subject complement 59

6 AGREEMENT 61

a Subject and verb 62
  (1) Misleading endings and intervening words 62
  (2) Subjects joined by *and* 63
  (3) Singular subjects joined by *or* or *nor* 63
  (4) Inverted word order; *there* + verb + subject 64
  (5) Relative pronoun as subject 64
  (6) *Each, neither, everyone,* etc., as subject 65
  (7) Collective noun as subject 65
  (8) Subject of linking verb with predicate noun 66
  (9) Titles, words as words, and plural nouns with singular verbs 66
b Pronoun and antecedent; number and gender 68
  (1) *Everyone, each,* etc., as antecedent 68
  (2) Antecedents joined by *and* or by *or, nor* 69
  (3) Collective noun as antecedent 70

Contents

7 VERB FORMS

72

a Misuse of principal parts; confusion of verbs — 77
   (1) Misuse of principal parts — 77
      PRINCIPAL PARTS OF VERBS — 78
   (2) Confusion of *set/sit* and *lay/lie* — 81
b Meaning and sequence of tenses — 82
   (1) Meaning of tense forms — 82
   (2) Logical tense forms in sequence — 84
c Subjunctive mood — 86
   (1) *That* clauses after *demand, suggest,* etc. — 86
   (2) Expression of wishes or hypothetical condition — 87
   (3) Use of *had* in an *if* clause — 87
d Needless shifts in tense or mood — 88

MECHANICS

91

8 MANUSCRIPT FORM

92

a Proper materials — 92
   (1) Handwritten papers — 92
   (2) Typewritten papers — 93
   (3) Word-processed papers — 93
b Clear and orderly arrangement — 93
   (1) Margins — 93
   (2) Indention — 94
   (3) Paging — 94
   (4) Title and heading — 94
   (5) Quoted lines — 94
   (6) Punctuation — 94
   (7) Binding — 95
c Legibility of manuscript — 95
   (1) Handwriting — 95
   (2) Typing or printing — 95
d Word division — 95
   (1) One-letter syllables — 96
   (2) Two-letter endings — 96
   (3) Misleading divisions — 96
   (4) Hyphenated words — 96

(5) *-ing* words 96
(6) Consonants between vowels 97
(7) Abbreviations and acronyms 97
e Careful proofreading and revision 97
(1) Revision and proofreading before submission
to instructor 97
(2) Revision after instructor's corrections 98
A PARAGRAPH MARKED BY AN INSTRUCTOR 99
THE PARAGRAPH BEING REVISED BY THE STUDENT 99
THE PARAGRAPH RESUBMITTED BY THE STUDENT 100
f Keeping a record of revisions 101
g Using a word processor 101

9 CAPITALS 104

a Proper names, derivatives, and shortened forms 105
(1) Names and nicknames, trademarks 105
(2) Geographical names 105
(3) Peoples and their languages 105
(4) Organizations, government agencies, institutions, companies 106
(5) Days of the week, months, holidays 106
(6) Historical documents, periods, events 106
(7) Religions and their adherents, holy books,
holy days, words denoting the Supreme
Being 106
(8) Personifications 106
(9) Words derived from proper names 107
(10) Shortened forms of capitalized words 107
b Titles of persons before the name 107
c Titles of books, plays, student papers, etc. 108
d *I* and *O* 109
e First word of sentence and of quoted speech 109
f Unnecessary capitals 109
STYLE SHEET FOR CAPITALS 110

10 ITALICS 112

a Titles of publications, shows, software programs,
etc. 112
b Foreign words and phrases 113

Contents

c Names of ships, airplanes, satellites, and space-craft   114

d Words, letters, or figures spoken of as such   114

e Emphasized words   115

11   ABBREVIATIONS, ACRONYMS, AND NUMBERS   117

a *Mr., Dr., Jr., MD,* etc.   117

b Names of states, months, units of measurement, etc.   118

POSTAL ABBREVIATIONS   118

c *Street, Park, Mount, Company,* etc.   119

d Book divisions and course names   119

e Acronyms   121

f Numbers   121

PUNCTUATION   125

12   THE COMMA   126

a Before coordinating conjunction linking main clauses   127

b After introductory words, phrases, clauses   129

(1) Adverb clauses before main clauses   130

(2) Introductory phrases before main clauses   130

(3) Introductory transitional expressions, conjunctive adverbs, interjections, and *yes* or *no*   131

c Between items in a series   132

(1) Words, phrases, and clauses   132

(2) Coordinate adjectives   133

d With parenthetical and miscellaneous elements   134

(1) Nonrestrictive clauses, phrases, appositives   134

(2) Contrasted elements, geographical names, dates, and addresses   137

(3) Parenthetical expressions, interjections, words in direct address, absolute phrases   138

e For the prevention of misreading   139

13 SUPERFLUOUS COMMAS 141

a Between subject and verb, verb and object   142
b Misuse with coordinating conjunction   142
c Slightly parenthetical words and phrases   142
d Restrictive clauses, phrases, appositives   143
e First and last items in a series   143

14 THE SEMICOLON 145

a Between main clauses without coordinating conjunction   146
b Between items in a series containing commas   148
c Misuse with parts of unequal rank   149

15 THE APOSTROPHE 152

a Possessive case   152
  (1) Singular nouns and indefinite pronouns   153
  (2) Pural nouns   153
  (3) Last word of compounds   153
  (4) Indicating individual ownership   153
b Omissions in contractions and in numbers   154
c Plurals of lower-case letters and abbreviations   155
d Misuse with pronouns and plural nouns   155

16 QUOTATION MARKS 157

a Direct quotations and dialogue; indention of long quotations   157
  (1) Double and single quotation marks   157
  (2) Dialogue   158
  (3) Long quotations of prose and poetry   159
b Minor titles and subdivisions of books   161
c Words used in a special sense   162
d Overuse   162
e Placement with other marks of punctuation   163
  (1) Period and comma   163
  (2) Colon and semicolon   163
  (3) Question mark, exclamation point, dash   164

Contents

17 THE PERIOD AND OTHER MARKS   **165**

  a The period   166
    (1) Declarative sentence, mildly imperative sentence   166
    (2) Some abbreviations   166
  b The question mark   167
  c The exclamation point   168
  d The colon   168
    (1) For an explanation or summary, a series, or a quotation   169
    (2) For time, between titles and subtitles   169
    (3) Superfluous use   170
  e The dash   171
    (1) For sudden break in thought, abrupt change in tone, or faltering speech   171
    (2) For emphasis of a parenthetical element   171
    (3) After an introductory list or series   172
  f Parentheses   172
  g Brackets   173
  h The slash   174
  i Ellipsis points   175
    (1) For an omission within a quoted passage   175
    (2) For a reflective pause or hesitation   177

SPELLING AND DICTION   **179**

18 SPELLING AND HYPHENATION   **180**

  a Mispronunciation   181
  b Words of similar sound   182
    WORDS FREQUENTLY CONFUSED   183
  c Prefixes and roots   184
  d Adding suffixes   185
    (1) Dropping or retaining a final unpronounced *e*   185
    (2) Doubling a final consonant before a suffix   186
    (3) Changing or retaining a final *y* before a suffix   186
    (4) Retaining a final *l* before *-ly*   187

Contents

21 WORDINESS AND NEEDLESS REPETITION 240

a Meaningless words and phrases 241
(1) Tautologies 241
(2) Unnecessary words 241
(3) Unnecessary expletive constructions 242
b Revising to eliminate wordiness 243
c Needless repetition 245
d Revising to eliminate needless repetition 246

22 OMISSION OF NECESSARY WORDS 248

a Articles, pronouns, conjunctions, prepositions 248
(1) Articles and pronouns 248
(2) Conjunctions and prepositions 249
b Verbs and auxiliaries 250
c Words needed to complete comparisons 251
d Phrases or clauses after *so, such, too* 252

EFFECTIVE SENTENCES 253

23 SENTENCE UNITY 254

a Clear relationship of ideas 254
b Excessive or poorly ordered detail 255
c Mixed metaphors and mixed constructions 256
(1) Mixed metaphors 256
(2) Mixed constructions 257
d Faulty predication 257
e Awkward definitions 258
(1) Faulty *is-when, is-where, is-because* constructions 258
(2) Clear, precise definitions 259

24 SUBORDINATION AND COORDINATION 261

a Combining short, related sentences 262
(1) Adjectives and adjective phrases 263
(2) Adverbs and adverb phrases 263

(5) Adding -*s* or -*es* to form plurals of nouns — 187
e Confusion of *ei* and *ie* — 188
WORDS FREQUENTLY MISSPELLED — 189
f Hyphenation — 195
   (1) For words serving as single adjective — 195
   (2) With spelled out compound numbers — 196
   (3) To avoid ambiguity or an awkward combination of letters or syllables — 196
   (4) With certain prefixes and suffixes, between a prefix and a capitalized word — 197

19   GOOD USAGE AND GLOSSARY   198

  a Dictionary use — 199
    (1) Spelling, syllabication, pronunciation — 200
    (2) Parts of speech and inflected forms — 200
    (3) Definitions and examples of usage — 201
    (4) Synonyms and antonyms — 201
    (5) Origin: Development of the language — 202
    (6) Special usage labels — 207
  b Informal words — 207
  c Newly coined words and slang — 208
  d Regional words — 209
  e Nonstandard words and usages — 210
  f Archaic and obsolete words — 210
  g Technical words and jargon — 210
  h Overwriting, ornate style, distracting combinations of sounds — 211
  i **Glossary of Usage** — 212

20   EXACTNESS   227

  a Exact words — 228
    (1) Precise denotation — 228
    (2) Appropriate connotation — 229
    (3) Specific and concrete words — 231
    (4) Figurative language — 233
  b Idiomatic expressions — 235
  c Fresh expressions — 236

(3) Appositives and contrasting elements 263
(4) Subordinate clauses 264
b Subordinating and coordinating clauses 264
(1) Subordinating compound sentences 265
(2) Coordinating to give ideas equal emphasis 265
(3) Faulty or illogical coordination 266
c Avoiding faulty or excessive subordination 266

25 MISPLACED PARTS, DANGLING MODIFIERS
269

a Needless separation of related sentence parts 269
(1) Placement of single-word modifiers 269
(2) Placement of prepositional phrases 270
(3) Placement of adjective clauses 270
(4) Avoidance of "squinting" constructions 271
(5) Separation of sentence base; split infinitives 271
b Dangling modifiers 272
(1) Participial phrases 272
(2) Phrases containing gerunds and infinitives 272
(3) Elliptical adverb clauses 273

26 PARALLELISM
274

a Balance of words, phrases, clauses, sentences 275
(1) Words and phrases 275
(2) Clauses 276
(3) Sentences 276
b Repetition of a preposition, an article, etc. 277
c Correlatives 278

27 SHIFTS
280

a In tense, mood, voice 280
b In person and number 281
c From indirect to direct discourse 282
d In tone or style 282
e In perspective or viewpoint 283

28 REFERENCE OF PRONOUNS
285

a Ambiguous reference 286
b Remote or awkward reference 286

Contents

c Broad or implied reference — 287
(1) Expressed ideas — 288
(2) Implied words and ideas — 288
d Awkward use of *you* or *it* — 288

29 EMPHASIS — 291

a Placement of important words — 291
b Periodic sentences — 292
c Ascending order of climax — 294
d Active voice and forceful verbs — 295
(1) Active voice versus passive voice — 295
(2) Action verb or forceful linking verb versus forms of *have* and *be* — 295
e Repeating important words — 296
f Inverting word order — 297
g Balancing sentence construction — 298
h Changing sentence length — 298

30 VARIETY — 300

a Sentence length — 301
b Sentence beginnings — 303
(1) Adverb or adverb clause — 303
(2) Prepositional phrase or verbal phrase — 303
(3) Sentence connectives — 303
(4) Appositives, absolute phrases, introductory series — 304
c Avoiding loose, stringy compound sentences — 306
(1) Compound sentences made into complex — 306
(2) Compound predicates in simple sentences — 306
(3) Appositives in simple sentences — 306
(4) Prepositional and verbal phrases in simple sentences — 306
d Varying conventional subject-verb sequence — 307
e Question, exclamation, or command — 308

LARGER ELEMENTS — 311

31 LOGICAL THINKING — 312

a Inductive reasoning — 312
b Deductive reasoning — 314

c Common fallacies 318
  (1) *Non sequitur* 318
  (2) Hasty generalization 319
  (3) *Ad hominem* 319
  (4) Bandwagon. 319
  (5) Red herring 319
  (6) *Either . . . or* fallacy 319
  (7) False analogy 319
  (8) Equivocation 320
  (9) Slippery slope 320
  (10) Oversimplification 320
  (11) Begging the question 320
  (12) False cause 320

32 THE PARAGRAPH   **322**

a Unity 324
  (1) Sentences related to the central thought 324
  (2) Main idea stated in topic sentence 325
b Coherence and transitions 329
  (1) Clear, logical order 329
  (2) Pronouns as links 335
  (3) Repetition of words, phrases, ideas 336
  (4) Conjunctions and other transitional expressions 336
  (5) Parallel structures 337
  (6) Transitions between paragraphs 339
c Adequate development 341
  (1) Specific details 342
  (2) Examples 343
d Strategies of paragraph development 344
  (1) Narration 344
  (2) Description 345
  (3) Process 347
  (4) Cause and effect 347
  (5) Comparison and contrast 349
  (6) Classification and division 350
  (7) Definition 352

33 THE WHOLE COMPOSITION   **356**

a Considering purpose, audience, occasion 359
b Finding an appropriate subject 366

c Exploring and focusing the subject   368
  (1) Exploring   368
  (2) Limiting and focusing   372
d Formulating a focused, directed thesis   373
e Choosing methods for arranging ideas   377
  INFORMAL WORKING PLANS   377
  OUTLINES   379
  CLASSICAL ARRANGEMENT   381
f Writing the first draft   382
  (1) Effective introductions   383
  (2) Effective conclusions   386
  (3) Appropriate titles   388
g Revising and editing   389
  REVISER'S CHECKLIST   390
  EDITING CHECKLIST   392
  AN ESSAY UNDERGOING REVISION   393
h Writing under pressure   400
  (1) Essay tests   400
  (2) In-class essays   403

34   THE RESEARCH PAPER   **405**

a Choosing and limiting a subject   406
b Finding library materials, preparing a bibliography   408
  (1) Books and periodicals   408
  (2) Nonprint sources   417
  (3) Evaluating sources   418
  (4) Preparing a working bibliography   418
c Taking notes on sources   420
d Making working plans or outlines   423
e Using sources responsibly   423
  (1) Plagiarism   424
  (2) Direct quotations   425
  (3) Paraphrase   426
  (4) Summary   428
f MLA style documentation   429
  (1) Parenthetical citations   429
  (2) Works cited   436
    SAMPLE BIBLIOGRAPHICAL ENTRIES   438
    COMMON ABBREVIATIONS   447

(3) Revisions and proofreading 449
SAMPLE RESEARCH PAPER IN MLA STYLE 451
FOOTNOTES AND ENDNOTES 480
g APA style documentation 483
SAMPLE RESEARCH PAPER IN APA STYLE 489
h Documentation style according to discipline 504
STYLE BOOKS AND MANUALS 504

35 WRITING FOR SPECIAL PURPOSES 506

a Reading and writing about literature 507
(1) Principles of good writing 507
(2) Reading with care 508
(3) Analyzing, interpreting, evaluating 509
(4) Choosing and developing a subject 510
(5) Writing about fiction 511
SAMPLE STUDENT PAPER ABOUT FICTION 517
(6) Writing about poetry 521
SAMPLE STUDENT PAPER ABOUT POETRY 525
(7) Writing about drama 529
SAMPLE STUDENT PAPER ABOUT DRAMA 531
(8) Using proper form 536
b Writing effective letters, résumés, memos, and reports 538
(1) Letters and résumés 538
(2) Memos 547
(3) Reports 549

GLOSSARY OF GRAMMATICAL AND RHETORICAL TERMS 551

INDEX I-1

GRAMMAR

Sentence Sense 1

Sentence Fragments 2

Comma Splice and Fused Sentence 3

Adjectives and Adverbs 4

Case 5

Agreement 6

Verb Forms 7

1
SENTENCE SENSE

Master the essentials of the sentence as an aid to clear thinking and effective writing.

Writing a good sentence is an art, and you can master that art by developing your awareness of what makes a sentence work. Your familiarity with English may already enable you to recognize an awkward or incorrect sentence. This handbook is designed to help you understand why some of your writing may not work and how you can improve it. As you become more familiar with the relationships among sentence elements, you will be strengthening your writing skills and will be better able to make your meaning clear to your reader.

The two essential elements of the English sentence are the *subject* and the *predicate*. (For explanations of any unfamiliar terms, see **Grammatical and Rhetorical Terms**, beginning on page 551.) In each of the following sentences, a plus sign connects the first part of the sentence—the complete subject (the simple subject and all the words associated with it)—with the second part—the complete predicate (the verb and all the words associated with it).

The word-processing **software + has arrived** safely.
The **attendant +** cheerfully **washed** my windshield.
These **forms + should have been ordered** in January.
The **tomato + is** a fruit. **It + tastes** good in salads.

The pattern of these sentences is **SUBJECT + PREDI-
CATE**, the basic order of English sentences.

1a

Learn to recognize verbs.

A verb functions as the predicate of a sentence or as an
essential part of the predicate.

SUBJECT + PREDICATE.
Martin   **swims.**
Martin   usually **swims** a mile every day.

Predicates may be compound:

Martin usually **swims** a mile every morning and still **arrives**
at the office by eight.   [compound predicate]

You can learn to recognize a verb by observing its *meaning* and its *form.* Often defined as a word expressing action,
occurrence, or existence (a state of being), a verb is used to
make a statement, to ask a question, or to give a command
or direction.

They **moved** to Atlanta.   **Is** this true?
The rain **stopped.**   **Consider** the options.

In the present tense, all verbs change form to indicate a
singular subject in the third person: *I ask—she asks; we
eat—she eats.* When converted from the present to the
past tense, nearly all verbs change form: *ask—asked; eat—
ate.* (See also section **7**.)

PRESENT TENSE		PAST TENSE
I **run**. Wayne **runs**.		I **ran**.
You **wait**. He **waits**.		We **waited**.
We **quit**. She **quits**.	BUT	She **quit**.

When used with *have, has,* or *had,* most verbs end in *-d* or *-ed* (*have moved, had played*), but some have a special ending (*has eaten*). Used with a form of *be,* all progressive verbs end in *-ing,* as in *was eating.*

Tom **has moved**.	They **have taken** the tests.
He **is moving**.	We **had been taking** lessons.

As these examples show, a verb may consist of two or more words. Such a unit follows the pattern **auxiliary + verb**. Since auxiliaries, or helping verbs, precede the verb, they are often called *verb markers.* (See section **7**.)

> The fight **had started**.   He **will be studying** late.
> Amy **ought to decide** now.   [Compare "Amy *should decide* now."]

Other words may intervene between the auxiliary and the verb:

> **Have** the members **paid** their dues? I **have** not **paid** mine.
> Television **will** never completely **replace** the radio.

Although not a verb, the contraction for *not* may be added to many auxiliaries: *haven't, doesn't, aren't, can't.* The full word *not* following an auxiliary is written separately; an exception is *cannot.*

Phrasal verbs   Sometimes a verb combines with a particle such as *across, away, down, for, in, off, out, up,* or *with* to create a meaning different from that of the verb as a single word. For example, the meaning of the verb *turned,* even when the adverb *out* occurs nearby, is different from the meaning of the combination *turned out.*

Stan **blew up** the balloon.   [single-word verb and adverb]
The rocket **blew up**.   [phrasal verb]
I **put** her picture **up** with tape.   [single-word verb and adverb]
I **put up** with the noise.   [phrasal verb]
I **called off** the engagement.   [phrasal verb with direct object]

These combined forms, called *phrasal verbs,* function grammatically in exactly the same ways that single-word verbs do.

■ **Exercise 1**   Underline the verbs (including any auxiliaries and particles) in the following sentences (adapted from *Reader's Digest*).

1. Developing nations are now facing many serious difficulties.
2. The flock of wheeling birds descended.
3. The fire gobbled up some of the most expensive real estate on earth.
4. Parts of the wreckage may never be found.
5. Philip's manner has given his statements the force of commands.
6. Is exercise important for healthy hearts and lungs?
7. There are approximately ten million college students.
8. His own political history makes his new attitude uncompromising.
9. Gnats and small flies invade the sheath and pollinate the blossoms.
10. He pushed the bike away from the rack, grasped the handlebars firmly, and swung his leg over the bar.

1b

Learn to recognize subjects, objects, and complements.

SUBJECTS OF VERBS

All grammatically complete sentences, except for imperatives (which are commands or requests in which the subject, *you,* is understood), contain stated subjects of verbs. In the following sentences, the subjects are in boldface, and the verbs are in italics.

Louisiana *produces* delicious yams.
Doesn't **North Carolina** also *grow* yams?

Take, for example, Louisiana and North Carolina.
[imperative]

Subjects of verbs may be compound:

Louisiana and **North Carolina** grow yams.
[compound subject]

To identify the grammatical subject of a sentence, first find the verb; then use the verb in a question beginning with *who* or *what* as shown in the following examples:

The two dogs in the cage barked.	The shack was built by Al.
Verb: **barked**	Verb: **was built**
WHO or WHAT barked? **The dogs** (not the cage) **barked**.	WHAT was built? **The shack** (not Al) **was built**.
Subject: **dogs**	Subject: **shack**

Subjects of verbs are nouns or pronouns (or word groups serving as nouns). See **1c**.

Subjects usually precede verbs in sentences. Common exceptions to the *subject + verb* pattern occur when subjects are used in questions and after the expletive *there* (which is never the subject).

Was the **statement** true?   [verb + subject]
Did these **refugees survive**?   [auxiliary + subject + verb]
There **were** no **objections**.   [expletive + verb + subject]

OBJECTS OF VERBS

Verbs denoting action often require objects to complete the meaning of the predicate. When they do so they are called *transitive* verbs. See section **7**, page 76. In the following sentences, the objects are in boldface.

The clerk sold **him** the expensive **briefcase**.   [direct object: *briefcase*—indirect object: *him*]
Kay met the **mayor** and his **wife**.   [compound direct object]

Like the subjects of verbs, direct and indirect objects of verbs are generally nouns or pronouns.

To identify a direct object, find the subject and the verb; then use them in a question ending with *whom* or *what* as shown in the following example:

Karen completely ignored the reporters.
Subject and verb: **Karen ignored**
Karen ignored WHOM or WHAT? **reporters**
Direct object: **reporters**

Notice that direct objects in sentences like the following are directly affected by the action of the verb.

A tornado leveled a city in West Texas.   [*Tornado,* the subject, acts. *City,* the object, receives the action.]

Knowing how to change an active verb to the passive voice can also help you to identify an object, since the object of an active verb can usually be made the subject of a passive verb. See section **7**, page 76.

ACTIVE   The Eagles finally **defeated** the **Lions**.
    [*Lions* is the direct object of *defeated.*]
PASSIVE   The **Lions were** finally **defeated** by the Eagles.
    [*Lions* is the subject of *were defeated.*]

Notice that a form of *be* (such as *is, are, was*) is added when an active verb is changed to a passive.

Some verbs (such as *give, offer, bring, take, lend, send, buy,* and *sell*) may have both a direct object and an indirect object. An indirect object generally states *to whom* or *for whom* (or *to what* or *for what*) something is done.

Richard sent Audrey an invitation.
Subject + verb + direct object: **Richard sent invitation**
Richard sent an invitation TO WHOM? **Audrey**
Indirect object: **Audrey**

■ **Exercise 2**   Circle the subjects of the verbs in Exercise 1 on page 5. Then put a wavy line under all nine direct objects and the indirect object.

SUBJECT AND OBJECT COMPLEMENTS

Nouns, pronouns, and adjectives are used as subject and object complements. See **1c** for a discussion of the forms of nouns, pronouns, and adjectives. A **subject complement** refers to, identifies, or qualifies the subject. Subject complements help to complete the meaning of intransitive linking verbs (*be* and forms of *be: am, is, are, was, were, been;* verbs like *be: seem, become;* and the sensory verbs: *feel, look, smell, sound, taste,* and so on). See section **7**.

> Diane is my **partner**.   [*Partner* identifies *Diane,* the subject.]
> Several tourists became **homesick**.   [*Homesick* describes or qualifies *tourists,* the subject.]

An **object complement** refers to, identifies, or qualifies the direct object. Object complements help to complete the meaning of verbs such as *make, name, elect, call, paint*.

> We elected Judy **president**.
> The flaw made it **worthless**.

▲ Note: Subjects, verbs, direct and indirect objects of verbs, subject complements, and object complements may be compound.

> She likes **peas** and **spinach**.   [compound direct object]
> They sent **Elyse** and **Mike** complimentary tickets.   [compound indirect object]
> The cathedrals are **old** and **famous**.   [compound subject complement]
> They will name the baby **Jude** or **Judith**.   [compound object complement]

Word order   Becoming thoroughly aware of English word order—usually **SUBJECT + VERB + OBJECT** or **COMPLEMENT**—will help you recognize subjects, objects, and complements. Study carefully the five most commonly used sentence patterns, observing the importance of word order—especially in pattern 2—in determining meaning.

PATTERN 1

SUBJECT + VERB.

The **children did** not **listen**.
The **lights** on the patrol car **flashed** ominously.

PATTERN 2

SUBJECT + VERB + OBJECT.

Mice frighten elephants.
Elephants frighten mice.
Our **team won** the gold **medal**.

PATTERN 3

SUBJECT + VERB + INDIRECT OBJECT + DIRECT OBJECT.

Mark showed George the **map**.
The **company will** probably **send me** a small **refund**.

In some sentences—especially questions—the direct object does not always take the position indicated by these basic patterns.

What **medal** did our team win?
[direct object + auxiliary + subject + verb]

PATTERN 4

SUBJECT + LINKING VERB + SUBJECT COMPLEMENT.

My son's **name is Aaron**.
The **fence was white**.

PATTERN 5

> ## SUBJECT + VERB + DIRECT OBJECT + OBJECT COMPLEMENT.

I **named** my son Aaron.
I **painted** the fence white.

■ **Exercise 3** Label all subjects and objects of verbs, indirect objects, subject complements, and object complements in the quotations below. Be prepared to discuss the basic sentence patterns (and any variations) and the types of verbs used.

1. An idea has built a nation. —NORMAN FORD
2. Inventions are the hallmark of mankind. —JAKE PAGE
3. Art and games need rules, conventions, and spectators.
   —MARSHALL McLUHAN
4. Sensible people find nothing useless. —LA FONTAINE
5. In the *Odyssey,* Homer gives us detailed information of wind and stars. —MAURICIO OBREGÓN
6. We must put down our old industrial tasks and pick up the tasks of the future. —JOHN NAISBITT
7. There is no little enemy. —BENJAMIN FRANKLIN
8. The multitude of books is making us ignorant. —VOLTAIRE
9. America has not always been kind to its artists and scholars.
   —LYNDON B. JOHNSON
10. Modern English, especially written English, is full of bad habits which spread by imitation and which can be avoided if one is willing to take the necessary trouble. —GEORGE ORWELL

1c

Learn to recognize all the parts of speech.

Understanding the function of a word in a sentence and recognizing its form are both essential for recognizing its part of speech. The chart that follows shows the relationship between parts of speech, form, and function.

Attentive waiters usually offered us refills at Joe's cafe.

	FORM	FUNCTION	PART OF SPEECH
Attentive	-*ive* ending	modifier	adjective
waiters	-*s* (plural)	subject	noun
usually	-*ly* ending	modifier	adverb
offered	-*ed* (past tense)	verb of predicate	verb
us	objective case	indirect object	pronoun
refills	plural	direct object	noun
at	invariable	connector	preposition
Joe's	's (possessive)	modifier	noun
cafe	singular	object of preposition	noun

Notice here that one part of speech—the noun (a naming word that forms the plural with -*s* and the possessive with '*s*)—is used as a subject, a direct object, a modifier, and an object of a preposition.

A dictionary labels words according to their part of speech. Some words have only one classification—for example, *notify* (verb), *sleepy* (adjective), *practically* (adverb). Other words have more than one label because they can function as two or more parts of speech. Each classification depends upon the use of a word in a given sentence. The word *living*, for instance, is first treated as a form of the verb *live* (as in *are living*) and is then listed separately and defined as an adjective (*a living example*) and as a noun (*makes a living*). Another example is the word *up*:

They dragged the sled **up** the hill.   [preposition]
She follows the **ups** and downs of the market.   [noun]
"They **have upped** the rent again," he complained.   [verb]
Kelly **ran up** the bill.   [part of phrasal verb]
The **up** escalator is jerking again.   [adjective]
Hopkins says to look **up**, to "look **up** at the skies!"   [adverb]

Words are traditionally grouped into eight classes or parts of speech: *verbs, nouns, pronouns, adjectives, adverbs, prepositions, conjunctions*, and *interjections*. Verbs, nouns, adjectives, and adverbs (called vocabulary or lexical words) make up more than 99 percent of all words listed in the dictionary. But pronouns, prepositions, and conjunctions—although small in number—are important because they are used over and over in our speaking and writing. Prepositions and conjunctions (called function or structure words) connect and relate other parts of speech.

Of the eight word classes, only three—prepositions, conjunctions, and interjections—do not change their form. For a summary of the form changes of the other parts of speech, see **inflection**, page 562.

Carefully study the forms and functions of each of the eight parts of speech listed on the following pages. For additional examples or more detailed information, see the corresponding entries in **Grammatical and Rhetorical Terms**, beginning on page 551.

VERBS   *notify, notifies, is notifying, notified*
             write, writes, is writing, wrote, has written

A verb functions as the predicate of a sentence or as an essential part of the predicate: see **1a**.

> Herman **writes**.   He **has written** five poems.
> He **is** no longer **writing** those dull stories.

Two suffixes frequently used to make verbs are *-ize* and *-ify*:

> *terror* (noun)—*terrorize, terrify* (verbs)

▲ Note: Verbals (infinitives, participles, and gerunds) cannot function as the predicate of a sentence: see **1d**, pages 17–19.

NOUNS   *nation, nations; nation's, nations'*
             woman, women; kindness, kindnesses

Carthage, United States, William, NASA
the money, an understanding, a breakthrough

Nouns function as subjects, objects, complements, appositives, and modifiers, as well as in direct address and in absolute constructions. See **noun**, page 565. Nouns name persons, places, things, ideas, animals, and so on. The articles *a, an,* and *the* signal that a noun is to follow (a *chair,* an *activity,* the last *race*).

McKinney drives a **truck** for the **Salvation Army**.

Suffixes frequently used to make nouns are *-ance, -ation, -ence, -ism, -ity, -ment, -ness,* and *-ship.*

relax, depend (verbs)—*relaxation, dependence* (nouns)
kind, rigid (adjectives)—*kindness, rigidity* (nouns)

▲ Note: Words such as *father-in-law, Labor Day, swimming pool,* and *breakthrough* are generally classified as *compound nouns.*

PRONOUNS   *I, me, my, mine, myself; you, your, yours, yourself*
he, him, his; she, her, hers; it, its
we, us, our; they, them, their
this, these; who, whom, whose; which, that
one, ones; everybody, anyone

Pronouns may substitute for nouns in sentences. They change form according to their function (see section **5**).

They bought **it** for **her**.   **Everyone** knows **that**.

ADJECTIVES   *shy, sleepy, attractive, famous, historic*
three men, this class, another one
young, younger, youngest; good, better, best

The articles *a, an,* and *the* are variously classified as adjectives, determiners, or function words. Adjectives modify or qualify nouns and pronouns (and sometimes gerunds). Adjectives are generally placed near the words they modify.

> **These difficult** decisions, whether **right** or **wrong**, affect all of us.
> **Competitive** runners look **healthy**.

In the second of these two examples, *healthy* is a predicate adjective (subject complement), a word that modifies the subject and helps to complete the meaning of a linking verb (*be, am, is, are, was, were, been, seem, become, feel, look, smell, sound, taste,* and so on): see **4b**.

Suffixes such as *-al, -able, -ant, -ative, -ic, -ish, -less, -ous,* and *-y* may be added to certain verbs or nouns to form adjectives:

> *accept, repent* (verbs)—*acceptable, repentant* (adjectives)
> *angel, effort* (nouns)—*angelic, effortless* (adjectives)

ADVERBS *rarely* saw, call *daily, soon* left, left *sooner*
very short, *too* angry, *never* shy, *not* fearful
practically never loses, *nearly always* cold

As the examples show, adverbs modify verbs, adjectives, and other adverbs. In addition, an adverb may modify a verbal, a phrase, a clause, or even the rest of the sentence in which it appears:

> I noticed a plane **slowly** circling overhead.
> **Honestly**, Ben did catch a big shark.

The *-ly* ending nearly always converts adjectives to adverbs:

> *rare, honest* (adjectives)—*rarely, honestly* (adverbs)

PREPOSITIONS *on* a shelf, *between* us, *because of* rain,
to the door, *by* them, *before* class

A preposition always has an object, which is usually a noun or a pronoun. The preposition establishes a relationship such as space, time, accompaniment, cause, or manner between its object and another word in the sentence. The preposition with its object (and any modifiers) is called a *prepositional phrase*.

Byron expressed **with great force** his love **of liberty**.

The preposition may follow rather than precede its object, and it can be placed at the end of the sentence:

What was he complaining **about**? [*What* is the object of the preposition.]

Words commonly used as prepositions:

about	besides	inside	since
above	between	into	through
across	beyond	like	throughout
after	but	near	till
against	by	of	to
along	concerning	off	toward
among	despite	on	under
around	down	onto	underneath
at	during	out	until
before	except	outside	up
behind	excepting	over	upon
below	for	past	with
beneath	from	regarding	within
beside	in	round	without

Phrasal prepositions (two or more words):

according to	by way of	in spite of
along with	due to ˙	instead of
apart from	except for	on account of
as for	in addition to	out of
as regards	in case of	up to
as to	in front of	with reference to
because of	in lieu of	with regard to
by means of	in place of	with respect to
by reason of	in regard to	with the exception of

CONJUNCTIONS

cars *and* trucks, in the boat *or* on the pier

will try *but* may lose, *neither* Amy *nor* Bill

I worked, *for* Dad needed money.

The river rises *when* the snow melts.

Conjunctions serve as connectors. The coordinating conjunctions (*and, but, or, nor, for, so,* and *yet*), as well as the correlatives (*both–and, either–or, neither–nor, not only–but also, whether–or*), connect sentence elements (words, phrases, or clauses) of equal grammatical rank. See also section **26**. The subordinating conjunctions (such as *because, if, since, till, when, where, while*) connect subordinate clauses with main clauses: see **1d**, pages 21–24.

▲ Note: Words like *consequently, however, nevertheless, then,* and *therefore* (see the list on page 39) are used as conjunctive adverbs (or adverbial conjunctions):

Don seemed bored in class; **however**, he did listen and learn.

INTERJECTIONS *Wow! Oh,* that's a surprise.

Interjections are exclamations. They may be followed by an exclamation point or by a comma.

■ **Exercise 4** Using your dictionary as an aid if you wish, classify each word in the following sentences according to its part of speech. Then, using one word from each of these sentences as a different part of speech, write five sentences of your own.

1. He struts with the gravity of a frozen penguin. —TIME
2. Neither intelligence nor integrity can be imposed by law.
   —CARL BECKER
3. They pick a President and then for four years they pick on him.
   —ADLAI STEVENSON

4. Of all persons, adolescents are the most intensely personal; their intensity is often uncomfortable to adults.
—EDGAR Z. FRIEDENBERG

5. We can remember minutely and precisely only the things which never really happened to us. —ERIC HOFFER

1d

Learn to recognize phrases and subordinate clauses.

Observe how a short simple sentence may be expanded by adding modifiers, not only single words but also word groups that function as adjectives or adverbs.

The hijacked plane has landed.   [subject (noun phrase) + predicate (verb phrase)]

Expansion:

The **first** hijacked plane has landed **safely**.   [single-word modifiers added]

The first hijacked plane **to arrive at this airport** has landed safely **on the south runway**.   [phrases added]

The first hijacked plane **that we have ever seen** at this airport has landed safely on the south runway, **which has been closed to traffic for a year**.   [subordinate clauses added]

A word group used as a single part of speech (noun, verb, adjective, or adverb) is either a phrase or a subordinate clause.

PHRASES

A phrase is a sequence of grammatically related words without a subject, a predicate, or both.

the hijacked plane   [noun phrase—no predicate]

has landed   [verb phrase—no subject]

at this airport, on the south runway, to traffic, for a year
[prepositional phrases—neither subject nor predicate]

Pete, *my brother* [appositive phrase—neither subject nor predicate]

For a list of types of phrases with examples, see **phrase**, page 568.

As you learn to recognize phrases, give special attention to verb forms in word groups used as a noun, an adjective, or an adverb. Such verb forms (called *verbals* and classified as participles, gerunds, and infinitives) are much like verbs in that they have different tenses, can take subjects and objects, and can be modified by adverbs. However, they cannot function as the predicate of a sentence.

VERBAL PHRASES IN SENTENCES

Shoppers **milling around** did not buy much. [participial phrase (see page 567) modifying the noun *shoppers*]

Some people win arguments by **just remaining silent**. [gerund phrase (page 561), object of the preposition *by*]

The group arrived in a van **loaded with heavy equipment**. [participial phrase modifying the noun *van*]

Vernon went to Boston **to visit relatives**. [infinitive phrase (see page 562) modifying the verb *went*]

As the examples illustrate, participial, gerund, and infinitive phrases function as single parts of speech and are therefore only parts of sentences.

(1) Phrases used as nouns

VERBAL PHRASES

Gerund phrases are always used as nouns. Infinitive phrases are often used as nouns (although they may also function as modifiers). Occasionally a prepositional phrase serves as a noun (as in "*After supper* is too late!").

NOUNS	PHRASES USED AS NOUNS
The **decision** is important.	**Choosing a major** is important. [gerund phrase—subject]
She likes the **job**.	She likes **to do the work**. [infinitive phrase—direct object]
He uses my room for **storage**.	He uses my room for **storing his auto parts**. [gerund phrase—object of a preposition]
He wants two things: **money** and **power**.	He wants two things: **to make money** and **to gain power**. [infinitive phrases in a compound appositive—see page 53]

APPOSITIVE PHRASES

An appositive phrase identifies, explains, or supplements the meaning of a noun it adjoins.

> Johnny cake, **a kind of cornbread**, is native to New England. Anthony Burgess, **one of the most prolific writers in the English-speaking world**, admits, "I might revise a page twenty times." —DONALD M. MURRAY

■ **Exercise 5** Underline the gerund phrases and the infinitive phrases (including any modifiers) used as nouns in the following sentences. Put a wavy line under any appositives.

1. Taking criticism from others is painful but useful.
2. Angry and proud, Claire resolved to fight back.
3. Running down a crowded sidewalk, the boy, a danger to everyone, collided with a dignified gentleman in uniform.
4. Merely to argue for the preservation of parkland is not enough.
5. All human acts—even saving a stranger from drowning or donating a million dollars to the poor—may be ultimately selfish.

(2) Phrases used as modifiers

Prepositional phrases nearly always function as adjectives or adverbs. Infinitive phrases are also used as adjectives or adverbs. Participial phrases are used as adjectives. Absolute phrases are used as adverbs. See also **sentence modifier**, page 572.

ADJECTIVES

It was a **sorrowful** day.

Appropriate language is best.

Destructive storms lashed the Midwest.

The **icy** bridge was narrow.

PHRASES USED AS ADJECTIVES

It was a day **of sorrow**. [prepositional phrase]

Language **to suit the occasion** is best. [infinitive phrase]

Destroying many crops of corn and oats, storms lashed the Midwest. [participial phrase containing a prepositional phrase]

The bridge **covered with ice** was narrow. [participial phrase containing a prepositional phrase]

ADVERBS

Drive **carefully**.

I nodded **respectfully**.

Therefore, I could feel the warm sun on my face.

PHRASES USED AS ADVERBS

Drive **with care on wet streets**. [prepositional phrases]

I nodded **to show respect**. [infinitive phrase]

My eyes closed against the glare, I could feel the warm sun on my face. [See page 551—absolute phrase]

The preceding examples demonstrate how phrases function in the same way as single-word modifiers. Remember, however, that phrases are not merely substitutes for single words. Phrases can express more than can be packed into a single word:

> The gas gauge fluttered **from empty to full**.
> He telephoned his wife **to tell her of his arrival**.
> The firefighters **hosing down the adjacent buildings** had very little standing room.

■ **Exercise 6**   Underline each phrase in the following sentences. Then state whether the phrase functions as a noun, an adjective, an adverb, or an appositive.

1. I expect a job offer like that one only once in a lifetime.
2. Dazzled by Baryshnikov's speed and grace, the audience gave him a standing ovation.
3. Crawling through the thicket, I suddenly remembered the box of shells left on top of the truck.
4. The people to watch closely are the ones ruling behind the political scene.
5. They worked fast, one man sawing logs and the other loading the truck.
6. A wave curling over the surfer swallowed him for a moment.
7. The skipper, a slender blond woman, swung the tiller sharply to the right.
8. Not wanting to wait for the rest of us, Andrew went home in a cab.
9. She took the job to get a better salary and to move to a more pleasant area of the country.
10. My brother bought a foreign car, small but fuel-efficient.

SUBORDINATE CLAUSES

A subordinate clause is a sequence of related words containing both a subject and a predicate and beginning with a subordinating conjunction or a relative pronoun. Unlike a main clause (an independent unit—see **1e**), a subordinate clause is grammatically dependent and may function within a sentence as an adverb, an adjective, or a noun. It often conveys less important information than does the main clause.

> I had to leave the meeting early **because I became ill.**
> [adverb clause]
> Simple illustrations, **which the instructor drew on the board,** explained the process.   [adjective clause]
> Geologists know **why earthquakes occur.**   [noun clause—direct object]

The following conjunctions are commonly used to introduce, connect, and relate subordinate clauses to other words in the sentence.

Words commonly used as subordinating conjunctions:

after	inasmuch as	supposing [that]
although	in case [that]	than
as	in order that	that
as [far/soon] as	insofar as	though
as if	in that	till
as though	lest	unless
because	no matter how	until
before	now that	when, whenever
even if	once	where, wherever
even though	provided [that]	whether
how	since	while
if	so that	why

The relative pronouns also serve as markers of those subordinate clauses called *relative clauses*:

> that   what   which   who, whoever
> whom, whomever   whose

(3) Subordinate clauses used as nouns

NOUNS	NOUN CLAUSES
The **news** may be false.	**What the newspapers say** may be false. [subject]

I do not know his **address**.	I do not know **where he lives**. [direct object]
Give the tools to **Rita**.	Give the tools to **whoever can use them best**. [object of a preposition]

The conjunction *that* before a noun clause may be omitted in some sentences:

I know **she is right**. [Compare "I know *that she is right*."]

(4) Subordinate clauses used as modifiers

Two types of subordinate clauses, the adjective clause and the adverb clause, are used as modifiers.

Adjective clauses Any clause that modifies a noun or a pronoun is an adjective clause. Adjective clauses, which nearly always follow the words modified, usually begin with relative pronouns but may begin with words such as *when,* *where,* or *why*.

ADJECTIVES	ADJECTIVE CLAUSES
Everyone needs **loyal** friends.	Everyone needs friends **who are loyal**.
The **golden** window reflects the sun.	The window, **which shines like gold**, reflects the sun.
Peaceful countrysides no longer exist.	Countrysides **where one can find peace of mind** no longer exist.

If it is not used as a subject, the relative pronoun in an adjective clause may sometimes be omitted:

He is a man **I admire**. [Compare "He is a man *whom I admire*."]

Adverb clauses An adverb clause usually modifies a verb but may modify an adjective, an adverb, or even the rest of the sentence in which it appears. Adverb clauses are ordinarily introduced by subordinating conjunctions.

ADVERBS	ADVERB CLAUSES
Soon the lights went out.	**When the windstorm hit,** the lights went out.
No alcoholic beverages are sold **locally**.	No alcoholic beverages are sold **where I live**.
The price is **too** high for me.	The price is higher **than I can afford**.
Speak **very** distinctly.	Speak as distinctly **as you can**.

Some adverb clauses may be elliptical. See also **25b**.

> If I can save enough money, I'll go to Alaska next summer. **If not**, I'll take a trip to St. Louis.   [Clearly implied words are omitted.]

■ **Exercise 7**   Find the subordinate clauses in the following sentences (adapted from *Time* magazine) and label each as a noun clause, an adjective clause, or an adverb clause.

1. The candidate refused to renounce the current NATO doctrine that threatens the first use of nuclear weapons.
2. As the days grew shorter, her spirits darkened.
3. Both small nations claimed victory in the battle, which immediately became a symbol of the stalemated global war.
4. What excited scientists most was the unmistakable traces of dry riverbeds and deltas etched into the rocky Martian surface.
5. If, like a musical Rip Van Winkle, a nineteenth-century man awoke today in a concert hall, he would find that things had hardly changed.

1e

Learn to recognize main clauses and the various types of sentences.

Independent units of expression, a main clause and a simple sentence have the same grammatical structure: **subject + predicate**. Generally, however, the term *main*

Sentences may also be classified according to purpose and are punctuated accordingly:

DECLARATIVE	He refused the offer. [statement]
IMPERATIVE	Refuse the offer. [request or command]
INTERROGATIVE	Did he refuse the offer? He refused, didn't he? He refused it? [questions]
EXCLAMATORY	What an offer! He refused it! [exclamations]

■ **Exercise 8**   Underline the main clauses in the following sentences (selected from *Natural History*). Put subordinate clauses in brackets: see **1d**. (Noun clauses may be an integral part of the basic pattern of a main clause, as in the second sentence.)

1. Practice never really makes perfect, and a great deal of frustration invariably accompanies juggling.
2. Nature is his passion in life, and colleagues say he is a skilled naturalist and outdoorsman.
3. The two clouds have a common envelope of atomic hydrogen gas that ties them firmly together.
4. Transportation comes to a halt as the steadily falling snow, accumulating faster than snowplows can clear it away, is blown into deep drifts along the highways.
5. Agriculture is the world's most basic industry; its success depends in large part on an adequate supply of water.
6. Probably because their whirling sails were new and strange to Cervantes, windmills outraged the gallant Don Quixote.
7. There have been several attempts to explain this rhythm, but when each hypothesis was experimentally explored, it had to be discarded.
8. Allegiance to a group may be confirmed or denied by the use or disuse of a particular handshake, as Carl's experience indicates.
9. Some black stem rust of wheat has been controlled by elimination of barberry, a plant that harbored the rust.
10. We know that innocent victims have been executed; fortunately, others condemned to death have been found innocent prior to execution.

■ **Exercise 9**   Classify the sentences in Exercise 8 as *compound* (there are two), *complex* (five), or *compound-complex* (three).

clause refers to an independent part of a sentence containing other clauses.

SIMPLE SENTENCES

I had lost my passport.
I did not worry about it.

MAIN CLAUSES IN SENTENCES

I had lost my passport, but **I did not worry about it.**   [A coordinating conjunction links the two main clauses.]

Although I had lost my passport, **I did not worry about it.** [A subordinate clause precedes the main clause.]

Sentences may be classified according to their structure as *simple, compound, complex,* or *compound-complex.*

1. A simple sentence has only one subject and one predicate (either or both of which may be compound):

   Dick started a coin collection.   [SUBJECT + VERB + OBJECT.]

2. A compound sentence consists of at least two main clauses:

   Dick started a coin collection, and his brother bought an album of rare stamps.   [MAIN CLAUSE, and MAIN CLAUSE. See **12a.**]

3. A complex sentence has one main clause and at least one subordinate clause:

   As soon as Dick started a coin collection, his brother bought an album of rare stamps.   [ADVERB CLAUSE, MAIN CLAUSE. See **12b.**]

4. A compound-complex sentence consists of at least two main clauses and at least one subordinate clause:

   As soon as Dick started a coin collection, his brother bought an album of rare stamps; on Christmas morning they exchanged coins and stamps.   [ADVERB CLAUSE, MAIN CLAUSE; MAIN CLAUSE. See **14a.**]

■ **Exercise 10**   First identify the main and subordinate clauses in the sentences in the following paragraph; then classify each sentence according to structure.

[1]Jim angrily called himself a fool, as he had been doing all the way to the swamp.   [2]Why had he listened to Fred's mad idea?   [3]What did ghosts and family legends mean to him in this age of computers and solar-energy converters?   [4]He had enough mysteries of his own of a highly complex sort, which involved an intricate search for values.   [5]But now he was chasing down ghosts, and this chase in the middle of the night was absurd.   [6]It was lunacy!   [7]The legends that surrounded the ghosts had horrified him as a child, and they were a horror still.   [8]As he approached the dark trail that would lead him to the old mansion, he felt almost sick.   [9]The safe, sure things of every day had become distant fantasies.   [10]Only this grotesque night—and whatever ghosts might be lurking in the shadows—seemed hideously real.

2
SENTENCE FRAGMENTS

As a rule, avoid sentence fragments.

The term *fragment* refers to a group of words beginning with a capital letter and ending with a period. Although written as if it were a sentence, a fragment is only a part of a sentence—such as a phrase or a subordinate clause.

FRAGMENTS	SENTENCES
Larry always working in his yard on Saturdays.	Larry always works in his yard on Saturdays.
Because he enjoys the flowers and shrubs.	He enjoys the flowers and shrubs.
Which help to screen his house from the street.	He enjoys the flowers and shrubs which help to screen his house from the street—for example, a tall hedge with a border of petunias.
For example, a tall hedge with a border of petunias.	

As you study the preceding examples, notice that the first fragment is converted to a sentence by substituting *works* (a verb) for *working* (a verbal) and the second by omitting *because* (a subordinating conjunction). The last two fragments (a subordinate clause and a phrase) are made parts of a sentence.

Similarly, you can eliminate any fragment in your own papers (1) by making it into a sentence or (2) by connecting it to an existing sentence. If you cannot easily distinguish structural differences between sentences and nonsentences, study section **1**, especially **1d**.

Test for a sentence Before handing in a composition, proofread each word group written as a sentence. One way to eliminate many sentence fragments is to be sure that each word group has at least one subject and one predicate.

FRAGMENTS WITHOUT A SUBJECT, A PREDICATE, OR BOTH

And always looked for an easier way to do the job.   [no subject]
Water sparkling in the moonlight.   [no predicate]
With no forethought whatsoever.   [no subject, no predicate]

Further, make sure you have not written a subordinate clause as a sentence. Look first for subordinating conjunctions and relative pronouns (see page 21). When followed by a subject and a predicate, these connectors signal a subordinate clause. Check to be sure the clause is combined with a main clause (see **1d**).

FRAGMENTS WITH SUBJECT AND PREDICATE

When he tried for days to change my mind.   [subject and verb: *he tried;* subordinating conjunction: *when*]
Which sparkles in the moonlight.   [subject and verb: *which sparkles;* relative pronoun: *which*]

You need not avoid all fragments. Written dialogue that mirrors speech habits often contains grammatically incomplete sentences or expressions that have an understood subject or verb (see also **9e**). Exclamations and answers to questions are often single words, phrases, or subordinate clauses written as sentences.

> Where does Peg begin a mystery story? **On the last page.**
> **Too bad!**   **No shoes, no service.**

Occasionally, writers deliberately use fragments for emphasis.

> The American grain calls for plain talk, for the unvarnished
> truth. **Better to err a little in the cause of bluntness than**
> **soften the mind with congenial drivel. Better a challenging**
> **half-truth than a discredited cliché.** —WRIGHT MORRIS
> [Note the effective repetition and the parallel structure in the
> bold-faced fragments.]

> What I most remember is certain moments, revelations,
> epiphanies, in which the sensuous little savage that I then
> was came face to face with the universe. **And blinked.**
> —WALLACE STEGNER

Despite their suitability for some purposes, sentence
fragments are comparatively rare in formal expository writing. In formal papers, sentence fragments are to be used—
if at all—sparingly and with care.

2a

**Do not capitalize and punctuate a phrase as you would a
sentence.**

FRAGMENT   Astronauts venturing deep into space may not
come back to earth for fifty years. **Returning on-**
ly to discover an uninhabitable planet.
[participial phrase]

REVISED   Astronauts venturing deep into space may not
come back to earth for fifty years. They may return only to discover an uninhabitable planet.
[fragment made into a sentence]

FRAGMENT   Soon I began to work for the company. **First in**
the rock pit and later on the highway.
[prepositional phrase]

REVISED   Soon I began to work for the company, first in
the rock pit and later on the highway.

OR   Soon I began to work for the company. First I worked in the rock pit and later on the highway.

FRAGMENT   Sarah was elected president of her class. **And was made a member of Mortar Board.**   [part of a compound predicate]

REVISED   Sarah was elected president of her class and was made a member of Mortar Board.
OR   Sarah was elected president of her class. She was also made a member of Mortar Board.

FRAGMENT   The new lawyer needed a secretary. **Preferably someone with experience.**   [appositive]

REVISED   The new lawyer needed a secretary, preferably someone with experience.
OR   The new lawyer needed a secretary. She preferred someone with experience.

■ **Exercise 1**   Revise each item below to eliminate the sentence fragment either by including it in the sentence next to it or by making it into a sentence. Explain why you chose to revise as you did in each case.

1. Dennis finally left home. Earnestly seeking to become an individual in his own right.
2. The panel discussed the proposed amendment to the Constitution. A single issue dividing voters.
3. They did not recognize Walter. His beard gone and hair cut.
4. These commercials have a hypnotic effect. Not only on children but on adults too.
5. I killed six flies with one swat. Against the law of averages but possible.

2b

Do not capitalize and punctuate a subordinate clause as you would a sentence.

FRAGMENT   Thousands of young people became active workers in the community. **After these appeals had changed their apathy to concern.**   [detached adverb clause]

REVISED   Thousands of young people became active work-
            ers in the community after these appeals had
            changed their apathy to concern.   [fragment in-
            cluded in the preceding sentence]

FRAGMENT   We were trying to follow the directions. **Which
            were confusing and absurd**.   [detached adjective
            clause]

REVISED   We were trying to follow the directions, which
            were confusing and absurd.   [fragment included
            in the preceding sentence]

            OR   We tried to follow the directions. They
            were confusing and absurd.   [fragment made into
            a sentence]

            OR   We tried to follow the confusing, absurd
            directions.   [fragment reduced to adjectivals that
            are included in the preceding sentence]

■ **Exercise 2**   Revise each item below to eliminate the sentence fragment either by including it in the preceding sentence or by making it into
a sentence. Explain why you chose to revise as you did in each case.

1. I decided to give skiing a try. After I had grown tired of watching
   other people fall.
2. Pat believes that everyone should go to college. And that all tests
   for admission should be abolished.
3. Many students were obviously victims of spring fever. Which affected class attendance.
4. Paul faints whenever he sees blood. And whenever he finds himself
   in high places.
5. I am making a study of cigarette advertisements. That use such
   slogans as "less tar, more taste" and "the lowest in tar and nicotine."

■ **Exercise 3**   The paragraph below contains nine fragments. Revise
the paragraph so it contains no fragments. You might attach a fragment
to an adjacent sentence, make it into a sentence of its own, or revise the
fragment or the sentences surrounding it to include the information con-
tained in the fragment, adding additional words if necessary. Give your
reasons for revising each fragment as you did.

¹The little paperback almanac I found at the newsstand has given me
some fascinating information. ²Not just about the weather and

changes in the moon. ³There are also intriguing statistics. ⁴A tub bath, for example, requires more water than a shower. ⁵In all probability, ten or twelve gallons more, depending on how dirty the bather is. ⁶And one of the Montezumas downed fifty jars of cocoa every day. ⁷Which seems a bit exaggerated to me. ⁸To say the least. ⁹I also learned that an average beard has thirteen thousand whiskers. ¹⁰That, in the course of a lifetime, a man could shave off more than nine yards of whiskers, over twenty-seven feet. ¹¹If my math is correct. ¹²Some other interesting facts in the almanac. ¹³Suppose a person was born on Sunday, February 29, 1976. ¹⁴Another birthday not celebrated on Sunday until the year 2004. ¹⁵Because February 29 falls on weekdays till then—twenty-eight birthdays later. ¹⁶As I laid the almanac aside, I remembered that line in *Slaughterhouse-Five*: "So it goes."

3
COMMA SPLICE AND FUSED SENTENCE

Do not link two main clauses with only a comma (comma splice) or run two main clauses together without any punctuation (fused sentence).

The terms *comma splice* and *fused sentence* (also called comma fault and run-on sentence) refer to errors in punctuation that occur only in compound (or compound-complex) sentences.

> COMMA SPLICE   (only a comma between main clauses): The wind was cold, they decided not to walk.
> FUSED SENTENCE   (no punctuation between the main clauses): The wind was cold they decided not to walk.

You can correct comma splices and fused sentences (1) by placing a period after the first main clause and writing the second main clause as a sentence, (2) by using a semicolon to separate the main clauses, or (3) by using a comma before you insert an appropriate coordinating conjunction (*and, but, or, nor, for, so, yet*) to link and relate the main clauses.

REVISIONS

The wind was cold. They decided not to walk.
The wind was cold; they decided not to walk.
The wind was cold, so they decided not to walk.

When you use the second method of revision, keep in mind that the semicolon separates two grammatically equal units of thought: **Subject + predicate; subject + predicate.** As you proofread your papers to check for comma splices and as you make revisions, do not overuse the semicolon or use it between parts of unequal grammatical rank: see **14c**.

Often a more effective way to revise a comma splice or fused sentence is to make one clause subordinate to the other: see **24b**.

REVISIONS

The wind was so cold that they decided not to walk.
Because the wind was cold, they decided not to walk.

A subordinate clause may be reduced to a phrase and used as a part of a simple sentence: *"Because of the cold wind* they decided not to walk."

If you cannot always recognize a main clause and distinguish it from a phrase or a subordinate clause, study section **1**, especially **1d** and **1e**.

3a

Use a comma between main clauses *only* when they are linked by the coordinating conjunctions *and, but, or, for, nor, so,* or *yet.* See also **12a**.

COMMA SPLICE   Women's roles have changed radically since 1963, women now can choose to stay home or to get a job.

REVISED   Women's roles have changed radically since 1963, **for** women now can choose to stay home or to get a job.
  [coordinating conjunction *for* added after the comma]

OR   Women's roles have changed radically since 1963**;** women now can choose to stay home or to get a job.   [A semicolon separates the main clauses: see **14a**.]

COMMA SPLICE   She was not an outstanding success at her first job, she was not a complete failure either.

REVISED   She was not an outstanding success at her first job**, nor** was she a complete failure.   [Note the shift in the word order of subject and verb after the coordinating conjunction *nor*.]
OR   She was **neither** an outstanding success at her first job **nor** a complete failure.   [a simple sentence with a compound complement]

COMMA SPLICE   I ran over some broken glass in the parking lot, it did not puncture my tires.

REVISED   I ran over some broken glass in the parking lot**, but** it did not puncture my tires.   [the coordinating conjunction *but* added after the comma]
OR   **Although** I ran over some broken glass in the parking lot**,** it did not puncture my tires.   [Addition of *although* makes the first clause subordinate: see **12b**.]

To avoid a fused sentence, use a period or a semicolon between main clauses not linked by *and, but, or, for, nor, so,* or *yet.*

FUSED SENTENCE   She wrote him a love letter he answered it in person.

REVISED   She wrote him a love letter**.** **H**e answered it in person.   [each main clause written as a sentence]
OR   She wrote him a love letter**;** he answered it in person.   [main clauses separated by a semicolon: see **14a**]

▲ Note 1: Either a comma or a semicolon may be used between short main clauses not linked by *and, but, or, for, nor, so,* or *yet* when the clauses are parallel in form and unified in thought:

School bores them**,** preaching bores them**,** even television bores them.   —ARTHUR MILLER

One is the reality**;** the other is the symbol.   —NANCY HALE

▲ Note 2: The comma is used to separate a statement from a tag question.

> You can come, can't you? He rides a bike, doesn't he? They couldn't be wrong, could they—not all those millions!
> —WILLIAM GOLDING

■ **Exercise 1**   Connect each pair of sentences below in two ways, first with a semicolon and then with a coordinating conjunction: *and, but, for, or, nor, so,* or *yet.*

EXAMPLE
They should have walked a mile every day. That would have improved their physical fitness.
  a. *They should have walked a mile every day; that would have improved their physical fitness.*
  b. *They should have walked a mile every day, and that would have improved their physical fitness.*

1. There used to be turtles in that pond. I remember seeing them when I was a child.
2. Some call his theory nonsense. Others think it has revolutionary significance.
3. Dexter goes hunting. He carries his camera instead of his rifle.
4. He may haggle fiercely over details. He also has the best interests of this project firmly in mind.

■ **Exercise 2**   Use a subordinating conjunction (see the list on page 22) to combine each of the four pairs of sentences in Exercise 1. For the use of the comma, refer to **12b**.

EXAMPLE
Because *it would have improved their physical fitness, they should have walked a mile every day.*

■ **Exercise 3**   Proofread the following sentences (selected and adapted from *National Geographic* and *Natural History*). Place a check mark after a sentence with a comma splice and an *X* after a fused sentence. Do not mark correctly punctuated sentences.

1. In this method, a drawing was made on a plank of hardwood, the wood was cut away around it.
2. The orchid needs particular soil microbes those microbes vanished when the virgin prairie was plowed.

3. The mammals are partial to peanut butter and rolled oats, which we used to lure them into our live traps.
4. Attempts to extinguish such fires have often failed some have been burning for decades.
5. The winds lashed our tents all night, by morning we had to dig ourselves out from under a snowdrift.
6. The ringleaders abandoned the cub they had attacked we stayed with the dying cub to follow its fate.
7. South Pass country is still short on roads and people, so I was delighted to discover an experienced guide in Charley Wilson, son of Pony Express rider Nick Wilson.
8. The song that awakened me carried an incredible sense of mournfulness, it seemed to be the prolonged cry of a lone animal calling in the night.
9. Between the islands of North and South Bimini is a five-mile long, two-mile wide lagoon except for the deep waters near Alicetown, the lagoon averages about three feet deep.
10. One afternoon I was searching for sharks from an airboat, a flat-bottomed craft capable of operating in only a few inches of water, even with plugs of wax jammed deep in my ears, the roar of the engine behind my head was deafening.

■ **Exercise 4**   Use various methods of revision (see pages 34–35) as you correct the comma splices or fused sentences in Exercise 3.

3b

Be sure to use a semicolon before a conjunctive adverb or transitional expression placed between main clauses. See also **14a**.

COMMA SPLICE   TV weather maps have various symbols, for example, a big apostrophe means drizzle.

REVISED   TV weather maps have various symbols; for example, a big apostrophe means drizzle.   [MAIN CLAUSE; *transitional expression,* MAIN CLAUSE.]

FUSED SENTENCE   The tiny storms cannot be identified as hurricanes therefore, they are called neutercanes.

REVISED   The tiny storms cannot be identified as hurricanes; therefore, they are called neutercanes.   [MAIN CLAUSE; *conjunctive adverb,* MAIN CLAUSE.]

Below is a list of frequently used conjunctive adverbs and transitional phrases.

CONJUNCTIVE ADVERBS

also	incidentally	nonetheless
anyway	indeed	otherwise
besides	instead	still
consequently	likewise	then
finally	meanwhile	therefore
furthermore	moreover	thus
hence	nevertheless	
however	next	

TRANSITIONAL PHRASES

after all	even so	in the second place
as a result	for example	on the contrary
at any rate	in addition	on the other hand
at the same time	in fact	
by the way	in other words	

Unlike a coordinating conjunction, which has a fixed position between the main clauses it links, many conjunctive adverbs and transitional phrases may either begin the second main clause or take another position in it.

> She doubted the value of daily meditation; **however**, she decided to try it.   [The conjunctive adverb begins the second main clause. See also **14a**, page 146.]
>
> She doubted the value of daily meditation; she decided, **however**, to try it.   [The conjunctive adverb (set off by commas) appears later in the clause.]
>
> COMPARE   She doubted the value of daily meditation, **but** she decided to try it.   [The coordinating conjunction has a fixed position.]

■ **Exercise 5** Write five correctly punctuated compound sentences using various conjunctive adverbs and transitional phrases to connect and relate main clauses.

3c

Do not let a divided quotation trick you into making a comma splice. See also **16a**.

COMMA SPLICE   "Who won the lottery?" he asked, "how much money was in the pot?"

REVISED   "Who won the lottery?" he asked. "How much money was in the pot?"

COMMA SPLICE   "Injustice is relatively easy to bear," says Mencken, "it is justice that hurts."

REVISED   "Injustice is relatively easy to bear," says Mencken; "it is justice that hurts."

■ **Exercise 6**   Divide the following quotations without creating a comma splice, as shown in the example below.

EXAMPLE
Eric Sevareid has said, "Let those who wish compare America with Rome. Rome lasted a thousand years."
"Let those who wish compare America with Rome," Eric Sevareid has said. "Rome lasted a thousand years."

1. "I am saddest when I sing. So are those who hear me," Artemus Ward commented.
2. W. C. Fields once said, "I am free of all prejudice. I hate everyone equally."
3. "I know of no successful surgical procedure that will replace macaroni in the spine with a rigid backbone. This is strictly a do-it-yourself project," says Ann Landers.
4. According to Harrison E. Salisbury, "There is no shortcut to life. To the end of our days, life is a lesson imperfectly learned."
5. John Kenneth Galbraith commented, "Money is a singular thing. It ranks with love as man's greatest source of joy—and with death as his greatest source of anxiety."

■ **Exercise 7**   Correct the comma splices and fused sentences in the following paragraph. Do not revise a correctly punctuated sentence.

[1]"Age is just a frame of mind," Nellie often says, "you're as old or as young as you think you are." [2]Does she really believe this, or is she just making conversation? [3]Well, when she was sixteen, her father said, "Baby Nell, you're not old enough to marry Johnny, besides he's a

Democrat." ⁴So Nellie ran away from her Missouri home in Oklahoma she found another Democrat, Frank, and married him. ⁵When Nellie was thirty-nine, Frank died. ⁶A year later she shocked everyone by marrying a Texan named William, he was a seventy-year-old veteran of the Spanish-American War. ⁷"Billy thinks young," Nellie explained, "and he's just as young as he thinks he is." ⁸Maybe she was right that happy marriage lasted eighteen years. ⁹Nellie celebrated her seventieth birthday by going to Illinois, there she married Tom, who in her opinion was a youngster in his late sixties. ¹⁰But her third marriage didn't last long, because Tom soon got hardening of the arteries and died of a heart attack, however, Nellie's arteries were fine. ¹¹In 1975, when Nellie was eighty-three, she found and finally married her old Missouri sweetheart, then eighty-seven-year-old Johnny whisked her away to his soybean farm in Arkansas. ¹²Nellie's fourth wedding made front-page news, and then the whole town echoed Nellie's words: "Life doesn't begin at sixteen or at forty. ¹³It begins when you want it to, age is just a frame of mind."

■ **Exercise 8** First review section **2** and study section **3**. Then proofread the following for sentence fragments, comma splices, and fused sentences. Make appropriate revisions. Put a check mark after each sentence that needs no revision.

1. We sold our property, then we bought a motor home to tour the country in.
2. The cabin was originally built to house four people a family often lives in it now. Not to mention all the dogs and cats.
3. Val signed up for the university chorus, however, he really doesn't sing very well.
4. The Kiwanis Club sponsors a flea market every year, it is not, however, an easy way to make money.
5. Wallace Stevens, the poet, walked to work at the insurance company where he was an executive.
6. Most of my professors require that students be on time for classes. The reason being that students who come in late disturb the other students.
7. Our choir will go to Holland in May, when the tulip gardens are especially beautiful.
8. A long article in the magazine describes botulism, this is an acute form of food poisoning.
9. That is absurd. It's nonsense. An argument that is riddled with stupid assumptions.
10. After class, I often drop by the college bookstore. Usually buying best-selling paperbacks, then never getting around to reading any of them.

4
ADJECTIVES
AND ADVERBS

Distinguish between adjectives and adverbs and use the appropriate forms.

Adjectives and adverbs are modifiers. Modifiers qualify or limit the meaning of other words. As you study the following examples, observe that (1) the adjectives modify nouns or pronouns and (2) the adverbs modify verbs, adjectives, or other adverbs.

ADJECTIVES	ADVERBS
a **brief**, **dramatic** one	a **briefly** dramatic one
armed squads	**very heavily** armed squads
She looked **angry**.	She looked **angrily** at me.
a **quick** review	reviewed **quickly**

Adverbs may also modify verbals (gerunds, infinitives, participles) or even whole clauses. See **1c**, page 14.

The *-ly* ending can be an adjective-forming suffix as well as an adverb-forming one.

NOUNS TO ADJECTIVES	earth–earthly, ghost–ghostly
ADJECTIVES TO ADVERBS	rapid–rapidly, lucky–luckily

A number of words ending in *-ly* (such as *deadly, cowardly*), as well as many not ending in *-ly* (such as *far, fast, little, well*), may function either as adjectives or as adverbs. Some adverbs have two forms (such as *quick, quickly; slow, slowly; loud* and *clear, loudly* and *clearly*).

When in doubt about the correct use of a given modifier, consult your dictionary. Look for the labels *adj.* and *adv.*, for examples of usage, and for any usage notes.

4a

Use adverbs to modify verbs, adjectives, and other adverbs.

NOT   Cicely Tyson played Miss Jane Pittman just perfect.

BUT   Cicely Tyson played Miss Jane Pittman just **perfectly**. [The adverb modifies the verb *played*.]

NOT   The plane departs at a reasonable early hour.

BUT   The plane departs at a **reasonably** early hour.   [The adverb modifies the adjective *early*.]

Most dictionaries still label the following as informal usage: *sure* for *surely, real* for *really*, and *good* for the adverb *well*.

INFORMAL   The Broncos played **real good** during the first quarter.

FORMAL   The Broncos played **very well** during the first quarter.   [appropriate in both formal and informal usage—see also **19b**]

■ **Exercise 1**   In the phrases below, convert adjectives into adverbs, following the pattern of the examples.

  EXAMPLE
  abrupt reply—*replied abruptly*   [OR *abruptly replied*]

1. calm behavior
2. prompt reward
3. careless remark
4. sincere belief
5. regular visit
6. special appeal

EXAMPLE
complete happiness—*completely happy*

7. near possibility
8. total incompatibility

9. former prosperity
10. recent illness

■ **Exercise 2** In the following sentences, convert any informal or unacceptable modifier into an adverb acceptable in college writing. Put a check mark after each sentence that needs no revision.

1. People today don't take politics very serious.
2. When I get tired of balancing my checkbook, the pocket calculator surely does help.
3. Our national known team played well but did not win.
4. The passengers on Flight 562 were lucky to escape as easy as they did.
5. With my new job, I don't get to eat as regular as I would like.
6. The cost of housing went up very sudden.
7. My fingers get on the wrong keys when I have to type that rapid.
8. Last night the stars seemed exceptional bright.
9. He treats people most brutally when he is unsure of himself.
10. They were well-trained and swam graceful.

4b

Distinguish between adverbs used to modify the verb and adjectives used as complements.

NOT   The honeysuckle smells sweetly in the morning.

BUT   The honeysuckle smells **sweet** in the morning.   [The adjective *sweet* is a subject complement.]

NOT   We painted the sign careful.   [The adjective *careful* does not modify the noun *sign*.]

BUT   We painted the sign **carefully**.   [The adverb *carefully* modifies the verb *painted*.]

When used as a subject complement, an adjective always modifies the subject. (See also **1b**.)

They look **fashionable**.
The soup tastes **different** with these herbs in it.

When used as an object complement, an adjective always modifies the object.

These herbs make the soup **different**.
They considered the style **fashionable**.

Either an adverb or an adjective may follow a direct object; the choice depends on meaning, on the word modified:

Anne considered Morris **angrily**.   [The adverb *angrily* modifies the verb *considered*.]
Anne considered Morris **angry**.   [An object complement, *angry* modifies the noun *Morris*.]

▲ Caution: Do not omit the *-d* or *-ed* of a past participle used as an adjective. (See also **7a**, page 78.)

NOT   The typist was experience.

BUT   The typist was experienced.   [Compare "an experienced typist."]

■ **Exercise 3**   Using adjectives as complements, write two sentences that illustrate each of the following patterns.

Subject + linking verb + subject complement.

Subject + verb + direct object + object complement.

■ **Exercise 4**   Look up each pair of modifiers in your dictionary. Give special attention to specific examples of usage and to any usage notes. Then write sentences of your own to illustrate the formal use of each modifier.

EXAMPLE
bad, badly—*I felt bad. I played badly.*

1. slow, slowly   3. awful, awfully   5. most, mostly
2. real, really   4. good, well   6. quick, quickly

4c

Use the appropriate forms of adjectives and adverbs for the comparative and the superlative. See also **22c**.

Many adjectives and adverbs change form to indicate degree. As you study the following examples, notice that *positive* refers to the simple, uncompared form of the adjective or adverb. In general, many of the shorter adjectives (and a few adverbs) form the *comparative* degree by the addition of *-er* and the *superlative* by the addition of *-est*. Some two-syllable adjectives, especially those ending in a vowel sound (such as *dirty, shallow*), regularly take the *-er* and *-est* endings. The longer adjectives and most adverbs form the comparative by the use of *more* (or *less*) and the superlative by the use of *most* (or *least*). A few modifiers have irregular comparatives and superlatives.

POSITIVE	COMPARATIVE	SUPERLATIVE
cold	colder	coldest
sturdy	sturdier	sturdiest
fortunate	more/less fortunate	most/least fortunate
near	nearer	nearest
warmly	more/less warmly	most/least warmly
good, well	better	best
bad, badly	worse	worst
little	less OR littler	least OR littlest
far	farther, further	farthest, furthest

(1) Use the comparative to denote a greater degree or to refer to two in a comparison.

The metropolitan area is much **bigger** now.
Bert can run **faster** than his father.
Dried apples are **more** nutritious per pound than fresh apples.   [a comparison of two groups]

With the use of *other*, the comparative form may refer to more than two.

Bert can run **faster** than the *other* players.

▲ Note: In certain expressions, no degree is intended although the comparative form is used: *outer* space, *higher* mathematics, *lower* Manhattan.

(2) Use the superlative to denote the greatest degree or to refer to three or more in a comparison.

The interests of the family are **best** served by open communication.

Bert is the **fastest** of the three runners.
OR   Bert is the **fastest** runner of all.

The superlative occasionally refers to two, as in "Put your *best* foot forward!"

▲ Note: Current usage, however illogical it may seem, accepts comparisons of many adjectives or adverbs with absolute meanings, such as "a *more perfect* society," "the *deadest* campus," and "*less completely* exhausted." But many writers make an exception of *unique*—using "*more nearly* unique" rather than "more unique." They consider *unique* an absolute adjective—one without degrees of comparison.

(3) Do not use a double comparative or superlative.

NOT   Our swimming hole is much more shallower than Lake Murray.   [double comparative: *-er* and *more*]

BUT   Our swimming hole is much **shallower** than Lake Murray.   [deletion of the comparative *more*]

NOT   That was the most funniest situation.   [double superlative: *-est* and *most*]

BUT   That was the **funniest** situation.   [deletion of the superlative *most*]

■ **Exercise 5**   Give the comparative and superlative of each adjective or adverb.

1. quick
2. quickly
3. thirsty
4. hollow
5. modest
6. ill
7. realistically
8. frightened
9. scared
10. inactive

■ **Exercise 6**   Fill in each blank by using the appropriate comparative or superlative form of the modifier given at the beginning of each sentence.

1. *bad*   That is absolutely the _____ grade I have ever received.
2. *useful*   The _____ tool of all is the screwdriver.
3. *lively*   A _____ music video has never before been produced.
4. *mellow*   As one grows older, one usually grows _____.
5. *little*   Some smokers are _____ considerate than others.
6. *strong*   Who in that quartet has the _____ voice?
7. *tiny*   Even the _____ flaw lessens the value of the gem.
8. *thin*   His chili is _____ than mine.
9. *good*   Of the two applicants Jamie seems _____ qualified.
10. *mature*   Naturally, a person's outlook on life is _____ at eighteen than at sixteen.

4d

Avoid awkward or ambiguous use of a noun form as an adjective.

Many noun forms are used effectively to modify other nouns (as in *reference* manual, *windfall profits* tax, *House Ways and Means* Committee), especially when appropriate adjectives are not available. But such forms should be avoided when they are either awkward or confusing.

AWKWARD   Many candidates entered the president race.

BETTER   Many candidates entered the presidential race.

CONFUSING   The Representative Landor recess maneuvers led to victory.

BETTER   Representative Landor's maneuvers during the recess led to victory.

4e

Do not use the double negative.

The term *double negative* refers to the use of two negatives to express a single negation. Like the double comparison, the double negative is grammatically redundant.

NOT   He did **not** keep **no** records.   [double negative: *not* and *no*]

BUT   He did **not** keep any records.   [one negative: *not*]

NOT   **Couldn't nobody** help him.   [double negative -*n't* and *nobody*]

BUT   **Nobody** could help him.   [one negative, *nobody*]

If used with an unnecessary negative such as *not, nothing,* or *without,* the modifiers *hardly, barely,* and *scarcely* are still considered unacceptable.

NOT   I **couldn't hardly** quit in the middle of the job.

BUT   I **could hardly** quit in the middle of the job.

NOT   The motion passed **without scarcely** a protest.

BUT   The motion passed **with scarcely** a protest.

The use of two negatives to express a positive is acceptable and can be effective.

We cannot afford to stand by and do nothing. [a positive meaning: We have to do something about it.]

▲ Caution: Many writers avoid the idiom, *"can't* help *but* disagree,"* substituting *"can't help* disagreeing"* or *"can't but* disagree.*"

■ **Exercise 7** Eliminate double negatives in the following sentences.

1. They don't have no home.
2. It was so noisy I couldn't hardly hear myself think.
3. We never do nothing but talk about the weather.
4. We needed gas but couldn't buy none.
5. The club didn't scarcely have any money left.

■ **Exercise 8** After you have reread rules **4a** through **4e** and have studied the examples, correct all errors in the use of adjectives or adverbs in the sentences below. Also eliminate any awkward use of nouns as adjectives. Put a check mark after any sentence that needs no revision.

1. I was always told the Bible was the best-selling book in the world, and I'm sure it still sells good.
2. Adding chopped onions and jalapeño peppers to the chili makes it taste real well.
3. According to the National Weather Service, September is suppose to be our most wettest month, but we haven't barely received a drop of rain.
4. It was easily the largest deficit in history.
5. Although yesterday's news commentary was relatively unbias, it was more duller than usual.
6. The repair estimates mechanic was out to lunch.
7. I've always wanted to run for public office, so I've entered the mayor campaign.
8. My friend Karl is much contenter now that he is going to college full time.
9. A football game between a well-coached team and a group of naturally good athletes is usually close.
10. A favorite device of detective novels authors is to make seeming innocent characters look suspicious.

5
CASE

Choose the case form that shows the function of nouns and pronouns in sentences.

Case refers to the form of a noun or pronoun that shows its relation to other words in a sentence. For example, the different case forms of the boldfaced pronouns below, all referring to the same person, show their different uses.

> **I** [the subject] believe that **my** [modifier] uncle will help **me** [direct object].

I is in the subjective (or nominative) case; *my*, in the possessive (or genitive); *me*, in the objective.

As you study the following tables, observe that the pronouns *I, we, he, she, they,* and *who* have distinctive forms for all three cases.

PERSONAL PRONOUNS

	SUBJECTIVE	POSSESSIVE	OBJECTIVE
Singular			
1st person	I	my, mine	me
2nd person	you	your, yours	you
3rd person	he, she, it	his, her, hers, its	him, her, it

Plural

1st person	we	our, ours	us
2nd person	you	your, yours	you
3rd person	they	their, theirs	them

▲ Note: The pronouns *my*, *our*, *your*, *him*, *her*, *it*, and *them* are used as parts of *-self* pronouns. Edited American English—that is, formal or standard English—does not accept *myself* as a substitute for *I* or *me*:

John and **I** [NOT myself] work at the gas station on Oak Street.

See **intensive/reflexive pronoun**, page 562.

THE RELATIVE PRONOUNS *Who, Which,* AND *That*

	SUBJECTIVE	POSSESSIVE	OBJECTIVE
Singular	who	whose	whom
OR	which	whose	which
Plural	that	that	that

Who, whose, and *whom* ordinarily refer to people, *which* to things, and *that* to either. The possessive pronoun *whose* (in lieu of an awkward *of which*) sometimes refers to things:

The poem, **whose** author is unknown, has recently been set to music.

See also **12d**.

USE OF CASES

The subject of a verb and a subject complement are in the *subjective* case.

SUBJECTIVE **We** left early. **Who** noticed? [subjects of verbs]
That was **he** at the door. [subject complement]

The *possessive* case indicates ownership or a comparable relationship: see **15a**. Nouns and pronouns in the possessive case ordinarily serve as modifiers, but a few pronouns (such as *mine* and *theirs*) take the position of nouns and function as subjects, objects, and so on.

POSSESSIVE   **Their** cat likes **its** new leash.   [modifiers]
                That book is **mine**.   [subject complement]

Nouns and some indefinite pronouns have a distinctive form only in the possessive case: a student's opinion, the students' opinions, everyone's vote. See **15a**. The object of a verb, verbal, or a preposition is in the *objective* case.

OBJECTIVE   Fran blamed **me**.   [direct object]
             Feeding **them** is a nuisance.   [object of verbal]
             I fried **him** two eggs.   [indirect object]
             To **whom** was it addressed?   [object of preposition]

An *appositive* has the same case as the word that it refers to.

SUBJECTIVE   Some people—for example, **he** and **I**—did not agree.   [*He* and *I* refer to *people,* the subject.]
OBJECTIVE   The officer ticketed both drivers, **Rita** and **him**.   [*Rita* and *him* identify *drivers,* the object.]

5a

Do not let a compound construction trick you into choosing inappropriate forms of pronouns.

Subjects, subject complements:

She and her brother play golf on Saturday mornings.
I thought **he or Dad** would come to my rescue.
It was **Maria and I** who solved the problem.   [See **5f**.]

▲ Note 1: As a rule, speakers and writers place first-person pronouns last in a compound construction—usually as a matter of courtesy (rather than for emphasis).

Objects of prepositions:

> between **you and me**   to **the chef and her**
> except **Elmer and him**   with **Carla and me**

Objects of verbs or verbals, subjects of infinitives:

> Clara may appoint **you or me**.   [direct object]
> They lent **Tom and her** ten dollars.   [indirect object]
> He gets nowhere by scolding **Bea or him**.   [object of gerund]
> Dad wanted **Sue and me** to keep the old car.   [subject of infinitive]

Appositives:

> Two members of the cast, **he and I**, assisted the director. [Compare "**He and I**, two members of the cast, assisted the director."]
> The director often calls on her two assistants: **him and me**. [Compare "The director often calls on **him and me**, her two assistants."]
> "Let us, just **you and me**," he drawled, "sit down and reason together."   [Informal English accepts *Let's you and I. . . .*]

▲ Note 2: Do not let an appositive following *we* or *us* cause you to choose the wrong form.

> NOT   Us students need this. Don told we students about it.
> BUT   **We** students need this. Don told **us** students about it.

■ **Exercise 1** Choose the correct pronoun within the parentheses in each of the following sentences.

1. When choosing a career, young people like Lucille and (I, me) have more options today than ever before.
2. (She, Her) and (I, me) applied for a small federal grant.
3. It was Dean and (she, her) who volunteered to do the publicity.
4. Are Mitch and (they, them) still looking for a job?
5. Between Lana and (she, her) there is little cooperation.
6. Mr. Liu will hire a new programmer, either Sam or (he, him).
7. Leaving Scot and (he, him) at home, we went to town to pick up Elizabeth and (she, her).
8. My family and (I, me, myself) expected Bobby and (she, her) to declare bankruptcy any day.

9. Two employees in our office, Tom and (he, him), talked with the boss before the meeting.
10. After the meeting the boss talked with two employees in our office, Tom and (he, him).

5b

Determine the case of each pronoun by its use in its own clause.

(1) *Who* or *whoever* as the subject of a clause

The subject of a verb in a subordinate clause takes the subjective case, even when the whole clause is used as an object:

> I forgot **who** won the Superbowl in 1989.   [In its own clause, *who* is the subject of the verb *won*. The complete clause *who won the Superbowl in 1989* is the object of the verb *forgot*.]
> He has respect for **whoever** is in power.   [*Whoever* is the subject of *is*. The complete clause *whoever is in power* is the object of the preposition *for*.]

(2) *Who* or *whom* before *I think, he says,* and so on

Such expressions as *I think, he says, she believes,* and *we know* may follow either *who* or *whom*. The choice depends on the use of *who* or *whom* in its own clause:

> Gene is a man **whom** we know well.   [*Whom* is the direct object of *know*. Compare "We know him well."]
> Gene is a man **who** we know is honest.   [*Who* is the subject of the second *is*. Compare "We know that Gene is a man *who* is honest."]

(3) Pronoun after *than* or *as*

In sentences such as the following, which have implied (rather than stated) elements, the choice of the pronoun form is important to meaning:

She admires Kurt more than **I**. [meaning "more than I do"]
She admires Kurt more than **me**. [meaning "more than she admires me"]
He talks about food as much as **she**. [meaning "as much as she does"]
He talks about food as much as **her**. [meaning "as much as he talks about her"]

Formal usage still requires the use of the subjective case of pronouns in sentences such as the following:

Mr. Ames is older than **I**. [Compare "older than I am."]

■ **Exercise 2** Using the case form in parentheses, convert each pair of sentences below into a single sentence.

EXAMPLES

I understand the daredevil. He motorcycled across the Grand Canyon. (*who*)
I understand the daredevil who motorcycled across the Grand Canyon.
Evelyn consulted an astrologer. She had met him in San Francisco. (*whom*)
Evelyn consulted an astrologer whom she had met in San Francisco.

1. Hercule Poirot is a famous detective. Agatha Christie finally kills him off in *Curtain*. (*whom*)
2. We heard terrifying stories of terrorist activity from my brother. My brother had just returned from two years of active duty in the Middle East. (*who*)
3. After the home run, hundreds of fans were smiling and slapping each other on the back. The fans had been halfheartedly watching a routine game. (*who*)
4. The district attorney called for the maximum sentence. The defense attorney had shouted at the district attorney earlier. (*whom*)

■ **Exercise 3** In sentences 1, 2, and 3 below, insert *I think* after each *who*; then read each sentence aloud. Notice that *who,* not *whom,* is still the correct case form. In sentences 4 and 5, complete each comparison by using first *they* and then *them.* Prepare to explain the differences in meaning.

1. George Eliot, who was a woman, wrote *Adam Bede.*
2. It was Dieter Jordan who first vaulted sixteen feet at my university.
3. Sylvia Plath, who was a poet, wrote about her feelings of inadequacy.
4. My supervisor likes you as much as _____.
5. The director praised her more than _____.

5c

As a rule, use *whom* for all objects. See also **5b**.

Depending on the situation and your audience, use *whom* (rather than the informal *who*) as the object of the verb in sentences:

> **Whom** do they recommend?   [object of the verb *do recommend*]
> For **whom** did the board of directors vote?   [object of the preposition *for*]
> Danny told Chet **whom** to call. Danny told Chet to call **whom**?   [object of the infinitive *to call*—see also **5e**]

In subordinate clauses:

> The artist **whom** she loved has gone away.   [object of the verb *loved* in the adjective clause]
> This is a friend **whom** I write to once a year.   [object of the preposition *to* in the adjective clause]

Whom may be omitted (or *that* substituted) in sentences where no misunderstanding would result:

> The friend he relied on moved away.
> This is a person I try to avoid.

▲ Note: When a preposition follows its object, informal English accepts *who* rather than *whom*.

> Who is the gift for? I don't know who to give it to.

■ **Exercise 4**   Assume that your situation and audience demand your most careful attention to usage of *who* and *whom*. Change *who* to *whom* when the pronoun functions as an object. Put a check mark after sentences containing *who* correctly used as the subject of a verb or as a subject complement.

1. Who did you invite?
2. Who wants to know?
3. He knows who they will promote.
4. He knows who will be promoted.
5. The witness who the lawyer questioned next could remember nothing.
6. Guess who I ran into at the airport?
7. Someone must know who they are and where they came from.
8. In a friendly discussion she knows exactly who to ask what.
9. To find out who deceived who, read to the end of the novel.
10. In the crowded airport, whoever I asked for directions pointed me back the way I had come.

5d

As a rule, use the possessive case immediately before a gerund.

> I resented **his** criticizing our every move.   [Compare "I resented his criticism, not him."]
> **Harry's** refusing the offer was a surprise.   [Compare "Harry's refusal was a surprise."]

The *-ing* form of a verb can be used as a noun (gerund) or as an adjective (participle). The possessive case is not used before participles:

> **Caroline's** radioing the Coast Guard solved our problem. [*Radioing* is a gerund. Compare "*Her action* solved our problem."]
> The **man** sitting at the desk solved our problem.   [*Sitting* is a participle. Compare "*He* solved our problem."]

▲ Note 1: Avoid an awkward possessive before a gerund.

> AWKWARD   The board approved of something's being sent to the poor overseas.

BETTER   The board approved of sending something to the
          poor overseas.

▲ Note 2: Do not omit 's to show possessive case before
nouns:

Karl's street   [NOT Karl street]

5e

Use the objective case for the subject or the object of an infinitive.

They expected Nancy and **me** to do the scriptwriting.
    [subject of the infinitive *to do*]
I did not want to challenge Victor or **him**.   [object of the infinitive *to challenge*]
I didn't want **her** to fail.   [subject of infinitive *to fail*]

5f

Use the subjective case for the subject complement.

That certainly could be **she** sitting near the front.
It was **I** who first noticed the difference.   [Compare "I was the one who first noticed the difference."]

Informal English accepts *It's me* (*him, her, us,* and *them*).

■ **Exercise 5**   Find and revise all case forms that would be inappropriate. Put a check mark after each sentence that needs no revision.

1. As for I and my wife, we prefer the mountains to the seashore, but she likes to camp out more than I.
2. There was no one who would listen to us, no one whom we could turn to for help.
3. It was Pete and he who I blamed for me being fired.
4. John racing the motor did not hurry Scot or me.
5. It is true that the Staffords eat more fried foods than us; no wonder we are thinner than them.

6. Do Aaron and she want you and me to help them paint the car?
7. Let's you and me tell Harvey who to put in charge of the organization.
8. Just between you and me, I think that her family and she could do these things for themselves.
9. We students wanted higher standards in high school, but most of us graduating seniors did not speak up much.
10. The librarian wanted us—Kurt Jacobs and I—to choose one of the American Heritage books.

6
AGREEMENT

Make a verb agree in number with its subject; make a pronoun agree in number with its antecedent.

A verb and its subject or a pronoun and its antecedent agree when their forms indicate the same number or person. Notice below that the singular subject takes a singular verb and that the plural subject takes a plural verb. (If you cannot easily recognize verbs and their subjects, study **1a** and **1b**.)

SINGULAR   The **car** in the lot **looks** shabby.   [*car looks*]
PLURAL   The **cars** in the lot **look** shabby.   [*cars look*]

Lack of subject-verb agreement occurs chiefly in the use of the present tense. Except for forms of *be* and *have* (*you were, he has eaten*), verbs in other tenses do not change form to indicate the number or person of their subjects. For a list of various forms of *be* and the subjects they take, see page 73.

When a pronoun has an antecedent (the word the pronoun refers to), the two words should agree in number. (See also section **28**.)

SINGULAR   A **wolf** has **its** own language.   [*wolf–its*]
PLURAL   **Wolves** have **their** own language.   [*wolves–their*]

▲ Note: A pronoun also agrees with its antecedent in gender. Agreement in gender is usually easy and natural:

the **boy** and **his** mother   [masculine]
the **girl** and **her** mother   [feminine]
the **garden** and **its** weeds   [neuter]

6a

Make a verb agree in number with its subject.

As you study the following rules and examples, remember that *-s* (or *-es*) marks plural nouns but singular verbs (those present-tense verbs with third-person singular subjects).

subject + s	OR	verb + s
The egotists like attention.		The egotist likes attention.
Tomatoes ripen best in the sun.		A tomato ripens best in the sun.

▲ Note: Be sure that you do not omit the *-s* on the third-person singular form of the verb:

The telephone **rings** constantly.   [NOT *ring*]

(1) Do not be misled by subjects and verbs with endings not clearly sounded or by nouns, pronouns, or phrases intervening between the subject and the verb.

NOT   Scientist are puzzled. BUT **Scientists** are puzzled.
NOT   She ask me every time I see her. BUT She **asks**. . . .

The **repetition** of the drumbeats **helps** to stir emotions.
Every **one** of you **is invited** to the panel discussion.

As a rule, the grammatical number of the subject is not changed by the addition of expressions beginning with such words as *accompanied by, along with, as well as, in addi-*

tion to, including, no less than, not to mention, together with.

> **Unemployment** as well as taxes **influences** votes.
> **Taxes**, not to mention unemployment, **influence** votes.

(2) Subjects joined by *and* are usually plural.

> My **parents** and my **uncle do** not **understand** this.
> The **band** and the **team were leading** the parade.
> **Building a good marriage** and **building a good log fire** are similar in many ways. —JOSEPHINE LOWMAN
> [gerund phrases—Compare "Two actions are similar."]

▲ Exceptions: Occasionally, such a compound subject takes a singular verb because the subject denotes one person or a single unit.

> Its **inventor** and chief **practitioner is** a native son of Boston, Robert Coles. —MARTHA BAYLES
> **Pushing** and **shoving** in public places **is** characteristic of Middle Eastern culture. —EDWARD T. HALL

Every or *each* preceding singular subjects joined by *and* calls for a singular verb:

> Every silver knife, fork, and spoon **has** to be counted.
> Each cat and each dog **has** its own toy.

Placed after a plural subject, *each* does not affect the verb form:

> The cat and the dog each **have** their own toys.

(3) Singular subjects joined by *or, either . . . or,* or *neither . . . nor* usually take a singular verb.

> Paula or her secretary **answers** the phone on Saturday.
> Either the mayor or the governor **is** the keynote speaker.
> Neither praise nor blame **affects** her.

If one subject is singular and one is plural, the verb usually agrees with the nearer subject:

> Neither the quality nor the prices **have** changed.
> Neither the prices nor the quality **has** changed.
> [Compare "The prices *and* the quality *have* not changed."]

The verb also agrees with the nearer subject in person in sentences like the following.

> Either Nat or **you were** ready for any emergency call.
> Either you or **Nat was** ready for any emergency call.

(4) Do not let inverted word order (VERB + SUBJECT) or the structure *there* + VERB + SUBJECT cause you to make a mistake in agreement.

VERB + SUBJECT

> Hardest hit by the high temperatures and the drought **were** American **farmers**.   —TIME

> Among our grandest and longest-lived illusions **is** the **notion** of the noble savage.   —JOHN PFEIFFER

There + VERB + SUBJECT

> There **are** a few unanswered **questions**.
> There **were anger** and **hatred** in that voice.   —JOHN CIARDI

(5) A relative pronoun (*who, which, that*) used as subject has the same number as its antecedent.

> It is the **pharmacist who** often **suggests** a new brand.
> Tonsillitis is among those **diseases that are** curable.
> This is the only **one** of the local papers **that prints** a daily horoscope.   [*That* refers to *one* because only one paper prints a daily horoscope; the other papers do not.]
> He is **one** of those **who agree** with my decision.   [*Who* refers to *those,* a plural pronoun. The plural form of the verb is necessary for agreement.]
> It is not better things but better **people that make** better living.   —CARLL TUCKER [Compare "Better people (not better things) make better living."]

(6) When used as subjects, such words as *each, either, neither, one, everybody,* and *anyone* regularly take singular verbs.

Neither likes the friends of the other.
Each of them **does have** political ambitions.
Everybody in the office **has** tickets.

Subjects such as *all, any, half, most, none,* and *some* may take a singular or a plural verb; the context generally determines the choice of the verb form.

Evelyn collects stamps; **some are** worth a lot. [Compare "Some of them are worth a lot."]
The honey was marked down because **some was** sugary. [Compare "Some of it was sugary."]

(7) Collective nouns and phrases denoting a fixed quantity take a singular verb when they refer to the group as a unit and take a plural verb when they refer to individuals or parts of the group.

Singular (regarded as a unit):

My **family has** its traditions.
The number is very small.
A **billion dollars is** a lot of money.
The **majority** of it **was** wasted.
Two-thirds of this **has** been finished.

Plural (regarded as individuals or parts):

A number were absent.
The **majority** of us **are** for it.
Two-thirds of these **have** been finished.

Although the use of *data* as a singular noun has gained currency in recent years, many writers still maintain the distinction between the singular *datum* and the plural *data*. The use of *media* as a singular subject is not accepted in formal English.

Professor Pollinger had for the last ten years devoted himself . . . to the collection of every possible **datum** about William Sharp. —AMANDA CROSS [Note use of singular.]
The **data were** accurate.
Marshall McLuhan defined television as "a hot **medium**."
[singular]
The **media have** shaped public opinion. [plural, referring to
television, newspapers, and so on]

**(8) A linking verb agrees with its subject, not with its com-
plement (predicate noun).**

His **problem is** frequent headaches.
Frequent **headaches are** his problem.

▲ Note: Because the number of the pronoun *what* depends
on the number of the word (or word group) referred to, the
verb does agree with its complement in sentences like this:

What I do, at these times, **is** to change the way the system
works. —LEWIS THOMAS [Compare "That is what I do."]

**(9) Titles of single works, words spoken of as words, and
nouns plural in form but singular in meaning usually
take singular verbs. In all doubtful cases, consult a
good dictionary.**

Harry and Tonto **sticks** in the memory. [The movie, not the
characters, sticks in the memory.]
"Autumn Leaves" **is** a beautiful song.
Kids **is** informal for *children*.

Nouns that are regularly treated as singular include *economics, electronics, measles, mumps, news,* and *physics*.

News **is** traveling faster than ever before.
Physics **has** fascinated my roommate for months.

Some nouns (such as *athletics, politics, series, deer,* and
sheep) can be either singular or plural, depending on
meaning:

Statistics is an interesting subject. **Statistics are** often misleading.

A **series** of natural disasters **has** occurred recently. Two **series** of natural disasters **have** occurred recently.

The **sheep strays** when the gate is left open. **Sheep stray** when the gate is left open.

■ **Exercise 1** The following sentences are all correct. Read them aloud, stressing the italicized words. If any sentence sounds wrong, read it aloud two or three more times so that you will gain practice in saying and hearing the correct forms.

1. The *timing* of these strikes *was* poorly *planned*.
2. There *are* several *books* and three *maps* in the car.
3. Neither the *wrench* nor the *hubcap was* missing.
4. Every *one* of my cousins, including Larry, *has* brown eyes.
5. Al was the *only one* of the speakers *who was* interesting.
6. *Doesn't it make* sense?
7. *Neither* employee *respects* the dress code.
8. *A number* in this group *are* affected.
9. There *were* several *reasons* for this.
10. The *data* for the experiment *were collected* in three groups.

■ **Exercise 2** Choose the correct form of the verb within parentheses in each sentence below. Make sure that the verb agrees with its subject according to the rules of formal English.

1. Neither Professor Barr nor Professor Neill (think, thinks) that the problem is solved.
2. Attitudes about responsibility, of course, (vary, varies).
3. Every one of the items (was, were) inventoried last month.
4. A low wall and a high hedge (provide, provides) privacy for the entrance.
5. Neither of them even (know, knows) when to stop.
6. There (comes, come) to my mind now the names of the two or three people who were most influential in my life.
7. The sweepstakes prize (was, were) ten million dollars.
8. A rustic lodge, as well as a game refuge and fishing waters, (is, are) close by.
9. Such computers, which (stores, store) personal data, (jeopardizes, jeopardize) the privacy of millions.
10. An understanding of mathematics (is, are) facilitated by a knowledge of number theory.

6b

Make a pronoun agree in number and gender with its antecedent.

SINGULAR	A lawyer represents **his or her** clients.
PLURAL	Lawyers represent **their** clients.
MASCULINE	John represents **his** clients.
FEMININE	Mary represents **her** clients.

(1) Such singular antecedents as *man, woman, person, everybody, one, anyone, each, either, neither, sort,* and *kind* are referred to by a singular pronoun.

Each of these companies had **its** books audited.   [NOT their]
One has to live with **oneself**.   [NOT themselves]
A woman has a right to follow **her** conscience.   [feminine singular antecedent]

▲ Note: Avoid the use of pronouns that exclude either sex or that stereotype male and female roles:

NOT	As **a person** grows up, **he** must assume responsibilities. [excludes females]
NOT	As **a person** grows up, **she** must assume responsibilities. [excludes males]
BUT	As **people** grow up, **they** must assume responsibilities. [includes both sexes]

The following sentences also stereotype male and female roles:

A **professor** should be thoroughly familiar with **his** material.
A **secretary** should be thoroughly familiar with **her** filing system.

Include both sexes by using one of the following options:

A **professor** should be thoroughly familiar with **his or her** material.   [Substitute compound phrase.]

The filing system should be thoroughly familiar to the secretary. [Recast in passive voice, but see also **29d**.]

Professors should be thoroughly familiar with **their** material. [Recast in plural.]

A secretary should be thoroughly familiar with the filing system. [Avoid the pronoun altogether.]

Any of these options may change your meaning; some work more smoothly than others. Many people consider the compound phrase *his or her* stylistically awkward; many also find the forms *his/her* and *he/she* ugly and bureaucratic. You can always rewrite your sentence to avoid them. The most effective options are usually to recast the sentence in the plural or to avoid the pronoun altogether.

(2) Two or more antecedents joined by *and* are referred to by a plural pronoun; two or more singular antecedents joined by *or* or *nor* are referred to by a singular pronoun.

Andrew and Roger lost **their** self-confidence.
Did **Andrew or Roger** lose **his** self-confidence?

If one of two antecedents joined by *or* or *nor* is singular and one is plural, the pronoun usually agrees with the nearer antecedent:

Neither the **package nor** the **letters** had reached **their** destination. [*Their* is closer to the plural antecedent *letters.*]

Stray **kittens or** even an abandoned grown **cat** has **its** problems finding enough food to survive long. [*Its* is closer to the singular antecedent *cat.*]

▲ Note: When following this rule is awkward, as in sentences such as "Roger or Melissa will bring her book," recast the sentence to avoid the problem: "Roger will bring his book, or Melissa will bring hers."

(3) Collective nouns are referred to by singular or plural pronouns, depending on whether the collective noun has a singular or plural sense. See also **6a(7)**.

Special care should be taken to avoid treating a collective noun as both singular and plural within the same sentence.

INCONSISTENT	The choir **is** writing **their** own music. [singular verb, plural pronoun]
CONSISTENT	The choir **is** writing **its** own music. [both singular]
CONSISTENT	The group of students **do** not agree on methods, but **they** unite on basic aims. [both plural]

■ **Exercise 3** Following the rules of formal usage, choose the correct pronoun or verb form in parentheses in each sentence.

1. A number of writers (has, have) expressed (his, his and her, his/her, their) concern about sexist usage.
2. If any one of the sisters (needs, need) a ride to church, (she, they) can call Trudy.
3. Neither the pilot nor the flight attendants mentioned the incident when (he, they) talked to reporters.
4. The Washington team (was, were) opportunistic; (it, they) took advantage of every break.
5. If the board of directors (controls, control) the company, (it, they) may vote (itself, themselves) bonuses.

■ **Exercise 4** Make the language of the following sentences inclusive rather than sexist.

1. A doctor who treats his own child shows poor judgment.
2. The nurse looks efficient in her starched, white uniform.
3. Every lawyer should make sure his receptionist knows which parking place is hers.
4. The child's teacher gave her report to the social worker, who put it on her desk so that she would have it ready for the psychiatrist when he gave his testimony.
5. The policeman asked the little old lady who was robbed if the robber had put her money in his pocket.

■ **Exercise 5** All of the following sentences are correct. Change them as directed in parentheses, revising other parts of the sentence to secure agreement of subject and verb, pronoun and antecedent.

1. A sign in the lab reads: "This computer does only what you tell it to, not what you want it to." (Change *this computer* to *these computers.*)
2. Perhaps this sign was put up by some frustrated students who were having trouble with their computer manuals. (Change *some frustrated students* to *a frustrated student.*)
3. The sign in the lab reminds me of similar problems. A chef, for example, whose vegetables or casserole is ruined in a microwave might think: "This oven reads buttons, not minds." (Change *vegetables or casserole* to *casserole or vegetables.* Change *This oven* to *These ovens.*)
4. All too often what comes out of our mouths is the very opposite of what we intend to say but exposes what we really think. (Change *what* to *the words that.* Change *our* to *one's.*)
5. Two of my instructors, together with a few of my classmates, were talking about such Freudian slips the other day. (Change *Two* to *One.*)
6. Who knows what kind of label is attached to one's computer errors! (Change *kind* to *kinds.*)
7. Then there is the mirror. (Change *the mirror* to *mirrors.*) There are times when people don't like to face mirrors. (Change *people* to *a person.*)
8. At such times a person has to face how he or she actually looks, not how he or she wants to look. (Change *a person* to *people.*)
9. There is another thought that comes to mind. (Change *another thought* to *other thoughts.*)
10. Mirrors reflect images in reverse, so not even in a mirror do we ever see ourselves as we really are. (Change *we* to *one.*)

7

VERB FORMS

Use the appropriate form of the verb.

The forms of verbs and auxiliaries may indicate not only number and person of their subjects (see **6a**) but also tense, voice, and mood. A change in the form of a verb shows a specific meaning or a grammatical relationship to another word or group of words in a sentence.

Regular and irregular verbs　The way a verb forms its past tense determines its classification as regular or irregular. A regular verb takes the *-d* or *-ed* ending to denote the past tense.

> REGULAR　　*believe (believes), believed*
> 　　　　　　*attack (attacks), attacked*

Irregular verbs do not take the *-d* or *-ed* ending. They are inflected in various other ways to indicate past tense: see **irregular verb**, page 563.

> IRREGULAR　　*run (runs), ran*
> 　　　　　　*eat (eats), ate, eaten*

A few irregular verbs (like *cut* or *hurt*) have the same form in the present and the past tense.

Auxiliary verbs Auxiliary verbs are combined with basic verb forms to indicate voice, mood, and tense. The following words are commonly used as auxiliaries:

have	be	will	may
has	am	shall	might
had	are	can	must
do	is	would	ought to
does	was	should	has to
did	were	could	have to
	been		used to

In addition, the present and past forms of *get* and *keep* may serve as auxiliaries:

I *got* robbed.   I *kept* running.

Other words may intervene between the auxiliary and the basic verb.

Have the members paid their dues? I have not paid mine. Television will never completely replace the radio.

Although not a verb, the contraction for *not* may be added to many auxiliaries: *haven't, doesn't, aren't, can't.* The full word *not* following an auxiliary is written separately (*do not, have not*); an exception is *cannot.*

Forms of the verb *be* The most irregular verb in the English language is *be.* It has eight forms: *am, are, is, was, were, be, been, being.*

That may **be** true.   He **was being** difficult.

The following is a list of forms of *be* used with various subjects in the present and the past tense.

	First	*Second*	*Third*	
PRESENT	I am	you are	he/she/it is	[singular]
	we are	you are	they are	[plural]
PAST	I was	you were	he/she/it was	[singular]
	we were	you were	they were	[plural]

A form of *be* is used with the present participle to form the progressive: **is** *attacking,* **will** be *eating.* A form of *be* is used with a past participle to form the passive: **was** *attacked, had* **been** *eaten.*

Tense   *Tense* refers to the form of the verb that indicates time. There are different ways of classifying the number of tenses in English. If you consider only the form changes of single-word verbs, there are only two tenses (present and past); if you consider progressive forms and certain auxiliaries, there are twelve. The usual practice, however, is to distinguish six tenses: three simple tenses (*try, tried, will try*) and three perfect tenses (*have tried, had tried, will have tried*). A perfect tense is distinguished from a simple tense in that it refers not only to the time in which the action began but also to the time in which the action is completed. See **7b(2)** for a fuller explanation.

The forms of the verb used in the following conjugation are *see* (*sees*), *saw, seen* (called the principal parts), and *seeing* (sometimes called the fourth principal part: see **7a**).

INDICATIVE MOOD

Active Voice		*Passive Voice*	

PRESENT TENSE

Singular	*Plural*	*Singular*	*Plural*
1. I see	we see	I am seen	we are seen
2. you see	you see	you are seen	you are seen
3. one (he/she/it) sees	they see	one (he/she/it) is seen	they are seen

PAST TENSE

1. I saw	we saw	I was seen	we were seen
2. you saw	you saw	you were seen	you were seen
3. one saw	they saw	one was seen	they were seen

FUTURE TENSE

1. I shall (will) see	we shall (will) see	I shall (will) be seen	we shall (will) be seen
2. you will see	you will see	you will be seen	you will be seen
3. one will see	they will see	one will be seen	they will be seen

PRESENT PERFECT TENSE

1. I have seen	we have seen	I have been seen	we have been seen
2. you have seen	you have seen	you have been seen	you have been seen
3. one has seen	they have seen	one has been seen	they have been seen

PAST PERFECT TENSE

1. I had seen	we had seen	I had been seen	we had been seen
2. you had seen	you had seen	you had been seen	you had been seen
3. one had seen	they had seen	one had been seen	they had been seen

FUTURE PERFECT TENSE (seldom used)

1. I shall (will) have seen	we shall (will) have seen	I shall (will) have been seen	we shall (will) have been seen
2. you will have seen	you will have seen	you will have been seen	you will have been seen
3. one will have seen	they will have seen	one will have been seen	they will have been seen

SUBJUNCTIVE MOOD

Active Voice   *Passive Voice*

PRESENT TENSE

Singular: if I, you, one see   if I, you, one be seen
Plural: if we, you, they see   if we, you, they be seen

PAST TENSE

Singular: if I, you, one saw   if I, you, one were seen
Plural: if we, you, they saw   if we, you, they were seen

PRESENT PERFECT TENSE

Singular: if I, you, one have seen   if I, you, one have been seen
Plural: if we, you, they have seen   if we, you, they have been seen

PAST PERFECT TENSE

(Same as the Indicative)

IMPERATIVE MOOD

PRESENT TENSE

see   be seen

Verb forms in the indicative mood are generally used for making assertions or asking questions; those in the imperative mood for commands and requests; and those in the subjunctive mood (see also **7c**) for hypothetical or conditional situations.

Voice   *Voice* indicates the relationship between the action of the verb and the subject of the verb. Two kinds of relationships are possible: **active** and **passive**. Active voice indicates that the subject of the sentence is the doer of the action. Passive voice indicates that the action of the verb is done to the subject of the sentence. When an active verb is made passive, a form of *be* is used.

ACTIVE   Burglars often **steal** jewelry.   [The subject acts. The object is *jewelry*.]

PASSIVE   Jewelry **is** often **stolen** by burglars.   [The subject is acted upon. The prepositional phrase identifying the doer of the action could be omitted.]

Transitive and intransitive verbs   Notice that the object of the active verb becomes the subject of the passive verb. This transformation is possible only with **transitive** verbs. A transitive verb takes an object, and it may be made passive.

An **intransitive** verb may not take a direct object (although it may take a subject complement) and may not be made passive.

TRANSITIVE These figures **deceive** many people. [The direct object is *people*.]

INTRANSITIVE The figures **seemed** reliable. [The subject complement is *reliable*.]

The figures **rose** annually. [intransitive complete]

7a

Avoid misusing the principal parts of verbs and confusing similar verbs.

NOT Has the president spoke to the press about this? [misuse of a principal part of the verb *speak*]

BUT **Has** the president **spoken** to the press about this?

NOT The hand-carved chairs set on the porch for years. [confusion of past forms of the similar verbs *set* and *sit*]

BUT The hand-carved chairs **sat** on the porch for years.

(1) Avoid misusing the principal parts of verbs.

The principal parts of a verb include the present form (*see*), which is also the stem of the infinitive (*to see*), the past form (*saw*), and the past participle (*seen*). (See "Principal Parts of Verbs" on page 78.) The present participle (*seeing*) is often considered a fourth principal part.

The PRESENT FORM may function as a single-word verb or may be preceded by auxiliaries.

I **ask**, he **does ask**, we **will begin**, it **used to begin**

The PAST FORM functions as a single-word verb.

He **asked** a few questions.   The show **began** at eight.

When used as part of a simple predicate, the PAST PARTICIPLE as well as the PRESENT PARTICIPLE always has at least one auxiliary.

> He **has asked** them. I **was asked**. I **will be asking** questions.
> They **have begun**. **Had** he **begun**? It **is beginning** to snow.

Both the past and the present participle serve not only as parts of a simple predicate but also as modifiers: "pastries *baked* last week," "heat waves *rising* from the road." Nouns modified by participles are not sentences: see **2a**.

▲ Caution: Do not omit a needed *-d* or *-ed* because of pronunciation. For example, although it is easy to remember a clearly pronounced *-d* or *-ed* (*added, repeated*), it is sometimes difficult to remember a needed *-d* or *-ed* in such expressions as *had priced them* or *opened it*. Observe the use of the *-d* or *-ed* in these sentences:

> Yesterday I ask**ed** myself: "Is the judge prejudice**d**?" [NOT Yesterday I ask myself is the judge prejudice?]
> He use**d** to smoke. [NOT He use to smoke.]
> I am not suppose**d** to be the boss. [NOT I am not suppose to be the boss.]
> She talk**ed** to Ellen yesterday. [NOT She talk to Ellen yesterday.]

The following list of principal parts includes both regular and irregular verbs that are sometimes misused.

Principal Parts of Verbs

PRESENT	PAST	PAST PARTICIPLE
arise	arose	arisen
ask	asked	asked
attack	attacked	attacked
awaken	awakened	awakened
become	became	become
begin	began	begun

Principal Parts of Verbs (cont.)

PRESENT	PAST	PAST PARTICIPLE
blow	blew	blown
break	broke	broken
bring	brought	brought
burst	burst	burst
choose	chose	chosen
cling	clung	clung
come	came	come
creep	crept	crept
dive	dived OR dove	dived
do	did	done
drag	dragged	dragged
draw	drew	drawn
drink	drank	drunk
drive	drove	driven
drown	drowned	drowned
eat	ate	eaten
fall	fell	fallen
fly	flew	flown
forgive	forgave	forgiven
freeze	froze	frozen
give	gave	given
go	went	gone
grow	grew	grown
happen	happened	happened
know	knew	known
ride	rode	ridden
ring	rang	rung
rise	rose	risen
run	ran	run
see	saw	seen
shake	shook	shaken
shrink	shrank OR shrunk	shrunk OR shrunken
sing	sang OR sung	sung
sink	sank OR sunk	sunk
speak	spoke	spoken
spin	spun	spun

Principal Parts of Verbs (cont.)

PRESENT	PAST	PAST PARTICIPLE
spring	sprang OR sprung	sprung
steal	stole	stolen
sting	stung	stung
stink	stank OR stunk	stunk
swear	swore	sworn
swim	swam	swum
swing	swung	swung
take	took	taken
tear	tore	torn
throw	threw	thrown
wake	woke OR waked	waked OR woken
wear	wore	worn
wring	wrung	wrung
write	wrote	written

▲ Note: Mistakes with verbs sometimes involve spelling errors. Use care when you write troublesome verb forms such as the following:

PRESENT	PAST	PAST PARTICIPLE	PRESENT PARTICIPLE
lead	led	led	leading
loosen	loosened	loosened	loosening
lose	lost	lost	losing
pay	paid	paid	paying
study	studied	studied	studying

■ **Exercise 1** Respond to the questions in the past tense with a past tense verb; respond to the questions in the future tense with a present perfect verb (*have* or *has* + a past participle). Follow the pattern of the examples.

EXAMPLES
Did she criticize Don? *Yes, she criticized Don.*
Will they take it? *They have already taken it.*

1. Did he give it away?
2. Will you run a mile?
3. Did the man drown?
4. Will they begin that?
5. Did the wind blow?
6. Will she choose it?
7. Did it really happen?
8. Will the river rise?
9. Did you do that?
10. Will they steal it?
11. Did you spin your wheels?
12. Will they freeze it?
13. Did he cling to that belief?
14. Will they go to the police?
15. Did she know them?
16. Will the fire alarm ring?
17. Did the sack burst?
18. Will he eat it?
19. Did you grow these?
20. Will Bert speak out?

(2) Do not confuse *set* with *sit* or *lay* with *lie*.

Sit means "be seated," and *lie down* means "rest in [or get into] a horizontal position." To *set* or *lay* something down is to place it or put it somewhere.

Learn the distinctions between the forms of *sit* and *set* and those of *lie* and *lay*.

PRESENT (INFINITIVE)	PAST	PAST PARTICIPLE	PRESENT PARTICIPLE
(to) sit	sat	sat	sitting
(to) set	set	set	setting
(to) lie	lay	lain	lying
(to) lay	laid	laid	laying

As a rule, the verbs (or verbals) *sit* and *lie* are intransitive; they do not take objects. *Set* and *lay* are usually transitive and therefore take objects. Transitive verbs may be passive as well as active. (If you cannot easily recognize objects of verbs, see **1b**.)

Sit down. **Sitting** down, I thought it over. He **sat** up.
Lie down. I **lay** down. It **was lying** here. **Has** it **lain** here long?
Somebody **had set** the pup in the cart. It **had been set** there.
We **ought to lay** these aside. These **should be laid** aside.

■ **Exercise 2**   Substitute the correct forms of *sit* and *lie* for the italicized word in each sentence. Follow the pattern of the example. Do not change the tense of the verb.

EXAMPLE

The lawn mower has been *rusting* in the yard.
The lawn mower has been *sitting* in the yard.
The lawn mower has been *lying* in the yard.

1. My neighbor's baby never wants to *slow* down.
2. Elizabeth's cat *stayed* under the house during the storm.
3. Melody *remained* in that position for half an hour.
4. Caleb often *sleeps* in the car.
5. Have they *been* there all along?

■ **Exercise 3**   Without changing the tense of the italicized verb, substitute the correct form of one of the verbs in parentheses at the end of each sentence.

1. Last month they *established* the plans for next week's party. (lie/lay)
2. I often *stand* there and watch the tide come in. (sit/set)
3. After he mowed the grass, Dick decided to *recline* for a nap. (lie down/lay down)
4. Ron *was sprawling* on the couch. (sit/set)
5. Bill *was putting* up the Christmas tree. (sit/set)

7b

Learn the meaning of tense forms. Use logical tense forms in sequence.

(1) Learn the meaning of tense forms.

Although tense refers to time (see page 74), the tense forms do not always agree with divisions of actual time. The present tense, for example, is by no means limited to the present time. As you study the following examples, observe that auxiliaries as well as single-word verbs indicate time.

PRESENT TENSE

I **see** what you meant by that remark.   [now, present time]
Maureen **uses** common sense.   [habitual action]
Mistakes **are** often **made**.   [passive verb, habitual action]
Blind innocence **sees** no evil.   [universal or timeless truth]
In 1939 Hitler **attacks** Poland.   [historical present]

Conrad **writes** about what he **sees** in the human heart. [literary present]

Officially, winter **begins** next week. [present form, used with the adverbial *next week* to denote future time]

I **am learning** from my mistakes. [a progressive form denoting past, present, and (probably) future]

PAST TENSE—past time, not extending to the present

I **saw** the accident. [at a definite time before now]
They **used** makeshift tools. [action completed in the past]
We **were enjoying** our reunion. [continuing action in the past]
The accident **was seen** by two people. [passive]
Talk shows **used to be** worse. [Compare "*were* worse then."]

FUTURE TENSE—at a future time, sometime after now

He **will see** his lawyer.
Shall we **use** a different strategy?
He **will be seeing** his lawyer. [progressive]
A different strategy **will be used**. [passive]

PRESENT PERFECT TENSE—sometime before now, up to now

I **have seen** the movie. [sometime before now]
She **has used** her savings wisely. [up to now]
Has Kevin **been using** his talents?
Deer **have been seen** in those woods.

PAST PERFECT TENSE—before a specific time in the past

Carla **had talked** to me before the game started.
After he **had used** his savings, he applied for a loan.
Had they **been sailing** along the coast?
At his death their home **had been** on the market for ten years.

FUTURE PERFECT TENSE—before a specific time in the future

The top executive **will have seen** the report by next week.
By the year 2000 I **will have been seeing** my dreams in action. [a rarely used passive, progressive, future-perfect verb]

▲ Note: Sometimes the simple past tense is used for the past perfect:

Carla **talked** to me before the game started.

Far more frequently the simple future replaces the future perfect:

> The top executive **will see** the report by next week.
> By the year 2000 I **will be seeing** my dreams in action.

■ **Exercise 4**   Prepare to discuss differences in the meaning of the tense forms separated by slashes.

1. It *has snowed/had snowed* for days.
2. Michael *trimmed/did trim/was trimming* the hedge.
3. Charlotte *teaches/is teaching* French.
4. He *complained/has complained* to the president about this.
5. My mother-in-law *had sold/will have sold* her car by then.
6. Time *passes/does pass/has passed/had been passing* rapidly.
7. In 1840 Thomas Carlyle *calls/called* time a great mystery, a miracle.

(2) Use logical tense forms in sequence.

VERBS

Notice in the following examples the relationship of each verb form to actual time:

> When the speaker **entered**, the audience **rose**.   [Both actions took place at the same definite time in the past.]
> I **have ceased** worrying because I **have heard** no more rumors.   [Both verb forms indicate action at some time before now.]
> When I **had been** at camp four weeks, I **received** word that my application **had been accepted**.   [The *had* before *been* indicates a time prior to that of *received*.]

INFINITIVES

Use the present infinitive to express action occurring at the same time as, or later than, that of the main verb; use the present perfect infinitive for action prior to that of the main verb:

I would have liked **to live** (NOT *to have lived*) in Shakespeare's time. [present infinitive—for the same time as that of the main verb]

She wanted **to win**. She wants **to win**. [present infinitives—for time later than *wanted* or *wants*]

I would like **to have won** that prize. [present perfect infinitive— for time prior to that of the main verb. Compare "I wish I *had won*."]

PARTICIPLES

Use the present form of participles to express action occurring at the same time as that of the main verb; use the present perfect form for action prior to that of the main verb:

Walking along the streets, he met many old friends. [The walking and the meeting were simultaneous.]

Having climbed that mountain, they felt a real sense of achievement. [The climbing took place first; then came their sense of achievement.]

■ **Exercise 5** Choose the verb form inside parentheses that is the logical tense form in sequence.

1. When the song (ended, had ended), the jukebox stopped.
2. The winners cheered when the legislation (had been passed, was passed).
3. I plan (to move, to have moved) tomorrow.
4. We should have planned (to have gone, to go) by bus.
5. (Having finished, Finishing) the project, Leslie went home.
6. (Having bought, Buying) the tickets, John took the children to the exhibit.
7. The president had left the meeting before it (had adjourned, adjourned).
8. It is customary for students (to register, to have registered) early for summer classes.
9. Patrice had not expected (to meet, to have met) our group until Thursday.
10. My roses have begun blooming because the weather (was, has been) warm.

7c

Use the appropriate form of the verb for the subjunctive mood.

Although the subjunctive mood is alive in fixed expressions such as *far be it from me, be that as it may, as it were,* and *God bless you,* it has been largely displaced by the indicative. But a few distinctive forms for the subjunctive still occur.

FORMS FOR THE SUBJUNCTIVE

For the verb *be*:

> PRESENT, singular or plural: **be**
> PAST, singular or plural: **were**

(Contrast the indicative forms of *be* with various subjects on page 73.)

For all other verbs with third-person singular subjects:

> PRESENT, singular only: **see**   [The -*s* ending is dropped.]

Examples

It is necessary that Ron **see** him first.
Suppose he **were** to die before she does.
One debater insisted that the other not **avoid** the question.

Alternatives

Ron **has to see** him first.
Suppose he **dies** before she does.
One debater urged the other not **to avoid** the question.

Should and *would* (past forms of *shall* and *will*) are also used for the subjunctive.

(1) Use the subjunctive in *that* clauses after such verbs as *demand, recommend, urge, insist, request, suggest, move.*

I move that the report **be** approved.

The counselor suggested that he **discover** the library.

OR   The counselor told him *to discover* the library.

(2) Especially in formal English, use the subjunctive to express wishes or (in *if* or *as if* clauses) a hypothetical, highly improbable, or contrary-to-fact condition.

I wish I **were** in Madison. **Would** I **were** there now!

If I **were** you, I'd accept the offer.

Drive as if every other car on the road **were** out to kill you.

—ESQUIRE

Especially in formal English, *should* is still used in conditional clauses:

If she **should** resign, we **would** have grave difficulty locating a competent replacement.

OR   If she *resigns,* we *will* have grave difficulty locating a competent replacement.

The indicative is displacing this use of the subjunctive, just as *will* is displacing *shall*—except in questions such as "*Shall we tell?*"

(3) Do not use *would have* for *had* in an *if* clause that expresses an imagined condition.

NOT   If he would have arrived earlier, he wouldn't have lost the sale.

BUT   If he **had** arrived earlier, he wouldn't have lost the sale.

OR   **Had** he arrived earlier, he wouldn't have lost the sale.

■ **Exercise 6**   Prepare to discuss the use of the subjunctive in the following sentences.

1. Had Linda been here, she would have explained everything.
2. We insist that he be punished.
3. I wish that peace were possible.
4. If there should be a change in policy, we would have to make major adjustments.

5. Americans now speak of Spain as though it were just across the river.
6. Present-day problems demand that we be ready for any emergency.
7. One reporter insisted that the president answer her directly.
8. If I were you, I would apply tomorrow.
9. The man acts as if he were the owner.
10. It is necessary that we be prepared in case of attack.

■ **Exercise 7**   Compose five sentences illustrating various uses of the subjunctive.

7d

Avoid needless shifts in tense or mood. See also **27a**.

INCONSISTENT   He **walked** up to me in the cafeteria and **tries** to start a fight.   [shift in tense from past to present]

BETTER   He **walked** up to me in the cafeteria and **tried** to start a fight.

INCONSISTENT   It is necessary to restrain an occasional foolhardy park visitor. If a female bear **were** to mistake his friendly intentions and **supposes** him a menace to her cubs, he would be in trouble.   [shift in mood from subjunctive to indicative]   But females with cubs **were** only one of the dangers. [a correct sentence if standing alone, but here inconsistent with present tense of preceding sentence and therefore misleading] All bears are wild animals and not domesticated pets. It **is** therefore an important part of the park ranger's duty to watch the tourists and above all **don't** let anyone try to feed the bears.   [shift in mood from indicative to imperative]

BETTER   It is necessary to restrain an occasional foolhardy park visitor. If a female bear **were** to mistake his friendly intentions and **suppose** him a menace to her cubs, he would be in trouble. But females with cubs **are** only one of the dangers. All bears are wild animals and not domesticated pets. It **is** therefore an important part of the park ranger's duty to watch the tourists and above all not to let anyone try to feed the bears.

■ **Exercise 8** In the following passage correct all errors and inconsistencies in tense and mood as well as any other errors in verb usage. Put a check mark after any sentence that is satisfactory as it stands.

¹Across the Thames from Shakespeare's London lay the area known as the Bankside, probably as rough and unsavory a neighborhood as ever laid across the river from any city. ²And yet it was to such a place that Shakespeare and his company had to have gone to build their new theater. ³For the Puritan government of the city had set up all sorts of prohibitions against theatrical entertainment within the city walls. ⁴When it became necessary, therefore, for the company to have moved their playhouse from its old location north of the city, they obtain a lease to a tract on the Bankside. ⁵Other theatrical companies had went there before them, and it seemed reasonable to have supposed that Shakespeare and his partners would prosper in the new location. ⁶Apparently the Puritans of the city had no law against anyone's moving cartloads of lumber through the public streets. ⁷There is no record that the company met with difficulty while the timbers of the dismantled playhouse are being hauled to the new site. ⁸The partners had foresaw and forestalled one difficulty: the efforts of their old landlord to have stopped them from removing the building. ⁹Lest his presence complicate their task and would perhaps defeat its working altogether, they waited until he had gone out of town. ¹⁰And when he came back, his lot was bare. ¹¹The building's timbers were all in stacks on the far side of the river, and the theater is waiting only to be put together. ¹²It is a matter of general knowledge that on the Bankside Shakespeare continued his successful career as a showman and went on to enjoy even greater prosperity after he had made the move than before.

MECHANICS

Manuscript Form **8**

Capitals **9**

Italics **10**

Abbreviations, Acronyms, and Numbers **11**

8

MANUSCRIPT FORM

Put your manuscript in acceptable form. Revise and proofread with care.

A clean, well-formatted manuscript contributes to your credibility with your reader. A messy manuscript suggests haste, carelessness, and incompetence. Manuscripts prepared in class typically do contain neatly crossed-out words and passages as well as clearly indicated insertions of words or even large blocks of writing. Manuscripts prepared outside of class should require few, if any, corrections.

8a

Use the proper materials.

Unless you are given other instructions, follow these general practices:

(1) Handwritten papers   Use regular notebook paper, size $8\frac{1}{2} \times 11$ inches, with widely spaced lines. (Narrow spaces between lines do not allow sufficient room for corrections.) Use black or blue ink. Write on only one side of the paper.

(2) Typewritten papers   Use regular white typing paper (not sheets torn from a spiral notebook), size $8\frac{1}{2} \times 11$ inches. Or use a good grade of bond paper (neither onionskin nor erasable bond). Use a fresh black ribbon and avoid fancy typefaces such as script or all capitals. Double-space between lines. Type on only one side of the paper.

(3) Word-processed papers   Check with your instructor to make sure the typeface and the paper you plan to use will be satisfactory. Letter-quality print from a good daisy-wheel or laser printer is always acceptable. If you have a dot matrix printer, set the word-processing program (or the printer) for near-letter-quality print; most readers find print that shows the separate dots hard to read. Use good quality, letter-sized cut sheets or equally good quality pin-feed paper that separates cleanly on all edges. Make sure the printer ribbon is fresh enough to type clear, dark characters.

8b

Arrange your writing in clear and orderly fashion on the page.

(1) Margins   One-inch margins (except for page numbers) on all sides give your reader room for comments and prevent a crowded appearance. The ruled vertical line on notebook paper marks the left margin.

(2) Indention   Indent the first lines of paragraphs uniformly, about an inch in handwritten copy and five spaces in typewritten copy.

(3) Paging   Use Arabic numerals—without parentheses or periods—in the upper right-hand corner to mark all pages. Type your last name immediately before the page number.

(4) Title and heading   Do not put quotation marks around the title or underline it (unless it is a quotation or the title of a book), and use no period after the title. Capitalize the first and last words of the title and all other words except articles, coordinating conjunctions, prepositions, and the *to* in infinitives. See also **9c**.

Unless your instructor requests a title page, type your name, your instructor's name, the course and section number, and the date in the top left-hand corner (one inch from the top and one inch from the left edge of the page), double-spacing after each line. Center the title and double-space between the lines of a long title. Double-space twice after the title. Begin your first paragraph on the fourth line below the title. If you use a title page, follow your instructor's directions about the form.

(5) Quoted lines   When you quote over four lines of another's writing to explain or support your ideas, set the quotation off by indention: see **16a(3)**. Acknowledge the source of quotations: see **34e**.

(6) Punctuation   Never begin a line with a comma, a colon, a semicolon, a hyphen, a dash, or a terminal mark of punctuation; similarly, never end a line with the first of a set of brackets, parentheses, or quotation marks.

(7) Binding   Unless your instructor tells you otherwise, staple or paper clip the pages of your paper; do not use pins, brads, or plastic folders.

8c

Write, type, or print out your manuscript for easy and accurate reading.

(1) Legible handwriting   Form each letter clearly; distinguish between *o* and *a, t* and *l,* and *b* and *f* and between capital and lowercase letters. Use solid dots, not circles, for periods. Make each word a distinct unit. Avoid flourishes.

(2) Legible typing or printing   Before producing your final draft, check the quality of the ribbon and the cleanness of the type. In a typed manuscript, do not strike over an incorrect letter; make neat corrections. Leave one space after a comma, a semicolon, or a colon; two after a period, a question mark, or an exclamation point. To indicate a dash, use two hyphens without spacing before, between, or after. Use a pen to insert marks that are not on your machine, such as accent marks, mathematical symbols, or brackets.

8d

Whenever possible, avoid dividing a word at the end of a line. Make such divisions only between syllables and according to standard practice.

You will seldom need to divide words if you leave a reasonably wide right margin. Remember that the reader expects a somewhat uneven right margin and so may be distracted or slowed down by a series of word divisions at the ends of consecutive lines.

When you do need to divide a word at the end of a line, use a hyphen to mark the separation of syllables. In college dictionaries, dots usually divide the syllables of words: **re · al · ly, pre · fer, pref · er · ence, sell · ing, set · ting**. But not every division between syllables is an appropriate place for dividing a word at the end of a line. The following principles are useful guidelines:

(1) **One-letter syllables**   Do not put the first or last letter of a word at the end or beginning of a line. Do not divide **o · mit, a · ble, spunk · y, bo · a**.

(2) **Two-letter endings**   Do not put the last two letters of a word at the beginning of a line. Do not divide **dat · ed, does · n't, safe · ly, grav · el, tax · is**.

(3) **Misleading divisions**   Do not make divisions that may cause a misreading: **sour · ces, on · ions, an · gel, colo · nel**.

The vertical lines in the following examples mark appropriate end-of-line divisions.

(4) **Hyphenated words**   Divide hyphenated words only at the hyphen.

   mass- | produced

   father- | in-law   OR   father-in- | law

(5) ***-ing* words**   Divide words ending in *-ing* between those consonants that you double when adding *-ing*.

   set- | ting   jam- | ming   plan- | ning

   [Compare sell- | ing.]

(6) Consonants between vowels Divide words between two consonants that come between vowels—except when the division does not reflect pronunciation.

pic-| nic   dis-| cuss   thun-| der BUT co-| bra

(7) Abbreviations and acronyms Do not divide abbreviations, initials, or capitalized acronyms.

BA [degree]   **USAF**   **CBS**   **UCLA**   **UNESCO**

▲ Caution: Do not divide one-syllable words, such as *twelfth, through,* or *grabbed.*

▲ Note: Many word-processing programs include an automatic hyphenation feature, but these features sometimes hyphenate words incorrectly. Check each hyphenation and make corrections as needed.

■ **Exercise 1** First, put a check mark after the word that should not be divided at the end of a line; then, with the aid of your dictionary, write out the other words by syllables and insert hyphens followed by a vertical line to indicate appropriate end-of-line divisions.

1. cross-reference
2. economic
3. fifteenth
4. NATO
5. gripped
6. gripping
7. guessing
8. against
9. present (gift)
10. present (give)
11. seacoast
12. eventual
13. recline
14. CPA
15. magical
16. WFAA-FM
17. matches
18. dissolve
19. cobwebs
20. patron

8e

Revise and proofread your manuscript with care.

(1) Revise and proofread your paper before submitting it to the instructor.

When writing an out-of-class paper, draft and revise until you have a version you feel comfortable with. Then put the paper aside for as long as you can before you rework it. It is often easier to see that you have not clearly stated your ideas or that you need to rework your sentences after you have been away from your writing for a while.

Careful revision is important for good writing. You will usually need to make extensive changes, but prepare a clean draft of your paper to submit to the instructor.

When doing in-class papers, use the last few minutes for proofreading and making corrections. As you proofread, focus your attention on manuscript form—on mechanics, punctuation, spelling. For examples of how to make corrections, see pages 99–100.

(2) Revise your paper after the instructor has marked it.

Become familiar with the numbers or abbreviations used by your instructor to indicate specific errors or suggested changes.

Unless directed otherwise, follow this procedure as you revise a marked paper:

(a) Find in this handbook the exact principle that deals with each error or recommended change.

(b) After the instructor's mark in the margin, write the letter designating the appropriate principle, such as **a** or **c**. If your instructor uses abbreviations rather than numbers, you can identify the appropriate principles by number and letter.

(c) If your instructor's suggestions involve more than mechanical corrections, rewrite the composition. If only minor changes are needed, make them on the marked paper using a pencil or pen of a different color from the original so they will stand out.

This method of revision will help you understand why a change is desirable and avoid repetition of the same mistakes.

Following are examples of a paragraph marked by an instructor and the same paragraph corrected by a student. Examine the corrected paragraph to see how deletions of words, corrections of misspellings, substitutions of words, and changes in capitalization and punctuation are made. Notice also the use of a caret (∧) at the point in the line where an addition is made.

A Paragraph Marked by an Instructor

9   Drug pushers affect Society directly and

9 indirectly. They affect Society directly because

20 they break the law and sell dangerous drugs to

3 innocent victims simply to make money, the indirect

23 effect is because the people who become addicted to

18 the drugs that these pushers sell loose the ability

12 to make rational decisions, and will probably

become criminals themselves to support their

2 habits. Thus contributing to the explosion of

9 crime in Society today. The pushers therefore

32 jeopardize their own safety and also the safety of

the innocent public.

The Paragraph Being Revised by the Student

Drug pushers affect ̷Society directly and

indirectly. They affect ̷Society directly because

they break the law and~~(~~sell dangerous drugs ~~to~~
solely for profit. They affect society indirectly
~~innocent victims simply to make money, the indirect~~
buy these drugs usually
~~effect is~~ because the people who become addicted, ~~to~~
lose
~~the drugs that these pushers sell loose~~ the ability
often
to make rational decisions, and ~~will probably~~

become criminals themselves to support their
drug pushers are a major catalyst in
habits. Thus, ~~contributing to~~ the explosion of

crime~~, in Society today. The pushers therefore~~

ing   *as well as that of*
jeopardiz~~ed~~ their own safety ~~and also the safety of~~
their victims,
~~the innocent public.~~

The Paragraph Resubmitted by the Student

Drug pushers affect society directly and
indirectly. They affect society directly because
they break the law and, jeopardizing their own
safety as well as that of their victims, sell
dangerous drugs solely for profit. They affect
society indirectly because the people who buy these
drugs usually become addicted, lose the ability to
make rational decisions, and often become criminals
themselves to support their habits. Thus, drug
pushers are a major catalyst in the explosion of
crime.

8f

Keep a record of your revisions to help you improve your writing.

To monitor your progress toward mastery of writing, your instructor may want you to record and analyze your errors. You can record the marks your instructor makes on each paper by grouping them in columns corresponding to each of the seven major divisions of this handbook, as the following Record of Revisions illustrates. In the spaces for Paper No. 1 are the numbers and letters from the margin of the revised paragraph. In the spelling column is the correctly spelled word rather than **18c**. You may wish to add to your record sheet other columns for date, grade, and instructor's comments.

RECORD OF REVISIONS

Paper No.	Grammar 1–7	Mechanics 8–11	Punctuation 12–17	Words Misspelled 18	Diction 19–22	Effective-ness 23–30	Larger Elements 31–34
1	2a 3a	9f	12a	lose	20c	23d	32b

8g
Use a word processor effectively.

A word-processing program can ease your writing process and help you produce a clear, tidy, error-free paper. These programs allow you to insert and delete whole paragraphs or even pages. Word processing can make the mechanics of revision easier because it allows you to rearrange words and blocks of writing by moving them to a part of the composition where you think they will be most effective. And word processing allows you to do this without having to retype everything. The computer simply makes room on the screen where you need it and takes space away where you don't.

When you have completed your drafting and revising, you can use the search function of the program to help ensure consistency in your use of terms and to show you if you have been repetitious. Style-checking programs can highlight many kinds of grammatical errors and mannerisms that may distract your reader from the point you are trying to make. You can also verify your spelling and find typographical errors with the spelling checkers most word-processing programs include, but be aware that no program can catch the use of one correctly spelled word for another: of, say, *hole* for *whole*. Usually these proofreading programs operate by highlighting or otherwise isolating on the screen the part of your composition that may contain a problem. Word processing makes revision easier, but you still must choose which revisions you need to make.

Word processors will lay out pages of your manuscript exactly to your specifications. You can have the computer number your pages; produce single, double, or other spacing; print a certain number of lines per page; underline or print words and phrases in boldface; and hyphenate words at the ends of lines. Unless your printer has proportional spacing, do not take advantage of the computer's capability to justify (make straight) the right margin. Justification inserts spaces between words so that every line is the same length, which can make reading the text more difficult.

Word processors are not foolproof. Because inserting and deleting are so easy, you can create strange kinds of errors by inadvertently leaving in parts of old sentences you have abandoned or by mistakenly taking out parts of sentences you want to keep but have been tinkering with, and you can lose all of it if you forget to save, or back up, the document regularly. And because word processors are easy to use, they can make a wordy writer even wordier, a terse writer even less fluent. Finally, using word-processing programs does not make careful proofreading unnecessary; indeed, proofreading your final copy is essential. Word-processing programs are only a mechanical means for manipulating language you create yourself. They cannot think for you; they only remind you to think for yourself.

9

CAPITALS

Capitalize words according to standard conventions. Avoid unnecessary capitals.

A study of the principles in this section should help you use capitals correctly. When special problems arise, consult a good recent college dictionary. Dictionaries list not only words and abbreviations that begin with capitals but also acronyms that have full capitals:

Halloween, World War II, Hon., PhD, NASA, FORTRAN

If usage is divided, dictionaries also give options:

sunbelt OR Sunbelt, old guard OR Old Guard, nos. OR Nos.

A recent dictionary is an especially useful guide when the capitalization of a word depends upon a given meaning: "*mosaic* pictures" but "*Mosaic* laws," "on *earth*" but "the planet *Earth*."

9a

Capitalize proper names and, usually, their derivatives and their shortened forms (abbreviations and acronyms).

PROPER NAMES

As you study the following examples, observe that common nouns like *college, company, memorial, park,* and *street* are capitalized when they are essential parts of proper names.

(1) Names and nicknames of persons or things, trademarks

Rose O'Brien, T. S. Eliot, Buffalo Bill, Gandhi, Henry V
Skylab, Liberty Bell, Flight 41D, Academy Award
Noah's Ark, Alamo, Olympics, Elm Street, Jeep Cherokee
Rolaids

(2) Geographical names

America, Middle East, Utah, Buckeye State, Dixie
Kansas City, Great Divide, Arctic Circle, Lake District
Pacific Northwest, Snake River, Estes Park, Great Falls
Ellis Island, Cape Cod

(3) Peoples and their languages

American, Asian, Aztec, Eskimo, Indians (BUT native American), Hispanics, Poles
English, Polish, Spanish, French, Russian, Yiddish, Latin

▲ Option: Blacks or blacks

(4) Organizations, government agencies, institutions, companies

Red Cross, National Guard, Associated Press, Congress
House Ethics Committee, Miami Dolphins, Phi Beta Kappa
Howard University, Hampton Institute, Federal Express
Republican party

(5) Days of the week, months, holidays

Tuesday, October, Thanksgiving, Groundhog Day
Veterans Day

▲ Note: The names of seasons are not capitalized: spring,
summer, fall, winter.

(6) Historical documents, periods, events

the Fifth Amendment, the Bill of Rights
Federal Housing Act, Stone Age, Vietnam War
Romantic Movement, Yalta Conference

(7) Religions and their adherents, holy books, holy days, words denoting the Supreme Being

Christianity, Hinduism, Islam, Judaism, Protestant
Catholic, Christian, Hindu, Moslem, Jew, Baptists
Methodists, Mormons

the Bible, Book of Mormon, Koran, Revelations, Talmud
Easter, Yom Kippur, Allah, God, Messiah, Yahweh

▲ Option: Some writers always capitalize pronouns (except
who, whom, whose) referring to the Deity. Other writers
capitalize such pronouns only when the capital is needed
to prevent ambiguity, as in "The Lord commanded the
prophet to warn *His* people."

(8) Personifications See also **20a(4)**.

I could feel Old Man Time breathing down the back of my neck.   —PATRICK McMANUS

▲ Note: Occasionally, a common noun is capitalized for emphasis or clarity, as in "The motivation for many politicians is Power."

DERIVATIVES

(9) Words derived from proper names

Americanize [verb]   Israelite, Christmas, Stalinism [nouns]
Germanic, Orwellian   [adjectives]

When proper names and their derivatives become names of a general class, they are no longer capitalized.

zipper   [originally a capitalized trademark]
chauvinistic   [derived from *Nicholas Chauvin*]

ABBREVIATIONS AND ACRONYMS

(10) Shortened forms of capitalized words See also **17a(2)**.

DC   L.A. OR LA   DVM   IRS   CBS   CST   AT&T
OPEC   UNESCO   NATO   AMEX   NOW
[words derived from the initial letters of capitalized word groups]

▲ Common exceptions: a.m. OR A.M.   p.m. OR P.M.

9b

Capitalize titles of persons that precede the name but not those that follow it.

Governor Paul Dix, Captain Holt, Aunt Mae
Paul Dix, our governor; Holt, the captain; Mae, my aunt
President Kennedy; the president of the United States

Words denoting family relationship are usually capitalized when serving as substitutes for proper names:

Tell Mother I'll write soon.   [Compare: My mother wants me to write.]

9c

In titles and subtitles of books, plays, student papers, and so on, capitalize the first and last words and all other words except articles, coordinating conjunctions, prepositions, and the *to* in infinitives.

The articles are *a, an, the*; the coordinating conjunctions are *and, but, or, nor, for, so, yet*. (Formerly, longer prepositions like *before, between,* or *through* in titles were capitalized; MLA style, however, favors lowercased prepositions, whatever the length.)

All Creatures Great and Small
"What It Takes to Be a Leader"
"Why Women Are Paid Less Than Men"
"Aerobics before Breakfast"
Looking Back: A Chronicle of Growing Up Old in the Sixties
[Not a preposition, *Up* is part of a phrasal verb.]

▲ Note: In a title capitalize the first word of a hyphenated compound. As a rule, capitalize the word following the hyphen if it is a noun or a proper adjective or if it is equal in importance to the first word.

A Substitute for the H-Bomb   [noun]
The Arab-Israeli Dilemma   [proper adjective]
"Hit-and-Run Accidents"   [parallel words]

Usage varies with respect to the capitalization of words following such prefixes as *anti-, ex-, re-,* and *self-*:

The Anti-Poverty War   OR   *The Anti-poverty War*

▲ Exception: Titles in an APA style reference list. See **34**.

9d

Capitalize the pronoun *I* and the interjection *O* (but not *oh,* except when it begins a sentence).

David sings, "Out of the depths I cry to thee, O Lord."

9e

Capitalize the first word of every sentence (or of any other unit written as a sentence) and of directly quoted speech.

Humorists often describe their zany relatives.

Oh, really! Do such jokes have a point? Not at all.

Most first drafts, in fact, can be cut by fifty percent without losing anything organic. (Try it; it's a good exercise.)
—WILLIAM ZINSSER   [a parenthetical sentence]

COMPARE   You do this by moving the cursor under the symbol for "carriage return" (it looks like an arrow) and then pressing DELETE. —WILLIAM ZINSSER [a parenthetical main clause]

One thing is certain: We are still free.   [an optional capital after the colon—see also **17d**.]

She often replies, "Maybe tomorrow, but not today."
OR   "Maybe tomorrow," she often replies, "but not today."
OR   "Maybe tomorrow," she often replies. "But not today." [See also **3c**.]

The difference between "Well!" and "Well?" is a difference of tone, hence of meaning.   —J. MITCHELL MORSE

▲ Note: For the treatment of directly quoted written material, see **16a(3)**.

9f

Avoid unnecessary capitals.

If you have a tendency to overuse capitals, review **9a** through **9e**. Also keep in mind this rule: common nouns may be preceded by the indefinite articles (*a, an*) and by such limiting modifiers as *every* or *several*.

> **a** speech course in radio and television writing
> COMPARE   Speech 245: Radio and Television Writing
>
> **every** university, **several** schools of medicine
> COMPARE   the University of Colorado School of Medicine

When preceded by *a, an*, or modifiers like *every* or *several*, capitalized nouns name one or many of the members of a class: *a St. Bernard*, *an Iowan*, *several Catholics*.

Study the following style sheet:

Style Sheet for Capitalization

CAPITALS	NO CAPITALS
Dr. Freda E. Watts	every doctor, my doctor
the War of 1812	a space war in 1999
English, Spanish, French	the language requirement
Harvard University	a university like Harvard
the U.S. Navy	a strong navy
December, Christmas	winter, holiday
the West, Westerners	to fly west, western regions
the Student Association	an association for students
Parkinson's disease	flu, asthma, leukemia
a Chihuahua, Ford trucks	a beagle, pickup trucks
two Democratic candidates	democratic procedures
our Bill of Rights	a kind of bill of rights

■ **Exercise 1**   Write brief sentences using each of the following words correctly:

(1) senator (2) Senator (3) university (4) University (5) north (6) North (7) street (8) Street (9) theater (10) Theater

■ **Exercise 2**   Supply capitals wherever needed.

1. i am not looking forward to the christmas holidays since i must spend all of my time studying spanish and economics in an effort to offset the poor grade i expect in political science.

2. we encouraged our neighbors to travel in the west since there are many interesting sights: pike's peak, colorado; the rocky mountains; glacier national park; the mojave desert; active volcanoes such as mount baker in washington; puget sound; and others.
3. at the end of his sermon on god's social justice as set forth in the bible, he said, "we democrats really ought to re-elect senator attebury."
4. the full title of robert sherrill's book is *the saturday night special and other guns with which americans won the west, protected bootleg franchises, slew wildlife, robbed countless banks, shot husbands purposely and by mistake, and killed presidents—together with the debate over continuing same.*

10
ITALICS

Use underlining to indicate italics in accordance with customary practices. Use italics sparingly for emphasis.

In handwritten or typewritten papers, italics are indicated by underlining. Typesetters put underlined words in italic type.

TYPEWRITTEN

It was on <u>60 Minutes</u>.

PRINTED

It was on *60 Minutes.*

10a

Titles of separate publications (books, magazines, newspapers, pamphlets) and titles of plays, films, radio and television programs, entire recordings, works of art, long poems, comic strips, and software programs are underlined (italicized).

As you study the following examples, note that punctuation forming a part of the title is italicized (underlined).

BOOKS

Where Are the Children?   *A Caribbean Mystery*

MAGAZINES

Reader's Digest   *The Atlantic* OR the *Atlantic*

NEWSPAPERS	*USA TODAY* the *New York Times*
PLAYS, FILMS	*A Delicate Balance* *The Last Emperor*
TV SHOWS	*Nightline* *Sesame Street*
RECORDINGS	*Sergeant Pepper's Lonely Hearts Club Band* *Great Verdi Overtures*
WORKS OF ART	Beethoven's *Moonlight Sonata* Verdi's *Aida* Michelangelo's *Pietà* Grant Wood's *American Gothic*
COMIC STRIPS	*Peanuts* *Doonesbury*
SOFTWARE	*The Caret Patch* *PC Write* *First Publisher*

Occasionally short works such as essays, songs, short poems, episodes of a television series, and short stories are italicized, particularly when many such titles appear in a single paper. The usual practice, however, is to place those titles in quotation marks. (See **16b**.)

"Can Anything Be Done?" is the most thought-provoking section of David Burnham's *The Rise of the Computer State.*

Jane Alexander starred in "Testament" on *American Playhouse.*

▲ Exceptions: Neither italics nor quotation marks are used in references to major religious texts, such as books of the Bible, or to legal documents.

The first few books of the Bible—Genesis, Exodus, Leviticus, Deuteronomy, Numbers—are derived from the Torah.

How many Americans have actually read the Bill of Rights?

10b

Foreign words and phrases are usually underlined (italicized) in the context of an English sentence.

The maxim of the French Revolution still echoes in our ears: *liberté, egalité, fraternité.*   —MORTIMER J. ADLER

The rice water weevil (*Lissorhoptrus oryzophilus*) is a potential threat to the California rice crop.   —SCIENTIFIC AMERICAN

Countless words borrowed from other languages are a part of the English vocabulary and are therefore not italicized:

amigo (Spanish)	karate (Japanese)	shalom (Hebrew)
blasé (French)	pizza (Italian)	non sequitur (Latin)

Dictionaries that label certain words and phrases as foreign are fairly dependable guides to the writer in doubt about the use of italics. The labels, however, are not always up-to-date, and writers must depend on their own judgment after considering current practices.

10c

Names of specific ships, airplanes, satellites, and space-craft are underlined (italicized).

U.S.S. *Enterprise*   the space shuttle *Challenger*

Names of trains and names of a general class or a trademark are not italicized: Orient Express, a PT boat, a Boeing 747, Telstar, ICBMs.

10d

Words, letters, or figures spoken of as such or used as illustrations are usually underlined (italicized).

In no other language could a foreigner be tricked into pronouncing *manslaughter* as *man's laughter*.   —MARIO PEI

The letters *qu* replaced *cw* in such words as *queen, quoth,* and *quick*.   —CHARLES C. FRIES

The first *3* and the final *0* of the serial number are barely legible.

▲ Note: Quotation marks may also be used to identify words used as such. (See also **16c**.)

10e

Use underlining (italics) sparingly for emphasis. Do not underline the title of your own paper.

Writers occasionally use italics to show stress, especially in dialogue, or to emphasize the meaning of a word.

> When he sees the child dragging a rotten tomato on a string, Bill Cosby asks, "What *are* you doing?"
>
> If they take offense, then that's *their* problem.
>
> No one can imagine a *systematic* conversation.
> —JACQUES BARZUN

But overuse of italics for emphasis (like overuse of the exclamation point) defeats its own purpose. If you tend to overuse italics to stress ideas, study section **29**. Also try substituting more specific or more forceful words for those you are tempted to underline.

A title is not italicized when it stands at the head of a book or article. Accordingly, the title at the head of your paper (unless it is also the title of a book or it includes the title of a book) should not be underlined. See also **8b(4)**.

■ **Exercise 1** Underline all words that should be italicized in the following sentences.

1. I bought a copy of Newsweek because I was interested in the article "The Search for Adam and Eve."
2. The New York Times reported that the Andria Doria, an Italian ocean liner that was sunk twenty or thirty years ago, has recently been salvaged.
3. Spelling errors involving the substitution of d for t in such words as partner and pretty reflect a tendency in pronunciation.
4. At the Baths of Caracalla in Rome I attended a performance of Puccini's Madama Butterfly, after which the audience praised the performers with cries of bravo!
5. Leonardo da Vinci's priceless fresco, The Last Supper, is in danger of being destroyed by mold.
6. I'm not sure I like colorized versions of classic films such as Casablanca.

7. I know people who have watched 60 Minutes every Sunday night for over fifteen years.
8. When I get stuck trying to think of a word, I use Roget's Thesaurus of Words and Phrases.
9. The saddest chapter of J. R. R. Tolkien's The Fellowship of the Ring is the last one, "The Breaking of the Fellowship."
10. NotaBene is a word-processing program designed especially for use in colleges and universities.

11

ABBREVIATIONS, ACRONYMS, AND NUMBERS

Use abbreviations only when appropriate; spell out the first-time use of acronyms, and spell out numbers that can be expressed simply.

Abbreviations and figures are desirable in tables, notes, and bibliographies and in some kinds of special or technical writing. In ordinary writing, however, only certain abbreviations and figures are appropriate. All the principles in this section apply to ordinary writing, which of course includes the kind of writing often required in college.

ABBREVIATIONS

11a

In ordinary writing, designations such as *Miss, Ms.* (or *Ms*), *Mr., Mrs., Dr.,* and *St.* precede a proper name, and those such as *Jr., Sr., II,* and *MD* follow.

Ms. Janet Gray   Dr. Bell   St. Louis
  [Compare "the young doctor," "the early life of the saint."]
Hal Grant, Sr.   E. R. Ames III   Alice Holt, MD

▲ Note 1: For punctuation rules about designations that follow the proper name, see **15a(3)**.

Not all abbreviations require periods: *IRS*, *NBC*, *NY*. *Miss* is not an abbreviation and should not be followed by a period. Abbreviations of degrees are often used without a proper name, as in "a *BA* in languages."

▲ Caution: Do not use redundant titles: Dr. E. T. Fulton OR E. T. Fulton, MD [NOT Dr. E. T. Fulton, MD]

▲ Note 2: Abbreviations such as *Prof.*, *Sen.*, *1st Lt.*, or *Capt.* should be used only before initials or full names (Prof. Grady E. Bruce) and not before last names alone.

11b

Spell out names of states, countries, continents, months, days of the week, and units of measurement.

> On Sunday, October 10, we spent the night in Tulsa, Oklahoma; the next day we flew to South America.
>
> Only four feet tall, Susan weighs ninety-one pounds.
>
> An acre is 4,047 square meters.

▲ Note: Use appropriate postal abbreviations on correspondence:

Postal Abbreviations

AL	Alabama	DC	District of Columbia
AK	Alaska	FL	Florida
AZ	Arizona	GA	Georgia
AR	Arkansas	GU	Guam
CA	California	HI	Hawaii
CO	Colorado	ID	Idaho
CT	Connecticut	IL	Illinois
DE	Delaware	IN	Indiana

Postal Abbreviations (cont.)

IA	Iowa	ND	North Dakota
KS	Kansas	OH	Ohio
KY	Kentucky	OK	Oklahoma
LA	Louisiana	OR	Oregon
ME	Maine	PA	Pennsylvania
MD	Maryland	PR	Puerto Rico
MA	Massachusetts	RI	Rhode Island
MI	Michigan	SC	South Carolina
MN	Minnesota	SD	South Dakota
MS	Mississippi	TN	Tennessee
MO	Missouri	TX	Texas
MT	Montana	UT	Utah
NE	Nebraska	VT	Vermont
NV	Nevada	VA	Virginia
NH	New Hampshire	VI	Virgin Islands
NJ	New Jersey	WA	Washington (state)
NM	New Mexico	WV	West Virginia
NY	New York	WI	Wisconsin
NC	North Carolina	WY	Wyoming

11c

Spell out *Street, Avenue, Road, Park, Mount, River, Company,* and similar words used as an essential part of proper names.

Fifth Avenue is east of Central Park.
The Ford Motor Company does not expect a strike soon.

11d

Spell out the words *volume, chapter,* and *page* and the names of courses of study.

The chart is on page 46 of chapter 9 in volume 2.
I registered for physical education and for child psychology.

In addition to the abbreviations listed in **11a**, the following abbreviations and symbols are permissible and usually desirable.

1. *Certain words used with dates or figures*

58 BC	AD 70	8:00 a.m. OR A.M.	8:31 EST OR
E.S.T.	No. 13 OR no. 13	$4.25	25.5 MPG OR
mpg			

2. *The District of Columbia and the United States used adjectivally*: Washington, DC, the U.S. Navy.

3. *The names of organizations, agencies, countries, persons, or things usually referred to by their capitalized initials*

USMC	FDA	MIT	NBC	NFL	USSR
JFK	VCRs	IQ	TV		

4. *Certain common Latin expressions* (the English equivalent is spelled out in brackets)

cf.	[compare]	etc.	[and so forth]
e.g.	[for example]	i.e.	[that is]
et al.	[and others]	vs. OR v.	[versus]

Abbreviations are commonly used in bibliographies.

▲ Note: Avoid the use of the ampersand (&) except in copying official titles or names of firms and in APA parenthetical documentation. See section **34**. The abbreviations *Inc.* and *Ltd.* are usually omitted in ordinary writing.

   U.S. News & World Report   Motorola   [NOT Motorola, Inc.]

ACRONYMS

Acronyms are words formed from the initial letters of other words or from the combination of syllables of other words: *AIDS* (**a**cquired **i**mmune **d**eficiency **s**yndrome), *sonar* (**so**und **na**vigation **r**anging).

11e

Spell out the meaning of any acronym that may not be familiar to your reader when you use it for the first time.

> Then there is the antisatellite intercepter (ASAT). Consider ASAT's cost and value.
> OR   Then there is ASAT (the antisatellite intercepter).

Your reader will probably be familiar with such terms as *NASA, NATO, laser,* and *SAT scores* but perhaps not with those such as *MIRV, modem, VAT.*

▲ Note: Some clipped forms—such as *info, rep, execs,* or *porn*—are avoided in formal writing. Others—such as *math, lab,* and *Cal Tech*—are generally acceptable.

■ **Exercise 1**   Strike out any inappropriate form.

1. Ms. Janet Hogan; a dr. but not a saint
2. 21 mpg; on TV; in Calif. and Ill.
3. on Magnolia St.; on Magnolia Street
4. on Aug. 15; on August 15
5. for Jr.; for John Evans, Jr.
6. before 6 A.M.; before six in the A.M.

NUMBERS

11f

Follow acceptable practices for writing numbers; be consistent.

When numbers are used infrequently in a piece of writing, writers tend to spell out those that can be expressed in one word or two and to use figures for the others. Where numbers occur frequently, the general practice is to spell out numbers from one to ten and to use figures for all others. Very large numbers may be expressed by a combination of words and numbers.

ALWAYS   over three inches
BUT   three-quarters of an inch   OR   .75 inches
ALWAYS   after 124 years
BUT   after twenty-two years   OR   after 22 years
ALWAYS   563 voters
BUT   five hundred voters   OR   500 voters

ten million bushels   OR   10,000,000 bushels   OR   10 million bushels

SPECIAL USAGE REGARDING NUMBERS

1. *Specific time of day*

   2 a.m.   OR   2:00 a.m.   OR   two o'clock in the morning
   4:30 p.m.   OR   half-past four in the afternoon

2. *Dates*

   May 7, 1993   OR   7 May 1993   [NOT May 7th, 1993]
   May sixth   OR   the sixth of May   OR   May 6   OR   May 6th

   the nineties   OR   the 1990s   OR   the 1990's

   the twentieth century

   in 1900   in 1992–1993   OR   in 1992–93

   from 1990 to 1995   OR   1990–1995   OR   1990–95
      [NOT from 1990–1995, from 1990–95]

3. *Addresses*

   Apartment 3C, 8 Redwood Drive, Prescott, Arizona
   86301   [OR Apt. 3c, 8 Redwood Dr., Prescott, AZ 86301]
   16 Tenth Street

   350 West 114 Street   OR   350 West 114th Street

4. *Identification numbers*

   Channel 13   Interstate 35   Henry VIII   Room 10

5. *Pages and divisions of books and plays*

   page 30   chapter 6   part 4
   in act 3, scene 2   OR   in Act III, Scene ii

6. *Decimals and percentages*

a 2.5 average   12½ percent   0.907 metric ton

7. *Numbers in series and statistics*

two cows, five pigs, and forty-two chickens
125 feet long, 50 feet wide, and 12 feet deep
scores of 17 to 13 and 42 to 3   OR   scores of 17–13 and
42–3
The members voted 99 to 23 against it.

8. *Large round numbers*

four billion dollars   OR $4 billion   OR
$4,000,000,000   [Figures are used for emphasis only.]
12,500,000   OR   12.5 million

9. *Numbers beginning sentences*

Six percent of the students voted.   [NOT 6 percent of the
students voted.]

10. *Repeated numbers* (in legal or commercial writing)

The agent's fee will not exceed one hundred (100)
dollars.
OR
The agent's fee will not exceed one hundred dollars
($100).

■ **Exercise 2**   Using desirable abbreviations and figures, change each
item to an acceptable shortened form.

1. on the fifteenth of June
2. Ernest Threadgill, a doctor
3. thirty million dollars
4. Janine Keith, a certified public accountant
5. one o'clock in the afternoon
6. by the first of December, 1990
7. at the bottom of the fifteenth page
8. four hundred years before Christ
9. in the second scene of the first act
10. a five-year plan (from 1990 to 1995)

PUNCTUATION

The Comma **12**

Superfluous Commas **13**

The Semicolon **14**

The Apostrophe **15**

Quotation Marks **16**

The Period and Other Marks **17**

12
THE COMMA

Learn to apply basic principles governing comma usage.

Pauses and variations in voice pitch help to convey the meaning of spoken sentences; similarly, commas help to clarify the meaning of written sentences.

> When the thief shot**,** Ashley James called the police.
> When the thief shot Ashley**,** James called the police.

The use of the comma depends primarily on the structure of the sentence and signals a small interruption. Inflexible rules governing the use of the comma are few, but there are several basic principles.

Commas

- **a.** precede coordinating conjunctions when they link main clauses;
- **b.** follow introductory adverb clauses and, usually, introductory phrases;
- **c.** separate items in a series (including coordinate adjectives);
- **d.** set off nonrestrictive and other parenthetical elements.

12a

A comma ordinarily precedes a coordinating conjunction that links main clauses.

$$\text{MAIN CLAUSE} \atop \text{Subject + predicate,} \quad \left\{ \begin{array}{c} \textbf{and} \\ \textbf{but} \\ \textbf{for} \\ \textbf{or} \\ \textbf{nor} \\ \textbf{so} \\ \textbf{yet} \end{array} \right\} \quad \text{MAIN CLAUSE} \atop \text{subject + predicate.}$$

The minutes would pass, and then suddenly Einstein would stop pacing as his face relaxed into a gentle smile.
—BANESH HOFFMANN

Fanny Lou Hamer was a Black woman who pioneered civil rights organizing in the South, but few Americans know of Hamer's work.   —META GAIL CARSTARPHEN

From one point of view, their migration was the fruit of an old prophecy, for indeed they emerged from a sunless world.
—N. SCOTT MOMADAY

Justice stands upon Power, or there is no Justice.
—WILLIAM S. WHITE

My old friend never forgot to send my children a Christmas remembrance, nor did she forget to send them birthday cards. —MICHELLE SHARP

They are helpless and humble, so he loves them.
—E. M. FORSTER

I have never known a man who would not cheat himself, yet I have known many who would cheat no one else.
—ALTON MIKELJOHN

The rule also applies to coordinating conjunctions that link the main clauses of a compound-complex sentence.

It has been ambitious and plucky of me to attempt to describe what is indescribable, and I have failed, as I knew I would.
—E. B. WHITE   [two main clauses and three subordinate clauses]

When the clauses are short, the comma may be omitted before *and, but,* or *or,* but seldom before *for, nor, so, yet.*

The next night the wind shifted and the thaw began.
—RACHEL CARSON

Sometimes, especially when the second main clause reveals a contrast or when one main clause contains commas, a semicolon separates main clauses. See also **14a**.

We do not, most of us, choose to die; nor do we choose the time or conditions of our death.   —JOSEPH EPSTEIN

▲ Note: As a rule, do not use a comma before a coordinating conjunction that links parts of a compound predicate.

Colonel Cathcart had courage and never hesitated to volunteer his men for any target available.   —JOSEPH HELLER
[compound predicate—no comma before *and*]

Only occasionally do writers use a comma to emphasize a distinction between the parts of the predicate, as in E. M. Forster's "Artists always seek a new technique, and will continue to do so as long as their work excites them."

▲ Caution: Do not place a comma after a coordinating conjunction linking main clauses.

I found Tim arrogant at first, but I grew to love him.   [NOT I found Tim arrogant at first but, I grew to love him.]

■ **Exercise 1**   Using the punctuation pattern of **12a**, link the sentences in the following items with an appropriate *and, but, or, nor, for, so,* or *yet.*

EXAMPLE
We cannot win the battle.   We cannot afford to lose it.
We cannot win the battle, nor can we afford to lose it.

1. A government official is accused of unethical conduct. Another Congressional investigation is launched.
2. Nonsmokers do not like to have smoke blown in their faces. They also dislike eating in smoke-filled restaurants.
3. Customers may return unwanted purchases to the appropriate department. They may choose to return merchandise to the complaint counter.
4. We decided to drive along the coast road. We wanted to see the ocean.
5. We had arranged to meet them in New Orleans. They did not arrive before we left.

■ **Exercise 2**   Follow rule **12a** as you insert commas before connectives linking main clauses in these sentences. (Remember that not all coordinating conjunctions link main clauses and that *but, for, so,* and *yet* do not always function as coordinating conjunctions.)

1. The students had finished taking the various tests and answering the long questionnaires and they had gone to lunch.
2. There are now special shoes for someone to fill for Bob has resigned and is going to business school.
3. I decided to withdraw from that eight-o'clock class so that I could sleep later but I plan to enroll again for the same class in January.
4. We had seen the stage play and the movie and the College Players' performance was the best of all.
5. Everyone in our group was invited to the party but Gary and Irene decided to go to the hockey game.

12b

A comma usually follows introductory words, phrases, and clauses.

> **ADVERB CLAUSE, MAIN CLAUSE.**

> **INTRODUCTORY PHRASE,**
> **INTRODUCTORY WORD,** } **subject + predicate.**

(1) Adverb clauses before main clauses

> When you write, you make a sound in the reader's head.
> —RUSSELL BAKER

> While writing his last novel, James recognized and faced his solitude. —LEON EDEL [an elliptical adverb clause—compare "While he was writing. . . . "]

> The expansion phase is a demanding one, but if the choice is made for life and for following our true convictions, our energy level is intensified. —GAIL SHEEHY [adverb clause preceding the second main clause]

A writer may omit the comma after an introductory adverb clause, especially when the clause is short, if the omission does not make for difficult reading.

> When we talk to people we always mean something quite different from what we say. —ANTHONY BURGESS

▲ Note: When the adverb clause follows the main clause, there is usually no need for a comma. Adverb clauses in this position, however, may be preceded by a comma if they do not affect the meaning of the main clause.

> Henry is now in good health, although he has been an invalid most of his life.

(2) Introductory phrases before main clauses

Prepositional phrases:

> In today's Baskin-Robbins society, everything comes in at least 31 flavors. —JOHN NAISBITT

The comma is often omitted after introductory prepositional phrases when no misreading would result:

> In a crisis we choose Lincoln and FDR. In between we choose what's-his-name. —JOHN NAISBITT

In the next example the comma is needed to prevent misreading:

Because of this, beauty differs radically from truth and goodness in one very important aspect. —MORTIMER J. ADLER

Other types of phrases:

Having attempted nothing, I had no sense of my limitations; having dared nothing, I knew no boundaries to my courage. —TREVANIAN [participial phrases before both main clauses]

These differences aside, the resemblance between 1972 and 1980 is very striking. —NORMAN MAILER [absolute phrase—see also **12d(3)**]

(3) Introductory transitional expressions, conjunctive adverbs, interjections, and an introductory *yes* or *no*.

Furthermore, benefits include maternity leave of eight weeks and other child-care leave, which either parent can take until the child's first birthday. —KATHRYN STECHERT [transitional expression—see the list on page 39]

Well, move the ball or move the body. —ALLEN JACKSON

Yes, I know that every vote counts. **No,** I didn't vote.

▲ Caution: Do not use a comma after phrases that begin inverted sentences. (See also **29f**.)

With prosperity came trouble. —MALACHI MARTIN

Of far greater concern than censorship of "bad" words is censorship of ideas. —DONNA WOOLFOLK CROSS

■ **Exercise 3** Decide whether to use a comma after adverb clauses or after phrases that begin the following sentences. Put a check mark after any sentence in which a comma would be incorrect.

1. If you have been thinking of making a fortune by working for someone else forget it.
2. As far as I know these county officials are not hypocrites.
3. At the same time I recognize that they had good intentions.
4. Before noon the voting lines were two blocks long.
5. Trying to pass three gravel trucks going downhill the driver lost control of his car.

6. Trying to outwit competitors is the concern of almost every major company.
7. With about as much subtlety as a sledgehammer these book titles imply that there are shortcuts to nearly everything your heart desires.
8. Under the back seat is an extra heater as well as some storage space.
9. The election far from over the media began to announce the results.
10. When you can help someone less fortunate than yourself.

12c

Commas separate items in a series (including coordinate adjectives).

Consisting of three or more items, a series is a succession of parallel elements. See section **26**. The punctuation of a series depends on its form:

> The air was *raw*, *dank*, and *gray*. [**a, b,** and **c**—a preferred comma before *and*]
>
> The air was *raw*, *dank* and *gray*. [**a, b** and **c**—an acceptable omission of comma before *and* when there is no danger of misreading]
>
> The air was *raw*, *dank*, *gray*. [**a, b, c**]
>
> The air was *raw* and *dank* and *gray*. [**a** and **b** and **c**]

(1) Words, phrases, and clauses in a series

> Student reactions were swift and intense: delight, disbelief, fear, horror, anticipation. —ALVIN TOFFLER
>
> Garfield lives. His likeness looks up from beach thongs, out from coffee mugs, down from wall posters and across the room from the morning newspaper. —HOLLY G. MILLER
>
> He always said percussion clunked, horns went braaaa, violins squeaked, and so on. —ELIZABETH SWADOS

▲ Exceptions: If items in a series contain internal commas, the semicolon is used instead of commas for clarity: see **14b**. For special emphasis, commas are sometimes used even when all the items in a series are linked by coordinating conjunctions.

> We cannot put it off for a month**,** or a week**,** or even a day.

(2) Coordinate adjectives

Use a comma between coordinate adjectives that are not linked by a coordinating conjunction. One test for coordinate adjectives is to interchange them; another is to put *and* between them. If the results make sense, the adjectives are coordinate.

> It is a waiting**,** silent**,** limp room.   —EUDORA WELTY   [*Waiting, silent*, and *limp* all modify *room*. Compare "It is a silent**,** limp waiting room."]

> They are young**,** alert social workers.   [*Young* and *alert* modify the word group *social workers*. Compare "They are young**,** social**,** alert workers."]

> She was a frowsy**,** middle-aged woman with wispy**,** drab-brown hair. She sat behind a long wooden table on a high platform overlooking her disciples with her narrow**,** piercing eyes.   —EVELYN KOSSOFF

■ **Exercise 4**   Using commas as needed, write sentences supplying coordinate adjectives to modify any five of the following ten word groups.

> EXAMPLE
> metric system   *Most countries use the familiar***,** *sensible metric system to measure distances.*

1. cinnamon doughnut
2. classical music
3. cheddar cheese
4. metal sculpture
5. software documentation
6. office buildings
7. baseball parks
8. elementary school
9. sports car
10. state fair

12d

Commas set off nonrestrictive and other parenthetical elements as well as contrasted elements, items in dates, and so on.

To set off a word or a word group with commas, use two commas unless the element is placed at the beginning of the sentence or at the end. (Expressions that come at the beginning of a sentence are treated by both **12b** and **12d**.)

> Americans are reluctant to complain, *as William F. Buckley has observed,* because we now leave management of our environment to specialists.

> *As William F. Buckley has observed,* Americans are reluctant to complain because we now leave management of our environment to specialists.

> Americans are reluctant to complain because we now leave management of our environment to specialists, *as William F. Buckley has observed.*

△ Caution: When two commas are needed to set off an element, do not forget one of the commas.

| CONFUSING | An experienced driver generally speaking, does not fear the open road. |
| CLEAR | An experienced driver, generally speaking, does not fear the open road. |

(1) Nonrestrictive clauses or phrases and nonrestrictive appositives are set off by commas. Restrictive elements are not set off.

ADJECTIVE CLAUSES OR PHRASES

Adjective clauses or phrases are nonrestrictive when they describe (rather than limit the meaning of) the noun or pronoun they modify; set off by commas, they are nonessential parenthetical elements that may be omitted. Restrictive clauses or phrases are limiting (rather than descriptive) modifiers; not set off by commas, they identify the noun or pronoun they modify by telling *which one* (or *ones*) and are essential elements that may not be omitted.

As you study the following examples, read each sentence aloud and notice not only meaning but also your pauses and intonation.

NONRESTRICTIVE	RESTRICTIVE OR ESSENTIAL
Clauses:	
My mother**, who listened to his excuses,** smiled knowingly.	Any mother **who listened to such excuses** would smile knowingly.
We will explore Mammoth Cave**, which has twelve miles of underground passageways.**	We will explore a cave **that has twelve miles of underground passageways.**
Phrases:	
In July these mountains**, covered with snow,** seem unreal.	In July mountains **covered with snow** seem unreal.
The old Renault**, glistening in the rain,** looked brand new.	An old car **glistening in the rain** looked brand new.
Such noise**, too loud for human ears,** can cause deafness.	A noise **too loud for human ears** can cause deafness.

▲ Note: Although many writers prefer to use *that* at the beginning of restrictive clauses, *which* is also acceptable.

Sometimes only the omission or the use of commas indicates whether a modifier is restrictive or nonrestrictive and thus determines the exact meaning of the writer.

The party opposed taxes **which would be a burden to working Americans.**   [meaning opposition to levying taxes of a certain kind]

The party opposed taxes **, which would be a burden to working Americans**.   [meaning opposition to levying taxes of any
kind, all of which would be a burden to working Americans]

APPOSITIVES

Appositives are either nonrestrictive (set off by commas) or
restrictive (not set off by commas). A nonrestrictive appositive supplies additional but nonessential details about the
noun or pronoun it refers to. A restrictive appositive limits
the meaning of the noun or pronoun it refers to by pointing
out *which one* (or *ones*).

NONRESTRICTIVE	RESTRICTIVE OR ESSENTIAL
Even Zeke Thornbush **, my very best friend,** let me down.	Even my friend **Zeke Thornbush** let me down.
Voyager photographed Saturn **, the ringed planet**.	*Voyager* photographed the planet **Saturn**.

Abbreviations after names are treated as nonrestrictive
appositives: "Was the letter from Frances Evans **, PhD,** or
from F. H. Evans **, MD**?"

■ **Exercise 5**   Use commas to set off nonrestrictive adjective clauses
or phrases and nonrestrictive appositives in the following sentences. Put
a check mark after any sentence that needs no commas.

1. I will interview Mary Smith who manages the bank.
2. I will interview the Mary Smith who manages the bank.
3. Vanessa Berry sitting near the window saw the accident.
4. Lilacs which have a beautiful fragrance are my favorite flowers.
5. Few people around here have ever heard of my hometown a little place called Bugtussle.
6. All players who broke the rules had to sit on the bench.
7. The word *malapropism* is derived from the name of a character in Sheridan's *The Rivals* a Mrs. Malaprop.
8. The woman who is waving the red scarf is Sally.
9. Spokane Falls which was founded in 1871 was renamed Spokane in 1891.
10. Charles M. Duke Jr. and astronaut John W. Young landed their lunar vehicle near Plum Crater.

(2) Contrasted elements, geographical names, and most items in dates and addresses are set off by commas.

CONTRASTED ELEMENTS

Racing is supposed to be a test of skill, not a dice game with death. —SONNY KLEINFIELD

His phrases dribbled off, but not his memories.
—JAMES A. MICHENER

Human beings, unlike oysters, frequently reveal their emotions. —GEORGE F. WILL

▲ Note: Usage is divided regarding the placement of a comma before *but* in such structures as the following:

Other citizens who disagree with me base their disagreement, not on facts different from the ones I know, but on a different set of values. —RENÉ DUBOS

Today the Black Hills are being invaded again, not for gold but for uranium. —PETER MATTHIESSEN

GEOGRAPHICAL NAMES, ITEMS IN DATES AND ADDRESSES

Pasadena, California, is the site of the Rose Bowl.
The letter was addressed to Mr. J. L. Karnes, Clayton, DE 19938.

Leslie applied for the job on October 3, 1988, and accepted it on Friday, March 3, 1989.
OR
Leslie applied for the job in October 1988 and accepted it on Friday, 3 March 1989.
[Note that commas may be omitted when the day of the month is not given or when the day of the month precedes rather than follows the month.]

■ **Exercise 6** Insert commas where needed in the following sentences.

1. Those are pill bugs not insects.
2. The publisher's address is 1250 Sixth Avenue San Diego CA 92101.

3. The meeting will be held in Seattle Washington and will begin on 18 March 1990.
4. Paul Revere Jones was born in Grand Forks Kansas on April 24 not on April 18.
5. The January 19 1989 issue of *The Wall Street Journal* states that the economy remains cause for concern.

(3) Parenthetical words, phrases, or clauses (inserted expressions), mild interjections, words in direct address, and absolute phrases are set off by commas.

PARENTHETICAL EXPRESSIONS

Language, then, sets the tone of our society.
—EDWIN NEWMAN

To be sure, beauty is a form of power. —SUSAN SONTAG

It's healthy to admire, I suppose, but destructive to idolize.
—TIM WHITAKER

"The trouble with ministers," said Mrs. Emerson, "is that they're not women." —ANNE TYLER [See also **16a(2)**.]

Guard your enthusiasms, however frail they may be.
—ARDIS WHITMAN [parenthetical clause]

The Age of Television has dawned in China, a generation later than in the West. —LINDA MATHEWS [appended element]

When they cause little or no pause in reading, expressions such as *also, too, of course, perhaps, at least, therefore,* and *likewise* are seldom set off by commas.

The times **also** have changed in ways that soften the rhetoric.
—HENRY FAIRLIE

Study circles are **therefore** the most pervasive method of bringing education to Swedes of all ages and walks of life.
—WILLIAM L. ABBOTT

MILD INTERJECTIONS AND WORDS USED IN DIRECT ADDRESS

> **Ah,** that's my idea of a good meal.   [interjection]
> Now is the time, **animal lovers,** to protest.   [direct address]

ABSOLUTE PHRASES

> **His temper being what it is,** I don't want a confrontation.
>
> He was thumping at a book, **his voice growing louder and louder**.   —JOYCE CAROL OATES

12e

Occasionally a comma (although not required by any of the major principles already discussed) may be needed for ease in reading.

Some commas are necessary to prevent misreading. Without commas the following sentences would confuse the reader, if only temporarily.

> Still, water must be transported to dry areas.
> The day before, I had talked with her on the phone.
> In 1984, 2.9 million employees were on the federal payroll.
>
> Those who can, pay and forego consumption of other essential goods.   —ERIC P. ECKHOLM
>
> The earth breathes, in a certain sense.   —LEWIS THOMAS

Sometimes a comma replaces a clearly understood word or group of words.

> Politicians sometimes make controversial remarks; bureaucrats, never.   —MARGARET McCARTHY

▲ Note: Writers occasionally use a comma to indicate the reader should pause, perhaps reflect, before going on. See **17e** and **17i(2)**.

■ **Exercise 7** Commas have been deleted from the following sentences. Insert commas where they are needed. Prepare to explain the reason for each comma used. Also prepare to point out where optional commas might be placed as a matter of stylistic preference.

1. When I was six we moved closer to civilization but by then the twig had been bent. —MARGARET A. ROBINSON
2. It was a middle-class neighborhood not a blackboard jungle; there was no war no hunger no racial strife. —RALPH A. RAIMI
3. My guess is that as the family breaks down friendships will grow in importance. —SUSAN LEE
4. But alas I do not rule the world and that I am afraid is the story of my life—always a godmother never a God. —FRAN LEBOWITZ
5. If all else fails try doing something nice for somebody who doesn't expect it. —GEORGE BURNS
6. As if to celebrate the arrival of the Antarctic spring a brilliant flash of light illuminated the date of September 22 1979 in the southern hemisphere. —S. T. COHEN
7. Incidentally supporting the tobacco habit is very expensive some adults having been known to sacrifice much-needed family grocery money for a carton of cigarettes. —DAVID TATELMAN
8. Police action in arresting drunks will never prevent drunkenness nor can it cure an alcoholic. —RAMSEY CLARK
9. His trainer was a woman of about forty and the two of them horse and woman seemed caught up in one of those desultory treadmills of afternoon from which there is no apparent escape.
   —E. B. WHITE
10. I had once tried to write had once reveled in feeling had let my crude imagination roam but the impulse to dream had been slowly beaten out of me. —RICHARD WRIGHT

■ **Exercise 8** For humorous effect, the writer of the following paragraph deliberately omits commas that can be justified by rules **12a**, **12b**, or **12d**. Edit the paragraph, putting in commas to contribute to ease of reading. Compare your version with someone else's and comment on any differences you find.

The commas are the most useful and usable of all the stops. It is highly important to put them in place as you go along. If you try to come back after doing a paragraph and stick them in the various spots that tempt you you will discover that they tend to swarm like minnows into all sorts of crevices whose existence you hadn't realized and before you know it the whole long sentence becomes immobilized and lashed up squirming in commas. Better to use them sparingly, and with affection, precisely when the need for each one arises, nicely, by itself.
—LEWIS THOMAS, *The Medusa and the Snail*

13
SUPERFLUOUS COMMAS

Do not use superfluous commas.

Unnecessary or misplaced commas are false or awkward signals that may confuse the reader. If you tend to use too many commas, remember that although the comma ordinarily signals a pause, not every pause calls for a comma. As you read each sentence in the following paragraph aloud, you may pause naturally at places other than those marked by a period, but no commas are necessary.

> Springboard divers routinely execute maneuvers in which their body rotates in space. The basic maneuvers are the somersault and the twist. In the somersault the body rotates head over heels as if the athlete were rotating about an axis extending from his left side to his right side through his waist. In the twist the body spins or pirouettes in midair as if the athlete were rotating about an axis extending from his head to his toes.
>
> —CLIFF FROHLICH, "The Physics of Somersaulting and Twisting"

To avoid using unnecessary commas, first review section **12** and then study and observe the following rules.

13a

Do not use a comma to separate the subject from its verb or the verb from its object.

The circled commas should be omitted.

Most older, married students⊙ must hold a job in addition to going to school.   [needless separation of subject and verb]

The lawyer said⊙ that I could appeal the speeding ticket. [needless separation of verb and direct object (a noun clause)]

13b

Do not misuse a comma before or after a coordinating conjunction. See **12a**.

The circled commas should be omitted.

I fed the dog⊙ and put it out for the night.

For two decades the surgeon-general's office has warned about the dangers of smoking, but⊙ millions of people still smoke.

13c

Do not use commas to set off words and short phrases unless they are clearly parenthetical.

The circled commas should be omitted.

Beverley Anne was born⊙ in Rochester⊙ in 1959.
Perhaps⊙ the valve is not correctly calibrated.

13d

Do not use commas to set off restrictive (necessary) clauses, restrictive phrases, or restrictive appositives.

The circled commas should be omitted.

> Everyone⊙ who owns an automobile⊙ needs to have collision insurance. [restrictive clause: see **12d(1)**]

> With strains of bagpipes in the background, crowds watched two men⊙ carrying lances as they charged each other on horseback. [restrictive phrase: see **12d(1)**]

13e

Do not use a comma before the first or after the last item of a series (including a series of coordinate adjectives).

The·circled commas should be omitted.

> Field trips were required in a few courses, such as⊙ botany, geology, and sociology.

> I've always wanted a low-slung, fast, elegant⊙ sports car.

■ **Exercise 1** Study the structure of the following sentence; then answer the question that follows by giving a specific rule number (such as **13a, 13d**) for each item. Be prepared to explain your answers in class.

> Now when you say "newly rich" you picture a middle-aged and corpulent man who has a tendency to remove his collar at formal dinners and is in perpetual hot water with his ambitious wife and her titled friends. —F. SCOTT FITZGERALD

Why is there no comma after (1) *Now,* (2) *say,* (3) *rich,* (4) *middle-aged,* (5) *man,* (6) *collar,* (7) *dinners,* or (8) *wife*?

■ **Exercise 2** Change the structure and the punctuation of the following sentences according to the pattern of the examples.

EXAMPLE

A motorcyclist saw our flashing lights, and he stopped to offer aid.
[an appropriate comma: see **12a**]

A motorcyclist saw our flashing lights and stopped to offer aid.
[second main clause reduced to a part of compound predicate—
comma no longer needed]

1. Our employers gave us very good annual evaluations, and they also
   recommended us for raises.
2. Much modern fiction draws upon current psychological knowledge,
   and it presents very believable characters.
3. Patrick likes Portland, and he may move there.

EXAMPLE

If any students destroyed public property, they were expelled.   [an
appropriate comma: see **12b**]

Any students who destroyed public property were expelled.
[introductory adverb clause converted to restrictive clause—
comma no longer needed]

4. When people make requests instead of giving orders, they generally
   get cooperation.
5. If students are willing to listen, they can learn much from Professor
   Young.

■ **Exercise 3**   In the following paragraph (adapted from *Time*) some of
the commas are needed and some are superfluous. Circle all unnecessary commas. Prepare to explain (see section **12**) each comma that you
allow to stand.

[1]Yet, punctuation is something more than a culture's birthmark; it
scores the music in our minds, and gets our thoughts moving to the
rhythm of our hearts.   [2]Punctuation, is the notation in the sheet music
of our words, telling us when to rest, or when to raise our voices.   [3]It
acknowledges that the meaning of our discourse, as of any symphonic
composition, lies, not in the units, but in the pauses, the pacing, and, the
phrasing.   [4]Commas adjust things, such as, the tone, the color, and the
volume, till the feeling comes into perfect focus.   [5]A world, which has
only periods, is a world without shade.   [6]It has a music without sharps,
and flats.   [7]It has a jackboot rhythm.   [8]Words cannot bend, and curve.

14
THE SEMICOLON

Use the semicolon between main clauses not linked by a coordinating conjunction and between coordinate elements containing commas.

Having the force of a coordinator, the semicolon is used chiefly between main clauses that are closely related. Compare the following structures.

> Some french fries are greasy. Others are not. I like them any way you fix them. [three simple sentences]

> Some french fries are greasy; others are not. I like them any way you fix them. [a semicolon linking the more closely related ideas]

The semicolon is a stronger mark of punctuation than the comma, but, like the comma, it is followed by a single space.

If you can distinguish between main and subordinate clauses and between phrases and clauses (see **1d** and **1e**), you should have little trouble using the semicolon. As you study the rules in this section, notice that the semicolon is used only between closely related coordinate elements.

14a

Use the semicolon between two main clauses not linked by a coordinating conjunction. See also **12a**.

The coordinating conjunctions are *and, but, for, or, nor, so, yet*.

> MAIN CLAUSE MAIN CLAUSE
> Subject + predicate; subject + predicate.

The dark is not mysterious; it is merely dark.
—ARCHIBALD MacLEISH

Small mammals tick fast, burn rapidly, and live for a short time; large mammals live long at a stately pace.
—STEPHEN JAY GOULD

Rule **14a** also applies in compound-complex sentences:

If the new business is a success, I'll take my share of the profits; if it isn't, I think I'll leave the country.

COMPARE If the new business is a success, I'll take my share of the profits. If it isn't, I think I'll leave the country.

Keep in mind that *however, therefore, for example, on the contrary,* and so on (see the list of conjunctive adverbs and transitional expressions on page 39) are not coordinating conjunctions. Often appearing at the beginning of a sentence, such adverbials frequently serve as transitional devices between sentences: see **32b(4)**. When placed between main clauses, they are preceded by the semicolon: see **3b**.

From the deck of the small sloop, the waves looked like immense hills; nevertheless, the tiny boat sailed on.

COMPARE From the deck of the small sloop, the waves looked like immense hills. Nevertheless, the tiny boat sailed on.

For years I continued to resent my father; as a result, I became more and more like him.

COMPARE For years I continued to resent my father. As a result, I became more and more like him.

The comma after a conjunctive adverb or transitional expression is often omitted when the adverbial is not considered parenthetical or when the comma is not needed to prevent misreading.

New Orleans is unique among American cities; indeed in many ways it is scarcely American. —PHELPS GAY

Sometimes, a semicolon (instead of the usual comma) precedes a coordinating conjunction when a sharp division between the two main clauses is desired. See also **12a**, page 127.

The female bees feed these lazy drones for a while; but they let them starve to death after the mating of the queen bee.

▲ Note: Occasionally, a comma separates short, very closely related main clauses.

We are strengthened by equality, we are weakened by it; we celebrate it, we repudiate it. —THOMAS GRIFFITH [a semicolon used between pairs of main clauses separated by commas]

When the second main clause explains or amplifies the first, a colon may be used between main clauses. See **17d**, page 169.

▲ Caution: Do not overwork the semicolon: see **14c**. Often it is better to revise compound sentences according to the principles of subordination: see **24**.

■ **Exercise 1** Use semicolons where needed to eliminate errors in punctuation.

1. An engagement is not a marriage a family quarrel is not a broken home.
2. All members of my family save things they will never use, for example, my sister saves old calendars and bent or rusty nails.
3. Popular science fiction and cult novels often have sequels, from *The Hitchhiker's Guide to the Galaxy,* for instance, came *The Restaurant at the End of the Universe, So Long, and Thanks for All the Fish,* and *Life, the Universe and Everything.*
4. He took a course in Chinese cooking, later, while showing us how to slice vegetables rapidly, he cut his thumb.
5. The motor in my car blew up, as a result, I had to use the city bus for a month.

14b

Use the semicolon to separate a series of items which themselves contain commas.

I subscribe to several computer magazines which include reviews of new, better-designed hardware**;** descriptions of inexpensive, commercial software programs**;** advice from experts**;** and actual utility programs which make keeping track of my files easier.

▲ Note: Although many disapprove, a semicolon occasionally appears before such expressions as *namely, for example,* or *for instance* when these expressions introduce a list or indicate a significant change of focus.

Cats enjoy a variety of foods**;** for example, fish, poultry, beef, pork, and vegetables.   [Compare "Cats enjoy a variety of foods: for example, . . . "]

You will not be incorrect if you use the semicolon only for connecting coordinate elements.

■ **Exercise 2**   Substitute a semicolon for any comma that could result in misreading.

1. Dennis based his conclusions on statements by Carl Rogers, a clinical psychologist interested in counseling, Noam Chomsky, the father of transformational linguistics, and Bertrand Russell, the famous logician, philosopher, and pacifist.
2. Many of the most interesting current authors are physicists and geologists, experts in various social sciences, such as sociology and psychology, and politicians and their advisors.

14c

Do not use a semicolon between parts of unequal grammatical rank.

Not between a clause and a phrase:

NOT   Along came Harvey; the dormitory clown.
BUT   Along came Harvey, the dormitory clown.   [appositive phrase]

NOT   We took a detour; the reason being that the bridge was under construction.
BUT   We took a detour, the reason being that the bridge was under construction.   [absolute phrase]

NOT   Lucy has three topics of conversation; her courses, her career, and her travels.
BUT   Lucy has three topics of conversation: her courses, her career, and her travels.   [noun phrases]

Not between a main clause and a subordinate clause:

NOT   If this report is true; then we should act now.
BUT   If this report is true, then we should act now.
   [introductory adverb clause]

NOT   We heard about the final decision; which really surprised us.
BUT   We heard about the final decision, which really surprised us.   [adjective clause]

NOT   The truck needed repairs; although it would still run.
BUT   The truck needed repairs, although it would still run.
   [adverb clause]

■ **Exercise 3** Find the semicolons used between parts of unequal rank and substitute a correct mark of punctuation. Do not change properly placed semicolons.

1. Carver found a job advertised in Sunday's paper; no experience required; then he made plans to apply in person for the job the next day.
2. Although my sister makes the best seafood gumbo I ever ate; I still try ordering it at a restaurant.
3. I dislike only two kinds of people; those who tell me what to do and those who don't do anything themselves.
4. Many times I've pushed the up button; after I've waited for as long as five minutes; the doors of two elevators open at once.
5. Eating hot, cheesy, thick-crust pizza; swooping down a snow-covered mountain; watching old Bogart movies—these are some of my favorite activities.

■ **Exercise 4** Compose four sentences to illustrate various uses of the semicolon.

■ **Exercise 5** This is an exercise on the comma and the semicolon. Study the following examples, which illustrate rules in sections **12** and **14**. Using these examples as guides, punctuate sentences 1–10 appropriately.

12a Pat poured gasoline into the hot tank, for he had not read the warning in his tractor manual.

12b Since Pat had not read the warning in his tractor manual, he poured gasoline into the hot tank.
In very large print in the tractor manual, the warning is conspicuous.

12c Pat did not read the tractor manual, observe the warning, or wait for the tank to cool.
Pat was a rash, impatient young mechanic.

12d Pat did not read his tractor manual, which warned against pouring gasoline into a hot tank.
Pat, a careless young man, poured gasoline into the hot tank of his tractor.
First, warnings should be read.

12e A week before, he had glanced at the manual.

14a Pat ignored the warning in the tractor manual; he poured gasoline into the hot tank.
Pat poured gasoline into the hot tank; thus he caused the explosion.

14b At the hospital Pat said that he had not read the warning; that he had, of course, been careless; and that he would never again, under any circumstances, pour gasoline into a hot tank.

1. Students today are more intent than ever on making good grades in their courses for they know that those grades can mean the difference between a good job and a mediocre one.
2. Professor Mikoyama a noted Japanese scientist invented a new kind of microchip.
3. The fruit stand where we stopped displayed baskets overflowing with fresh snap beans rosy peaches mounds of home-grown tomatoes and heads of leafy lettuce.
4. Five or six healthy energetic little boys splashed merrily in the water.
5. While Fred was setting up the tent and Nan built a fire I roamed near the camp looking for wood.
6. After carrying in all of our luggage Dick collapsed on the sofa.
7. In high school we were asked to memorize dates and facts such as 1066 the Battle of Hastings 1215 the signing of the Magna Carta 1917 the Russian revolution and 1945 the bombing of Hiroshima and Nagasaki.
8. They often talk about their dream of sailing to Hawaii on a large sloop to tell the truth however they seem perfectly happy with their small boat on Lake Minnetonka.
9. I mentioned I was hungry Jack thought I wanted to go out for dinner.
10. Larry and Lorna thought their romance would never end however I reminded them that fires burn out unless they are refueled regularly.

15

THE APOSTROPHE

Use the apostrophe to indicate the possessive case (except for personal pronouns), to mark omissions in contractions, and to form certain plurals.

15a

Use the apostrophe to indicate the possessive case of nouns (including acronyms) and indefinite pronouns.

The possessive (or genitive) case shows ownership or a comparable relationship: *Donald's* car, two *weeks'* pay. The possessive case of nouns and of indefinite pronouns may be indicated by the use of *'s* or by the apostrophe alone.

everybody's friend   the students' laughter

Occasionally, the idea of the possessive is indicated by the use of both an *of* phrase and *'s*:

that pie of Al's   [often called a double possessive]
COMPARE   this description of Al   [Al is described.]
          this description of Al's   [Al did the describing.]

A possessive may follow the word it modifies:

Is that new computer **Frank's** or **Jane's**?   [Compare "Frank's or Jane's computer."]

(1) For singular nouns (including acronyms) and indefinite pronouns, add the apostrophe and s.

Sue's idea   a day's work   NASA's aim   anyone's guess

▲ Option: Although most writers prefer adding 's to all proper nouns ending in s, some authorities prefer adding only the apostrophe: Keats's house OR Keats' house. Consistently follow one convention or the other. Common nouns ending in an s, x, or z sound follow the same rule as other common nouns: box's, horse's.

▲ Note: Forming the possessive of inanimate objects with 's is occasionally awkward: *the chair's cushion.* When that is the case, indicate possession with *of: the cushion of the chair.*

(2) For plural nouns ending in s, add only the apostrophe. For plurals not ending in s, add the apostrophe and s.

her sons' room   ten dollars' worth   the Ameses' home
BUT   men's watches   women's names   children's rights

(3) For compounds, add the apostrophe and s only to the last word.

his father-in-law's job   anyone else's ideas
the Dean of Students' rules   Ian James, Jr.'s book
[Notice that no comma follows *Jr.'s* although *Jr.* is normally set off by commas.]

(4) To indicate individual ownership, add the apostrophe and s to each name.

Joan's and Sam's apartments
Joe's and Betty's mail   [Compare *Joe's mail* and *Betty's mail*; *mail* is a collective noun. *Joe and Betty's mail* indicates mail belonging jointly to Joe and Betty.]

▲ Option: When no confusion would result, the apostrophe and *s* may be added either to the last name only or to both names:

Joe and Betty's house OR Joe's and Betty's house [Singular *house* indicates joint ownership.]

▲ Note: Proper names (organizations, geographical locations, and so on) sometimes do not have the apostrophe or the apostrophe and *s*.

Devil's Island   Devils Tower   Devil Mountain

■ **Exercise 1** Change the modifier after the noun to a possessive form before the noun, following the pattern of the examples.

EXAMPLES
the laughter of the crowd   *the crowd's laughter*
suggestions made by James   *James's suggestions*
                                                        OR *James' suggestions*

1. the acreage belonging to John L. Field III
2. the house built by the Weinbergs
3. the voices of Gregory and Philip
4. the hopes of my sister-in-law
5. the home of Jefferson Davis
6. worth a dollar
7. a turn belonging to somebody else
8. stories by O. Henry
9. coats for men
10. a book written by Anne and Betty

15b

Use the apostrophe to mark omissions in contractions and in numbers.

didn't   he'll   they're   there's   she'd
class of '91   o'clock [contraction of "of the clock"]

"Well, Curley's pretty handy," the swamper said skeptically. "Never did seem right to me. S'pose Curley jumps a big guy an' licks him. Ever'body says what a game guy Curley is."
—JOHN STEINBECK [See also **19b**.]

15c

Use the apostrophe and *s* to form certain plurals.

Use the apostrophe and *s* for the plural forms of lowercase letters and of abbreviations followed by periods.

> his *e*'s and *o*'s   no more *ibid.*'s
> [The **'s** is not italicized (underlined). See also **10d**.]

When needed to prevent confusion, the **'s** is used for the plural of capital letters and of words referred to as words.

> too many *I*'s   several *A*'s   two *plus*'s   the *ha ha*'s

Either **'s** or *s* may be used to form such plurals as the following:

> the 1900's   OR   the 1900s   his 7's   OR   his 7s
> two *B*'s   OR   two *B*s   the &'s   OR   the &s
> her *and*'s   OR   her *and*s   the VFW's   OR   the VFWs

15d

Do not use the apostrophe with personal pronouns or with plural nouns not in the possessive case.

> A friend of **theirs** knows a cousin of **yours**.
> The **sisters** design **clothes** for **babies**.

▲ Caution: Do not confuse *its* with *it's* or *whose* with *who's*:

> **Its** motor is small.   **It's** [It is] a small motor.
> **Whose** responsibility is it?   **Who's** [Who is] responsible?

■ **Exercise 2**   Insert apostrophes where needed.

1. Many students attitudes changed at the end of the 1980s.
2. Two of Mr. Hughes students won awards for their essays.
3. My bosss unpredictable rages are bad for company morale.

4. Margaret dislikes football; its roughness disturbs her.
5. Snapshots of the class of 94 cover Marilyns bulletin board.
6. "Its just one M.D.s opinion, isnt it?" Murray asked.
7. There are four *is* and four *ss* in *Mississippi.*
8. Theres a world of difference between Toms ability and theirs.
9. NATOs stability is still a political analysts concern.
10. Computers often confuse his account with someone elses.

16

QUOTATION MARKS

Use quotation marks for direct quotations (other than those in indented blocks), for some titles, and for words used in a special sense. Place other marks of punctuation in proper relation to quotation marks.

Quotation marks (like scissors) are always used in pairs. The first mark indicates the beginning of the quotation and the second the ending. Remember to use a closing quotation mark and to space after it.

16a
Use quotation marks for direct quotations and in all dialogue. Set off long quotations by indention.

(1) Use double quotation marks for direct quotations but none for indirect quotations. Use single quotation marks to enclose a quotation (or a minor title—see 16b) within a quotation.

"A good friend," observes Claudia Miniken, "makes hills easier to climb." [Quotation marks enclose only the quotation, not expressions like *she said* or *he replied*. The period comes within the quotation marks.]

> According to Disraeli, Gladstone was a person who did not have **"**a single redeeming defect. **"** [The quoted phrase is an integral part of the sentence.]

> Disraeli once said, **"**He [Gladstone] has not a single redeeming defect. **"** [Not a part of the direct quotation, the information inserted in brackets contributes to clarity. See also **17g**.]

Single quotation marks (made on a typewriter with the apostrophe key):

> **"**Earl keeps calling my idea **'**the impossible dream,**' "** she said. [The period goes at the end of the sentence; the comma appears in the quotation within a quotation.]

> **"**Edgar Allan Poe's **'**A Predicament**'** is one of the funniest short stories I've ever read!**"** Chet exclaimed. [Note the title within a quotation and that the exclamation point—or a question mark—goes at the end of the quoted material, but see also **16e**.]

No quotation marks:

> Claudia Miniken said that hill-climbing is not so difficult when one has a good friend. [Quotation marks are not used for indirect quotations.]

In direct quotations, reproduce all quoted material *exactly* as it appears in the original, including capitalization and punctuation. If the quoted material contains an error, insert *sic* within brackets immediately after the error (see **17g** and **34e**).

(2) Use quotation marks for dialogue (directly quoted conversation).

In dialogue the standard practice is to write what each person says, no matter how short, as if it were a separate paragraph. Expressions such as *he said,* as well as closely related bits of narrative, are included with the direct quotations.

> Through an interpreter, I spoke with a Bedouin man tending nearby olive trees.

"Do you own this land?" I asked him.

He shook his head. "The land belongs to Allah," he said.

"What about the trees?" I asked. He had just harvested a basket of green olives, and I assumed that at least the trees were his.

"The trees, too, are Allah's," he replied.

I marveled at this man who seemed unencumbered by material considerations . . . or so I was thinking when, as if in afterthought, he said, "Of course, I own the *olives*."

—HARVEY ARDEN, "In Search of Moses"

▲ Note 1: When quoting more than one paragraph by a single speaker, use quotation marks at the beginning of each new paragraph but at the end of only the last paragraph.

▲ Note 2: Set off thoughts with double quotation marks, just as if they were stated: "Here we go again," I thought.

(3) Set off long quotations of prose and poetry by indention. Run short quotations into the text.

Prose Indent all lines of a long quotation (more than four lines) ten spaces from the left margin. In APA style, indent five spaces those quotations of more than forty words. Long quotations are double-spaced and are usually introduced by a colon. When you quote two or more paragraphs, indent the first line of each paragraph thirteen spaces rather than the usual ten unless the first line quoted does not begin the first paragraph quoted. In that case, indent the first line of the quotation ten spaces and the first lines of all subsequent paragraphs thirteen. Use quotation marks only if they appear in the original.

```
Metal coins replaced bartering.  Then paper money

became more convenient to use than metal coins not

only because it is easy to handle but also because,
```

as Cetron and O'Toole say in <u>Encounters with the</u>
<u>Future</u>, it has other advantages:

> Printing more zeroes is all it takes on a
> bill to increase its value. Careful
> engraving makes it easy to recognize and
> difficult to counterfeit. The fact that
> private individuals cannot create it at
> will keeps it scarce. Karl Marx once
> said that paper money was valued "only
> insofar as it represents gold" but that
> may never have been true. (188)

Today, checks and credit cards are even more
convenient than paper money.

An omission within a quotation is indicated by the use of
ellipsis points: see **17i**.

For the proper documentation of sources in a research
paper, see section **34**.

Poetry Except for very special emphasis, a quotation of
three (or fewer) lines of poetry is handled as other short
quotations are—run in with the text and enclosed in quotation marks. A slash with a space on each side indicates the
divisions between lines: see **17h**. Passages of more than
three lines are set off from the text—double-spaced and
indented ten spaces from the left margin unless unusual
spacing is meaningful in the poem. Quotation marks are
used only if they appear in the original. (Numbers in parentheses—placed two spaces after the close of the quotation—
may be used to indicate the line numbers of the poem.)

In "London" William Blake expressed his horror of

institutional callousness:

> How the Chimney-sweeper's cry
>
> Every black'ning Church appalls;
>
> And the hapless Soldier's sigh
>
> Runs in blood down Palace walls. (9—12)

■ **Exercise 1** Change each indirect quotation to a direct quotation and each direct quotation to an indirect one.

1. Doris said that she had a theory about me.
2. He says that he has read David Baltimore's "The Brain of a Cell."
3. A Weight Watcher, Eileen explained that she could eat as much as she wanted—of vegetables like spinach, eggplant, and zucchini.
4. Clyde asked, "Will you go to the opera with me?"
5. Last night Pruett said that he thought that Amanda's favorite expression was "Tell me about it!"

16b

Use quotation marks for minor titles (short stories, essays, short poems, songs, episodes of a radio or television series, articles in periodicals) and subdivisions of books.

> Coral Browne starred in "An Englishman Abroad," part of the *Great Performances* series.
>
> On the subway, I scanned Richard Sandza's "The Night of the Hackers" in an old issue of *Newsweek*.
>
> Andrew A. Rooney's *Pieces of My Mind* contains essays like "Procrastination" and "The Power of Negative Thinking."

Use double quotation marks to enclose a minor title appearing in a longer italicized (underlined) title. Use single marks for one within a longer title enclosed in double quotation marks.

> *Modern Interpretations of "My Last Duchess"*
> "An Introduction to 'My Last Duchess' "

▲ Note: Quotation marks are sometimes used to enclose titles of books, periodicals, and newspapers, but italics are generally preferred: see **10a**.

16c

Used sparingly, quotation marks may enclose words intended in a special or an ironic sense.

> His **"**castle**"** was a cozy little rattrap.
> OR   His so-called castle was a cozy little rattrap.   [The use of *so-called* eliminates the need for quotation marks.]

> And I do mean good and evil, not **"**adjustment and deviance,**"** the gutless language that so often characterizes modern discussions of psychological topics.   —CAROL TAVRIS

▲ Note: Either quotation marks or italics may be used in definitions such as the following. See also **10d**.

> **"**Ploy**"** means **"**a strategy used to gain an advantage.**"**
> *Ploy* means **"**a strategy used to gain an advantage.**"**
> *Ploy* means *a strategy used to gain an advantage.*

16d

Do not overuse quotation marks.

Do not use quotation marks to enclose a cliché (see **20c**).

> REVISE   A good debater does not "beat about the bush."
> TO   A good debater does not beat about the bush.
> BETTER   A good debater comes directly to the point.

Do not use quotation marks for a *yes* or *no* in indirect discourse or for diction that you may consider questionable.

> REVISE   A "wimp" can't say "no" to anyone.
> TO   A wimp can't say no to anyone.

Quotation marks are not used for titles that head compositions.

■ **Exercise 2** Insert quotation marks where needed in the following sentences.

1. In a short story entitled Cloning, scientists turn one Einstein into three Einsteins.
2. Here, stoked means fantastically happy on a surfboard.
3. David enjoyed reading the short story A Circle in the Fire.
4. *Learning to Live without Cigarettes* opens with a chapter entitled Sighting the Target.
5. Theresa said, My grandmother often said, When poverty comes in the door, love goes out the window.

16e

When using various marks of punctuation with quoted words, phrases, or sentences, follow the conventions of American printers.

(1) Place the period and the comma within the quotation marks.

> "Jenny," he said, "let's have lunch."
> She replied, "OK, but first I want to finish 'The Machine Stops.' "

> This problem illustrates what Hopkins called "inscape."

▲ Exception:

> The author states: "Time alone reveals the just" (471).
> [The period follows the parenthetical reference to the source of the quotation.]

(2) Place the colon and the semicolon outside the quotation marks.

> She spoke of "the protagonists"; yet I remembered only one in "The Tell-Tale Heart": the mad murderer.

(3) Place the question mark, the exclamation point, and the dash within the quotation marks when they apply only to the quoted matter. Place them outside when they do not.

Within the quotation marks:

> Pilate asked, "What is truth?"
> Gordon replied, "No way!"
> "Achievement—success!—," states Heather Evans, "has become a national obsession."
> Why do children keep asking "Why?"   [a question within a question—one question mark inside the quotation marks]

Outside the quotation marks:

> What is the meaning of the term "half-truth"?
> Stop whistling "All I do Is Dream of You"!
> The boss exclaimed, "No one should work for the profit motive!"— no exceptions, I suppose.

■ **Exercise 3**   Insert quotation marks where they are needed.

1. Who wrote The Star-Spangled Banner?
2. Get aholt, instead of get hold, is still used in that region.
3. One of my favorite songs is the old Beatles hit, Hey Jude.
4. Last spring I discovered Frost's poem The Road Not Taken.
5. No, Peg said, I didn't agree to do that. I may be a softie, but I haven't gone bananas yet!
6. Have you read Judy Syfers' essay I Want a Wife?
7. We were watching Black Orchid, a *Doctor Who* episode.
8. Her favorite short story is First Confession; mine is The Story of an Hour.
9. Why cry over spilled milk? my grandmother used to ask. Be glad you have the milk to spill.
10. Catherine said, Do the townspeople ever say to me You're a born leader? Yes, lots of times, and when they do, I just tell them my motto is Lead, follow, or get the heck out of the way!

17
THE PERIOD
AND OTHER MARKS

Use the period, question mark, exclamation point, colon, dash, parentheses, brackets, slash, and ellipsis points appropriately. For the use of the hyphen, see **18f**.

Notice how the marks in color below signal meaning and intonation.

> The days are dark. Why worry? The sun never stops shining!
>
> In *Lady Windermere's Fan* (1892) is this famous line: "I [Lord Darlington] can resist everything except temptation."
>
> According to *Consumer Reports*, "The electronic radio/ clock ... is extremely complicated—enough so to require five pages of instructions in the owner's manual."

Two spaces follow the period, question mark, exclamation point, and the last dot of four-dot ellipsis points; one space follows the colon, the ending parenthesis and bracket, and each of the dots in ellipsis points. No spaces follow the hyphen or dash.

THE PERIOD

17a

Use the period as an end mark and with some abbreviations.

(1) Use the period to mark the end of a declarative sentence and a mildly imperative sentence.

> Everyone should drive defensively. [declarative]
>
> Learn how to drive defensively. [mild imperative]
>
> She asks how drivers can cross the city without driving offensively. [declarative sentence containing an indirect question]
>
> "How can drivers cross the city without driving offensively?" she asked. [declarative sentence containing a direct quotation]
>
> "Get with it!" he hollered. [declarative sentence containing an exclamation]

(2) Use periods after some abbreviations.

> Mrs., Jr.   a.m., p.m.   vs., etc., et al.

Periods are not used with most abbreviations in ordinary writing (for example, *SSW, MVP, FM, mph*—see also page 118). The period is not used after clipped or shortened forms (*premed, lab, 12th*) or after the postal abbreviation of a state (*NJ, TX, KY*).

When in doubt about punctuating an abbreviation, consult a good college dictionary. Dictionaries often list options, such as *USA* or *U.S.A., CST* or *C.S.T.*

▲ Caution: When an abbreviation ending in a period appears last in the sentence, do not add a second period:

> The study was performed by Ben Werthman, et al.

THE QUESTION MARK

17b

Use the question mark after direct (but not indirect) questions.

Who started the rumor? [direct question]

She asked who had started the rumor. [indirect question]

Did you hear her ask, "Are you accusing me of starting the rumor?" [A direct question within a direct question is followed by one question mark inside the quotation mark: see **16e**.]

Did they clean the attic? the basement? the whole house? [A series of questions having the same subject and verb may be treated as elliptical; that is, only the first item need include both subject and verb.]

Declarative sentences may contain direct questions:

How can their differences be resolved? was the question.

After attending one session, ask yourself, was it worth it? [No period follows the question mark and no quotation marks enclose the question. The letter beginning a formal question not enclosed in quotation marks may be capitalized or not.]

When we ask ourselves, Why does evil happen? we seek a logical explanation for the irrational. [A question mark follows the interpolated question not enclosed in quotation marks.]

He said, "Who started the rumor?" [Put a question mark inside quotation marks only when it concludes a quoted direct question. Compare: Did he say, "I started the rumor"? See **16e**]

▲ Note: A question mark within parentheses is used to express the writer's uncertainty about the correctness of the preceding word, figure, or date:

Chaucer was born in 1340 (?) and died in 1400.

THE EXCLAMATION POINT

17c

Use the exclamation point after an emphatic interjection and after other expressions to show strong emotion, such as surprise or disbelief.

Boo!   What a game!   Look at that windshield!

Use the exclamation point sparingly; overuse diminishes its value. A comma is better after mild interjections and a period is better after mildly exclamatory expressions and mild imperatives.

Oh, look at that windshield.   How quiet the lake was.

▲ Caution: Do not use a comma or a period after an exclamation point.

"Watch out!" he yelled.   Jo exclaimed, "It's snowing!"

■ **Exercise 1**   Illustrate the chief uses of the period, the question mark, and the exclamation point by composing and correctly punctuating brief sentences of the types specified.

1. a direct question
2. a mild imperative
3. a declarative sentence containing a quoted exclamation
4. a declarative sentence containing an indirect question
5. a declarative sentence containing an interpolated question

THE COLON

17d

Use the colon as a formal introducer to call attention to what follows and as a mark of separation in scriptural and time references and between titles and subtitles.

(1) The colon may direct attention to an explanation or summary, a series, or a quotation.

I was a bilingual child, but of a certain kind: "socially disadvantaged," the son of working-class parents, both Mexican immigrants. —RICHARD RODRIGUEZ [Note that the first letter after a colon need not be capitalized unless it begins a quoted sentence.]

Of all the distinctions between man and animal, the characteristic gift which makes us human is the power to work with symbolic images: the gift of imagination.

—JACOB BRONOWSKI

Claire Safran points out two of the things that cannot be explained: "One of them is poltergeists. Another is teenagers." [A quoted sentence after a colon begins with a capital.]

The colon may introduce a second main clause when it explains or amplifies the first main clause:

The American conceives of fishing as more than a sport: it is his personal contest against nature. —JOHN STEINBECK

Similarly, a colon is occasionally used after one sentence to introduce the next sentence:

The sorrow was laced with violence: In the first week of demolition, vandals struck every night. —SMITHSONIAN

▲ Caution: Within a single sentence, use only one colon to direct attention.

(2) Use the colon between figures in time references and between titles and subtitles.

At 2:15 a.m. the phone rang.

Read *Megatrends: Ten New Directions Transforming Our Lives.*

▲ Note 1: Many writers prefer to use a colon in scriptural references: He quoted from Psalms 3:5. MLA recommends periods: Psalms 3.5.

▲ Note 2: The colon is also used after the salutation of a business letter and in bibliographical data: see **35b(1)**, **34f**, and **34g**.

(3) Do not use superfluous colons.

Be especially careful not to use an unnecessary colon between a verb and its complement or object, between a preposition and its object, or after *such as*.

> NOT   The winners were: Pat, Lydia, and Jack.
> BUT   The winners were Pat, Lydia, and Jack.
>> OR   There were three winners: Pat, Lydia, and Jack.
>> OR   The winners were as follows: Pat, Lydia, Jack.

> NOT   Many vegetarians do not eat dairy products, such as: butter, cheese, yogurt, or ice cream.
> BUT   Many vegetarians do not eat dairy products, such as butter, cheese, yogurt, or ice cream.

■ **Exercise 2** Punctuate the following sentences by adding colons. Put a check mark after any sentence that needs no change.

1. At 1230 a.m. he was still repeating his favorite quotation "TV is the opiate of the people."
2. The downtown streets are narrow, rough, and dirty.
3. Three states noted for their vacation areas are these Hawaii, Florida, and California.
4. During our tour of the library, our guide recommended that we find one of the following periodicals *Intellect, Smithsonian, Commentary,* or *The Chronicle of Higher Education*.
5. All their thoughts were centered on equal pay for equal work.

■ **Exercise 3** Decide whether to use a colon or a semicolon between the main clauses of the following sentences. See also **14a**.

1. These laws all have the same purpose they protect us from ourselves.
2. Some of these laws have an obvious purpose others seem senseless.
3. Few things are certain perhaps we could count them on one hand.
4. One thing is certain the future looks bright.

THE DASH

17e

**Use the dash to mark a break in thought, to set off a paren-
thetical element for emphasis or clarity, and to set off an
introductory series.**

On the typewriter, the dash is indicated by two hyphens
without spacing before, between, or after them. In handwriting, the dash is an unbroken line about the length of
two hyphens.

**(1) Use the dash to mark a sudden break in thought, an
abrupt change in tone, or faltering speech.**

A hypocrite is a person who —but who isn't?
—DON MARQUIS

When I was six I made my mother a little hat —out of her
new blouse. —LILLY DACHÉ

Aunt Esther replied, "I put the key on the —in the —no,
under the doormat, I think."

**(2) Use the dash to set off a parenthetical element for em-
phasis or (if it contains commas) for clarity.**

Lightning is an electrical discharge —an enormous spark.
—RICHARD E. ORVILLE

Instead, there has been a great deal of news in America about
the side effects —all bad —of the good news.
—BEN J. WATTENBERG

Sentiments that human shyness will not always allow one to
convey in conversation —sentiments of gratitude, of apology,
of love —can often be more easily conveyed in a letter.
—ARISTIDES

171

(3) Use the dash after an introductory list or series.

Notice that in the main part of each of the following sentences a word like *all, these, that, such,* or *none* points to or sums up the meaning of the introductory list.

> Keen, calculating, perspicacious, acute and astute—I was all of these. —MAX SHULMAN

> Farmer, laborer, clerk—that is a brief history of the United States. —JOHN NAISBITT

▲ Caution: Use dashes sparingly and not as easy or automatic substitutes for commas, semicolons, or end marks.

PARENTHESES

17f

Use parentheses to set off parenthetical, supplementary, or illustrative matter and to enclose figures or letters when used for enumeration.

> They call this illness Seasonal Affective Disorder (SAD).
> —LOWELL PONTE [a first-time use of an acronym in an article—see **11e**]

> Bernard Shaw once demonstrated that, by following the rules (up to a point!), we could spell *fish* this way: *ghoti.*
> —JOHN IRVING [an exclamatory parenthetical expression]

> In contrast, a judgment is subject to doubt if there is any possibility at all (1) of its being challenged in the light of additional or more accurate observations or (2) of its being criticized on the basis of more cogent or more comprehensive reasoning. —MORTIMER J. ADLER [In long sentences especially, the enumeration contributes to clarity.]

Notice in the next examples that the writer may choose between a parenthetical main clause and a parenthetical sentence. See also **9e**.

More stray cows came up to my lane (cows do like to get together as much as possible). —LEO SIMPSON

Strangely, he didn't seem to know much about cows. (That was when he told me that cows could not run downhill, and neither could bears.) —LEO SIMPSON

PUNCTUATION OF PARENTHETICAL MATTER

Dashes, parentheses, commas—all are used to set off parenthetical matter. Dashes set off parenthetical elements sharply and usually emphasize them:

Man's mind is indeed—as Luther said—a factory busy with making idols. —HARVEY COX

Parentheses usually de-emphasize the elements they enclose:

Man's mind is indeed (as Luther said) a factory busy with making idols.

Commas are the most frequently used separators:

Man's mind is indeed, as Luther said, a factory busy with making idols.

That face has moved men and women to poetry, and to tears.
—MAURICE SHADBOLT

▲ Note: Use parentheses sparingly and remember that the elements they enclose should still read smoothly within the sentence as a whole.

BRACKETS

17g

Use brackets to set off interpolations in quoted matter and to replace parentheses within parentheses.

The *Home Herald* printed the beginning of the mayor's speech: "My dear fiends [sic] and fellow citizens." [A bracketed *sic*—meaning "thus"—tells the reader that the error appears in the original.]

Deems Taylor has written: "Not for a single moment did he [Richard Wagner] compromise with what he believed, with what he dreamed."

Not every expert agrees. (See, for example, Malachi Martin's *Rich Church, Poor Church* [New York: Putnam's, 1984].)

THE SLASH

17h

Use the slash between terms to indicate that either term is applicable and to mark line divisions of quoted poetry. See also **16a(3)**.

Note that the slash is used unspaced between terms, but with a space before and after it between lines of poetry.

Today visions of the checkless/cashless society are not quite as popular as they used to be. —KATHRYN H. HUMES

Equally rare is a first-rate adventure story designed for those who enjoy a smartly told tale that isn't steeped in blood and/ or sex. —JUDITH CRIST

When in "Mr. Flood's Party" the hero sets down his jug at his feet, "as a mother lays her sleeping child / Down tenderly, fearing it may awake," one feels Robinson's heart to be quite simply on his sleeve. —WILLIAM H. PITCHARD

▲ Note: Extensive use of the slash to indicate either of two terms is applicable (as in *and/or*) can make writing choppy.

■ **Exercise 4** Correctly punctuate each of the following sentences by supplying commas, dashes, parentheses, brackets, or slashes. Prepare to explain the reason for all marks you add, especially those you choose for setting off parenthetical matter.

1. Gordon Gibbs or is it his twin brother? plays the drums.
2. Joseph who is Gordon's brother is a lifeguard at the beach.
3. "I admit that I" he began, but his voice broke; he could say no more.
4. This organization needs more of everything more money, brains, initiative.
5. Some of my courses for example, French and biology demand a great deal of work outside the classroom.
6. In the TV version of *The Lone Ranger*, Jay Silverheels 1918–1980 played the role of Tonto.
7. This ridiculous sentence appeared in the school paper: "Because of a personal fool sic the Cougars failed to cross the goal line during the last seconds of the game."
8. Body language a wink or yawn nose-rubbing·or ear-pulling folded arms or crossed legs can often speak much louder than words.
9. Gently rolling hills, rich valleys, beautiful lakes these things impress the tourist in Connecticut.
10. Some innovations for example the pass fail system did not contribute to grade inflation.

ELLIPSIS POINTS

17i

Use ellipsis points (three equally spaced periods) to mark an omission from a quoted passage and to mark a reflective pause or hesitation.

(1) Use ellipsis points to indicate an omission within a quoted passage.

ORIGINAL   If—or is it when?—these computers are permitted to talk to one another, when they are interlinked, they can spew out a roomful of data on each of us that will leave us naked before whoever gains access to the information. (From Walter Cronkite, "Foreword," *The Rise of the Computer State* by David Burnham [New York: Random, 1983], viii.)

OMISSION WITHIN A QUOTED SENTENCE

As Walter Cronkite has observed, "If **. . .** these computers are permitted to talk to one another, **. . .**they can spew out a roomful of data on each of us that will leave us naked before whoever gains access to the information." [The comma before the second group of ellipsis points could be omitted, but it marks the end of an introductory adverb clause and contributes to the grammatical integrity of the sentence.]

OMISSION AT THE END OF A QUOTED SENTENCE

If an omission at the end of the quoted sentence coincides with the end of your sentence, use a period in addition to the three ellipsis points, leaving no space immediately after the last letter in your sentence. If a parenthetical reference is cited, place the period after the second parenthesis instead.

According to Walter Cronkite, "If—or is it when?—these computers are permitted to talk to one another, when they are interlinked, they can spew out a roomful of data on each of us **. . . .**" [OR "each of us **. . .** " (viii).]

OMISSION OF A SENTENCE OR MORE

Use a period before ellipsis points (that is, use four dots) to mark omissions within a quoted passage if a complete sentence stands on either side of the ellipsis. Also use a period before ellipsis points to mark the omission of a sentence or more (even a paragraph or more—see **16a[3]**) within a quoted passage.

ORIGINAL   There's an uncertainty in our minds about the engineering principles of an elevator. We've all had little glimpses into the dirty, dark elevator shaft and seen the greasy cables passing each other. They never look totally safe. The idea of being trapped in a small box going up and down on strings induces a kind of phobia in all of us. (From Andrew A. Rooney, *Pieces of My Mind* [New York: Atheneum, 1984], 121.)

Of the common fear of riding in an elevator, Andrew A. Rooney writes, "We've all had little glimpses into the dirty, dark elevator shaft• • • • The idea of being trapped in a small box going up and down on strings induces a kind of phobia in all of us." [Thirteen words have been omitted from the original, but a sentence comes before and after the period and ellipsis points.]

Andrew A. Rooney writes about the fear of riding in an elevator: "We've all had little glimpses into the dirty, dark elevator shaft and seen the greasy cables passing each other. They never look totally safe. The idea of being trapped • • • induces a kind of phobia in all of us." [Ten words have been omitted from the original, all within a single sentence.]

To indicate the omission of a full line or more in quoted poetry, use spaced periods covering the length either of the line above it or of the omitted line.

The hoary prince in majesty appeared,
High on a throne of his own labors reared.
• •
His brows thick fogs, instead of glories, grace,
And lambent dullness played around his face.
—JOHN DRYDEN

(2) Use ellipsis points sparingly to mark a reflective pause or hesitation.

Love, like other emotions, has causes• • • and consequences.
—LAWRENCE CASLER

Ellipsis points to show a pause may also come after the period at the end of a sentence:

All channels are open. The meditation is about to begin• • • —TOM ROBBINS

■ **Exercise 5** Beginning with "According to John Donne," or with "As John Donne has written," quote the following passage, omitting the words placed in brackets. Use three or four periods as needed to indicate omissions.

> No man is an island [entire of itself]; every man is a piece of the continent, a part of the main. [If a clod be washed away by the sea, Europe is the less, as well as if a promontory were, as well as if a manor of thy friend's or of thine own were.] Any man's death diminishes me because I am involved in mankind [and therefore never send to know for whom the bell tolls; it tolls for thee].
>
> —JOHN DONNE

■ **Exercise 6**   First, observing differences in meaning and emphasis, use ellipsis points for the dash, commas, and italicized words in the following sentences. Then write two sentences of your own to illustrate the use of ellipsis points to mark a pause or hesitation.

1. My father was dying—*and, I wondered,* what would happen to us?
2. Our lives would have been different if *he had lived.*

■ **Exercise 7**   Punctuate the following sentences (selected and adapted from *The Atlantic*) by supplying appropriate end marks, commas, colons, dashes, and parentheses. Do not use unnecessary punctuation. Be prepared to explain the reason for each mark you add, especially when you have a choice of correct marks (for example, commas, dashes, or parentheses).

1. Freeways in America are all the same aluminum guardrails green signs white lettering
2. "Is it is it the green light then" was all I managed to say
3. I tell you again What is alive and young and throbbing with historic current in America is musical theater
4. Things aren't helped by the following typo "The second study involved 177,106 of the approximately 130,000 refugees"
5. "Judy" she exploded "Judy that's an awful thing to say" She raised an arm to slap her daughter but it wouldn't reach
6. Emily formerly Mrs. Goyette caught McAndless' sleeve where no one could see and tugged it briefly but urgently
7. At last she had become what she had always wished to be a professional dancer
8. My own guess is that sociobiology will offer no comfort to thinkers conservatives or liberals who favor tidy ideas about what it means to be human
9. As one man put it "Rose Bowl Sugar Bowl and Orange Bowl all are gravy bowls"
10. "Good and" can mean "very" "I am good and mad" and "a hot cup of coffee" means that the coffee not the cup is hot

SPELLING AND DICTION

Spelling and Hyphenation **18**

Good Usage and Glossary **19**

Exactness **20**

Wordiness and Needless Repetition **21**

Omission of Necessary Words **22**

18

SPELLING
AND HYPHENATION

Spell every word according to established usage as shown by your dictionary. Hyphenate words in accordance with current usage.

SPELLING

Spelling problems are highly visible, and misspellings may make a reader doubt whether the writer can present information clearly and correctly. Therefore, always proofread to detect misspellings as well as slips of the pen or errors in typing. One time-tested way to improve spelling is to record and study correct spellings of words that you have misspelled—it helps you detect patterns of misspelling: see **8f**.

If you write with a word-processing program, investigate compatible spelling checkers—computer programs that identify most spelling errors. But be aware of their limitations—for example, their inability to recognize a misspelling for words that sound alike, such as *them* for *then*.

If you have any doubt about a correct spelling, even if you use a spelling checker, consult your dictionary. Check the meaning to be sure you have found the word you had in mind. Watch for such restrictive labels as *British* or *chiefly British*:

| BRITISH | connexion | humour | centre | offence | realize |
| AMERICAN | connection | humor | center | offense | realize |

In ordinary writing, do not use spellings labeled *obsolete* or *archaic*, *dialectal* or *regional*, *nonstandard* or *slang*.

| NOT | afeard | heighth | chaw | boughten |
| BUT | afraid | height | chew | bought |

If your dictionary lists two unlabeled alternatives, either form is correct—for example, *fulfil* or *fulfill*, *symbolic* or *symbolical*, *girlfriend* or *girl friend*. The first option listed is usually the more common or preferred form.

18a

Do not misspell a word because of mispronunciation.

Mispronunciation frequently leads to misspelling. In the following words, trouble spots are in boldface.

athlete	drowned	mischievous	quantity
barbarous	everyone	modern	surprise
candidate	gratitude	perspire	umbrella

As you check pronunciation in the dictionary, notice carefully which letters represent /ə/, *schwa*, the symbol for a neutral vowel sound in unaccented syllables, usually an indistinct *uh* sound, as in *confidence*.

A word that is difficult to spell may have alternate pronunciations. Of these, one may be a better guide to spelling. Here are examples of such words:

| arctic | government | literature | veteran |
| February | interest | sophomore | where |

Do not misspell words like *and* or *than* because they are not stressed in speech: Wouldn't you rather have steak than (NOT *then*) ham and (NOT *an*) eggs?

18b

Distinguish between words of similar sound; use the spelling required by the meaning.

Words such as *forth* and *fourth* or *sole* and *soul* sound alike but have vastly different meanings. Be sure to choose the right word for your context.

A number of frequently confused spellings may be studied in groups:

Contractions and possessive pronouns

It's my turn next.	Each group waits **its** turn.
You're next.	**Your** turn is next.
There's no difference.	**Theirs** is no different.

Single words and two-word phrases

He wore **everyday** clothes.	He wears them **every day**.
Maybe we will go.	We **may be** going.
You ran **into** my car.	We can run **in to** check it.
Nobody was there.	The police found **no body**.

Singular nouns ending in *-nce* and plural nouns ending in *-nts*

Assistance is available.	I have two **assistants**.
For **instance**, Jack can go.	They arrived **instants** ago.
My **patience** is frayed.	Some **patients** waited hours.

As you study the following list, use your dictionary to check the meaning of words you are not thoroughly familiar with. You may find it helpful to devise examples of usage such as these:

accept—have accepted	**except**—anything except money
its—enjoy its warmth	**it's**—it is warm
passed—passed the test	**past**—a lurid past

Words Frequently Confused

accept, except
access, excess
adapt, adopt
advice, advise
affect, effect
aisles, isles
alley, ally
allude, elude
allusion, illusion
already, all ready 10
altar, alter
altogether, all together
always, all ways
angel, angle
ascent, assent
assistance, assistants
baring, barring, bearing
birth, berth
board, bored
born, borne 20
break, brake
breath, breathe
buy, by
canvas, canvass
capital, capitol
censor, censure, sensor
choose, chose
cite, site, sight
clothes, cloths
coarse, course 30

complement, compliment
conscience, conscious
council, counsel
credible, creditable
cursor, curser
dairy, diary
decent, descent, dissent
desert, dessert
detract, distract
device, devise 40
dominant, dominate
dual, duel
dyeing, dying
elicit, illicit
envelop, envelope
fair, fare
faze, phase
formerly, formally
forth, fourth
forward, foreword 50
gorilla, guerrilla
hear, here
heard, herd
heroin, heroine
hole, whole
holy, wholly
horse, hoarse
human, humane
instance, instants
its, it's 60

later, latter
led, lead
lesson, lessen
lightning, lightening
lose, loose
maybe, may be
minor, miner
moral, morale
of, off
passed, past   70
patience, patients
peace, piece
persecute, prosecute
perspective, prospective
personal, personnel
plain, plane
pray, prey
precede, proceed
predominant, predominate
presence, presents   80
principle, principal
prophecy, prophesy

purpose, propose
quiet, quite
respectfully, respectively
right, rite, write
road, rode
sense, since
shown, shone
stationary, stationery   90
statue, stature, statute
straight, strait
taut, taunt
than, then
their, there, they're
through, thorough
to, too, two
tract, track
waist, waste
weak, week   100
weather, whether
were, where
who's, whose
your, you're

18c

Distinguish between the prefix and the root.

The root is the base to which prefixes and suffixes are
added. Notice in the following examples that no letter is
added or dropped when the prefix is added to the root.

dis-	**dis**agree, **dis**appear	mis-	**mis**spent, **mis**spell
im-	**im**mortal, **im**moral	re-	**re**elect [OR **re**-elect]
un-	**un**necessary, **un**noticed	ir-	**ir**rational, **ir**regular

18d

Apply the rules for adding suffixes.

(1) Dropping or retaining a final unpronounced e

Drop the -*e* before a suffix beginning with a vowel:

| age | aging | scarce | scarcity |
| desire | desirable | fame | famous |

Retain the -*e* before a suffix beginning with a consonant:

| care | careful | safe | safety |
| mere | merely | manage | management |

▲ Options: *judgment* or *judgement, likable* or *likeable*

▲ Some exceptions: *acreage, mileage, argument, ninth, truly, wholly*

To keep the sound /s/ of -*ce* or /j/ of -*ge*, do not drop the final *e* before -*able* or -*ous*:

noticeable   changeable   outrageous   courageous

Similarly, keep the *e* before -*ance* in *vengeance.*

■ **Exercise 1**   Practice adding suffixes to words ending in an unpronounced *e*.

EXAMPLES
-ing: rise, lose, guide   *rising, losing, guiding*
-ly, -er, -ness: late   *lately, later, lateness*

1. -ly: like, safe, sure
2. -able, -ing, -ment: excite
3. -ing: come, notice, hope
4. -ing, -less: use
5. -ous: continue, courage
6. -ful: care, hope, use
7. -ing, -ment, -able: argue
8. -ly, -ing: complete
9. -able: desire, notice
10. -ing, -ment: manage

185

(2) Doubling a final consonant before a suffix

Double a final consonant before a suffix beginning with a
vowel if both (a) the consonant ends a stressed syllable or
a one-syllable word and (b) the consonant is preceded by a
single vowel.

One-syllable words:		*Words stressed on last syllable:*	
drag	dragged	abhor	abhorrent
hid	hidden	begin	beginning
shop	shoppers	occur	occurrence
stun	stunning	regret	regrettable
wet	wettest	unwrap	unwrapped

Compare benefited, reference   [stressed on first syllable]

■ **Exercise 2**   Write the present participle (*-ing* form) and the past
tense of each verb: *rob*—robbing, robbed.

admit	conceal	hope	plan	stop
brag	grip	jog	rebel	audit

(3) Changing or retaining a final *y* before a suffix

Change the *-y* to *i* before suffixes—except *-ing*.

apply → applies, applied, appliance BUT applying
study → studies, studied BUT studying
happy → happily, happiness, happier, happiest

▲ Exceptions: Verbs ending in *y* preceded by a vowel do not
change the *y* before *-s* or *-ed*: *stay, stays, stayed*. Following
the same pattern of spelling, nouns like *joys* or *days* have *y*
before *s*. The following irregularities in spelling are especially troublesome:

lays, laid   pays, paid   [Compare: says, said.]

(4) Retaining a final *l* before *-ly*

Do not drop a final *l* when you add *-ly*:

real–really   usual–usually   cool–coolly   formal–formally

■ **Exercise 3**   Add the designated suffixes to the following words.

1. -able: vary, ply
2. -er: funny, carry
3. -ous: vary, luxury
4. -ly: easy, final
5. -ed: supply, stay

6. -ing: study, worry
7. -d: pay, lay
8. -hood: lively, likely
9. -ness: friendly, lonely
10. -ly: usual, cool

(5) Adding *-s* or *-es* to form the plural of nouns

Form the plural of most nouns by adding *-s* to the singular:

few toys   some states   many scientists
several safes   two spoonfuls   none of the tables
both brothers-in-law   [chief word pluralized]
the Dudleys, the Berrys, and the Longorias   [proper names]

▲ Note 1: To form the plural of some nouns ending in *f* or *fe*, change the ending to *ve* before adding the *-s: a thief, two thieves; one life, our lives.*

Add *-es* to singular nouns ending in *s, z, ch, sh,* or *x*:

too many bosses   six boxes   the Rodriguezes
some peaches   sudden crashes   both Charleses
   [Note that each plural above makes an extra syllable.]

Add *-es* to singular common nouns ending in *y* preceded by a consonant, after changing the *y* to *i*:

ninety–nineties   industry–industries   party–parties

▲ Note 2: Although *-es* is often added to a singular noun ending in *o* preceded by a consonant, usage varies:

echoes	heroes	potatoes	vetoes [-es only]
autos	memos	pimentos	pros [-s only]
nos/noes	mottos/mottoes	zeros/zeroes [-s or -es]

▲ Exceptions: Irregular plurals (including retained foreign spellings) are not formed by adding -s or -es.

SINGULAR	woman	goose	analysis	datum	species
PLURAL	women	geese	analyses	data	species

SINGULAR	criterion	alumnus	alumna
PLURAL	criteria	alumni	alumnae

■ **Exercise 4**   Supply plural forms (including any optional spelling) for the following words, applying **18d**. (If a word is not covered by the rules, use your dictionary.)

1. belief
2. theory
3. church
4. genius
5. Kelly
6. bath
7. hero
8. story
9. wish
10. forty
11. radius
12. scarf
13. wife
14. speech
15. tomato
16. phenomenon
17. halo
18. child
19. handful
20. rodeo

18e

Apply the rules to avoid confusion of *ei* and *ie*.

When the sound is /ē/ (as in *me*), write *ie* (except after *c*, in which case write *ei*).

                            (after *c*)

chief	grief	pierce	wield		ceiling	deceive
field	niece	relief	yield		conceit	perceive

When the sound is other than /ē/, usually write *ei*.

counterfeit	foreign	heifer	heir	sleigh	vein
forfeit	freight	height	neighbor	stein	weigh

▲ Exceptions: friend, mischief, seize, sheik

■ **Exercise 5** Fill in the blanks with the appropriate letters: *ei* or *ie*.

1. p____ce
2. ach____ve
3. rec____ve
4. n____gh
5. fr____ght
6. ap____ce
7. bel____f
8. conc____ve
9. th____r
10. dec____t
11. n____ce
12. sh____ld
13. w____rd
14. shr____k
15. pr____st

Words Frequently Misspelled

You may find it helpful to study the following list in units of ten or twenty words at a time. Consult your dictionary for the exact meanings of any words you are not sure of.

absence	affected	apology
acceptable	affectionately	apparent
accessible	aggravate	appearance
accidentally	aggressive	appoint
accommodate	alcohol	appreciate
accompanied	allotted	appropriate
accomplish	all right	approximately
accumulate	a lot of	arguing
accuracy	always	argument
achievement 10	amateur 30	arrangement 50
acquaintance	among	arrest
acquire	analysis	article
acquitted	analyze	aspirin
across	annihilate	assassination
actually	announcement	associate
address	annual	athlete
admission	anxiety	athletics
adolescent	anywhere	attacked
advice	apartment	attendance
advised 20	apiece 40	attendant 60

authentic		challenge		conscious	
average		changeable		consistency	
awkward		changing		consistent	
bachelor		characteristic		contradict	
balance		chief		control	
bargain		children		controlled	
basically		chocolate		controlling	
beginning		choice		controversial	
belief		choose		convenience	
believed	70	chosen	100	convenient	130
beneficial		coarsely		coolly	
benefited		column		correlate	
biscuit		coming		counterfeit	
boundaries		commercial		courteous	
breath		commission		criticism	
breathe		commitment		criticize	
brilliant		commitment		cruelty	
bulletin		committed		curiosity	
bureaucracy		committee		curious	
burglar	80	comparative		dealt	140
		compelled	110		
business		competence		deceive	
busy		competition		decided	
cafeteria		completely		decision	
calendar		conceited		defense	
candidate		conceivable		define	
career		concentrate		definitely	
category		condemn		definition	
ceiling		confidence		descend	
cemetery		conscience		describe	
certain	90	conscientious	120	description	150

desirable
despair
desperate
destroy
develop
dictionary
difference
different
dilemma
dining   160

disagree
disappearance
disappoint
disapprove
disastrous
discipline
discussion
disease
dispensable
disturbance   170

divide
divine
dormitory
ecstatic
effect
efficiency
eighth
elaborately
eligible
eliminate   180

embarrass
emphasize
empty
enemy
entirely
environment
equipment
equipped
escape
especially   190

everything
evidently
exaggerate
exceed
excellence
excellent
except
exercise
exhaust
existence   200

expense
experience
explanation
extraordinary
extremely
familiar
fascinate
favorite
February
finally   210

financially
forehead
foreign
forfeit
forty
forward
friend
gauge
generally
government   220

governor
grammar
grammatically
grief
guaranteed
guard
guidance
happened
harass
height   230

hero
heroes
hindrance
humor
hypocrisy
hypocrite
ignorant
illogical
imaginary
imagine   240

imitate		literature		ninety	
immediately		lively		ninth	
immense		loneliness		noticeable	
incidentally		lonely		noticing	
incredible		lose		nuclear	
independent		lying		nuisance	
indispensable		magazine		occasionally	
inevitable		maintenance		occur	
infinite		maneuver		occurred	
influential	250	manual	280	occurrence	310
initiative		manufacture		omission	
innocence		marriage		omitted	
intellectual		material		opinion	
intelligence		mathematics		opponent	
intelligent		meant		opportunity	
interest		medicine		opposite	
interpret		mere		optimism	
interrupt		messenger		organize	
introduce		miniature		origin	
irrelevant	260	minutes	290	original	320
irresistible		mischievous		paid	
irritated		missile		pamphlet	
knowledge		morning		parallel	
laboratory		mortgage		particular	
legitimate		muscles		pastime	
leisure		mysterious		peculiar	
liable		naturally		performance	
library		necessary		perhaps	
license		nickel		permanent	
lightning	270	niece	300	permissible	330

personal
physical
physician
planned
pleasant
poison
possess
possession
possible
possibly 340

practically
prairie
precede
preferred
prejudiced
preparation
prepare
presence
prevalent
privilege 350

probably
procedure
proceed
profession
professor
prominent
pronunciation
propaganda
prophecy
prophesy 360

psychology
publicly
pumpkin
purpose
pursue
quantity
quiet
quite
quizzes
realize 370

really
receipt
receive
receiving
recognize
recommend
reference
referred
referring
regular 380

relieve
remembrance
repetition
representative
reproduce
restaurant
rhythm
ridiculous
roommate
sacrifice 390

safety
salary
schedule
secretary
seize
separate
sergeant
severely
sheriff
shining 400

similar
simply
since
sincerely
skiing
sophomore
specimen
speech
sponsor
strength 410

strict
stubbornness
studying
subtlety
succeed
successful
succession
sufficient
suicide
summary 420

superintendent		trafficked		vigilance
supersede		tragedy		villain
suppose		transferred		violence
suppress		tremendous		visible
surely		tried		vitamins
surprise		tries		waive
surround		trouble		warrant
susceptible		truly		warring
suspicious		twelfth		weather
swimming	430	tyranny	460	Wednesday	490
symbol		unanimous		weird
sympathize		unconscious		where
technique		undoubtedly		wherever
temperament		unmistakably		whether
temperature		unnecessary		whichever
tendency		until		wholly
than		usage		whose
their		useful		wield
themselves		useless		wintry
then	440	using	470	withdrawal	500
therefore		usually		woman
thorough		vacuum		women
thought		valuable		worshiped
through		varies		wreck
till		various		write
tobacco		vegetable		writing
together		vengeance		written
tomorrow		venomous		yield
tournament		vice		
traffic	450	view	480	

194

18f

Hyphenate words to express the idea of a unit and to avoid ambiguity. For the division of words at the end of a line, see **8d**.

Notice in the following examples that the hyphen links (or makes a compound of) two or more words that function as a single word.

> We planted forget-me-nots and Johnny-jump-ups. [nouns]
> He hand-fed them. I double-parked. Hard-boil an egg.
> [verbs]
> Was it an eyeball-to-eyeball confrontation? [adjective]

Consult a good recent dictionary when you are not sure of the form of compounds, since some are connected with hyphens (*eye-opener, cross-examine*), some are written separately (*eye chart, cross fire*), and others are written as one word (*eyewitness, crossbreed*).

(1) Use the hyphen to join two or more words serving as a single adjective before a noun.

> a well-built house
> BUT   a house that is well built
>
> caramel-filled chocolates
> BUT   chocolates filled with caramel
>
> a twelve-year-old son
> BUT   a son who is twelve years old
>
> "I reject get-it-done, make-it-happen thinking," he says.
> —THE ATLANTIC

In a series, hyphens are carried over:

> second-, third-, or fourth-generation Americans

▲ Note: The hyphen is generally omitted after an adverb ending in -*ly*:

quick-frozen foods   quickly frozen foods

■ **Exercise 6**   Convert the following word groups according to the pattern of the examples.

EXAMPLES
an ordeal lasting two months   *a two-month ordeal*
ideas that shake the world   *world-shaking ideas*

1. a garage for three cars
2. girls who chew gum
3. pipes covered with rust
4. cheese two years old
5. a club for bird lovers

6. books costing thirty dollars
7. conference that lasts a week
8. parents who solve problems
9. dams that control floods
10. a freeway with eight lanes

(2) Use the hyphen with spelled out compound numbers from twenty-one to ninety-nine (or twenty-first to ninety-ninth).

forty-six, fifty-eighth

▲ Note: Usage varies regarding the hyphenation of spelled out fractions. The hyphen is required, however, only when the fraction functions as a compound modifier. See also **18f(1)**.

almost one-half full   OR   eating only one half of it
a two-thirds vote   OR   two thirds of the voters

(3) Use the hyphen to avoid ambiguity or an awkward combination of letters or syllables between prefix and root or suffix and root.

a dirty movie-theater   [Compare "a dirty-movie theater."]
to re-sign a petition   [Compare "to resign a position."]
semi-independent, shell-like   BUT   semifluid, childlike

(4) Use the hyphen with the prefixes ex- ("former"), *self-*, *all-*; with the suffix *-elect*; and between a prefix and a capitalized word.

ex-wife   self-help   all-inclusive   mayor-elect
mid-September   non-Biblical   anti-American

▲ Note: The hyphen is also used with figures or letters such as *mid-1990s* or *T-shirt*, as well as with zip codes having more than five numbers: Dallas, TX 75392-0041.

■ **Exercise 7** Refer to **18f** and to your dictionary as you convert each phrase (or words within each phrase) to a compound or to a word with a prefix. Use hyphens when needed.

EXAMPLES

glasses used for water	*water glasses* OR *waterglasses*
not Communistic	*non-Communistic*
a job that pays $45,000 a year	*a $45,000-a-year job*

1. knowledge of oneself
2. men who chew tobacco
3. ham smoked with hickory
4. a light used at night
5. in the shape of an L

6. a brush for all purposes
7. trees covered with ice
8. flights from L.A. to Rome
9. a weekend lasting three days
10. a computer five years old

19
GOOD USAGE
AND GLOSSARY

Use a good dictionary to help you select the words that express your ideas exactly.

You can find valuable information about words in a good college dictionary, such as one of the following:

The American Heritage Dictionary
Funk & Wagnalls Standard College Dictionary
The Random House Dictionary
Webster's New Collegiate Dictionary
Webster's New World Dictionary

Occasionally you may need to refer to an unabridged dictionary or to a special dictionary.

Unabridged dictionaries

The Oxford English Dictionary. 2nd ed. 20 vols. 1989–.
Webster's Unabridged Dictionary of the English Language. 1989.
Webster's Third New International Dictionary. 1986.

Special dictionaries

Cowie, A. P., and R. Mackin. *Oxford Dictionary of Current Idiomatic English*. Vol. 1–. 1975–.

Follett, Wilson. *Modern American Usage: A Guide*. 1966.

Hayakawa, S. I., and the Funk and Wagnalls dictionary staff. *Modern Guide to Synonyms and Related Words*. 1968.

Mawson, C. O. S. *Dictionary of Foreign Terms*. 2nd ed. Rev. Charles Berlitz. 1979.

Morris, William, and Mary Morris. *Harper Dictionary of Contemporary Usage*. 2nd ed. 1985.

Onions, C. T. *Oxford Dictionary of English Etymology*. 1966.

Partridge, Eric. *Dictionary of Catch Phrases*. Rev. ed. 1986.

———. *Dictionary of Slang and Unconventional English*. 8th ed. 1985.

Roget's International Thesaurus. 4th ed. 1977.

Webster's Collegiate Thesaurus. 1976.

19a

Use a good dictionary intelligently.

Examine the introductory matter as well as the arrangement and presentation of material in your dictionary so that you can easily find the information you need. Note meanings of any special abbreviations your dictionary uses.

A sample dictionary entry follows. First, note the definitions of *empty* as an adjective, as a transitive verb, as an intransitive verb, as a noun, and as part of an idiomatic phrase (with *of*). Next, observe the examples of usage. Finally, note the various other kinds of information (labeled in color) that the dictionary provides.

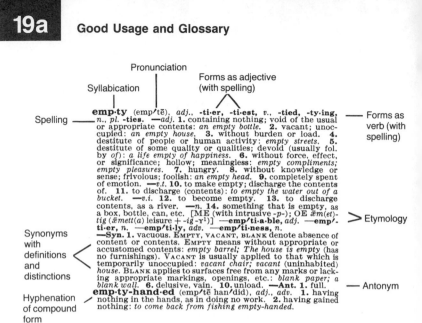

Pronunciation

Syllabication

Forms as adjective (with spelling)

Spelling —— **emp·ty** (emp′tē), *adj.*, **-ti·er, -ti·est,** *v.*, **-tied, -ty·ing,** *n., pl.* **-ties.** —*adj.* **1.** containing nothing; void of the usual or appropriate contents: *an empty bottle.* **2.** vacant; unoccupied: *an empty house.* **3.** without burden or load. **4.** destitute of people or human activity: *empty streets.* **5.** destitute of some quality or qualities; devoid (usually fol. by *of*): *a life empty of happiness.* **6.** without force, effect, or significance; hollow; meaningless: *empty compliments; empty pleasures.* **7.** hungry. **8.** without knowledge or sense; frivolous; foolish: *an empty head.* **9.** completely spent of emotion. —*v.t.* **10.** to make empty; discharge the contents of. **11.** to discharge (contents): *to empty the water out of a bucket.* —*v.i.* **12.** to become empty. **13.** to discharge contents, as a river. —*n.* **14.** something that is empty, as a box, bottle, can, etc. [ME (with intrusive *-p-*); OE *ǣm(et)tig (ǣmett(a)* leisure *+ -iġ* -Y¹)] —**emp′ti·a·ble,** *adj.* —**emp′·ti·er,** *n.* —**emp′ti·ly,** *adv.* —**emp′ti·ness,** *n.* —— Forms as verb (with spelling)

> Etymology

Synonyms with definitions and distinctions
—**Syn. 1.** vacuous. EMPTY, VACANT, BLANK denote absence of content or contents. EMPTY means without appropriate or accustomed contents: *empty barrel; The house is empty* (has no furnishings). VACANT is usually applied to that which is temporarily unoccupied: *vacant chair; vacant* (uninhabited) *house.* BLANK applies to surfaces free from any marks or lacking appropriate markings, openings, etc.: *blank paper; a blank wall.* **6.** delusive, vain. **10.** unload. —**Ant. 1.** full. —— Antonym

Hyphenation of compound form
emp·ty-hand·ed (emp′tē han′did), *adj., adv.* **1.** having nothing in the hands, as in doing no work. **2.** having gained nothing: *to come back from fishing empty-handed.*

(1) Spelling, syllabication, and pronunciation

Your dictionary describes both written and spoken language: you can check spelling and word division as well as pronunciation of unfamiliar words. Notice above the way words are divided into syllables (syllabication) by the use of dots or accent marks. (For end-of-line division of words, see **8d.**) A key to the sound symbols is provided at the bottom of the entry pages as well as in the front of the dictionary. A primary stress mark (′) normally follows the syllable that is most heavily accented. Secondary stress marks follow lightly accented syllables.

■ **Exercise 1** With the aid of your dictionary, write out the words below using sound symbols and stress marks to show the correct pronunciation (or a correct one if options are given).

1. performance   3. harass   5. nuclear   7. tuque   9. advertisement
2. incongruous   4. Mozart   6. interest   8. patois   10. minutia

(2) Parts of speech and inflected forms

Your dictionary labels the possible uses of words in sentences—for instance, *adj.* (adjective), *adv.* (adverb), *v.t.* (verb, transitive). It also lists ways that nouns, verbs, and modifiers change form to indicate number, tense, or comparison or to serve as other parts of speech (for example, under *repress, v.t.,* you may also find *repressible, adj.*).

■ **Exercise 2** With the aid of your dictionary, classify each of the following words as a verb (transitive or intransitive), a noun, an adjective, an adverb, a preposition, or a conjunction. Give the principal parts of each verb, the plural (or plurals) of each noun, and the comparative and superlative of each adjective and adverb. (Note that some words are used as two or more parts of speech.)

1. permit	3. sweet-talk	5. subtle	7. late	9. crisis
2. lonely	4. tattoo	6. for	8. bring	10. fine

(3) Definitions and examples of usage

Observe whether your dictionary gives the most common meaning of a word first or arranges the definitions in historical order. Notice also that examples of a word used in phrases or sentences often clarify the definition.

■ **Exercise 3** Study the definitions of any five of the following pairs of words, paying special attention to any examples of usage in your dictionary; then write sentences to illustrate the shades of difference in meaning.

1. quit–resign
2. sensual–sensuous
3. lethargy–lassitude
4. insolent–rude
5. pity–sympathy
6. inspire–motivate
7. contradict–deny
8. brutal–cruel
9. rash–imprudent
10. draw–draft (as verbs)

(4) Synonyms and antonyms

Lists and discussions of synonyms in dictionaries often help to clarify the meaning of closely related words. Studying denotations and connotations of words (see **20a**) with similar meanings will help you choose words more exactly and convey more subtle shades of meaning. Lists of antonyms help by providing words that have opposite meanings.

▲ Note: For more complete lists of synonyms, antonyms, and related and contrasted words, refer to a special dictionary or a thesaurus. The following is a sample thesaurus entry.

> **empty** *adj.* 1 *Our voices echoed in the empty house:* vacant, unoccupied, uninhabited, bare, void. 2 *He didn't want to retire and lead an empty life:* aimless, meaningless, without substance, vacuous, insignificant, worthless, purposeless, futile, unfulfilled, idle, hollow; shallow, banal, trivial, inane, insipid, frivolous. —*v.* 3 *Empty the glass before putting it in the dishwasher. The Mississippi empties into the Gulf of Mexico:* pour out, drain, dump, void, evacuate; discharge, flow, debouch.
> *Ant.* 1 full, stuffed, crammed, packed, jammed; occupied, inhabited. 2 meaningful, significant, substantial, useful, valuable, worthwhile, purposeful, fulfilled, busy, full, rich, vital, interesting, serious. 3 fill, pack, put in, stuff, cram, jam; receive.

Before choosing a synonym or a closely related word from such a list, look it up in the dictionary to make sure that it expresses your meaning exactly. Although *void, idle,* and *inane* are all listed as synonyms of *empty,* they have different meanings.

■ **Exercise 4** With the aid of your dictionary or thesaurus, list two synonyms and one antonym for each of the following words. Put each of these words in a sentence.

1. ugly   2. pleasure   3. defy   4. support   5. stingy

(5) Origin and development of the language

In college dictionaries the origin of a word—also called its *derivation* or *etymology*—is shown in square brackets. For example, after *expel* might be this information:

[<L *expellere* <*ex-* out + *pellere* to drive, thrust]

This means that *expel* is derived from (<) the Latin (L) word *expellere*, which is made up of *ex-*, meaning "out," and *pellere*, meaning "to drive or thrust." Breaking up a word, when possible, into *prefix—root—suffix* will often help show the basic meaning of a word.

	prefix		*root*		*suffix*
interruption	**inter-** between	+	**rupt** to break	+	**-ion** act of
transference	**trans-** across	+	**fer** to carry	+	**-ence** state of

The bracketed information given by a good dictionary is an especially rich source of information about the historical development of the language. The parenthetical abbreviations for languages here and on the next few pages are those commonly used in bracketed derivations in dictionaries.

English is one of the Indo-European (IE) languages, a group of languages apparently derived from a common source. Within this group, many of the more familiar words are remarkably alike. The word *mother*, for example, is *mater* in Latin (L), *meter* in Greek (Gk.), and *matar* in ancient Persian and in the Sanskrit (Skt.) of India. Such words, descended from or borrowed from the same form in a common parent language, are called *cognates*. The large number of cognates and the many correspondences in sound and structure in most of the European and some of the Asian languages indicate that they are derived from this common language, which was spoken in parts of Europe about six thousand years ago. By the beginning of the Christian era, speakers of this language had spread over most of Europe and as far east as India, and the original Indo-European had developed into eight or nine language families. Of these, the chief ones that influenced English were the Germanic in northwestern Europe (from which English is descended), and the Hellenic (Greek) and the Italic (Latin) groups in the Mediterranean basin.

After the fall of the Roman Empire in the fifth century, the several Latin-speaking divisions developed independently into the modern Romance languages, chiefly Italian, French, and Spanish. Long before the fall of Rome the Germanic group was breaking up into three families: (1) East Germanic, represented by the Goths, an important people in the last century of the Roman Empire; (2) North Germanic, or Old Norse (ON), from which modern Danish (Dan.), Swedish (Sw.), Norwegian (Norw.), and Icelandic (Icel.) derive; and (3) West Germanic, the direct ancestor of English, Dutch (Du.), and German (Ger.).

The English language may be said to have begun about the middle of the fifth century, when the West Germanic Angles, Saxons, and Jutes began the conquest of what is now England and either absorbed or drove out the Celtic-speaking inhabitants. (Celtic—from which Scots Gaelic, Irish Gaelic, Welsh, and other languages later developed—is another member of the Indo-European family.) The next six or seven hundred years are known as the Old English (OE) or Anglo-Saxon (AS) period of the English language. The fifty or sixty thousand words then in the language were chiefly Anglo-Saxon, with a small mixture of Old Norse words as a result of the Danish (Viking) conquests of England beginning in the eighth century.

The transitional period from Old English to Modern English—about 1100 to 1500—is known as Middle English (ME). The Normans, or "Northmen," had settled in northern France during the Viking invasions and had adopted Old French (OF) in place of their native Old Norse. The Normans conquered England in 1066, and, crossing over the English Channel by the thousands, they made French the language of the ruling classes throughout the land, while most people continued to speak English. The use of French began to decline by about 1250 and by 1385 English was once again the language of the courts and of the schools. But the English that emerged at that time had lost most of its Anglo-Saxon inflections and had taken on thousands of French words (derived originally from Latin). Nonetheless, it was still basically English, not French, in its structure.

The kinds of changes that occurred during the development of the English language (until it was partly stabilized by printing, introduced in London in 1476) are suggested by the following passages, two from Old English and two from Middle English.

PROSE:

Ǣlc þāra þe þās mīn word gehīerþ, and þā wyrcþ, biþ gelīc
Thus each who hears these my words, and does them, is like

þǣm wīsan were, sē his hūs ofer stān getimbrode. þā cōm þǣr
a wise man, who builds his house on a stone. Then there came

regen and micel flōd, and þǣr blēowon windas, and āhruron on
rain and a great flood, and blowing winds, and a roaring in

þæt hūs, and hit nā ne fēoll: sōþlīce hit wæs ofer stān getimbrod.
that house, and it did not fall: truly it was built on stone.
[Matthew 7:24–25, tenth century]

Therfor ech man that herith these my wordis, and doith hem, shal be maad lijk to a wise man, that hath bildid his hous on a stoon. And reyn felde doun, and flodis camen, and wyndis blewen, and russchiden into that hous; and it felde not doun, for it was foundun on a stoon.
[Matthew 7:24–25, fourteenth century]

POETRY:

Hē ǣrest gescēop	eorðan bearnum
He first created	*for earth's children*
heofon tō hrōfe,	hālig Scyppend.
heaven as a roof,	*holy creator.*

[From Caedmon's Hymn, about eighth century]

A knight ther was, and that a worthy man,
That fro the tyme that he first bigan
To ryden out, he loved chivalrye,
Trouthe and honour, fredom and curteisye.
[From Chaucer's Prologue to the *Canterbury Tales,* about 1385]

A striking feature of Modern English (that is, English since 1500) is its immense vocabulary. As already noted, Old English used fifty or sixty thousand words, largely native Anglo-Saxon; Middle English used perhaps a hundred thousand words, many taken through the French from Latin and others taken directly from Latin; and unabridged dictionaries today list over four times as many. English borrowed most heavily from Latin but drew some words from languages throughout the world. As the English pushed out to colonize and to trade in many parts of the globe, they brought home new words as well as goods. From India came *bungalow* and *dungaree*, and from Spain *patio* and *barbecue*. In North America, English borrowed such American Indian words as *teepee* and *succotash* and such African words as *okra, zombie*, and perhaps *yam*. Modern science and technology have drawn heavily from the Greek. As a result of all this borrowing, English has become one of the richest and most cosmopolitan of languages.

In the process of enlarging its vocabulary, English lost most of its original Anglo-Saxon words. But those that are left make up the most familiar, most useful part of the vocabulary. Practically all the articles, conjunctions, prepositions, and pronouns are native Anglo-Saxon; so are many familiar nouns, verbs, adjectives, and adverbs. These native words occur over and over in writing and speaking, much more frequently than the borrowed words. Indeed, if every word is counted every time it is used, the percentage of native words runs very high—usually between 70 and 90 percent. Milton's percentage was 81, Tennyson's 88, Shakespeare's about 90, and that of the King James Bible about 94. English has been enriched by its extensive borrowings without losing its individuality. Although it varies in sound, structure, and vocabulary according to the part of the world in which it is spoken, it is still, fundamentally, the *English* language. As George Bernard Shaw once commented, the English and the Americans are one people divided by a common language.

■ **Exercise 5**   With the aid of your dictionary, give the etymology of each of the following words:

1. cute
2. hallmark
3. ketchup
4. laugh

5. lunatic
6. noodle
7. OK

8. quasar
9. velcro
10. veal

(6) Special usage labels

In your dictionary, you will find special usage labels for words or particular definitions of words that differ from general (or unlabeled) usage. Here is a sampling of labels frequently used, each of them found in two or more college dictionaries:

unalienable	*archaic, obsolete*	inalienable
lift	*informal, colloquial*	plagiarize
nowheres	*nonstandard, dialect, colloquial*	not anywhere, nowhere
nerd	*slang*	an ineffectual person

The classification of usage is often difficult and controversial because the language is constantly changing. Good writers try to choose the words, whatever their labels, that exactly fit the audience and the occasion.

■ **Exercise 6**   Classify the following words and phrases according to the usage labels in your dictionary. If a word has no special usage label, classify it as *formal*. If a given definition of a word has a usage label, give the meaning after the label.

EXAMPLES
job—formal
bluejohn—dialectal for *skim milk*
nutty—informal for *silly,* slang for *insane*

1. ain't
2. dorm
3. dude
4. funky

5. gofer
6. lest
7. lout

8. macho
9. ort
10. vittle

19b

Use informal words only when appropriate to the audience.

Words or expressions labeled *informal* or *colloquial* (meaning "characteristic of speech") in college dictionaries are standard English and are used by writers every day, particularly in informal writing, especially dialogue. On occasion, informal words can be used effectively in formal writing, but they are usually inappropriate. Unless an informal expression is specifically called for, use the unlabeled words in your dictionary.

INFORMAL	dopey	gypped	bellybutton
FORMAL	stupid	swindled	navel

Contractions are common in informal English, especially in dialogue: see examples on page 154. But contracted forms (like *won't* or *there's*) are usually avoided in college writing, which is not as casual as conversational English is.

■ **Exercise 7**   Make a list of ten words or phrases you would consider informal. Then check your dictionary to see how (or if) each definition you have in mind is labeled.

19c

Use newly coined words or slang only when appropriate to the audience.

Newly coined words are usually fresh and interesting, but may be unfamiliar to your reader since they are often regional. A few years ago no one had ever heard of a *docudrama*, and even today many find *advertorial* and *geriphobia* unfamiliar. If you are unsure whether or not your reader will understand the new word you use, define it or find another.

Slang words, including certain coinages and figures of speech, are variously considered as breezy, racy, extremely informal, nonstandard, facetious, taboo, offbeat, or vigorous. On occasion, slang can be used effectively, even in formal writing. Below is an example of the effective use of the word *spiel*, still labeled by dictionaries as *slang*:

> Here comes election year. Here come the hopefuls, the conventions, the candidates, the spiels, the postures, the press releases, and the TV performances. Here comes the year of the hoopla.   —JOHN CIARDI

A few years ago the word *hoopla* was also generally considered as slang, but now dictionaries disagree: one classifies this word *standard* (unlabeled); another, *colloquial* (*informal*); still another, *slang*. Like *hoopla*, words such as *spiel*, *uptight*, *schlep*, *dork*, and *wimp* have a particularly vivid quality; they soon may join former slang words such as *sham* and *mob* as part of the general English vocabulary. On the other hand, they may also disappear from common usage.

Slang can easily become dated—which is a good reason to be cautious about using it in writing. Also, much slang is trite, tasteless, and imprecise. For instance, when used to describe almost anything disapproved of, *gross* becomes inexact, flat.

■ **Exercise 8**   Replace the italicized words in the following sentences with more exact words or specific phrases.

1. After dress rehearsal the whole cast *goofed off.*
2. Lately the weather has been *lousy* on weekends.
3. Jean's new haircut is *dynamite.*
4. That *wisecrack ticked* him *off.*

19d

Use regional words only when appropriate to the audience.

Regional or dialectal usages (also called localisms or provincialisms) should normally be avoided in writing outside the region where they are current since their meanings may

not be widely known. Speakers and writers, however, may
safely use regional words known to the audience they are
addressing.

REGIONAL   We were **fixing** to swim in Joe's **tank**.
FORMAL   We were ready to swim in Joe's pond.   [OR *lake*]

19e
Avoid nonstandard words and usages.

Words and expressions labeled by dictionaries as *nonstandard* or *illiterate* should be avoided in most writing—for example, *snuck* should not be used for *sneaked* or "They's no
use" for "There's no use."

19f
Avoid archaic and obsolete words.

All dictionaries list words (and meanings for words) that
have long since passed out of general use. Such words as
rathe (early) and *yestreen* (last evening) are still found in
dictionaries because, once the standard vocabulary of great
authors, they occur in our older literature and must be defined for the modern reader.

A number of obsolete or archaic words—such as *worser*
(for *worse*) or *holp* (for *helped*)—are still in use but are now
nonstandard.

19g
**Use technical words and jargon only when appropriate to
the audience.**

When writing for the general reader, avoid all unnecessary
technical language. The careful writer will not refer to an

organized way to find a subject for writing as a *heuristic* or a need for bifocals as *presbyopia*. (Of course, the greater precision of technical language makes it desirable when the audience can understand it, as when one physician writes to another.)

Jargon is technical slang that is tailored specifically for a particular occupation. It can be an efficient shortcut for specialized concepts, but you should use jargon only when you can be sure that you and your readers understand it.

19h

Avoid overwriting, an ornate or flowery style, or distracting combinations of sounds.

Overwriting, as well as distracting combinations of sounds, calls attention to words rather than to ideas. Such writing makes for slow, difficult reading.

ORNATE   The majority believes that the approbation of society derives primarily from diligent pursuit of allocated tasks.

BETTER   Most people believe success results from hard work.

■ **Exercise 9**   Using simple, formal, straightforward English, rewrite the following sentences (from Edwin Newman's *A Civil Tongue*).

1. We have exceptional game plan capabilities together with strict concerns for programming successful situations.
2. In order to improve security, we request that, effective immediately, no employees use the above subject doors for ingress and egress to the building.
3. We will also strategize with the client on ways to optimize usage of the spots by broadcast management.
4. Muzak helps human communities because it is a nonverbal symbolism for the common stuff of everyday living in the global village.
5. These precautions appeared to be quite successful in dissuading potential individuals with larcenous intent.

19i

Consider your purpose and your audience as you consult the following glossary to determine appropriate usage.

The following short glossary covers only the most common usage problems in written English. See **18b** for a supplementary list of frequently confused words. The entries in this glossary are authoritative only to the extent that they describe current usage, and justification for each can usually be found in at least two of the leading dictionaries.

As you study the descriptions of usage in this glossary, keep in mind that to be in charge of your own writing you must master not only the informal style most people use in personal letters and other kinds of self-expression, but also the very formal style used for most college writing—the style often referred to as edited American English.

FORMAL	Words or expressions listed in dictionaries without special usage labels; appropriate in college writing.
INFORMAL	Words or expressions that dictionaries label *informal* or *colloquial*—not generally appropriate in college writing.
NOT ACCEPTABLE	Words or expressions labeled in dictionaries as *archaic, illiterate, nonstandard, obsolete, slang, substandard*—not accepted in formal or informal writing.

USAGE GLOSSARY

a, an Use *a* before the sound of a consonant: **a** yard, **a** U-turn, **a** one-base hit. Use *an* before a vowel sound: **an** empty can, **an** M.D., **an** ax, **an** X-ray.

above Acceptable as a modifier or as a noun in such references as "in the paragraph above" or "none of the above." Some writers, however, avoid "the above."

accidently, accidentally *Accidentally* is the correct form.

ad   Informal for *advertisement*. Use the full word in formal writing.

affect, effect   The verb *affect* means "to influence, attack" or "to touch the emotions." The noun *effect* means "result of a cause."

> Smoking **affects** the heart.   His tears **affected** her deeply.
> Drugs have side **effects**.   The **effect** on sales was good.

When used as a verb, *effect* means "to produce an effect": The medicine **effected** a complete cure.

aggravate   Widely used for *annoy* or *irritate*. Many writers, however, restrict the meaning of *aggravate* to "intensify, make worse": Noises **aggravate** a headache.

a half a   Omit one of the *a*'s: half a loaf, a half loaf.

ahold of   Informal for "a hold of, a grasp upon something," as in "to get **ahold of** a rope."

ain't   Unacceptable in writing unless used in dialogue or for humorous effect.

allusion, illusion   An *allusion* is a casual or indirect reference. An *illusion* is a false idea or an unreal image.

> The author's **allusion** to a heaven on earth amused me.
> The author's concept of a heaven on earth is an **illusion**.

alot   A misspelling of the overused phrase *a lot*.

already, all ready   *Already* means "before or by the time specified." *All ready* means "completely prepared."

> The theater was **already** full by seven o'clock.
> The cast was **all ready** for the curtain call.

alright   Not yet a generally accepted spelling of *all right*.

altogether, all together   *Altogether* means "wholly, thoroughly." *All together* means "in a group."

> That law is **altogether** unnecessary.
> They were **all together** in the library.

a.m., p.m. (OR A.M., P.M.)   Use only with figures.

> NOT   The wedding begins at ten thirty in the **a.m.**
> BUT   The wedding begins at 10:30 **a.m.** [OR at ten thirty in the morning]

among, between   Prepositions with plural objects (including collective nouns). As a rule, use *among* with objects denoting three or more (a group), and use *between* with those denoting only two (or twos).

> walked **among** the crowd, quarreling **among** themselves
> a choice **between** war and peace, reading **between** the lines

amount of, number of   *Amount of* is followed by singular nouns; *number of*, by plural nouns.

> an **amount of** money, light, work, or postage   [singular]
> a **number of** coins, lights, jobs, or stamps   [plural]

See also **number.**

an   See **a, an.**

and etc.   *Etc.* is an abbreviation of *et* ("and") *cetera* ("other things"). Omit the redundant *and*. See also **etc.**

and/or   Now acceptable in most writing. Some writers, however, avoid the form because they consider it distracting and bureaucratic.

and which, and who   Do not use *and* before only one *which* or *who* clause. See **24b(3)**.

a number, the number   See **number.**

anyone, any one; everyone, every one   Distinguish between each one-word and two-word compound. *Anyone* means "any person at all"; *any one* refers to one of a group. Similarly, *everyone* means "all," and *every one* refers to each one in a group.

> Was **anyone** hurt?   Was **any one** of you hurt?
> **Everyone** should attend.   **Every one** of them should attend.

anyways, anywheres   Unacceptable for *anyway, anywhere*.

as (1) As a conjunction, use *as* to express sameness of degree, quantity, or manner: Do *as* I do. As a preposition, use *as* to express equivalence: I think of Tom **as** my brother [Tom = brother]. Use *like* to express similarity: Tom is **like** a brother.

(2) Use *if*, *that*, or *whether* instead of *as* after such verbs as *feel*, *know*, *say*, or *see*: I do not know if [NOT as] my adviser is right.

(3) In subordinate clauses, prefer *because* to introduce a causal relationship or *while* to introduce a time relationship.

Because [NOT as] it was raining, we watched TV.
OR **While** [NOT as] it was raining, we watched TV.

as far as Unacceptable as a substitute for the phrasal preposition *as for:* **As for** fasting [NOT as far as fasting], many doctors discourage losing weight that way.

as to Use *about* in such sentences as "We were unsure **about** [NOT as to] where he went."

at Unacceptable after *where*. See **where . . . at, where . . . to.**

awful, awfully Overworked for *ugly*, *shocking*, or *very*.

awhile, a while *Awhile,* an adverb, is not used as the object of a preposition: We rested **awhile**. [Compare: We rested for **a while**.]

back of Informal for *behind* or *in back of*.

backwards Use *backward* [NOT backwards] as an adjective: a **backward** motion.

bad, badly The adverb *badly* is preferred after most verbs. But either *bad* or *badly* is now acceptable in the sense of "sorry," and writers now usually prefer *bad* after such verbs as *feel* or *look*.

The organist plays **badly**.
Charles feels **bad**.

because See **23e.**

being as, being that Unacceptable for *since*, *because*.

beside, besides   Always a preposition, *beside* usually means "next to," sometimes "apart from": Marvin was sitting **beside** Betty. As a preposition, *besides* means "in addition to" or "other than": **Besides** countless toys, these children have their own TV set. As an adverb, *besides* means "also" or "moreover": The burglars stole our silver—and my stereo **besides**.

better, had better   Do not omit the *had* in your writing: We **had better** consider history as we plan for our future.

between   See **among, between.**

bias, prejudice   Synonyms in the sense of "a preconceived opinion" or "a distortion of judgment." But a bias may be in favor of or may be against, whereas a prejudice is against.

borrow off, borrow from   Use *borrow from* in your writing.

bottom line   An overworked cliché for "outcome" or "the final result."

bring   Unacceptable for *take*.

bunch   Informal if used to refer to a group of people.

but what   Informal after *no* or *not* following expressions such as "no doubt" or "did not know": There was no doubt but what they would win. [Compare formal usage: There was no doubt that they would win.]

but which, but who   See **24b.**

can, may   *Can* refers to ability and *may* refers to permission.

> **Can** student nurses give injections?   [Are they able to?]
> **May** student nurses give injections?   [Are they permitted to?]

can't hardly, can't scarcely   Use *can hardly, can scarcely.*

censor, censure   *Censor* means "to remove or suppress because of morally or otherwise objectionable ideas"; *censure* refers to the assignment of blame, "an official rebuke."

center about, center around   Informal for "to be focused on or at" or for "to center on."

compare to, compare with *Compare to* means "regard as similar" and *compare with* means "examine to discover similarities or differences."

> The speaker **compared** the earth **to** a lopsided baseball.
> Putting one under the other, the expert **compared** the forged signature **with** the authentic one.

complementary, complimentary *Complementary* means "completing" or "supplying needs." *Complimentary* means "expressing praise" or "given free."

> His talents and hers are **complementary**.
> Admiring their performance, he made several **complimentary** remarks.

conscious, conscience An adjective, *conscious* means "aware, able to feel and think." A noun, *conscience* means "the sense of right and wrong": When I became **conscious** of my guilt, my **conscience** bothered me.

consensus of opinion Redundant. Omit *of opinion*.

continual, continuous *Continual* means "successive," and *continuous* means "unbroken."

could of Unacceptable for *could have*. See **of**.

couple, couple of Informal for *two* or for *several* in such phrases as "a couple aspirin," "a couple more gallons of paint," or "just a couple of seconds."

different from In the United States the preferred preposition after *different* is *from*: The Stoic philosophy is **different from** the Epicurean. But the less formal *different than* is accepted by many writers if the expression is followed by a clause: The outcome was **different than** I had expected.

differ from, differ with *Differ from* means "to be unlike." *Differ with* means "to disagree."

disinterested, uninterested *Disinterested* means "impartial" or "lacking prejudice": a **disinterested** referee. *Uninterested* means "indifferent, lacking in interest."

don't   Unacceptable when used for *doesn't*: He **doesn't** [NOT don't] agree.

due to   Usually avoided in formal writing when used as a preposition in place of *because of* or *on account of*: **Because of** [NOT due to] holiday traffic, we arrived an hour late.

effect   See **affect, effect.**

emigrate from, immigrate to   The prefix *e-* (a variant of *ex-*) means "out of"; *im-* (a variant of *in-*) means "into." To *emigrate* is to go out of one's own country to settle in another. To *immigrate* is to come into a different country to settle. The corresponding adjective or noun forms are *emigrant* and *immigrant*. [Compare *export, import.*]

> Many workers **emigrated from** Sweden to America in the 1890s.
> These **immigrant** workers contributed to the growth of our economy.

eminent, imminent   *Eminent* means "distinguished." *Imminent* means "about to happen, threatening."

> Charlotte is an **eminent** scientist.
> Bankruptcy seemed **imminent**.

enthuse   Informal for "to show enthusiasm."

etc.   Many writers prefer to substitute *and so on* or *and so forth*. Since *etc.* means "and other things," *and etc.* is redundant.

everyone, every one   See **anyone, any one.**

except, accept   To *except* is to exclude or to make an exception of. To *accept* is to approve or to receive.

> These laws **except** [exclude] juveniles.
> These schools **accept** [admit] juveniles.

expect   Informal for *suppose* or *presume*.

explicit, implicit   *Explicit* means "expressed directly or precisely." *Implicit* means "implied or expressed indirectly."

The advertisement was **explicit**: "All sales final."
Reading between the lines, I understood the **implicit** message.

fantastic Overworked for "extraordinarily good" or "wonderful, remarkable."

farther, further Some writers prefer *farther* in references to geographic distance: six miles **farther**. *Further* is used as a synonym for *additional* in more abstract references: **further** delay, **further** proof.

fewer, less *Fewer* (used with plural nouns) refers to number and *less* (used with singular nouns) to amount: There were **fewer** dogs in the yard today, so we used **less** dog food.

figure Informal for *believe, think, conclude,* or *predict,* all of which are more precise.

fixing to Regional for "planning to."

former Refers to the first named of two. If three or more items are named, use *first* and *last* instead of *former* or *latter*: The Folger and the Huntington are two famous libraries; the **former** is in Washington, D.C., and the **latter** is in San Marino, California.

further See **farther, further.**

go, goes Inappropriate in written language for *say, says*: I **say** [NOT go] "Hello there!" Then he **says** [NOT goes] "Glad to see you!"

good *Good* is not an adverb: Watson played **well** [NOT good] under pressure.

great Overworked for more precise words such as *skillful, good, clever, enthusiastic,* or *very well,* as in "really **great** at guessing the answers" or "with everything going **great** for us."

had drank, had drunk Today some authorities accept *had drank* as a part of our general vocabulary, but many do not. *Had drunk* is fully established usage.

had of, had have Use *had.*

NOT   I wish I had of [OR had've] said that.
BUT   I wish I **had** said that.

had ought, hadn't ought   Use *ought, ought not,* or *oughtn't.*

half a, a half, a half a   Use *half a* or *a half* in your writing.

hanged, hung   *Hanged* refers specifically to "put to death by hanging." *Hung* is the usual past participle.

hardly, scarcely   See **4e**.

hisself   Use *himself.*

hopefully   Inappropriate for *I hope* or *it is hoped.*

illusion   See **allusion, illusion**.

immigrate   See **emigrate from, immigrate to**.

implicit   See **explicit, implicit**.

imply, infer   *Imply* means "suggest without actually stating" and *infer* means "draw a conclusion based on evidence."

His attitude **implies** that money is no problem.
I **infer** from his attitude that money is no problem.

incidently   Use *incidentally.*

include   When precisely used, *include* (*includes, included*) precedes an incomplete rather than a complete list.

in fact   Usually wordy and often redundant.

input   Useful as a computer term but overworked in the sense of "a voice in" or "an active role," as in "Students had no input in these decisions."

in regards to, with regards to   Use *in regard to, with regard to,* or *as regards.*

irregardless   Use *regardless.*

its, it's   *Its* is a possessive pronoun ("for *its* beauty"). *It's* is a contraction of *it is* ("*It's* beautiful!") or of *it has* ("*It's* been a beautiful day!").

-ize Verb-forming suffix overused in recent coinages: *colorize*— use *add color to; prioritize*—use *give priority to.*

kind, sort Singular forms are modified by *this* or *that*, plural forms by *these* or *those.*

> **This kind** of argument is deceptive.
> **These kinds** of arguments are deceptive.

kind of, kind of a Use *kind of*: "this *kind of* tour."

later, latter Comparative forms of *late*. In modern English, *later* (like *sooner*) refers to time; *latter* (like *former*) refers to the second of two. See also **former.**

lay, lie Use *lay* (*laid, laying*) in the sense of "put, place": Dick *laid* the spoon on the table. Use *lie* (*lay, lain, lying*) in the sense of "to rest or recline." See also **7a(2)**.

> I should **lie** down [NOT lay].
> Had he **lain** down [NOT laid]?
> The truck **was lying** [NOT laying] on its side.

learn Unacceptable for *teach, instruct, inform.*

leave Unacceptable for *let* except when followed by an object and *alone*, as in "**Leave** [OR **let**] them alone." "**Let** her go." [NOT Leave her go.]

less See **fewer, less.**

let's us Redundant. Use *let's* or *let us.*

liable, likely *Liable* implies responsibility; *likely* suggests probability.

> They are **liable** for all the damage.
> They are **likely** to arrive early.

like Although widely used as a conjunction in spoken English, *as, as if*, and *as though* are preferred for written English. See **as.**

lose, loose *Lose* is a verb: did **lose**, will **lose**. *Loose* is chiefly an adjective: a **loose** belt.

lots In college writing, replace with a more specific word or amount, such as *many, much, five hundred.*

may be, maybe Do not confuse the verb phrase *may be* with the adverb *maybe.*

> The story **may be** [OR might be] true.
> **Maybe** [OR Perhaps] the story is true.

me and Unacceptable as part of a compound subject.

> UNACCEPTABLE   Me and Drake took an early flight.
> ACCEPTABLE   Drake and I took an early flight.

might could Use *could* or *might be able.*

morale, moral *Morale* (a noun) refers to mood or spirit. *Moral* (chiefly an adjective) refers to correct conduct or ethical character.

> the **morale** of our team   a **moral** judgment

most Use *almost* in expressions such as "almost everyone," "almost all." Use *most* only as a superlative: most writers.

much *Much,* used with singular nouns, refers to amount: **much** money, **much** courage; *many,* used with plural nouns, refers to numbers: **many** children, too **many** facts. See also **fewer, less.**

myself Use only when the antecedent precedes it in the same sentence.

> My sister and I [NOT myself] prefer soccer.
> BUT   I hurt **myself** this morning.

nauseous Often confused with *nauseated. Nauseous* means "causing nausea"; *nauseated* means "suffering from nausea."

no . . . nor Use *no . . . or* in compound phrases: no water or [NOT nor] food.

not . . . no/none/nothing Double negative. See **4e.**

nowhere near Use *not nearly.*

nowheres Use *nowhere.*

number As subjects, *a number* is generally plural and *the number* is singular. Make sure that the verb agrees with the subject. See also **amount of, number of.**

> **A number** of options are available.
> **The number** of options is limited.

of Do not write *of* for an unstressed *have.*

> NOT I might of [OR may of, could of, would of, must of, should of, ought to of] said that.
> BUT I might **have** [OR may **have**, could **have**, would **have**, must **have**, should **have**, ought to **have**] said that.

off of Use *off* in phrases such as "fell off the ladder."

oftentimes Use *often.*

OK, O.K., okay All three are acceptable spellings. It is often better to replace *OK* with a more specific word.

per Unacceptable in sentences such as "I have acted per your request." Many authors prefer to use *per* only in Latin phrases, such as *per capita.*

plus Many writers do not use or accept *plus* as a substitute for *and* between main clauses (see **12a**) or for conjunctive adverbs like *moreover, besides, in addition* placed between main clauses or sentences.

p.m. See **a.m., p.m.**

principal, principle Distinguish between *principal*, an adjective or noun meaning "chief" or "chief official," and the noun *principle*, meaning "fundamental truth."

> A **principal** factor in his decision was his belief in the **principle** that men and women are born equal.

raise, rise *Raise (raised, raising)* means "to lift or cause to move upward, to bring up or increase." *Rise (rose, risen, rising)* means "to get up, to move or extend upward, ascend." *Raise* (a transitive verb) takes an object; *rise* (an intransitive verb) does not.

Retailers **raised** prices.
Retail prices **rose** sharply.

rarely ever   Use *hardly* instead of *rarely* or omit the *ever*.

He **hardly ever** mentions money.
He **rarely** mentions it.

real   Use only as an adjective: He was in **real** trouble.

reason . . . is because   See **23e**

respective, respectful   *Respective* refers to considering two or more items individually; *respectful* means "showing proper respect."

rise   See **raise.**

says   See **goes.**

scarcely   See **hardly, scarcely.**

seldom ever   See **hardly ever.**

sensuous, sensual   *Sensuous* refers to gratification of the senses in response to art, music, nature, and so on; *sensual* refers to gratification of the physical senses.

set, setting   Use *set* in the sense of "to place something." See **lay** and **7a(2)**

sit   Use *sit* in the sense of "be seated." See **lay** and **7a(2)**

so, so that   *So that* is preferred when there is even a remote possibility of ambiguity.

AMBIGUOUS   We stay with Uncle Ed so we can help him out.
[Does *so* mean *therefore* or *so that*?]
PREFERRED   We stay with Uncle Ed **so that** we can help him out.

Overused as an intensifier, *so* generally begins a comparison.

some   Unacceptable as a substitute for such words as *remarkable, memorable*: That was a **memorable** [NOT some] speech.

someone, some one   See **anyone, any one.**

somewheres   Use *somewhere*.

sort, sort of a   See **kind, kind of a.**

stationary, stationery   *Stationary* means "in a fixed position"; *stationery* means "writing paper and envelopes."

subsequently   Do not confuse with *consequently*. *Subsequently* means "afterward, occurring later." *Consequently* means "as a result, therefore."

> The last three pages of the novel are missing; **consequently**, [NOT subsequently] I do not know the ending.

such   Overused and vague as a substitute for *very*.

suppose to, supposed to   Be sure to add the *-d*: was **supposed to** do that. See **7a**.

sure   Use *surely* or *certainly* as adverbs: At the sound of the shot, the crowd **certainly** [NOT sure] scattered.

their, there, they're   *Their* is the possessive form of *they*; *there* is ordinarily an adverb or an expletive; *they're* is a contraction of *they are*.

> **There** is no explanation for **their** refusal.
> **They're** installing a traffic light **there**.

theirself, theirselves   Use *themselves*.

them   Unacceptable when used adjectivally: **those** apples OR **these** apples [NOT them apples].

then   Sometimes incorrectly used for *than*. Unlike *then*, *than* does not relate to time.

these kind, these sort, those kind, those sort   See **kind, sort.**

this here, that there, these here, them there   Use *this, that, these, those.*

thusly   Use *thus*.

to, too   Distinguish the preposition *to* from the adverb *too*: If it isn't **too** cold Saturday, let's go **to** the state fair.

try and   Use *try to*.

used to could   Unacceptable for *used to be able*.

use to, used to   Be sure to add the *-d* to *use* unless the auxiliary is accompanied by *did* in questions or in negative constructions: He **used** [NOT use] **to** sail.

very   Omit when superfluous (as in "very unique" or "very perfect"). If you tend to overuse *very* as an intensifier, try using more exact words; in place of "very strange," for example, try *outlandish, grotesque,* or *bizarre*.

ways   Informal for *way* when referring to distance, as in "It's a long **way** to Chicago."

whenever   Use *when* unless the reference is to repeated action.

where   Use *that* in sentences such as "I saw in the paper **that** the strike had been settled."

where . . . at, where . . . to   Omit the superfluous *at, to*.

> NOT   Where is she at? Where is she going to?
> BUT   Where is she? Where is she going?

which   Use *who* or *that* to refer to persons.

-wise   An overused adverb-forming suffix. Recent coinages such as *computerwise, advertisingwise,* or *cost-benefit-analysiswise* are generally unacceptable in college writing.

with regards to   Use *with regard to* or *in regard to*.

would of   Use *would have*. See **of.**

your, you're   *Your* is the possessive of *you*: on **your** desk. *You're* is a contraction of *you are*: **You're** a winner.

you was   Use *you were*.

20
EXACTNESS

Choose words that are exact, idiomatic, and fresh.

Especially when writing, strive to choose words which express your ideas and feelings exactly. If you can make effective use of the words you already know, you need not use a thesaurus in the hope of making your writing seem more sophisticated. Good writing often consists of short, familiar words:

> The ball was loose, rolling free near the line of scrimmage. I raced for the fumble, bent over, scooped up the ball on the dead run, and turned downfield. With a sudden burst of speed, I bolted past the line and past the linebackers. Only two defensive backs stood between me and the goal line. One came up fast, and I gave him a hip feint, stuck out my left arm in a classic straight-arm, caught him on the helmet, and shoved him to the ground. The final defender moved toward me, and I cut to the sidelines, swung sharply back to the middle for three steps, braked again, and reversed my direction once more. The defender tripped over his own feet in confusion. I trotted into the end zone, having covered seventy-eight yards on my touchdown run, happily flipped the football into the stands, turned and loped casually toward the sidelines. Then I woke up.
>
> —JERRY KRAMER, *Farewell to Football*

Adding to your vocabulary, however, will help you choose the right word to suit your purpose, occasion, and audience. So make valuable new words your own by mastering their spelling, meaning, and exact use.

20a

Select the word that expresses your ideas exactly.

(1) Choose words to denote precisely what you mean. Avoid wrong, inexact, or ambiguous usage.

WRONG	From the figures before me I implied that our enrollment had increased significantly this year. [*Imply* means "to state indirectly."]
RIGHT	From the figures before me I **inferred** that our enrollment had increased significantly this year. [*Infer* means "to conclude from evidence."]
INEXACT	Patrice felt ill, and she went home early. [*And* adds or continues.]
EXACT	Patrice felt ill, **so** she went home early. [*So* states result.]
AMBIGUOUS	I knew enough German to understand I would have to drive six miles—but no more. [Confusion involves whether "no more" refers to number of miles to drive or adequacy of writer's German.]
CLEAR	I **knew only enough** German to understand I would have to drive six miles. OR I knew enough German to understand I would have to **drive only** six miles.

■ **Exercise 1** The italicized words in the following sentences are wrong, inexact, or ambiguous. Replace such words with exact ones.

1. The faculty was concerned about the *affects* of the new admission standards.
2. My father's curly hair and dimples gave him a *childish* appearance.
3. Todd *flouts* his wealth.

4. Bart *procrastinated* about where he ate dinner.
5. We must persuade voters to *adapt* antismoking laws.
6. Perhaps she just missed getting that job by some *misfortunate* chance.
7. I frequently consult the classified ads, *and* I can seldom find what I want.
8. She didn't say it but she *intimidated* it.
9. Hurricanes are *seasonable*.
10. Boyd was worried even though he found her story *incredulous*.

■ **Exercise 2** With the aid of your dictionary, give the exact meaning of each italicized word in the quotations below. (Italics have been added.) Pay particular attention to any usage notes.

1. Ignorance of *history* is dangerous. —JEFFREY RECORD

   Those who cannot remember *the past* are condemned to repeat it.
   —GEORGE SANTAYANA

2. The capacity for rage, spite and aggression is part of our endowment as *human beings*. —KENNETH KENISTON

   Man, all down his history, has defended his uniqueness like a point of honor. —RUTH BENEDICT

3. Travel is no cure for melancholia; space-ships and time machines are no *escape* from the human condition. —ARTHUR KOESTLER

   Well, Columbus was probably regarded as an *escapist* when he set forth for the New World. —ARTHUR C. CLARKE

4. Once, a full high school education was the best achievement of a minority; today, it is the *barest minimum* for decent employment or self-respect. —ERIC SEVAREID

   Study and planning are an *absolute prerequisite* for any kind of intelligent action. —EDWARD BROOKE

5. We had a *permissive* father. He *permitted* us to work.
   —SAM LEVENSON

(2) Choose the word with the connotation, as well as the denotation, appropriate to the idea you wish to express.

The *denotation* of a word is what the word signifies, its explicit meaning. According to one dictionary, the word *beach* denotes "the shore of a body of water, especially when sandy or pebbly." The *connotation* of a word is what the word suggests or implies. *Beach*, for instance, may connote natural beauty, warmth, surf, water sports, fun, sunburn, crowds, or even gritty sandwiches. Context has much to do with which connotations a word evokes; in a treatise on shoreline management, *beach* evokes scientific, geographic connotations, whereas in a fashion magazine it evokes images of bathing suits.

■ **Exercise 3** Give one denotation and one connotation for each of the following words.

1. golden	2. valley	3. star	4. Alaska	5. liberal
6. computer	7. aerobics	8. justice	9. success	10. baboon

■ **Exercise 4** Prepare for a class discussion of word choice. After the first quotation below are several series of words that the author might have used but did not select. Note the differences in meaning when an italicized word is substituted for the related word at the head of each series. Be prepared to supply your own alternatives for each of the words that follow the other four quotations.

1. Creeping gloom hits us all. The symptoms are usually the same: not wanting to get out of bed to start the day, failing to smile at ironies, failing to laugh at oneself. —CHRISTOPHER BUCKLEY
   a. gloom: *sadness, depression, melancholy*
   b. hits: *strikes, assaults, infects, zaps*
   c. usually: *often, frequently, consistently, as a rule*
   d. failing: *too blue, unable, neglecting, too far gone*
2. It was a night of still cold, zero or so, with a full moon—a night of pure magic. —WALLACE STEGNER
   a. night   b. still   c. pure   d. magic
3. The morning tides are low, the breeze is brisk and salty, and the clams squirt up through the sand and tunnel back down almost faster than you can dig. —ANN COMBS
   a. morning   b. brisk   c. squirt   d. tunnel
4. Stereotypes economize on our mental effort by covering up the blooming, buzzing confusion with big recognizable cut-outs.
   —ROBERT L. HEILBRONER
   a. economize   b. effort   c. blooming   d. recognizable
   e. cut-outs

5. No emotion is so corrosive of the system and the soul as acute envy. —HARRY STEIN
   a. corrosive   b. system   c. soul   d. acute   e. envy

(3) Choose the specific and concrete word rather than the general and abstract one.

A *general* word is all-inclusive, indefinite, sweeping in scope. A *specific* word is precise, definite, limited in scope.

GENERAL	SPECIFIC	MORE SPECIFIC / CONCRETE
food	fast food	pizza
prose	fiction	short stories
place	city	Cleveland

An *abstract* word deals with concepts, with ideas, with what cannot be touched, heard, or seen. A *concrete* word has to do with particular objects, with the practical, with what can be touched, heard, or seen.

ABSTRACT	democracy, loyal, evil, hate, charity
CONCRETE	mosquito, spotted, crunch, wedding

Often, writers tend to use too many abstract or general words, leaving their writing drab and lifeless. As you select words to fit your context, avoid combining an abstract word for subjects, a linking verb, and an abstract word for the complement. Find more concrete words for the subject or the complement or use a transitive verb. Be as specific and concrete as you can. For example, instead of the word *bad*, consider using a more precise adjective.

bad planks: rotten, warped, scorched, knotty, termite-eaten

bad children: rowdy, rude, ungrateful, selfish, perverse

bad meat: tough, tainted, overcooked, contaminated

To test whether or not a word is specific, ask one or more of these questions about what you want to say: Exactly who? Exactly what? Exactly when? Exactly where? Exactly how? As you study the following examples, notice what a difference specific, concrete words can make in the expression of an idea. Notice, too, how specific details can be used to expand or develop ideas.

VAGUE   I always think of a good museum as one that is very big.

SPECIFIC   I always think of a good museum as one I get lost in.   —EDWARD PARKS

VAGUE   Before long a lot of desktop tools will be replaced by terminals.

SPECIFIC   Before long the functions of most desktop business tools—calculator, telephone, typewriter, memo pad, and appointment book, to name a few—will be replaced with a single "engine," or terminal.
—PAUL CAMPBELL

VAGUE   I remember my pleasure at discovering new things about language.

SPECIFIC   I remember my real joy at discovering for the first time how language worked, at discovering, for example, that the central line of Joseph Conrad's *Heart of Darkness* was in parentheses.
—JOAN DIDION

All writers use abstract words and generalizations when these are vital to the communication of ideas, as in the following sentence:

He is immortal, not because he alone among creatures has an inexhaustible voice, but because he has a soul, a spirit capable of compassion and sacrifice and endurance.
—WILLIAM FAULKNER

To be effective, however, the use of these words must be based upon clearly understood and well-thought-out ideas.

■ **Exercise 5**   Replace the general words and phrases in italics with specific ones.

1. I always think of a shopping mall as *very big*.
2. *A lot of people* are threatened by *pollution*.

3. The *movie* was *great*.
4. Aunt Grace served *the same thing* every Sunday.
5. I explained my overdraft to my parents by telling them I had bought *some things I needed*.
6. Backpacking has *numerous advantages*.
7. The *dog walked* over to his *food*.
8. My father looked at my grade in science and said *what I least expected to hear*.
9. *Various aspects of the television show* were criticized *in the newspaper*.
10. The police searched the whole *area* thoroughly.

(4) Use figurative language appropriately.

Commonly found in nonfiction prose as well as in fiction, poetry, and drama, figurative language uses words in an imaginative rather than a literal sense. Simile and metaphor are the chief *figures of speech*. A *simile* is the comparison of dissimilar things using *like* or *as*. A *metaphor* is an implied comparison of dissimilar things not using *like* or *as*.

SIMILES

The first thing people remember about failing at math is that it felt like sudden death. —SHEILA TOBIAS

She shot me a glance that would have made a laser beam seem like a birthday candle. —LARRY SERVAIS

The bowie knife is as American as a half-ton pickup truck.
—GEOFFREY NORMAN

The two men passed through the crowd as easily as the Israelites through the Red Sea. —WILLIAM X. KIENZLE

He was like a piece of rare and delicate china which was always being saved from breaking and which finally fell.
—ALICE WALKER

METAPHORS

Dress is language. —LANCE MORROW

Successful living is a journey toward simplicity and a triumph over confusion. —MARTIN E. MARTY

233

The white spear of insomnia struck two hours after midnight, every night.   —GAIL SHEEHY

Wolf pups make a frothy ribbon of sound like fat bubbling.
—EDWARD HOAGLAND   [a metaphor and a simile]

Single words are often used metaphorically:

These roses must be **planted** in good soil.   [literal]

A man's feet must be **planted** in his country, but his eyes should survey the world.   —GEORGE SANTAYANA
[metaphorical]

We always **sweep** the leaves out of the garage.   [literal]

She was letting her imagination **sweep** unchecked round every rock and cranny of the world that lies submerged in the depths of our unconscious being.   —VIRGINIA WOOLF
[metaphorical]

Similes and metaphors are especially valuable when they are concrete and point up essential relationships that cannot otherwise be communicated. (For faulty metaphors, see **23c**.) Similes and metaphors can also be extended throughout a paragraph of comparison. See **32d(5)**.

There are many other common figures of speech. *Personification* is the attribution to the nonhuman (objects, animals, ideas) of characteristics possessed only by the human.

Time talks. It speaks more plainly than words. . . . It can shout the truth where words lie.   —EDWARD T. HALL

Paradox is a seemingly contradictory statement that actually makes sense when thoughtfully considered.

Only where love and need are one
And the work is play for mortal stakes . . .
                                   —ROBERT FROST

Overstatement (also called *hyperbole*) and *understatement* are complementary figures of speech often used for ironic or humorous effect.

I for one, don't expect till I die to be so good a man as I am at this minute, for just now I'm fifty thousand feet high—a

tower with all the trumpets shouting. —G. K. CHESTERTON
[overstatement]

You have a small problem; your employer has gone bankrupt.
[understatement]

Irony involves a deliberate incongruity between what is stated and what is meant (or what the reader expects). In verbal irony, words are used to express the opposite of what they literally mean; for example, in Shakespeare's *Julius Caesar*, Marc Antony stirs a mob to anger against Brutus by repeatedly stating, "Brutus is an honorable man." An *allusion* is a brief reference to a work or a person, place, event, or thing (real or imaginary) which serves as a kind of shorthand to convey a great deal of meaning compactly. The administration of President John F. Kennedy was often referred to as "Camelot," an allusion to the domain of the legendary King Arthur. An *image* represents a sensory impression in words; for example, Tennyson describes the sea as seen from the point of view of an eagle as "wrinkled."

■ **Exercise 6** Write sentences containing the specified figure of speech.

1. Metaphor 2. Simile 3. Personification 4. Overstatement or understatement 5. Allusion

20b

Choose expressions that are idiomatic.

Be careful to use idiomatic English, not unidiomatic approximations. *She talked down to him* is idiomatic. *She talked under to him* is not. Occasionally the idiomatic use of prepositions may prove difficult. If you are uncertain which preposition to use with a given word, check the word in the dictionary. For instance, *agree* may be followed by *about, on, to,* or *with.* The choice depends on the context. Writers often have trouble with expressions such as these:

according **to** the plan   [NOT with]
accuse **of** perjury   [NOT with]
bored **by** it   [NOT of]
comply **with** rules   [NOT to]
conform **to/with** standards   [NOT in]
die **of** cancer   [NOT with]
in accordance **with** policy   [NOT to]
independent **of** his family   [NOT from]
inferior **to** ours   [NOT than]
happened **by** accident   [NOT on]
jealous **of** others   [NOT for]

Many idioms—such as *all the same, put up a fight,* and *to mean well*—cannot be understood from the individual meanings of their elements. Some are metaphorical: *turn something over in one's mind.* Such expressions cannot be meaningfully translated word for word into another language. Used every day, they are at the very heart of the English language. As you encounter idioms that are new to you, master their meanings just as you would any new word.

■ **Exercise 7**   Write sentences using each of the following idioms correctly. Use your dictionary when necessary.

1. agree with, agree to, agree on
2. differ from, differ with, differ about
3. wait on, wait for
4. get even with, get out of hand
5. on the go, on the spot

20c

Choose fresh expressions instead of trite, worn-out ones.

Such expressions as *bite the dust, breath of fresh air,* or *leave no stone unturned* were once striking and effective. Excessive use, however, has drained them of their original force and made them clichés. Some euphemisms (pleasant-sounding substitutions for more explicit but possibly offensive words) are not only trite but wordy and/or awkward—for example, *correctional facility* for *jail* or *pre-owned* for *used*. Many political slogans and the catchy phraseology of advertisements soon become hackneyed. Faddish or trendy expressions like *interface, impacted, viable, input,* or *be into* (as in "I am into dieting") are so overused that they quickly lose their force.

Nearly every writer uses clichés from time to time because they are so much a part of the language, especially of spoken English. But experienced writers will often give a fresh twist to an old saying or a well-known literary passage.

> If a thing is worth doing, it is worth doing badly.
> —G. K. CHESTERTON

> Into each life a little sun must fall.   —L. E. SISSMAN

> Washington is Thunder City—full of the sound and fury signifying power.   —TOM BETHELL   [Compare Shakespeare's "full of sound and fury, / Signifying nothing."   —*Macbeth*]

Proverbs and familiar expressions from literature or the Bible, many of which have become a part of everyday language, can often be used effectively in your own writing.

> Slowly but steadily, in the following years, a new vision began gradually to replace the dream of political power—a powerful movement, the rise of another ideal to guide the unguided, another **pillar of fire by night** after a clouded day.
> —W. E. B. DU BOIS   [Compare Exodus 13:21: "And the Lord went before them . . . by night in a pillar of fire, to give them light."]

Good writers, however, do not rely too heavily on the words of others; they choose their own words to communicate their own ideas.

■ **Exercise 8**   From the following list of trite expressions—only a sampling of the many in current use—select ten that you often use or hear, and replace them with carefully chosen words or phrases. Then write a paragraph using six of these words.

EXAMPLES
A bolt from the blue *a shock*
beyond the shadow of a doubt *undoubtedly*

1. a crying shame
2. after all is said and done
3. as cold as ice
4. at the crack of dawn
5. bored to tears/death
6. to make a long story short
7. drop a bombshell
8. get in a rut
9. hoping against hope
10. horse of a different color
11. in the last analysis
12. in this day and age
13. launch a campaign
14. over and done with
15. sea of red ink
16. shun like the plague
17. slept like a log
18. smell a rat
19. stick to your guns
20. the depths of despair
21. the powers that be
22. the spitting image of
23. throw in the towel
24. with a ten-foot pole

■ **Exercise 9** Choose five of the ten items below as the basis for five original sentences. Use language that is exact, idiomatic, and fresh.

EXAMPLES
the appearance of her hair
Her hair poked through a broken net like stunted antlers.
—J. F. POWERS
OR
Her dark hair was gathered up in a coil like a crown on her head.
—D. H. LAWRENCE

1. the look on his face
2. her response to fear
3. the way she walks
4. the condition of the streets
5. spring in the air
6. the noises of the city
7. the appearance of the room
8. the scene of the accident
9. the final minutes of play
10. the approaching storm

■ **Exercise 10** Read the two paragraphs below in preparation for a class discussion of the authors' choice of words—their use of exact, specific language to communicate their ideas.

[1] Eating artichokes is a somewhat slow and serious business. [2] You must concentrate, focusing on each leaf as you break it off at its fleshy base, dip it in its sauce and draw it carefully to your mouth (being careful not to drip). [3] Between your front teeth it goes, and you scrape off the deliciously blanketed flesh. [4] Languorously you work this combination of flavors and sensations to the back of your mouth, where all the subtle-

ties of the artichoke unfold and mingle with the sharp, rich sauce; and now your taste buds get the full, exciting impact. [5]Down it goes, and you pluck another leaf, sometimes methodically, working around the base of this thistle bud, sometimes with abandon. [6]Yet you can never really "bolt" an artichoke; there is always a measure of pause with each leaf, as it is torn, dipped and tasted.

—MARTHA ROSE SHULMAN, "An Artichoke Memoir"

[1]The biblical story does not present the departure from Egypt as an everyday occurrence, but rather as an event accompanied by violent upheavals of nature. [2]Grave and ominous signs preceded the Exodus: clouds of dust and smoke darkened the sky and colored the water they fell upon with a bloody hue. [3]The dust tore wounds in the skin of man and beast; in the torrid glow vermin and reptiles bred and filled air and earth; wild beasts, plagued by sand and ashes, came from the ravines of the wasteland to the abodes of men. [4]A terrible torrent of hailstones fell, and a wild fire ran upon the ground; a gust of wind brought swarms of locusts, which obscured the light; blasts of cinders blew in wave after wave, day and night, night and day, and the gloom grew to a prolonged night, and blackness extinguished every ray of light. [5]Then came the tenth and most mysterious plague: the Angel of the Lord "passed over the houses of the children of Israel . . . when he smote the Egyptians, and delivered our houses" (Exodus 12:27). [6]The slaves, spared by the angel of destruction, were implored amid groaning and weeping to leave the land the same night. [7]In the ash-gray dawn the multitude moved, leaving behind scorched fields and ruins where a few hours before had been urban and rural habitations.

—IMMANUEL VELIKOVSKY, *Ages in Chaos*

21
WORDINESS AND NEEDLESS REPETITION

Avoid wordiness. Repeat a word or phrase only when it is needed for emphasis or clarity.

Wordiness is the use of more words than necessary to express an idea.

WORDY   In the early part of the month of August, a hurricane was moving threateningly toward Houston.

REVISED   In early August, a hurricane was threatening Houston.

Needless repetition of words or phrases distracts the reader and blurs meaning.

REPETITIOUS   This **interesting** instructor knows how to make an un**interesting** subject **interesting**.

REVISED   This instructor knows how to make a dull subject interesting.

For the effective use of repetition in parallel structures, for emphasis, and as a transitional device, see **26b**, **29e**, and **32b(3)**, respectively.

WORDINESS

21a

Make every word count; omit words or phrases that add nothing to the meaning.

(1) Avoid tautology (the use of different words that say the same thing).

WORDY	Commuters going back and forth to work or school formed car pools.
CONCISE	Commuters formed car pools.
WORDY	Each writer has a distinctive style, and he or she uses this in his or her own works.
CONCISE	Each writer has a distinctive style.

Notice the useless words in brackets below:

yellow [in color]	circular [in shape]
at 9:45 p.m. [that night]	return [back]
[basic] essentials	rich [and wealthy] nations
bitter [-tasting] salad	small [-size] potatoes
but [though]	to apply [or utilize] rules
connect [up together]	[true] facts

Avoid grammatical redundancy—such as a double subject (subject + subjective pronoun), double comparison, or double negative.

my sister [she] is   [more] easier than   could[n't] hardly

(2) Do not use many words when a few will express the idea well. Omit unnecessary words.

WORDY	**In the event that** the grading system is changed, expect complaints **on the part of** the students.
CONCISE	**If** the grading system is changed, expect complaints **from** the students. [Two words take the place of eight.]

WORDY   **As far as sexism is concerned, it seems to me that
a woman can be as guilty of sexism as a man.**

CONCISE   A woman can be as guilty of sexism as a man.
[Unnecessary words are deleted.]

One or two words can replace expressions such as these:

at this point in time   **now**
has the capability of working   **can work**
made contact by personal visits   **visited**
on account of the fact that   **because**
somewhere in the neighborhood of $2500   **about $2500**

One exact word can say as much as many. (See also **20a**.)

spoke in a low and hard-to-hear voice   **mumbled**
persons who really know their particular field   **experts**

Notice below that the words in brackets are not necessary.

because [of the fact that]   was [more or less] hinting
[really and truly] fearless   by [virtue of] his authority
fans [who were] watching TV   the oil [that exists] in shale

(3) Avoid unnecessary expletive constructions.

There followed by a form of *to be* is an expletive—a word
that signals you will put the subject after the verb. (See also
29f.) This weak construction can rob the subject of the force
it gains from being first in the sentence.

WORDY   There were three squirrels in the yard.
CONCISE   Three squirrels were in the yard.

It also is an expletive when it lacks an antecedent and is
followed by a form of *to be*.

WORDY   It is easy to learn to type.
CONCISE   Learning to type is easy.

▲ Note: In a few instances, no logical subject exists and the
impersonal *it* construction is necessary: *It is going to snow.*

■ **Exercise 1**   Revise each sentence to eliminate tautology.

1. The exact date has not been set and is not known to us.
2. During the last two innings, many senseless mistakes occurred without any apparent reason for them.
3. Long lines of starving refugees in need of food were helped by the Red Cross volunteer people.
4. Perhaps maybe the chief cause or reason for obesity in people who are overweight is lack of exercise.
5. The tall skyscraper buildings form a dark silhouette against the evening sky.

■ **Exercise 2**   Substitute one or two words for each item.

1. in this day and age
2. has the ability to sing
3. was of the opinion that
4. in a serious manner
5. prior to the time that
6. did put in an appearance
7. located in the vicinity of
8. has a tendency to break
9. during the same time that
10. involving too much expense

■ **Exercise 3**   Delete unnecessary words below.

1. It seems to me to be obvious.
2. Because of the fact that Larry was there, the party was lively.
3. Other things being equal, it is my opinion that all of these oil slicks, whether they are massive or not so big, do damage to the environment to a greater or lesser degree.
4. As for the nature of biased newscasts, I can only say that I realize that reporters have to do some editing, though they may not use the finest type of judgment when they are underscoring, as it were, some of the stories and downplaying others.

21b

Eliminate needless words by combining sentences or by simplifying phrases and clauses.

Note differences in emphasis as you study the following examples.

WORDY   The grass was like a carpet. It covered the whole playground. The color of the grass was blue-green.

CONCISE   A carpet of blue-green grass covered the whole playground.

WORDY   A few of the listeners who had become angry called in so that they would have the opportunity of refuting the arguments set forth by Ian.

CONCISE   A few angry listeners called in to refute Ian's arguments.

■ **Exercise 4** Following the pattern of the examples, condense the following sentences.

EXAMPLE
These were theories which were, in essence, concerned with politics.
These were political theories.

1. These are pitfalls that do, of course, pose a real danger.
2. This is an act which, in truth, partakes of the nature of aggression.

EXAMPLE
It was a house built with cheap materials.
It was a cheaply built house.

3. It was a garden planned with a great deal of care.
4. It was a speech delivered with a lot of passion.

EXAMPLE
The stories written by Carson McCullers are different from those composed by Flannery O'Connor.
Carson McCullers's stories are different from Flannery O'Connor's.

5. The dishes prepared by her husband are not as good as those fixed by her father.
6. The ideas shared by the students were different from those promoted by the advertiser.

EXAMPLE
It is unfortunate. A few come to college so that they can avoid work.
Unfortunately, a few come to college to avoid work.

7. It is inevitable. Corporations produce goods so that they can make a profit.
8. It is predictable. Before an election legislators reduce taxation so that they can win the approval of voters.

EXAMPLE

The forces that were against gun control ran an advertisement that covered two pages.
The anti-gun control forces ran a two-page advertisement.

9. A group that is in favor of labor wants vacations that last two months.
10. One editorial against "nukes" stressed the need for plants that are state controlled.

■ **Exercise 5** Restructure or combine the following sentences to reduce the number of words.

1. These hazards are not visible, and they cause accidents, many of which are fatal ones.
2. The United States was being invaded. What I mean by that is a takeover of land. Foreign investors were buying up farms.
3. In spite of the fact that my parents did not approve of it, I was married to Evelyn last June.
4. The fire chief made the recommendation saying that wooden shingles should not be used on homes now being built or in the future.

NEEDLESS REPETITION

21c

Avoid needless repetition.

NEEDLESS	His father is not like her father. Her father takes more chances.
REVISED	Her father takes more chances than his father.
NEEDLESS	I think that he knows that that woman is not the one for him to marry.
REVISED	I think he knows he should not marry that woman.

21d

Eliminate needless repetition by using pronouns and elliptical constructions.

Use a pronoun instead of needlessly repeating a noun or substituting a clumsy synonym. If the reference is clear, several pronouns may refer to the same antecedent.

> NEEDLESS   The hall outside these offices was empty. The hall had dirty floors, and the walls of this corridor were full of gaudy portraits.
>
> REVISED   The hall outside these offices was empty. It had dirty floors, and its walls were full of gaudy portraits.

The writer of the following sentence uses an elliptical construction. The omitted words (shown here in brackets) will be understood by the reader without being repeated.

> Prosperity is the goal for some people, fame [is the goal] for others, and complete independence [is the goal] for still others. . . .   —RENÉ DUBOS

Sometimes, as an aid to clarity, commas are used to mark omissions that avoid repetition.

> Family life in my parents' home was based upon a cosmic order: Papa was the sun; Mamma, the moon; and we kids, minor satellites.   —SAM LEVENSON

For effective use of the repetition of words or phrases, see **29e**.

■ **Exercise 6** Revise each sentence to eliminate wordiness and needless repetition.

1. The manager returned the application back because of illegible handwriting that could not be read.
2. In this day and time, it is difficult today to find in the field of science a chemist who shows as much promise for the future as Joseph Blake shows.

3. From time to time during one's life, one needs to remember that one who is learning to walk has to put one foot before the other one.
4. When the fans in the stadium shout and yell, the shouting and yelling is deafening, and so the total effect of all this is that it is a contributing factor in decisions to stay home and watch the games on TV.
5. A distant hurricane or a seaquake can cause a tidal wave. This wave can form when either occurs.
6. A comedy of intrigue (or a situation comedy) is a comedy that relies on action instead of characterization for its comedy.
7. In my family, schoolwork came first, chores came second, fun and games came next, and discussions came last.
8. Numerous products can be made from tobacco. The nicotine from this plant is used in pesticides. A sugar extracted from tobacco helps control blood pressure.

22

OMISSION OF NECESSARY WORDS

Do not omit a word or phrase necessary to the meaning of the sentence.

If you omit necessary words in your compositions, your mind may be racing ahead of your pen, or your writing may reflect omissions in your spoken English.

> The analyst talked about the tax dollar goes. [The writer thought "talked about where" but did not write *where*.]
>
> You better be there on time! [In speaking, *had* may be omitted before *better*.]

To avoid omitting necessary words, proofread your compositions carefully and study **22a–22c**.

22a

Do not omit a necessary article, pronoun, conjunction, or preposition. See also **26b**.

(1) Omitted article or pronoun

INCOMPLETE	The first meeting was held on other campus.
COMPLETE	The first meeting was held on **the** other campus.

| INCOMPLETE | I know a man had a horse like that. |
| COMPLETE | I know a man **who** had a horse like that. |

To avoid ambiguity, it is often necessary to repeat a pronoun or an article before the second part of a compound.

AMBIGUOUS	A friend and helper stood nearby. [one person or two?]
CLEAR	A friend and **a** helper stood nearby. [two persons clearly indicated by repetition of *a*]
ALSO CLEAR	My mother and father were there. [clearly two persons—repetition of *my* before *father* not necessary]

(2) Omitted conjunction or preposition

| CONFUSING | Fran noticed the passenger who was sleeping soundly had dropped his wallet in the aisle. [The reader may be momentarily confused by "noticed the passenger."] |
| BETTER | Fran noticed **that** the passenger who was sleeping soundly had dropped his wallet in the aisle. |

| INFORMAL | I had never seen that type movie before. |
| BETTER | I had never seen that type **of** movie before. |

When two verbs requiring different prepositions are used together, do not omit the first preposition. See also **20b**.

| INCOMPLETE | Such comments neither contribute nor detract from his reputation. |
| COMPLETE | Such comments neither contribute **to** nor detract from his reputation. |

In sentences such as the following, if you omit the conjunction, use a comma in its place.

The English used the paints chiefly on churches at first**,** then later on public buildings and the homes of the wealthy. —E. M. FISHER [Compare "on churches at first *and* then later on public buildings."]

The fact is**,** very few people in this society make a habit of thinking in ethical terms. —HARRY STEIN [Compare "The fact is *that* very few people. . . ."]

■ **Exercise 1**   Insert needed words below.

1. Gary reminded Sheila Richard might not approve.
2. What kind course to take is the big question.
3. Winter and spring breaks the campus is dead.
4. She lent me a dollar then decided to take it back.
5. The trouble was my good pair shoes got stolen.
6. Boynton will not ask or listen to any advice.
7. Fires had burned for weeks were still not out.
8. The book which he referred was not in our library.
9. It is the exception proves the rule.
10. The recipe calls for a variety spices.

22b

Avoid awkward omission of verbs and auxiliaries.

AWKWARD	Preston has never and cannot be wholly honest with himself.
BETTER	Preston has never **been** and cannot be wholly honest with himself.
INCOMPLETE	Since I been in college, some of my values have changed.
COMPLETE	Since I **have** been in college, some of my values have changed.
INCOMPLETE	This problem easy to solve.
COMPLETE	This problem **is** easy to solve.
INCOMPLETE	As far as the speed limit, many drivers think they have to drive that fast.
BETTER	As for the speed limit, many drivers think they have to drive that fast.

▲ Option: In sentences such as the following, the omission or inclusion of the second verb is optional.

> The sounds were angry, the manner violent.
> —A. E. VAN VOGT [omission of second verb]
> The sounds were angry, the manner **was** violent.   [inclusion of second verb]

22c

Do not omit words needed to complete comparisons.

| INCOMPLETE | Broken bottles around a swimming area are more dangerous than picnic tables. |
| COMPLETE | Broken bottles around a swimming area are more dangerous than **around** picnic tables. |

| INCOMPLETE | Snow here is as scarce as Miami. |
| COMPLETE | Snow here is as scarce as **it is in** Miami. |

| INCOMPLETE | He is taller. |
| COMPLETE | He is taller **than I am**.   [BUT   Of the two brothers, he is the taller.] |

| INCOMPLETE | After I started believing in myself, the world offered me more challenges. |
| COMPLETE | After I started believing in myself, the world offered me more challenges **than before**. |

| INCOMPLETE | Small schools often accomplish better results. |
| COMPLETE | Small schools often accomplish better results **than large schools do**. |

In a comparison such as the following, the word *other* may indicate a difference in meaning:

O'Brien runs faster than any player on the team.   [O'Brien is apparently not on the team. In context, however, this may be an informal sentence meaning that O'Brien is the fastest of the players on the team.]

O'Brien runs faster than any **other** player on the team. [*Other* clearly indicates that O'Brien is on the team.]

■ **Exercise 2**   Supply needed words in verb phrases and in comparisons.

1. They been trying to make small cars safe.
2. The consumers better listen to these warnings.
3. Ed's income is less than his wife.
4. Bruce admires Cathy more than Aline.
5. Fiberglass roofs are better.
6. The scenery here is as beautiful as any place.

7. I always have and always will like to read the comics.
8. One argument was as bad, maybe even worse than, the other.
9. The ordinance never has and never will be enforced.
10. The crusty old man irritates his roommate more than the cranky young nurse.

22d

When used as intensifiers in formal writing, *so, such,* and *too* are generally (but not always) followed by a completing phrase or clause.

The line was **so** long that we decided to skip lunch.
Bill has **such** a hearty laugh that it is contagious.
Laura was **too** angry to think straight.

■ **Exercise 3**   Insert words where needed.

1. I had my senior year a strange type virus.
2. As far as Boston, I could see the people were proud of their history.
3. The group is opposed and angered by these attempts to amend the Constitution.
4. It good to talk with a person has a similar problem.
5. In our state the winter is as mild as Louisiana.
6. The concert we attended last night was so wonderful.
7. The lawyer had to prove whatever the witness said was false.
8. Here is the hole which the rabbit escaped.
9. If Jack gets a job which he is not trained, he will fail.
10. The stadium was already filled with people and still coming.

EFFECTIVE SENTENCES

Sentence Unity | **23**

Subordination and Coordination | **24**

Misplaced Parts, Dangling Modifiers | **25**

Parallelism | **26**

Shifts | **27**

Reference of Pronouns | **28**

Emphasis | **29**

Variety | **30**

23

SENTENCE UNITY

Write unified sentences.

Good writing is unified: it sticks to its purpose. Whether in sentences, paragraphs (see **32**), or whole compositions (**33**), unity is achieved when all the parts contribute to fulfilling the writer's aim. A sentence may lack unity because it combines unrelated ideas (see **23a**) or because it contains too many unrelated details (**23b**), mixed metaphors, mixed constructions (**23c**), or faulty predication (**23d**). Clear, precise definitions (**23e**) often depend upon careful attention to sentence unity.

23a

Make the relationship of ideas in a sentence immediately clear to the reader.

UNRELATED Alaska has majestic glaciers, but most Americans must travel great distances. [unity thwarted by a gap in the thought]

RELATED Alaska has majestic glaciers, but to see them most Americans must travel great distances.

■ **Exercise 1** All the sentences below contain ideas that are apparently unrelated. Adding words when necessary, rewrite each of the sen-

tences to indicate clearly a relationship between ideas. If you cannot establish a close relationship, put the ideas in separate sentences.

1. There are many types of bores at social gatherings, but I prefer a quiet evening at home.
2. A telephone lineman who works during heavy storms can prove a hero, and cowards can be found in any walk of life.
3. Jones was advised to hire a tutor in French immediately, but he kept on driving his Jaguar.
4. Macbeth was not the only man to succumb to ambition, and Professor Stetson, for example, likes to draw parallels between modern men and literary characters.
5. Yellowstone National Park offers truly unusual sights, but I couldn't get any vacation time last summer.

23b

Avoid excessive or poorly ordered detail.

EXCESSIVE   In 1788, when Andrew Jackson, then a young man of twenty-one years who had been living in the Carolinas, still a virgin country, went to Tennessee, a turbulent place of unknown opportunities, to enforce the law as the new prosecuting attorney, he had the necessary qualifications for the task.

CLEAR   In 1788, when Andrew Jackson went to Tennessee as the new prosecuting attorney, he had the necessary qualifications for the task.

As you strive to eliminate ineffective details, remember that length alone does not make a sentence ineffective. Your purpose sometimes requires a long, detailed sentence. If the details all contribute to the central thought, then parallel structure, balance, rhythm, effectively repeated connectives, and careful punctuation can make a sentence of even paragraph length coherent.

     The rediscovery of fresh air, of home-grown food, of the delights of the apple orchard under a summer sun, of the swimming pool made by damming the creek that flows through the meadow, of fishing for sun perch or catfish from an ancient rowboat, or of an early morning walk down a country lane when the air is cool—all of these things can stir memories of a simpler time and a less troubled world.

           —CASKIE STINNETT, "The Wary Traveler"

■ **Exercise 2**   Revise each sentence to eliminate excessive detail.

1. The fan that Joan bought for her brother, who frets about any temperature that exceeds seventy and insists that he can't stand the heat, arrived today.
2. Flames from the gas heater that was given to us three years ago by friends who were moving to Canada licked at the chintz curtains.
3. After finishing breakfast, which consisted of oatmeal, toast, and coffee, Sigrid called the tree surgeon, a cheerful man approximately fifty years old.
4. At last I returned the book that I had used for the report which I made Tuesday to the library.
5. A course in business methods helps undergraduates to get jobs and in addition helps them to find out whether they are fitted for business and thus to avoid postponing the crucial test, as so many do, until it is too late.

23c

Avoid mixed metaphors and mixed constructions.

(1) Do not mix metaphors. See also 20a(4).

MIXED	Playing with fire can get you into deep water.
BETTER	Playing with fire can result in burned fingers.
MIXED	Her climb up the ladder of success was nipped in the bud.
BETTER	Her climb up the ladder of success was soon halted.
OR	Her promising career was nipped in the bud.

▲ Note: Metaphors like these have become clichés, which means people use them without thinking about their meaning. You can avoid mixing metaphors by choosing fresh ones. See **20c**.

(2) Do not mix constructions.

When a writer begins a sentence with one kind of construction and completes it by shifting to another kind, the result is a mixed construction. (See also **23d**.)

MIXED	When Howard plays the hypochondriac taxes his wife's patience. [adverb clause + predicate]
REVISED	When Howard plays the hypochondriac, he taxes his wife's patience. [adverb clause, main clause]
	OR Howard's playing the hypochondriac taxes his wife's patience. [subject + predicate]
MIXED	It was an old ramshackle house but which was quite livable.
REVISED	It was an old ramshackle house, but it was quite livable.
	OR It was an old ramshackle house which was quite livable. [noun + adjective clause]

▲ Note: Sometimes a sentence is flawed by the use of a singular noun instead of a plural one: "Hundreds who attended the convention drove their own **cars** [NOT car]."

Similarly, do not allow speech habits to trick you into omitting a necessary plural: "Two contestants [NOT contestant] want to play."

23d

Avoid faulty predication.

Make sure that your verbs indicate actions that are possible for your subjects. Faulty predication occurs when the subject and predicate do not fit each other logically.

FAULTY	One book I read believes in eliminating subsidies. [A person, not a thing, believes.]
REVISED	The author of one book I read believes in eliminating subsidies.
	OR One book I read says that subsidies should be eliminated.

FAULTY   An example of discrimination is an apartment owner, especially after he has refused to rent to people with children.   [The refusal, not the owner, is an example of discrimination.]

REVISED   An example of discrimination is an apartment owner's refusal to rent to people with children.

■ **Exercise 3** Revise each sentence to eliminate faulty predication, a mixed construction, or a mixed metaphor.

1. Another famous story from American history is Christopher Columbus.
2. One example of a rip-off would be a butcher, because he could weigh his heavy thumb with the steak.
3. When people avoid saying or doing something tactless shows they have good manners.
4. Like a bat guided by radar, Maureen was always surefooted in her business dealings.
5. Could anyone be certain why George resigned or where did he find a better job?
6. For Don, money does grow on trees, and it also goes down the drain quickly.
7. Because her feet are not the same size explains the difficulty she has finding shoes that fit.
8. I felt like a grain of sand crying out in the wilderness.
9. When children need glasses causes them to make mistakes in reading and writing.
10. The forecast of subnormal temperatures in late March was predicted by the National Weather Service.

23e

Avoid awkward definitions. Define a word or an expression clearly and precisely. See also **32d(7)**.

(1) In formal writing avoid faulty *is-when, is-where,* or *is-because* constructions.

Constructions combining *is* with the adverbs *when, where,* or *because* are often illogical since forms of *to be* signify identity or equality between the subject and what follows.

FAULTY	Banishing a man is where he is driven out of his country. [Banishing is an act, not a place.]
REVISED	Banishing a man is driving him out of his country.
FAULTY	Unlike a fact, a value judgment is when you express personal opinions or preferences.
REVISED	Unlike a fact, a value judgment is a personal opinion or preference.
FAULTY	The reason the package arrived so late is because he didn't mail it soon enough.
REVISED	The package arrived so late because he didn't mail it soon enough.

(2) Write clear, precise definitions.

A short dictionary definition may be adequate when you need to define a term or a special meaning of a word that may be unfamiliar to your reader.

> Here *galvanic* means "produced as if by electric shock."
> [See also the note following **16c**.]

Giving a synonym or two may clarify the meaning of a term. Often such synonyms are used as appositives.

> A *dolt* is a dullard, a blockhead.

> *Magendo*, or black-market corruption, is flourishing.
> —KEN ADELMAN

> If you press your forefinger gently against your closed eyelid for a minute or less, you will probably start to see phosphenes: shapes and colors that march and swirl across your darkened field of view. —JEARL WALKER [word substitutions with restrictive details]

Writers frequently show—rather than tell—what a word means by giving examples.

> Many homophones (*be* and *bee*, *in* and *inn, see* and *sea*) are not spelling problems.

A formal definition first states the term to be defined and puts it into a class, then differentiates the term from other members of its class.

A phosphene [term] is a luminous visual image [class] that results from applying pressure to the eyeball [differentiation].

You may formulate your own definitions of the concepts you wish to clarify.

> Questions are windows to the mind.
>   —GERARD I. NIERENBERG   [use of a metaphor—see also 20a(4)]

Clichés are sometimes thought of as wisdom gone stale.
>   —JOSEPH EPSTEIN

■ **Exercise 4**   Define any two of the following terms in full sentences using first (*a*) a synonym and then (*b*) a formal definition.

1. blintz	3. love	5. neurotic	7. stupid	9. humanism
2. uncanny	4. peer	6. Bren gun	8. blanch	10. integrity

24

SUBORDINATION
AND COORDINATION

Use subordination to relate ideas concisely and effectively. Use coordination to give ideas equal emphasis.

Establishing clear relationships among ideas is one of the most important functions of subordination and coordination; indeed, one of the marks of a mature writer is the ability to do so.

Subordinate means "being of lower structural rank." In the following sentence, the italicized subordinate elements are grammatically dependent on the sentence base (subject + compound predicate) in boldface.

> *If we wish to trace the history of ideas,* **iconography becomes a candid camera** *trained upon the creator's mind.*
> —STEPHEN JAY GOULD

Although, as this example shows, grammatically subordinate structures may contain very important ideas, subordinating these ideas to the sentence base draws attention to the main clause and establishes relationships between the main clause and the explanatory or supporting subordinate clause(s).

Coordinate means "being of equal structural rank." Coordination gives equal grammatical emphasis to two or more ideas that you want your reader to consider equally important. In the following sentence, both main clauses (subject + predicate, and subject + predicate) are equally important to the writer's meaning: they are coordinate elements.

> Hearing them, **I'd grow nervous,** and **my clutching trust in their protection and power would be weakened.**
> —RICHARD RODRIGUEZ

Coordination gives equal emphasis not only to two or more clauses but also to two or more words, phrases, or sentences. See also section **26**.

> *tactless, abrasive* language   [coordinate adjectives]
> *on the roof* or *in the attic*   [compound prepositional phrases]
> *I have not gone on a diet.* Nor *do I intend to.*   [sentences linked by coordinating conjunction]

A study of this section should help you to use subordination effectively when you revise a series of short, choppy simple sentences (see **24a**) or stringy compound ones (**24b[1]**). It should also help you use coordination to secure the grammatical emphasis you want (**24b[2]**) and to eliminate faulty subordination (**24c**). If you cannot distinguish between phrases and clauses and between subordinate and main clauses, see **1d** and **1e**.

24a

Use subordination to combine a series of related short sentences into longer more effective units.

CHOPPY   He stood there in his buckskin clothes. One felt in him standards and loyalties. One also felt a code. This code is not easily put into words. But this code is instantly felt when two men who live by it come together by chance.

BETTER   As he stood there in his buckskin clothes, one felt in him standards, loyalties, a code which is not eas-

ily put into words, but which is instantly felt when
two men who live by it come together by chance.
—WILLA CATHER

When combining a series of related sentences, first choose
a sentence base (subject + predicate); then use subordinate
elements to relate the other ideas to the base. See **24a(4)**
for the meaning of subordinate conjunctions. (Coordination
is also used to combine short sentences, but inexperienced
writers tend to use too much of it: see **24b**.)

(1) Use adjectives and adjective phrases.

CHOPPY   The limbs were covered with ice. They sparkled in
         the sunlight. They made a breathtaking sight.
BETTER   *Sparkling in the sunlight,* the *ice-covered* limbs
         made a breathtaking sight.   [participial phrase and
           hyphenated adjectival]

(2) Use adverbs or adverb phrases.

CHOPPY   Season the chicken livers with garlic. Use a lot of it.
         Fry them in butter. Use very low heat.
BETTER   Season the chicken livers *heavily* with garlic, and
         slowly fry them in butter.   [Note the use of both
           subordination and coordination.]
    OR   *After seasoning the chicken livers heavily with
         garlic,* slowly fry them in butter.

CHOPPY   His face was covered with white dust. So were his
         clothes. The man looked like a ghost.
BETTER   *His face and clothes white with dust,* the man
         looked like a ghost.   [first two sentences combined in
           an absolute phrase]

(3) Use appositives and contrasting elements.

CHOPPY   These kindnesses were acts of love. They were no-
         ticed. But they were not appreciated.
BETTER   These kindnesses—*acts of love*—were noticed *but
         not appreciated.*

(4) Use subordinate clauses.

Subordinate clauses are linked and related to main clauses by markers (subordinating conjunctions and relative pronouns) which signal whether a clause is related to the sentence base by **time** (*after, before, since, until, when, while*), **place** (*where, wherever*), **reason** (*as, because, how, so that, since*), **condition** (*although, if, unless, whether*) or **additional information** (*that, which, who, whose*). See page 22 for a list of these markers.

CHOPPY   The blizzard ended. Then helicopters headed for the mountaintop. It looked dark and forbidding.

BETTER   *As soon as the blizzard ended*, helicopters headed for the mountaintop, *which looked dark and forbidding.*   [adverb clause and adjective clause]

■ **Exercise 1**   Combine the following short sentences into longer sentences by using effective subordination and coordination. (If you wish, keep a short sentence or two for emphasis: see **29h**.)

¹I have just read *The Idea of a University* by John Henry Newman.   ²I am especially interested in his views regarding knowledge.   ³He says that knowledge is its own reward.   ⁴It is not just a means to an end. ⁵Newman says knowledge is a treasure in itself.   ⁶I had looked upon knowledge only in terms of practical results.   ⁷One result would be financial security.   ⁸But that was before I read this essay.   ⁹Now I accept Newman's definition of knowledge.   ¹⁰Such knowledge is worth pursuing for its own sake.

24b

Do not string main clauses together when some ideas should be subordinated. Use coordination to give ideas equal emphasis.

Do not overwork coordinating connectives like *and, then, and then, so, and so, but, however, therefore.* For ways to revise stringy or loose compound sentences, see **30c**. Methods of subordination that apply to combining two or more sentences also apply to revising faulty or excessive coordination in a single sentence: see **24a**.

(1) Avoid stringing several compound sentences together; subordinate some ideas to others.

AWKWARD   I wanted to go to college, so I scraped and painted houses all summer, and that way I could earn my tuition.

BETTER   *Because I wanted to go to college,* I scraped and painted houses *to earn my tuition.*

AWKWARD   Burns won, and it was a landslide vote, but he had rigged the election.

BETTER   Burns, *who had rigged the election,* won by a landslide vote.

OR   *Having rigged the election,* Burns won by a landslide vote.

(2) Use coordination to give ideas equal emphasis.

The offer was tempting, but I didn't accept it.   [equal grammatical stress on the offer and the refusal]

COMPARE   Although the offer was tempting, I didn't accept it.   [stress on the refusal]

Although I didn't accept it, the offer was tempting.   [stress on the offer]

■ **Exercise 2**   Revise each sentence by using effective subordination and coordination.

1. First she selected a lancet and sterilized it, and then she gave the patient a local anesthetic and lanced the infected flesh.
2. Yesterday I was taking a shower, so I did not hear the telephone ring, but I got the message in time to go to the party.
3. Two ambulances tore by, and an oncoming bus crowded a truckload of laborers off the road, but nobody got hurt.
4. Jean Henri Dunant was a citizen of Switzerland, and he felt sorry for Austrian soldiers wounded in the Napoleonic Wars; therefore, he started an organization, and it was later named the Red Cross.
5. The administrators stressed career education, and not only did they require back-to-basics courses, but they also kept students informed about job opportunities.

(3) Avoid faulty or illogical coordination.

Faulty coordination fails to show a clear relationship among ideas. Coordinate only those ideas that are of equal importance and that go together logically. (See also **23d**.)

FAULTY   I tripped on the rug and I broke my ankle. [Subordinate the less important idea.]

BETTER   I broke my ankle because I tripped on the rug.

FAULTY   That was the only way in which Evelyn could have known that Mary concealed a secret and, if revealed, would cost her the elective office she desperately wanted.   [Rewrite to remove faulty coordination of predicates.]

BETTER   That was the only way Evelyn could have known that Mary concealed a secret which, if revealed, would cost Mary the elective office she desperately wanted.

FAULTY   Irene is a music major and who can play several instruments.   [Do not use *but* or *and* before *which, who,* or *whom* when introducing a single adjective clause.]

BETTER   Irene is a music major who can play several instruments.

FAULTY   You can walk to school or carry your lunch. [Rewrite such sentences completely.]

BETTER   If you walk to school, you may not want to carry an arm load of heavy books and your lunch.

24c

Avoid faulty or excessive subordination.

FAULTY   I have never before known a man like Ernie, who is ready to help anybody who is in trouble that involves finances.

BETTER   I have never before known a man like Ernie, who is ready to help anybody in financial trouble. [one subordinate clause reduced to a phrase, another reduced to an adjective]

EXCESSIVE   Some people who are insecure when they are involved in personal relationships worry all the time, at least when they are not busy with things they have to do, about whether their friends truly love them.

BETTER   Some insecure, idle people worry about whether their friends truly love them. [two subordinate clauses reduced to adjectives]

■ **Exercise 3**   Observing differences in emphasis, convert each pair of sentences below to (a) a simple sentence, (b) a compound sentence consisting of two main clauses, and (c) a complex sentence with one main clause and one subordinate clause.

EXAMPLE
Male sperm whales occasionally attack ships. These whales jealously guard their territory.

a. *Jealously guarding their territory, male sperm whales occasionally attack ships.*
b. *Male sperm whales occasionally attack ships; these whales jealously guard their territory.*
c. *Since male sperm whales jealously guard their territory, they occasionally attack ships.*

1. The men smuggled marijuana into Spain. They were sentenced to six years in prison.
2. The council first condemned the property. Then it ordered the owner's eviction.
3. Uncle Oliver applied for a patent on his invention. He learned of three hundred such devices already on the market.
4. The border guards delayed every tourist. They carefully examined passports and luggage.

■ **Exercise 4**   Prepare for a discussion of the subordination and the coordination of ideas in the paragraph below.

¹Going by canoe is often the best—and sometimes the only—way to go. ²Some difficult country can't be reached any other way, and once you arrive, the aches of paddling and sitting unsupported on a canoe seat seem a small price to pay for being there. ³One such place is the

Boundary Waters area along the border of northeastern Minnesota and Ontario. ⁴The terrain is rolling and pocked by thousands of glacier lakes. ⁵Some are no more than bowls of rock that hold the accumulated clear green water; others are spring-fed and dark. ⁶The maze of lakes, islands, and portage trails is inhabited by all sorts of wildlife: beaver, otter, loons, and bear. ⁷It is a landscape suited to the canoe and has in fact been canoe country since the time of the fur-trading voyageurs—hard Frenchmen whose freighters were up to twenty-five feet long and required eight paddlers.

—GEOFFREY NORMAN, "Rapid Transit"

25
MISPLACED PARTS, DANGLING MODIFIERS

Avoid needless separation of related parts of the sentence. Avoid dangling modifiers.

25a
Avoid needless separation of related parts of the sentence.

As a rule, place modifiers near the words they modify. Note how the meaning of the following sentences changes according to the position of modifiers:

> Rex **just** died with his boots on.
> Rex died with **just** his boots on.
> **Just** Rex died with his boots on.

> The man **who drowned** had tried to help the child.
> The man had tried to help the child **who drowned**.

(1) In formal English, modifiers such as *almost, only, just, even, hardly, nearly,* and *merely* are regularly placed immediately before the words they modify.

> The truck costs **only** $450.   [NOT only costs]
> He works **even** during his vacation.   [NOT even works]

■ **Exercise 1**   Circle each misplaced modifier; draw an arrow to show its proper position.

1. The explosion only killed one person.
2. The new computer program nearly cost a hundred dollars.
3. Bruce polished his antique Mercedes almost until he could see his face in the door panels.
4. He even daydreams when you talk to him about salary.
5. Compulsive talkers hardly show any interest in what other people may have to say.

(2) The position of a modifying prepositional phrase should clearly indicate what the phrase modifies.

MISPLACED	A garish poster attracts the visitor's eye **on the east wall**.
BETTER	A garish poster **on the east wall** attracts the visitor's eye.
MISPLACED	One student said that such singing was not music but a throat ailment **in class**.
BETTER	**In class** one student said that such singing was not music but a throat ailment.
OR	One student said **in class** that such singing was not music but a throat ailment.

■ **Exercise 2**   Circle each misplaced prepositional phrase below; draw an arrow to show its proper position.

1. The evening news carried the story of the Senator's loss of memory in every part of the country.
2. My neighbor barbecued steaks for his children with hickory sauce on them.
3. In the cafeteria the school serves spaghetti to hungry customers on paper plates.
4. The professor made it clear why plagiarism is wrong on Monday.

(3) Adjective clauses should be placed near the words they modify.

MISPLACED	We bought gasoline in Arkansas at a small country store **which cost $10.25**.

BETTER   At a small country store in Arkansas, we bought
          gasoline **which cost $10.25**.

**(4) Avoid "squinting" constructions—modifiers that may
refer to either a preceding or a following word.**

SQUINTING   Jogging **often** relaxes her.
BETTER   **Often**, jogging relaxes her.
             OR It relaxes her to jog **often**.

**(5) Avoid the awkward separation of the sentence base and
the awkward splitting of an infinitive.**

AWKWARD   **I had** in spite of my not living in a neighborhood
           as fine as Jane's a healthy **measure** of pride.
           [awkward separation of a verb from its object]
BETTER   In spite of my not living in a neighborhood as fine
           as Jane's, **I had** a healthy **measure** of pride.

AWKWARD   Hawkins is the man **to**, if we can, **nominate for**
           governor.   [awkward splitting of an infinitive]
BETTER   Hawkins is the man **to nominate** for governor if
           we can.

Sometimes, splitting an infinitive is not only natural but
desirable.

He forgot to **completely** latch it.   [Compare: He forgot completely to latch it.]

■ **Exercise 3**   Revise the sentences to eliminate squinting modifiers or
needless separation of related sentence parts.

1. Bill failed to, because he was sleepy, lock the back door.
2. Melissa said last week she had gone.
3. The game warden warned the hunter not to carry a rifle in a car that
   was loaded.
4. Arlene promised when she was going to the store to pick up some
   milk.
5. The puppy advertised in last night's paper which is already eight
   weeks old is a registered Labrador retriever.

25b

Avoid dangling modifiers.

Although any misplaced word, phrase, or clause can be said to dangle, the term *dangling* is applied primarily to verbal phrases that do not refer clearly and logically to another word or phrase in the sentence.

To correct a dangling modifier, rearrange the words in the sentence to make the modifier clearly refer to the right word, or add words to make the meaning clear and logical.

(1) Avoid dangling participial phrases.

DANGLING   **Discouraged by low grades**, dropping out seemed to make sense.

REVISED   **Because I was discouraged by low grades**, dropping out seemed to make sense.

OR   **Discouraged by low grades**, I thought dropping out made sense.

Placed after the sentence base, the participial phrase in the revision below refers to the subject.

DANGLING   The evening passed very pleasantly, **playing backgammon and swapping jokes**.

REVISED   **They** passed the evening very pleasantly, **playing backgammon and swapping jokes**.

(2) Avoid dangling phrases containing gerunds or infinitives.

DANGLING   **Instead of watching the late show**, a novel was read.

REVISED   **Instead of watching the late show**, Hilary read a novel.

DANGLING   **Not able to swim that far**, a lifeguard came to my rescue.

REVISED   **I was not able to swim that far**, so a lifeguard came to my rescue.

OR   **Because I was not able to swim that far**, a
lifeguard came to my rescue.

(3) Avoid dangling elliptical adverb clauses.

Elliptical clauses have words that are implied rather than
stated.

DANGLING   **When confronted with these facts**, not one word
was said.

REVISED   **When confronted with these facts**, **nobody** said a
word.

OR   **When they were confronted with these
facts**, not one word was said.

DANGLING   **Although only a small boy**, my father expected
me to do a man's work.

REVISED   **Although I was only a small boy**, my father expected me to do a man's work.

▲ Note: Sentence modifiers (see page 572) are considered
standard usage, not danglers.

To judge from reports, all must be going well.
His health is fairly good, **considering his age**.

■ **Exercise 4**   Revise the following sentences to eliminate dangling
modifiers. Put a check mark after any sentence that needs no revision.

1. While waiting for my friends to say goodbye, the moon rose above
the horizon.
2. By standing and repeating the pledge, the meeting came to an end.
3. Once mixed thoroughly, you must freeze the ingredients within an
hour.
4. Prepare to make an incision in the abdomen as soon as completely
anesthetized.
5. After walking for six blocks, it began to rain and we ran the rest of
the way.
6. Darkness having come, we stopped for the night.
7. Having deteriorated in the last year, he found the streets bumpy.
8. Ready to pitch camp, the windstorm hit.
9. My friends did not complain of the cold, realizing they would be
home soon.
10. Burned to the ground, the Welches had to build a new home.

26
PARALLELISM

Use parallel structure to express matching ideas.

Parallel (grammatically equal) sentence elements regularly appear in lists or a series, in compound structures, in comparisons using *than* or *as*, and in contrasted elements. As the examples below illustrate, parallelism contributes to ease in reading and provides clarity and rhythm.

> Music expresses, at different moments, **serenity or exuberance**, **regret or triumph**, **fury or delight**.   —AARON COPLAND
>
> **Listening** is as much a persuasive technique as **speaking**.
> —GERARD I. NIERENBERG   [a comparison with *as . . . as*]

Many parallel elements are linked by a coordinating conjunction (such as *and, or, but*) or by correlatives (such as *neither . . . nor, whether . . . or*). Others are not. In the following examples, verbals used as subjects and complements are parallel in form.

> **To define** flora is **to define** climate.   —NATIONAL GEOGRAPHIC
> **Seeing** is **deceiving**. It's **eating** that's **believing**.
> —JAMES THURBER

Parallel structures are also used in topic outlines; see **33e**, page 380.

Faulty parallelism disrupts the balance of coordinate elements:

FAULTY   We are not so much **what we eat** as **the thoughts we think**.   [The coordinate elements differ in grammatical form.]

REVISED   We are not so much **what we eat** as **what we think**.

OR   We are not so much **the food we eat** as **the thoughts we think**.

Parallel grammatical structure cannot correct the imbalance of elements that are not parallel in thought. Rethink the sentence.

FAULTY   We can choose ham, tuna salad, cottage cheese, or television.   [The first three elements are foods; the last is an activity.]

REVISED   We can eat or we can watch television.

26a

For parallel structure, balance nouns with nouns, prepositional phrases with prepositional phrases, main clauses with main clauses, and so on.

As you study the parallel words, phrases, clauses, and sentences that follow, notice that repetition can be used to emphasize the balanced structure.

(1) Parallel words and phrases

People begin to feel ‖ **faceless**
and ‖ **insignificant**.   —S. L. HALLECK

The two most powerful words in the world today are
not ‖ **guns and money,**
but ‖ **wheat and oil.**   —FREDERIC BIRMINGHAM

She had ‖ **no time to be human,**
‖ **no time to be happy.**   —SEAN O'FAOLAIN

(2) Parallel clauses

Almost all of us want things ‖ that we do not need
and fail to want things ‖ that we do need.
—MORTIMER J. ADLER

‖ Top soil, once blown away, can never be returned;
‖ virgin prairie, once plowed, can never be reclaimed.
—MARILYN COFFEY

(3) Parallel sentences

‖ When I breathed in, I squeaked.
‖ When I breathed out, I rattled.   —JOHN CARENEN

‖ The danger of the past was that men became slaves.
‖ The danger of the future is that men may become robots.
—ERICH FROMM

■ **Exercise 1**   Underline the parallel structures. Then write five sentences: one containing parallel words, one containing parallel phrases, one containing parallel clauses, and two that are themselves parallel.

1. Many plants are pollinated by animals, such as bees, birds, or bats.
   —NATIONAL GEOGRAPHIC
2. Carpets are bought by the yard and worn by the foot.
   —A. R. SPOFFORD
3. To say that some truths are simple is not to say they are unimportant.   —WILLIAM J. BENNETT
4. Reading through *The Origin* is like eating Cracker Jacks and finding an I O U note at the bottom of the box.   —JOHN FLUDAS
5. The earth's nearest neighbor has mountains taller than Everest, valleys deeper than the Dead Sea rift, and highlands bigger than Australia.   —NEWSWEEK
6. There might be some people in the world who do not need flowers, who cannot be surprised by joy, but I haven't met them.
   —GLORIA EMERSON
7. Booms typically attract an oversupply of trained specialists; busts generate an undersupply.   —CHRIS WELLES
8. Think before you speak. Read before you think.   —FRAN LEBOWITZ
9. They must accept the criticism of others and be suspicious of it; they must accept the praise of others and be even more suspicious of it.   —DONALD M. MURRAY

10. What I value is not the "friend" who, looming sympathetically above me when I have been dashed to the ground, appears gigantically generous in the hour of my reversal; more and more I desire friends who will endure my ecstasies with me, who possess wings of their own and who will fly with me. —GAIL GODWIN

26b

To make the parallel clear, repeat a preposition, an article, the *to* of the infinitive, or the introductory word of a phrase or clause.

The reward rests not ‖ **in** the task
            but ‖ **in** the pay.   —JOHN K. GALBRAITH

Life is ‖ **a** mystery
  and ‖ **an** adventure
which he shares with all living things.
                      —JOSEPH WOOD KRUTCH

It is easier ‖ **to love humanity as a whole**
     than ‖ **to love one's neighbor**.   —ERIC HOFFER

It is the things we think we know—
     ‖ **because** they are so elementary
or ‖ **because** they surround us—
that often present the greatest difficulties when we are actually challenged to explain them. —STEPHEN JAY GOULD

■ **Exercise 2** Insert words that are needed to bring out the parallel structure in the following sentences.

1. On our trip west I took several pictures of Pike's Peak and Mount Rushmore.
2. I want something cool to do this summer: to swim and sail.
3. They understood that I was busy and I could not go with them.
4. My grandmother told me that I could learn more by listening than talking.
5. They would lie on the battlefield without medical attention for an hour or day.

26c

**Use parallel structures with correlatives (*both . . . and;
either . . . or; neither . . . nor; not only . . . but also;
whether . . . or*).**

FAULTY Either they obey the manager or get fired.

PARALLEL Either ‖ **they obey the manager**
     or ‖ **they get fired.**

PARALLEL They either ‖ **obey the manager**
       or ‖ **get fired.**

FAULTY Whether drunk or when he was sober, he liked to
     pick a fight.

PARALLEL Whether ‖ **drunk**
      or ‖ **sober,**
     he liked to pick a fight.

FAULTY Not only practicing at 6 a.m. during the week, but
     the team also scrimmages on Sunday afternoons.

PARALLEL The team
     not only ‖ **practices at 6 a.m. during the week**
     but also ‖ **scrimmages on Sunday afternoons.**

    OR Not only does the team practice at 6 a.m.
      during the week, but it also scrimmages on
      Sunday afternoons. [The *also* may be omit-
      ted.]

■ **Exercise 3** Revise each sentence by using parallel structure to
express parallel ideas.

1. He has not only maintained but improved upon the high standards
   set by his predecessors.
2. Art likes to play the piano and listening to the Boston Pops.
3. There are two kinds of people where I work: the ones who do most
   of the work and lazy people.
4. Maureen was thoughtful and in a quiet mood when we left the
   theater.
5. My friend asked me whether the trip would be delayed or to be
   ready to start on Friday as planned.

■ **Exercise 4** First study the parallelism in the sentences below. Then use one of the sentences as a structural model for a sentence of your own.

1. What is true of coral and of all other forms of marine life is also true of whales. —JACQUES-YVES COUSTEAU
2. The day I liked best in New York was the fall evening when the lights went out. The elevators stopped, the subways stopped, the neon stopped. Factories, presses, and automatic doughnut fryers— everything ground to a halt. —MARGARET A. ROBINSON
3. Calm, relaxed people get ulcers as often as hard-pressed, competitive people do, and lower-status workers get ulcers as often as higher-status ones. —CAROL TAVRIS
4. Each word has been weighed, each thought has been evaluated, and each point carefully considered. —ZIG ZIGLAR

27
***
SHIFTS

Avoid needless shifts in grammatical structures, in tone or style, and in viewpoint.

Abrupt, unnecessary shifts—for example, from past to present, from singular to plural, from formal diction to slang, from one perspective to another—obscure meaning and make for difficult reading.

27a

Avoid needless shifts in tense, mood, and voice. See also section **7**.

SHIFT While they waited George **argued** against nuclear power while his brother **discusses** the effects of acid rain. [shift from past to present tense]

BETTER While they waited George **argued** against nuclear power while his brother **discussed** the effects of acid rain. [both verbs in the past tense]

SHIFT   If I **were** rich and if my vacation **was** longer, I would go to Japan.   [shift from subjunctive to indicative]

BETTER   If I **were** rich and if my vacation **were** longer, I would go to Japan.   [both verbs in subjunctive mood]

SHIFT   My grandmother **had to enter** a nursing home when she was ninety-nine, but it **was not liked** by her.   [shift from active to passive voice]

BETTER   My grandmother **had to enter** a nursing home when she was ninety-nine, but she **did not like** it. [both verbs in active voice]

When using the literary present, as in summarizing plots of novels and plays, avoid slipping from the present into the past tense.

Romeo and Juliet fall in love at first sight, marry secretly, and die [NOT *died*] together in the tomb within the same hour.

27b

Avoid needless shifts in person and in number. See also **6b**.

SHIFT   If a **person** is going to improve, **you** should work harder.   [shift from third person to second person]

BETTER   If **you** are going to improve, **you** should work harder.   [second person]

    OR   If **people** are going to improve, **they** should work harder.   [third person]

    OR   If **we** are going to improve, **we** should work harder.   [first person]

SHIFT   The senior class **is** planning to ask six faculty members to **their** spring dance.   [shift in number]

BETTER   The senior class **is** planning to ask six faculty members to **its** spring dance.

■ **Exercise 1**   Correct all needless shifts in tense, mood, voice, person, and number.

1. Before the game began, Karl comes over to our seats and asked us to wait for him later.
2. Raoul made the motion that the special election be held in January and that the city hall will be the polling place.
3. Maclean struggled to push the lawnmower up the hill and then it was dragged down again by her.
4. Every witness was questioned, and they were taken to police headquarters.
5. I was told billions of germs live on one's skin and that you should bathe often.

27c

Avoid needless shifts from indirect to direct discourse. See also **26a**.

SHIFT   Janet wondered **how the thief got the computer out** and **why didn't he steal the silver?** [shift from indirect to direct discourse]

BETTER   Janet wondered **how the thief got the computer out** and **why he didn't steal the silver.** [two indirect questions]

     OR   Janet asked, **"How did the thief get the computer out? Why didn't he steal the silver?"** [two direct questions]

SHIFT   Her assistant said **that she was out** and **would I please wait.** [shift from indirect to direct discourse]

BETTER   Her assistant said **that she was out and asked me please to wait.** [indirect discourse]

27d

Avoid needless shifts in tone or style.

INAPPROPRIATE   Journalists who contend that the inefficiency of our courts will lead to the total elimination of the jury system are **nuts**. [Replace *nuts* (slang) with a word like *wrong* or *uninformed*.]

INAPPROPRIATE   The darkness of the auditorium, the monotony of the ballet, and the strains of music drifting sleepily from the orchestra aroused in me a desire to **sack out**.   [Replace *sack out* (slang) with a word like *doze*.]

27e

Avoid needless shifts in perspective or viewpoint.

FAULTY PERSPECTIVE   The underwater scene was dark and mysterious; the willows lining the shore dipped gracefully into the water.   [The perspective abruptly shifts from beneath the surface of the water to above it.]

BETTER   The underwater scene was dark and mysterious; **above**, the willows lining the shore dipped gracefully into the water.

■ **Exercise 2**   Correct all needless shifts. Put a check mark after any sentence that needs no revision.

1. A woman stepped forward, grabs the mugger's belt, snatches the purses, and got lost in the crowd.
2. Vigorous exercise is good for everyone because stress is reduced and the body is strengthened.
3. Rob spends Thanksgiving in San Francisco but flies to Seattle for Christmas.
4. Linda asked whether Sam had arrived and did we know when he was expected.
5. Every cook has their own recipes for making vegetable soup.
6. She told them that there is somebody in the room.
7. If Louis really likes someone, he would make any sacrifice for them.
8. Bring your swimsuit. They will be useful.
9. The outside of the building looks like a fortress; the comfortable furnishings seem out of place.
10. The doctor asked me why I had not taken the medicine and did I want to go to the hospital?

■ **Exercise 3**   Revise the following paragraph to eliminate all needless shifts.

[1]He was a shrewd businessman, or so it had always seemed to me. [2]He has innocent-looking eyes, which are in a baby face, and spoke softly when he talks.   [3]When questioned about who recommended he make a recent stock purchase, he answers, "I work hard and do a lot of research."   [4]Not one name was mentioned by him; moreover, his reluctance to discuss his business transactions was evident.   [5]Take these comments for what they are worth; they may help one in your dealings with this sharp operator.

28
REFERENCE OF PRONOUNS

Make a pronoun refer unmistakably to its antecedent.
See also **6b**.

Each boldfaced pronoun below clearly refers to its italicized antecedent, a single word or a word group:

> *Languages* are not invented; **they** grow with our need for expression. —SUSANNE K. LANGER

> There is no *country* in the world **whose** population is stationary. —KENNETH BOULDING

> Thus, *being busy* is more than merely a national passion; **it** is a national excuse. —NORMAN COUSINS

Without any loss of clarity, a pronoun can often refer to a noun that follows:

> Unlike **their** predecessors, today's *social workers* cannot exclusively seek middle-class, home-owning, two-parent, one-career families for the children they want to place.
> —MARSHA TRUGOT

As you edit your compositions, check to see that the meaning of each pronoun is immediately obvious. If there is any chance of confusion, repeat the antecedent, use a synonym for it, or recast your sentence.

28a

Avoid an ambiguous reference.

When a pronoun could refer to either of two possible antecedents, the ambiguity confuses, or at least inconveniences, your reader. Recast the sentence to make the antecedent clear, or replace the pronoun with a noun. (A pronoun, of course, may clearly refer to two or more antecedents: *"Jack* and *Jill* met their Waterloo.")

AMBIGUOUS	Lisa wrote to Jennifer every day when she was in the hospital.
CLEAR	When Lisa was in the hospital, she wrote to Jennifer every day.
	OR When Jennifer was in the hospital, Lisa wrote to her every day.
AMBIGUOUS	After listening to Ray's proposal and to Sam's objections, I liked his ideas better.
CLEAR	I agreed with Sam after listening to his objections to Ray's proposal.

28b

Avoid a remote or an awkward reference.

Placing a pronoun too far away from its antecedent may force your reader to backtrack to get your meaning. Making a pronoun refer to a modifier can obscure your meaning. Recast the sentence to bring a pronoun and its antecedent closer together or substitute a noun for the obscure pronoun.

| REMOTE | A freshman found herself the unanimously elected president of a group of animal lovers, **who** was not a joiner of organizations. [*Who* is too far removed from the antecedent *freshman*. See also **25a(3)**.] |

BETTER	A **freshman who** was not a joiner of organizations found herself the unanimously elected president of a group of animal lovers.
OBSCURE	Before Ellen could get to the jewelry store, **it** was all sold. [reference to a modifier]
BETTER	Before Ellen could get to the jewelry store, all the **jewelry** was sold.

■ **Exercise 1** Revise each sentence below to eliminate any ambiguous, remote, or obscure pronoun reference.

1. Kate's dislike for Christine did not end until she invited her to play tennis with her cousins from England.
2. On the keyboard, the many function keys often confuse a computer novice that are not clearly identified.
3. In Morris's book he does not say what to do.
4. The lake is peaceful. Near the shore, water lilies grow in profusion, spreading out their green leaves and sending up white blossoms. It is well stocked with fish.
5. Mrs. Young spoke to Betty as she was walking down the hall.

28c

Use broad or implied reference only with discretion.

Pronouns such as *it, this, that, which,* and *such* may refer to a specific word or phrase or to the sense of a whole clause, sentence, or paragraph.

SPECIFIC REFERENCE	His nose was absolutely covered with warts of different sizes; it looked like a sponge, or some other kind of marine growth. —DAN JACOBSON [*It* refers to *nose.*]
BROAD REFERENCE	Some people think that the fall of man had something to do with sex, but that's a mistake. —C. S. LEWIS [The pronoun *that* refers to the sense of the whole clause.]

287

When used carelessly, broad reference can interfere with clear communication. Be especially careful with *this* and *that*.

(1) Avoid broad reference to an expressed idea.

VAGUE   Although the story referred to James, Henry misapplied it to himself, which is true in real life.

CLEAR   Although the story referred to James, Henry misapplied it to himself. Such mistakes occur in real life.

(2) As a rule, do not refer to a word or an idea not expressed but merely implied.

VAGUE   Lois said that she would stay in Yuma for at least a year. This suggests that she is happy there.   [*This* has no expressed antecedent.]

CLEAR   Lois said that she would stay in Yuma for at least a year. This remark suggests that she is happy there.

VAGUE   He wanted his teachers to think he was above average, as he could have been if he had used it to advantage.   [*It* has no expressed antecedent.]

CLEAR   He wanted his teachers to think he was above average, as he could have been if he had used his ability to advantage.

28d

Avoid the awkward use of *you* or *it*.

AWKWARD   It was no use in trying.

BETTER   There was no use trying.   OR   Trying was useless.

AWKWARD   When one cannot swim, you fear deep, stormy waters.   [The pronoun *you* (second person) refers to *one* (third person). See also **27b**.]

REVISED   The person who cannot swim fears deep, stormy waters.

AWKWARD   In McKenny's book **it** says that many mushrooms are edible.   [The pronoun *it* clumsily refers to *book*.]

REVISED   McKenny's book says that many mushrooms are edible.

In some contexts, the use of the impersonal, or indefinite, *you* is both natural and acceptable. Notice in the following example that *you* is equivalent in meaning to "people in general" or "the reader."

> The study of dreams has become a significant and respectable scientific exploration, one that can directly benefit **you**.
> —PATRICIA GARFIELD

Some writers, however, prefer not to use *you* in a formal context.

▲ Note: Avoid the awkward placement of *it* near another *it* with a different meaning.

AWKWARD   It would be unwise to buy the new model now, but it is a superior machine.   [The first *it* is an expletive. The second *it* refers to *model*.]

REVISED   Buying the new model now would be unwise, but it is a superior machine.

■ **Exercise 2**   Revise the following sentences as necessary to correct faults in reference. Put a check mark after any sentence that needs no revision.

1. Clearly, the freezer was broken; it melted all over the inside.
2. At the Chinese restaurant, the Murrays had a hard time eating with chopsticks, but that is their favorite food.
3. Copiers and other fine modern office machines enable business executives to accomplish more work because their assistants can manage them easily and quickly.
4. In the essay it says that the author dislikes the wilderness because of all the bugs.

5. Our language is rich in connectives that express fine distinctions of meaning.
6. I decided not to attend the family reunion, which was very disappointing to my grandparents.
7. Anne told Theresa that she was supposed to go to Chicago next week.
8. When building roads the Romans tried to detour around valleys as much as possible for fear that flood waters might cover them and make them useless.
9. The extra fees surprised many freshmen that seemed unreasonably high.
10. In Ellen's car she plays only Country and Western tapes.

29
EMPHASIS

Construct sentences to emphasize important ideas.

You may emphasize ideas by using exact diction (see section **20**), concise language (**21**), and appropriate subordination and coordination (**24**). This section presents other ways to gain emphasis.

29a
Place important words at the beginning or end of the sentence—especially at the end.

UNEMPHATIC   Good telephone manners are just as important as good table manners, however, for many reasons.   [Unimportant elements are placed at the end of the sentence.]

EMPHATIC   Good telephone manners, however, for many reasons, are just as important as good table manners.

OR   However, good telephone manners are for many reasons just as important as good table manners.   [Introductory transitional expressions do not ordinarily weaken a sentence beginning.]

UNEMPHATIC	In his book, Morrow argued against capital punishment, it seemed to me. [An unemphatic prepositional phrase begins the sentence, and an unnecessary qualification ends it.]
EMPHATIC	Morrow argued against capital punishment. [See also section **21**.]

Because the semicolon (see also section **14**) is a strong punctuation mark when used between main clauses, the words placed immediately before and after a semicolon tend to receive emphasis.

The colon and the dash often precede an emphatic ending. (See also **17d** and **17e**.)

> We have developed something new in politics: the professional amateur. —MEG GREENFIELD

> It was a night of still cold, zero or so, with a full moon—a night of pure magic. —WALLACE STEGNER

■ **Exercise 1** Giving special attention to the placement of important words, revise the following sentences to improve emphasis.

1. Rock music affects the brain's alpha waves, so they say.
2. A shot came from the direction Tim was hunting in.
3. In Colorado Springs there used to be a program to train young figure skaters for national competition.
4. It had never before entered my mind to challenge the decisions Marla made or to offer ideas of my own, however.

29b

Occasionally use a periodic instead of a loose sentence.

In a *loose* sentence, the main idea (grammatically a main clause or sentence base) comes first; less important ideas or details follow. In a *periodic* sentence, however, the main idea comes last, just before the period.

LOOSE	Such sticky labels do not accurately describe any generation—for example, labels like *lost, beat, now, silent,* or *me.*

PERIODIC   Such sticky labels as *lost, beat, now, silent,* or *me* do not accurately describe any generation.

LOOSE   Hair has always been a statement for men, variously representing strength (Samson), fashionable virtue (King Charles I of England, whose wigs were long-locked and elaborate), bravado (General Custer), and genius (Einstein).
   —OWEN EDWARDS   [The main idea comes first.]

PERIODIC   When you die, when you get a divorce, when you buy a house, when you have an auto accident, not to mention the hundreds of times during your lifetime when you are fleeced in your role as a consumer, a lawyer either must or should be involved.   —DAVID HAPGOOD   [The main idea comes last.]

Both types of sentences can be effective. The loose sentence is, and should be, the more commonly used. Although the periodic sentence is often the more emphatic, you should take care in your writing not to overuse it.

■ **Exercise 2**   Convert the loose sentences to periodic sentences, and the periodic to loose. Notice how your revisions vary the emphasis.

1. Italy remains cheerful, despite everything.   —AUBERON WAUGH

2. Even where people want better relations, old habits and reflexes persist.   —HEDRICK SMITH

3. The Milky Way Galaxy is entirely unremarkable, one of billions of other galaxies strewn through the vastness of space.
   —CARL SAGAN

4. And then she was sweet and apologetic, as always, as she had been all her life, nervously backing away from the arguments she should have had with my father, turning aside from the talks she should have had with me.   —JOYCE CAROL OATES

5. As Mays told me, almost with pride, "If I don't know anything about something, or if I don't understand it, I just oppose it."
   —BERKELEY RICE

29c

Occasionally arrange ideas in an ascending order of climax.

Notice in the following examples that the ideas are arranged in an order that places the writer's most dramatic or important idea last.

> Urban life is unhealthy, morally corrupt, and fundamentally inhuman. —RENÉ DUBOS [adjectives in the series arranged in climactic order]

> They could hear the roar of artillery, the crash of falling timbers, the shrieks of the wounded. [sentence climax reached with *shrieks of the wounded*]

> In the language of screen comedians four of the main grades of laugh are the titter, the yowl, the belly laugh and the boffo. The titter is just a titter. The yowl is a runaway titter. Anyone who has ever had the pleasure knows all about a belly laugh. The boffo is the laugh that kills. —JAMES AGEE [First, words are placed in climactic order, then sentences.]

▲ **Note:** Anticlimax—an unexpected shift from the dignified to the trivial or from the serious to the comic—is sometimes used for special effect.

> But I still fear it will all end badly, this Protective Syndrome. I see a future in which the government has stripped us of all worldly goods worth having: clothes hangers, toothpaste, Alka-Seltzer, toasters, pencil sharpeners, and maybe even thumb tacks. —S. L. VARNADO

■ **Exercise 3** Arrange the ideas in the following sentences in what you consider to be the order of climax.

1. Franklin used the ant as a symbol of industry, wisdom, and efficiency.
2. Among the images in the poem are sun-drenched orchards, diamond-eyed children, and golden-flecked birds.

3. He left the city because his health was failing, his taxes were going up, and his pet dog was tired of the leash.
4. Something must be done at once. Unless we act now, the city will be bankrupt in five years. The commission is faced with a deficit.
5. The would-be governor attended a community festival, autographed books for teenagers, promised prosperity to all, and wrote letters to senior citizens.

29d

Rely on the active voice and forceful verbs.

(1) Prefer the active voice to the passive voice.

A sentence in which the grammatical subject and the doer of the action are the same usually presents your ideas strongly and directly.

UNEMPHATIC	An adequate number of parking places are always needed by commuting students.
EMPHATIC	Commuting students always need an adequate number of parking places.

▲ Exception: If the receiver of the action is more important than the doer, the passive voice is more effective.

There in the tin factory, in the first moment of the atomic age, a human being was crushed by books.   —JOHN HERSEY

Freedom can be squashed by the tyrant or suffocated by the bureaucrat.   —WILLIAM F. RICKENBACKER

(2) Prefer an action verb or a forceful linking verb to a form of *have* or *be*.

Forms of *have* or *be*, when used without an action verb, rob your writing of energy and forcefulness. The real action of such a sentence often lies in a verbal phrase or in an object or complement.

UNEMPHATIC	Our college is always the winner of the conference. [The subject complement—*winner*—contains the real action.]
EMPHATIC	Our college always wins the conference. [The verb *win* presents the real action.]
UNEMPHATIC	The meat has a rotten smell. [Action is in the direct object—*smell*.]
EMPHATIC	The meat smells rotten. [The verb *smell* presents the real action.]
UNEMPHATIC	You can be more effective at solving problems by understanding the problem first. [Objects of prepositions contain the real action—*solving, understanding*.]
EMPHATIC	You can solve problems more effectively if you understand the problem first. [Verbs present the real action.]

■ **Exercise 4**   Make each sentence more emphatic by substituting the active for the passive voice or by substituting a more forceful verb for a form of *have* or *be*. Write five sentences of your own using forceful verbs.

1. Flies and mosquitoes are eaten by frogs.
2. My brother is a manipulator of other people.
3. Every Saturday, violence is taught to children by cartoons.
4. Bad pizza has a taste like cardboard.
5. It is usually required by the professor that the students have a ten-page paper to write each term.

29e

Gain emphasis by repeating important words.

Take Reggie Jackson of the Yankees. He spits constantly, even when he is figuring tax shelters in the dugout. He spits walking to the plate. He spits while he is there. He spits on balls. He spits on strikes.

Reggie Jackson spits with style. He has two distinct spits. There is the straight "ptui!" spit where he simply applies cheek and lip pressure.

His deluxe, superstar spit—typically flamboyant—is his through-the-teeth-line-drive-spit, however. He can fire away five to ten quick streams through the gap in his two front teeth faster than a Ron Guidry fastball. —LEWIS GRIZZARD

▲ Caution: This method of gaining emphasis will not be effective if you routinely repeat words. See **21**.

■ **Exercise 5** First make each sentence below more emphatic by substituting repetition for the use of synonyms; then write two sentences of your own using repetition for emphasis.

1. Usually we cheat to make people think we are better than we are; sometimes we deceive to avoid unpleasant consequences such as paying taxes.
2. He gripes all the time: he complains about the weather, fusses in heavy traffic, grumbles about high prices, and is critical of his meals.

29f

Gain emphasis by occasionally inverting the word order of a sentence. See also **30b**.

At the feet of the tallest and plushiest offices lie the crummiest slums. —E. B. WHITE [Compare "The crummiest slums lie at the feet of the tallest and plushiest offices."]

Then come all the greens in the spectrum—doubly welcome after a long winter. —HAL BORLAND

▲ Caution: This method of gaining emphasis, if overused, will make the style distinctly artificial.

▲ Note: "There is (are)" constructions can emphasize a topic the author will address later. (See also **21a**.)

There is such a thing as the freedom of exhaustion. Some people are so worn down by the yoke of oppression that they give up. . . . —MARTIN LUTHER KING, JR.

29g

Gain emphasis by using balanced sentence construction.

A sentence is balanced when grammatically equal structures—usually main clauses with parallel elements—are used to express contrasted (or similar) ideas: see section **26**. A balanced sentence emphasizes the contrast (or similarity) between parts of equal length and movement.

> To be French is to be like no one else; to be American is to be like everyone else. —PETER USTINOV

> Love is positive; tolerance negative. Love involves passion; tolerance is humdrum and dull. —E. M. FORSTER

■ **Exercise 6** Write emphatic sentences using balanced construction to show the contrast between the following:

1. summer and winter
2. youth and age
3. town and city
4. hypocrisy and candor

29h

Gain emphasis by abruptly changing sentence length.

> In the last two decades there has occurred a series of changes in American life, the extent, durability, and significance of which no one has yet measured. No one can.
> —IRVING HOWE   [The short sentence, which abruptly follows a much longer one, is emphatic.]

■ **Exercise 7** Write a short, emphatic sentence to follow each long sentence below. Then write another pair of sentences—one long and one short—of your own.

1. According to some minor prophets of doom, the next century will be a push-button era, a computer-controlled and robot-dominated one with life dependent on the movement of a forefinger.
2. In sequined costumes the skaters glide into the huge arena, smile at the applauding spectators, strike a brief pose, and then race into a

series of intricate leaps and spins, their feet perfectly balanced on thin wedges of shining steel.

■ **Exercise 8** Prepare for a class discussion of emphasis in the following passages.

1. No one reads anymore—blame television. Families are breaking up—blame television. High culture is being despoiled—blame television. . . . What a splendid all-purpose explanation television has become. —ARISTIDES

2. In fantasy, the timid can be bold and aggressive, the weak are strong, the clumsy are full of grace, the tongue-tied discover vast verbal resources. In the privacy of the mind, we can all rise up in righteous wrath, and vengeance is ours. —ADELAIDE BRY

■ **Exercise 9** Revise each sentence for emphasis. Be prepared to explain why your revision provides correct emphasis.

1. I think that creating viruses with DNA should stop even if it might help us find a cure for cancer.
2. Such jokes are offensive to many people because they have references to minorities or to religion.
3. Fields of wild flowers were all around us.
4. Fools talk about each other; ideas fill the conversations of the wise.
5. At any rate, the gun fired when the fleeing robber tripped over the patrolman's foot.
6. The storm broke in all its fury at the close of a hot day.
7. A fast pass was caught by Milburn, and a thirty-yard gain was made by him before the whistle was blown by the referee.
8. I asked her to marry me, two years ago, in a shop on Tremont Street, late in the fall.
9. The art of the people was crude, but a great deal of originality was shown by some of them.
10. I can identify the guilty person in every Agatha Christie novel by the simple device of choosing the least likely suspect whose alibi is airtight.

30
VARIETY

Vary the structure and the length of your sentences.

Inexperienced writers tend to rely too heavily—regardless of content or purpose—on a few comfortable, familiar structures. Seek sentence variety in your writing.

Compare the two paragraphs below. Both express the same ideas in virtually the same words; both use acceptable sentence patterns. It is the variety in sentence structure and length that makes the difference.

NOT VARIED

Most Americans highly value their freedom to do this or that. They value their ability to own this or that. Freedom to them means the right to become something or other. But I have a different point of view. I prize most the freedom not to do, not to have, and not to become. I can, as an American, choose not to vote, and I don't have to buy. Moreover, I can also choose not to be ambitious; I don't have to be successful. I can pursue my own kind of happiness. I prize this freedom the most.

[nine sentences: seven simple and two compound—all except two beginning with the subject]

VARIED

To do this or that, to own this or that, to become something or other—these freedoms are what most Americans value

highly. But I have a different point of view. What I prize most is the freedom not to do, not to have, not to become. As an American, I can choose not to vote, and I can choose not to buy. Although I am free to be ambitious and successful, I can choose not to be either. To pursue happiness—as I define it—is the freedom I prize most.
[six sentences: four complex, one compound, and one simple—two beginning with the subject]

▲ Note: If you have difficulty distinguishing various types of structures, review the fundamentals of the sentence treated in section **1**, especially **1d**.

30a

As a rule, avoid a series of short simple sentences. Vary the length. See also **29h**.

Rather than present your ideas in a series of choppy, ineffective sentences, learn how to relate your ideas precisely in a longer sentence. See section **24**.

CHOPPY   The Maine coast and the Oregon coast look very much alike. The houses by the sea, however, are different. It's a matter of architectural style.

EFFECTIVE   Although the Maine coast and the Oregon coast look very much alike, the architectural style of the houses by the sea is different.   [use of subordination to combine sentences]

CHOPPY   Some people simply put coffee in an enamel saucepan. Next, they pour very hot water over it. Then they wait until flavor develops. Finally, they add eggshell or a small amount of cold water. The idea is to get the floating grounds to settle to the bottom.

EFFECTIVE   Some people simply put coffee in an enamel saucepan, pour very hot water over it, wait until flavor develops, and get the floating grounds to settle to the bottom by adding eggshell or a small amount of cold water. [use of coordination to combine sentences]

▲ Note: Occasionally, as the example below illustrates, a series of brief, subject-first sentences may be used for special effect:

He stumbled, recovered, picked up his pace. Now he was running. He broke out of the ring. People were throwing things at him. An egg hurtled past his head. A tomato hit someone nearby and splattered onto his suit.   —GERRY NADEL
[The short sentences suggest staccato action.]

■ **Exercise 1**   Study the structure of the sentences below, giving special attention to the variety of sentence lengths.

As she picked her way toward the garden chairs beside the front porch, she poured out a customary torrent of complaint. Her eyesight was failing. She found herself swatting raisins on the kitchen table, thinking they were flies, and bringing her stick down on spiders that turned out to be scurrying tufts of lint. Her hearing was going, and she suffered from head noises. She imagined she heard drums beating.
—PETER DE VRIES

■ **Exercise 2**   Combine each of the following series of short simple sentences into one long sentence in which ideas are carefully related.

1. A supernova appeared in 1986. It was visible with the naked eye. That has not happened in four hundred years.
2. Suellen did not buy a new car. She bought a sailboat. It is 22 feet long. It can be sailed by one person.
3. There were thirty seconds of play left. Cooper stole the ball from Jackson. He dribbled down the court. He shot at the basket. The buzzer sounded. The ball bounced off the backboard. It bounced onto the floor.
4. My favorite ball club is the Minnesota Twins. They won yesterday. They defeated the Cleveland Indians. The game was thrill-packed. The right fielder drove in the winning run. He does that frequently.
5. J. Allen Boone is the author of *Kinship with All Life*. In this book Boone describes his ability to communicate with animals. He converses mentally with a dog. He orders ants to leave his home. They obey his orders. He even tames an ordinary housefly.

30b

Vary the beginnings of your sentences.

Most writers begin about half their sentences with the subject—far more than the number of sentences begun in any other way. But overuse of the subject-first beginning results in monotonous writing.

(1) Begin with an adverb or an adverb clause.

> **Suddenly** a hissing and clattering came from the heights around us. —DOUGLAS LEE [adverb]

> **Even though baseball is essentially the same**, the strategy of play then and now is different. —JAMES T. FARRELL [adverb clause]

(2) Begin with a prepositional phrase or a verbal phrase.

> **For the writer**, the wild dream is the first step to reality.
> —NORMAN COUSINS

> **To be really successful**, you will have to be trilingual: fluent in English, Spanish, and computer. —JOHN NAISBITT [infinitive phrase]

> **Looking out of the window high over the state of Kansas**, we see a pattern of a single farmhouse surrounded by fields, followed by another single homestead surrounded by fields.
> —WILLIAM OUCHI [participial phrase]

(3) Begin with a sentence connective—a coordinating conjunction, a conjunctive adverb, or a transitional expression.

Notice how each sentence connective relates the ideas in each set of sentences. See also **32b(4)**.

> For students who have just survived the brutal college-entrance marathon, this competitive atmosphere is all too

familiar. **But** others, accustomed to being stars in high school, find themselves feeling lost in a crowd of overachievers.
—NANCY R. GIBBS [The coordinating conjunction *but* makes a contrast.]

If any group has options to change and improve its life, it is the American middle class. **And** yet with freedom comes turmoil. —GAIL SHEEHY

Health experts are cautioning that many new oat products are high in saturated fats and calories. **Moreover**, oat enthusiasts are mistaken if they think scarfing down oats allows them to gorge on steak and French fries. —ANASTASIA TOUFEXIS [conjunctive adverb]

If the Soviet care and feeding of athletes at times looks enviable, it is far from perfect. **For one thing**, it can be ruthless.
—WILLIAM A. HENRY III [transitional expression]

(4) Begin with an apposition, an absolute phrase, or an introductory series.

A city of ancient origins, Varna lies on the Black Sea coast.
—COLIN RENFREW [appositive referring to the subject]

His eyebrows raised high in resignation, he began to examine his hand. —LIONEL TRILLING [absolute phrase]

Light, water, temperature, minerals—these affect the health of plants. [See also **17e(3)**.]

▲ Note: An occasional declarative sentence with inverted word order can contribute to sentence variety. See **29f**.

■ **Exercise 3** Prepare for a class discussion of the types of sentence beginnings in the following paragraph. For instance, White begins the first sentence with a long prepositional phrase that includes a verbal phrase. See **30b(2)**.

[1]In attempting to recapture this mild spectacle, I am merely acting as recording secretary for one of the oldest of societies—the society of those who, at one time or another, have surrendered, without even a show of resistance, to the bedazzlement of a circus rider. [2]As a writing

man, or secretary, I have always felt charged with the safekeeping of all unexpected items of worldly or unworldly enchantment, as though I might be held personally responsible if even a small one were to be lost.   [3]But it is not easy to communicate anything of this nature.   [4]The circus comes as close to being the world in microcosm as anything I know; in a way, it puts all the rest of show business in the shade.   [5]Its magic is universal and complex.   [6]Out of its wild disorder comes order; from its rank smell rises the good aroma of courage and daring; out of its preliminary shabbiness comes the final splendor.   [7]And buried in the familiar boasts of its advance agents lies the modesty of most of its people.   [8]For me the circus is at its best before it has been put together. [9]It is at its best at certain moments when it comes to a point, as through a burning glass, in the activity and destiny of a single performer out of so many.   [10]One ring is always bigger than three.   [11]One rider, one aerialist, is always greater than six.   [12]In short, a man has to catch the circus unawares to experience its full impact and share its gaudy dream.

—E. B. WHITE

■ **Exercise 4**   Recast each sentence (adapted from *Omni* magazine) twice to vary the beginning.

EXAMPLE

The green fireballs traveled at great speed and fascinated sky watchers throughout the Southwest.

a. *Traveling at great speed, the green fireballs fascinated skywatchers throughout the Southwest.*

b. *Throughout the Southwest, green fireballs traveling at great speed fascinated skywatchers.*

1. A limestone plateau studded with razor-sharp pinnacles stretched ahead of them.
2. The longest-running television series anywhere may be the British science fiction saga, *Dr. Who.*
3. Potential franchise buyers crowded around the booth that displayed small household robots and asked questions about how many tasks the machines could perform.
4. Rita Levi-Montalcini initiated study into the development of the central nervous system using the simplest scientific tools while she was hiding from the Nazis in a farmhouse.
5. A new, smart elevator samples the location, destination, and passenger load of each car, rerouting individual elevators to eliminate long waits in the hall and stops by elevators already too full to admit additional riders.

30c

Avoid loose, stringy compound sentences. See also **24b**.

To revise an ineffective compound sentence, try one of the following methods.

(1) Make a compound sentence complex.

COMPOUND Gazpacho is a cold Spanish soup, and it has a history going back to Roman times, and it is usually made with bread, tomatoes, green peppers, and garlic.

COMPLEX Gazpacho, which is a cold Spanish soup usually made with bread, tomatoes, green peppers, and garlic, has a history going back to Roman times.

(2) Use a compound predicate in a simple sentence.

COMPOUND She caught the bird expertly, and next she held it so its feet were still, and then she slipped a numbered yellow band around its left leg.

SIMPLE She caught the bird expertly, held it so its feet were still, and slipped a numbered yellow band around its left leg.

(3) Use an appositive in a simple sentence.

COMPOUND J. T. Nichols was an old-fashioned naturalist, and he spent his life studying birds and turtles on Long Island.

SIMPLE J. T. Nichols, an old-fashioned naturalist, spent his life studying birds and turtles on Long Island.

(4) Use a prepositional or verbal phrase in a simple sentence.

COMPOUND The rain was torrential, and we could not see where we were going.

SIMPLE	Because of the torrential rain, we could not see where we were going.
COMPOUND	I checked into the hotel about 4:30, and then I called the office about my return flight.
SIMPLE	After checking into the hotel about 4:30, I called the office about my return flight.
COMPOUND	The town was near the Atlantic Ocean, and the hurricane struck it, and it was practically demolished.
SIMPLE	The town, located near the Atlantic Ocean, was struck by the hurricane and practically demolished.

■ **Exercise 5** Using the methods illustrated in **30c**, revise the loose, stringy compound sentences below.

1. The house is small, and it is easy to keep clean, but it is too cramped.
2. Our friends the Comptons grew tired of the long, cold winters, so they moved to Arizona, but there they had to endure long, hot summers.
3. Plastic can be sliced in thin sheets to form computer disks, and it can be molded in cases for keyboards and monitors, and it can also be removed from one's wallet to purchase equipment one cannot afford.
4. Keith kept asking the library board about the budget, and he asked about increasing the amount spent on books and salaries, but he did not mention the amount spent for maintenance.

30d

Vary the conventional subject-verb sequence by occasionally separating subject and verb with words or phrases.

Each subject and verb below is in boldface.

SUBJECT-VERB	**Wizzard Wells was** a popular resort once, but **it is** a ghost town now.
VARIED	**Wizzard Wells**, once a popular resort, **is** a ghost town now.

| SUBJECT-VERB | **Rhode Island is** east of Connecticut, and **it has** a forty-mile coastline. |
| VARIED | **Rhode Island,** east of Connecticut, **has** a forty-mile coastline. |

■ **Exercise 6** Using the methods illustrated in **30d**, vary the conventional subject-verb sequence.

1. Marcella is like her sister, and she is an excellent driver.
2. San Francisco is south of Portland, Oregon, but it is colder in the summer.
3. The manager sympathized with the employees, and she supported their decision to ask for shorter hours.
4. Ron was hurrying to get home before the storm broke, and he flooded the engine of his car.
5. Doyle Washington was a popular football star years ago, and now he is manager of a health club.

30e

Occasionally, instead of the usual declarative sentence, use a question, an exclamation, or a command.

How can anybody assert that "growth" is a good thing? If my children grow, it is a very good thing; if I should suddenly start growing, it would be a disaster. —E. F. SCHUMACHER [Here a rhetorical question is followed by the usual declarative statement.]

Now I stare and stare at people, shamelessly. Stare. It's the way to educate your eye. —WALKER EVANS [A one-word imperative sentence provides variety.]

■ **Exercise 7** Prepare for a class discussion of sentence variety in the following paragraph.

¹Some people collect stamps or coins or antique cars. ²I collect practically useless scraps of information without really wanting to. ³Things that most people don't bother to remember accumulate in my mind like unused wire hangers in a coat closet. ⁴For instance, hardly

anybody except me remembers the names of the four models of the Edsel (Pacer, Ranger, Corsair and Citation), or the name of the only New York newspaper that supported Harry Truman in 1948 (the now-defunct New York *Star*). [5]Do you know there's enough concrete in Boulder Dam to build a six-lane highway from Seattle to Miami? [6]I do. [7]I also know the origin of the word *hitchhike* (two people traveling with one horse), and that the Japanese word for first lieutenant (*chūi*) is the same as the Swahili word for leopard. [8]Just don't ask me why.

—WILLIAM ATTWOOD, "The Birth of the Bikini"

LARGER ELEMENTS

Logical Thinking **31**

The Paragraph **32**

The Whole Composition **33**

The Research Paper **34**

Writing for Special Purposes **35**

31
LOGICAL THINKING

Base your writing on logical thinking. Avoid common fallacies.

In writing you can win readers and gain their confidence in three ways: by establishing your credibility so they will trust what you say, by appealing to their interests and concerns (see **33a**), and by using well-reasoned and well-supported arguments. This section treats logical thinking—the natural reasoning processes of induction and deduction that underlie arguments—and fallacies—the errors that can occur with arguments. Logical thinking and a knowledge of fallacies will help you not only to write but also to analyze the arguments of others—in reading, in political speeches, and in discussions with friends. You will learn to be critical of what you see and hear and to recognize problems in your own and other people's arguments.

31a

Learn how to use inductive reasoning in your writing.

Whenever you interpret evidence, you reason inductively. For example, if six apples in a basketful of apples are sweet, you assume that the rest of them are sweet. This use of probability to form a generalization is called an inductive leap. Inductive arguments, rather than producing scientific certainty, are thus intended to produce probable and believable conclusions.

Science's use of inductive reasoning is known as the scientific method. For instance, early medical studies equated diets high in fat with coronary disease. The scientific community, however, reserved judgment since the early studies were based on small samplings. Later studies with broader sampling, however, confirmed the early reports, and although all persons with coronary disease cannot be studied, the sampling is now large enough to make the conclusion with confidence.

Inductive reasoning is useful in writing not only for arriving at conclusions but also for persuading others to accept those conclusions. An inductive argument is built on evidence; as your evidence mounts, your reader draws the conclusion you intend. You must make sure that the amount of evidence is sufficient and not based on exceptional or biased sampling (see Hasty generalization, page 319). Be sure that you have not ignored information that invalidates your conclusion (called the "neglected aspect") or presented only evidence that supports a predetermined conclusion (known as "slanting").

In writing, inductive reasoning often employs examples. Since you cannot cite all the instances that support your well-reasoned generalization, one or a few examples closely related to the point you are making will provide evidence (see **32c**). In the following inductively organized paragraph, a number of examples support the last sentence.

> In Chicago last month, a nine-year-old boy died of an asthma attack while waiting for emergency aid. After their ambulance was pelted by rocks in an earlier incident, city paramedics wouldn't risk entering the Dearborn Homes project [where the boy lived] without a police escort. In Atlanta, residents of the Bankhead Courts project had their mail

service suspended for two days last month after a postman nearly lost his life in the cross fire of a gun battle. Mail carriers wouldn't resume service until police accompanied them on their rounds. This is the day-to-day reality of life now in America's urban ghettos. Their residents, under siege by what are essentially organized drug terrorists, deserve the benefit of an unapologetic assault on drug-driven crime.
—"Hot Towns," *Wall Street Journal*

How you organize your inductive reasoning varies with the situation. You may wish to state the conclusion first, in the form of a topic sentence (**32a[2]**) or a thesis statement (**33d**), and then present the supporting examples. Or you may wish to reverse the order by presenting the conclusion or the generalization after the evidence. Still another way is to let the reader draw the conclusion. These last two strategies work well when your conclusion is one your reader may resist.

31b

Learn how to use deductive reasoning in your writing.

When you reason inductively, you begin with a number of instances (facts or observations) and use them to draw a general conclusion; when you reason deductively, you begin with generalizations (premises) and apply them to a specific instance to draw a conclusion about that instance. Although the terminology may be new to you, you are already familiar with deductive reasoning. For example, you know that an A average is a prerequisite for Honors History, and since Jean is in Honors History you conclude that she probably has an A average. This argument can be expressed in a structure called a *syllogism*.

> **Major Premise:** All students in Honors History have an A average.
> **Minor Premise:** Jean is a student in Honors History.
> **Conclusion:** Therefore Jean has an A average.

Of course, your reader must accept the ideas or values that you choose as premises in order to accept the conclusion.

Sometimes premises are not stated.

> Jean is in Honors History so she must have an A average.

In this sentence, the unstated premise is that all students in Honors History have an A average. A syllogism with an unstated major or minor premise, or even an unstated conclusion, needs to be examined with care, since the omitted statement may well contain an inaccurate generalization. "She's on the basketball team so she must be a good swimmer" contains the unstated major premise that "All basketball players are good swimmers," an unacceptable premise since some basketball players cannot swim at all.

The Toulmin method   Another way of viewing the process of logical thinking is through the Toulmin method. This approach sees such arguments as the progression from accepted facts or evidence (data) to a conclusion (claim) by way of a statement (warrant), which establishes a reasonable relationship between the two. For example, in the argument,

> Honors History requires an A average, and since John is enrolled in that course, he must have an A average,

the conclusion or claim is that John has an A average and the evidence or data is that he is, in fact, in the class. The warrant, that an A average is a course prerequisite, ties the two statements together, making the conclusion follow from the data.

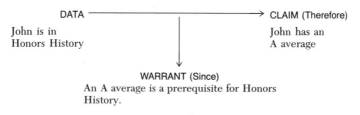

DATA ──────────────→ CLAIM (Therefore)

John is in   John has an
Honors History   A average

WARRANT (Since)
An A average is a prerequisite for Honors
History.

The warrant is often implied in arguments and, like the unstated premise in the syllogism, needs careful examination to be acceptable.

Of course, not all arguments are as simple as this example. For instance, the instructor in the Honors course may have made an exception in admitting John. In such cases, the writer can make allowances for exceptions to the major premise. Qualifiers such as *probably, possibly, doubtless,* and *surely* show the degree of certainty of the conclusion, and rebuttal terms such as *unless* allow the writer to anticipate objections.

> **Since** John is in Honors History, he **probably** has an A average, **unless** the instructor gave him special permission to enroll.

Notice that the boldfaced transitional words express logical relationships among ideas in the argument and corresponding elements in the sentence. The Toulmin model is less constrained than the syllogism and makes allowances for the important elements of probability, backing or proof for the premise, and rebuttal of the reader's objections in the model itself.

In the following paragraph, Edward I. Koch answers the argument that the death penalty should be banned because executions are barbaric. His claim is that opponents of capital punishment are troubled more by "the death itself" than by the method of execution. The data is the *New York Times* quote that "execution can never be made human through science," and the warrant is that the *New York Times* is a reliable source and accurately reflects the views of people opposed to capital punishment.

> *The death penalty is "barbaric."* Sometimes opponents of capital punishment horrify with tales of lingering death on the gallows, of faulty electric chairs, or of agony in the gas chamber. Partly in response to such protests, several states such as North Carolina and Texas switched to execution by lethal injection. The condemned person is put to death painlessly, without ropes, voltage, bullets, or gas. Did this answer

the objections of death penalty opponents? Of course not. On June 22, 1984, the *New York Times* published an editorial that sarcastically attacked the new "hygienic" method of death by injection, and stated that "execution can never be made humane through science." So it's not the method that really troubles opponents. It's the death itself they consider barbaric. —EDWARD I. KOCH, "Death and Justice"

■ **Exercise 1** Analyze the arguments in the following excerpt by asking yourself the following questions:

1. What is the conclusion or claim?
2. What are the premises on which the argument is based?
3. What is the evidence and what proof is there of the evidence?
4. What objections can be anticipated to the argument?

Whether in liquefied form, or used—as many recommend—as a substitute for oil or natural gas to produce electricity, coal is not so simple as it seems. You don't just dig it out of the ground and burn it like waste paper. It is a bulky commodity, and it has more than its share of disadvantages as a fuel.

Railroad facilities and barge canals must be greatly expanded and pipelines constructed to carry the coal in dry or slurry form thousands of miles. Underground mining is hazardous and expensive; open-pit, or strip, mining engenders stiff opposition because it threatens to scar the landscape—in the United States, some particularly beautiful Western landscapes would be an early target. Burned under electric-generating boilers, coal leaves behind vast tonnages of residue, and the gasses it releases upon burning are heavy with contaminants. Getting rid of coal's ashes—usually in the form of a fine powder, because coal must be pulverized before burning for maximum efficiency—is difficult. Expensive scrubbers must be installed in new plants that burn coal with a high sulfur content to prevent the creation of "acid rain." The huge quantities of carbon dioxide that would be released into the air by burning coal on a vastly expanded scale could raise further havoc with the earth's atmosphere. —ROGER STARR, "The Case for Nuclear Energy"

■ **Exercise 2** Supply the missing premise in the following statements and analyze the arguments by asking yourself the questions in Exercise 1.

1. He must be a nice person. He smiles all the time.
2. She's a good writer. She's easy to understand.

317

3. It's going to rain tomorrow. There is a circle around the moon.
4. The majority is always right. It says so in the Constitution.
5. He's probably a good swimmer. He's a magnificent tennis player.

31c

Avoid Fallacies.

A deductive argument must be both valid and true. A *true* argument is based on generally accepted, well-backed premises. Learn to distinguish between fact (based on measurable and verifiable data) and opinion (based on personal preferences). A *valid* argument is one that follows a reasonable line of thinking. The conclusion in the following syllogism is valid but untrue because the major premise is untrue.

All redheads are brilliant.
Jane is a redhead.
Therefore Jane is brilliant.

The following syllogism is invalid because the conclusion does not follow from the premises.

All Republicans are smart people.
All Democrats are smart people.
Therefore all Republicans are Democrats.

Fallacies are faults in premises (truth) or in reasoning (validity). They may result from misusing or misrepresenting evidence, from relying on faulty premises or omitting a needed premise, or from distorting the issues. The following are some of the major forms of fallacies.

(1) Non sequitur: A statement that does not follow logically from what has just been said—a conclusion that does not follow from the premises.

FAULTY Billy Joe is honest; therefore, he will get a good job.
[Many honest people do not get good jobs.]

(2) Hasty generalization: A generalization based on too little evidence or on exceptional or biased evidence.

> FAULTY   Teenagers are reckless drivers.   [Many teenagers are careful drivers.]

(3) *Ad hominem:* Attacking the person who presents an issue rather than dealing logically with the issue itself.

> FAULTY   His arguments might impress us more if he didn't have false teeth.   [His false teeth have nothing to do with his arguments.]

(4) Bandwagon: An argument saying, in effect, "Everyone's doing or saying or thinking this, so you should too."

> FAULTY   Everyone else is cheating, so why shouldn't I? [The majority is not always right.]

(5) Red herring: Dodging the real issue by drawing attention to an irrelevant issue.

> FAULTY   Why worry about a few terrorists when we ought to be doing something about acid rain?   [Acid rain has nothing to do with the actions of terrorists.]

(6) *Either . . . or* fallacy: Stating that only two alternatives exist when in fact there are more than two.

> FAULTY   We have only two choices: ban nuclear weapons or destroy the earth.   [In fact, other possibilities exist.]

(7) False analogy: The assumption that because two things are alike in some ways, they must be alike in other ways.

> FAULTY   Since the books are about the same length and cover the same material, one is probably as good as the other.   [The length and coverage of the books cannot predict whether one is as good as the other.]

(8) Equivocation: An assertion that falsely relies on the use of a term in two different senses.

> FAULTY   They belong to the same religion, but money is his real religion. [Religion in the first sense means an organized church; in the second sense it means a cause or principle.]

(9) Slippery slope: The assumption that if one thing is allowed it will only be the first step in a downward spiral.

> FAULTY   Handgun control will lead to a police state. [Handgun control has not led to a police state in England.]

(10) Oversimplification: A statement or argument that leaves out relevant considerations about an issue.

> FAULTY   People who pass tests are lucky. [People who pass tests have usually studied and prepared.]

(11) Begging the question: An assertion that restates the point just made. Such an assertion is circular in that it draws as a conclusion a point stated in the premise.

> FAULTY   He is lazy because he just doesn't like to work. [Being lazy and not liking to work mean essentially the same thing.]

(12) False cause: The assumption that because one event follows another, the first is the cause of the second. Sometimes called *post hoc, ergo propter hoc* ("After this, so because of this").

> FAULTY   The new mayor took office last January, and crime in the streets has already increased 25 percent. [The assumption is that having the new mayor caused the increase in crime, an assumption unlikely to be true.]

■ **Exercise 3** Identify the fallacies in the following statements. Prepare for a class discussion.

1. Most crime is the result of drug trafficking, so if we legalized all drugs we would do away with crime.
2. Women will vote for him because he is good-looking.
3. A person who cannot spell should not become a journalist.
4. If you walk self-confidently, you probably won't get mugged.
5. Our jails are full because a lot of people don't have enough money to buy necessities.
6. She's a woman, so she's no good at math.
7. Mary missed class twice last week. She must have been sick.
8. Bill is the most popular boy in the class. You should vote for him for president.
9. These razor blades give the smoothest shave; all the baseball players use them.
10. There are only two kinds of politicians; those interested in their own welfare and those interested in the welfare of the people.
11. He frowns all the time, so he must be sick.
12. Why can't I buy a car? All my friends have them.

32

THE PARAGRAPH

Write paragraphs that are unified, coherent, and adequately developed.

An essential unit of thought in writing, paragraphs develop the main idea of a paper in the same way that sentences develop the main idea of a paragraph. Sentences and paragraphs rarely stand alone and are best thought of as integral parts of the greater units—that is, the paragraphs and the essays—to which they belong. The beginning of a paragraph is indicated by the visual marker of indention to signal the reader that a new idea is being introduced. (Indention is also used in dialogue, as discussed in **16a[2]**.)

Good paragraphs are unified, coherent, and well developed. In paragraphs 1 and 2, observe how the sentences of each paragraph relate to a single main idea (unity), how ideas progress easily from sentence to sentence (coherence), and how specific details support the main idea (development). (For easy reference, the paragraphs in this section are numbered—except for those in need of revision.)

1   The modern typewriter keyboard was deliberately designed to be as inconvenient as possible. On earlier models of the typewriter, the keyboard was arranged so that the

most common letters in the English language were located in the middle row. Typists soon became so quick that they continually jammed the primitive machines. The inventor solved the problem by scrambling the letters on the keyboard and creating a deliberately inconvenient arrangement. This slowed down the typists and thus prevented them from accidentally jamming the typewriter. Although modern typewriters are virtually jam-proof, they still have the deliberately inefficient keyboard arrangement designed for the first primitive typing machines.

—PAUL STIRLING HAGERMAN,
The Odd, Mad World of Paul Stirling Hagerman

2   In all the world of living things, it is doubtful whether there is a more delicately balanced relationship than that of island life to its environment. This environment is a remarkably uniform one. In the midst of a great ocean, ruled by currents and winds that rarely shift their course, climate changes little. There are few natural enemies, perhaps none at all. The harsh struggle for existence that is the normal lot of continental life is softened on the islands. When this gentle pattern of life is abruptly changed, the island creatures have little ability to make the adjustments necessary for survival. —RACHEL CARSON, "The Birth of an Island"

Paragraphs have no set length. Typically, they average perhaps 100 words, ranging anywhere from 50 to 250 words. Paragraphs in books are usually longer than those written for the narrow columns of newspapers and magazines. Writers should be careful, however, not to construct extremely long paragraphs, especially those that exhaust one point or combine too many points. Short paragraphs often indicate inadequate development, although occasionally one-sentence paragraphs are used for emphasis (see paragraphs 32–34, page 340).

▲ Note: Introductory, concluding, and transitional paragraphs serve other purposes and are discussed in **32b[6]** and **33f**.

32a

Construct unified paragraphs.

In a unified paragraph, each sentence helps develop the central thought. Stating the central thought in a topic sentence will help you achieve unity.

(1) Make sure each sentence is related to the central thought.

Stick to your main idea; eliminate any information that is unrelated. Suppose, for instance, the main idea of your paragraph is "Computers help students in final editing." If you include sentences about searching for information through computers, you will disrupt the unity. Every sentence should pertain to how computers help with final editing. Notice in paragraph 3 how each sentence helps to show exactly what the writer means by the curious experiences referred to in the first sentence.

3   A number of curious experiences occur at the onset of sleep. A person just about to go to sleep may experience an electric shock, a flash of light, or a crash of thunder—but the most common sensation is that of floating or falling, which is why "falling asleep" is a scientifically valid description. A nearly universal occurrence at the beginning of sleep (although not everyone recalls it) is a sudden, uncoordinated jerk of the head, the limbs, or even the entire body. Most people tend to think of going to sleep as a slow slippage into oblivion, but the onset of sleep is not gradual at all. It happens in an instant. One moment the individual is awake, the next moment not. —PETER FARB, *Humankind*

As you check your paragraphs for unity, eliminate any information that does not clearly relate to the main idea, or add a sentence or a phrase to make its relevance to the main idea clear. Sometimes the relationship may be obvious to you but not to your reader. Sometimes too many major ideas may appear in a single paragraph. In that case you may need to reform or refocus your main idea either in your own mind or in a clearly stated topic sentence, or you may wish to develop each idea in a separate paragraph.

■ **Exercise 1** Note how each sentence in the following paragraph expresses a major idea. Select one sentence and develop it into a paragraph by using specific details and examples.

> My attitude toward high school has changed now that I am in college. I now wish that I had studied more in high school and paid more attention in class. It was easy to get a good grade and no one ever flunked a course. We didn't have to write much in any of my classes and as a result I feel pretty uncertain whenever I am asked to write anything. Also, we didn't have to read very much and now I have trouble getting through the long reading assignments that I have to do in my history course. I wish that I had taken a speed reading course in high school. In high school, I learned a lot of things outside of class but not much in class.

■ **Exercise 2** The following paragraph lacks unity since either the sentences do not relate to the main idea—the similarities between the coasts of Maine and Oregon—or the relationship to the main idea is not clear. Revise by making such connections clear and deleting unrelated sentences.

> When I visited the coast of Maine last summer, I noticed that it looked very much like the coast of Oregon. It was very cold and rainy in Maine and we had to wear coats even though it was late July. In Maine, the coastline is rocky and in many places evergreens march straight to the water. In other places, bluffs lined with evergreens overlook the sea. One day we saw a large sailboat driving hard toward some half-submerged rocks. In Oregon, pine-rimmed bluffs usually overlook the ocean, but sometimes the trees extend to a partly submerged rocky ledge or a pebble beach. Small islands, called sea stacks, dot this coastline much as the low, wooded islands lie offshore in Penobscot Bay. Lighthouses can be found here and there along both coastlines.

(2) State the main idea of the paragraph in a clearly constructed topic sentence.

A topic sentence embodies the central thought of a paragraph. Notice how the topic sentence of paragraph 4 (the first sentence) announces the idea of our reaction to eye behavior; it also suggests the approach of the paragraph by establishing an expectation that the writer will go on to provide an example.

4   Much of eye behavior is so subtle that we react to it only on the intuitive level. The next time you have a conversation with someone who makes you feel liked, notice what he does with his eyes. Chances are he looks at you more often than usual with glances a little longer than the normal. You interpret this as a sign—a polite one—that he is interested in you as a person rather than just in the topic of conversation. Probably you also feel that he is both self-confident and sincere.   —FLORA DAVIS,
        Inside Intuition: What We Know about Nonverbal Communication

Notice in paragraph 5 how the phrase "two flying-squirrel species" in the topic sentence suggests the approach the writer will follow.

5   There are two flying-squirrel species in North America, and their ranges overlap slightly. The northern species is found throughout Canada, Alaska and the Northern states. In mountains of the East and West, the species extends its range farther south but is restricted to the higher altitudes. The southern flying squirrel inhabits the forests of the Eastern states and southern Ontario, and a few isolated populations have also been found in Mexico and Central America. Fortunately for me, both species occur in Michigan, with their ranges meeting in the upper part of the state.   —NANCY WELLS-GOSLING, "The Little Squirrel That Flies"

The main idea of a paragraph is most often stated at or near the beginning, as in examples 4 and 5. It is sometimes also restated at the end to emphasize its importance. In paragraph 6, compare "the intolerable has become normal" with the final "Ugliness is accepted, no longer even noticed."

6   In the towns and cities of Ulster, the intolerable has become normal. The civic environment is scarred. In Belfast and Derry, it is hard to find a shop with windows; shop-

keepers have had so many broken that they are content to leave the boards up. Burned-out houses and shops are left as abandoned hulks. The army has run out its barbed wire, concrete and corrugated iron in dozens of checkpoints, barricades and gun emplacements. Ugliness is accepted, no longer even noticed.

—PAUL HARRISON, "The Dark Age of Ulster"

Occasionally, the topic sentence is not stated until the end of the paragraph, especially when the writer progresses from particulars—for instance, from specific examples—to a generalization, as in paragraph 7.

7   In the warmth of the inner Solar System a comet releases clouds of vapor and dust that form the glowing head and then leak into the tail, which is the cosmic equivalent of an oil slick. Pieces of the dust later hit the Earth, as meteors. A few survivors among the comets evolve into menacing lumps of dirt in tight orbits around the Sun. For these reasons comets are, in my opinion, best regarded as a conspicuous form of sky pollution.

—NIGEL CALDER, *The Comet Is Coming*

Occasionally, there is no topic sentence because the details unmistakably imply the central idea. Notice how the idea that perceptions change as persons change, although never explicitly stated, is clearly the central idea of the following paragraph.

8   Everything Chuck did that summer was kind, and helped me to grow normally. I would love to meet him now and thank him for all the strength I took from him. Every person probably encounters these "saints" again and again in his lifetime, without understanding their importance or being grateful. If I saw him now, the way he was then, I wonder if I would even appreciate Chuck. He was fresh out of the army, starting college on the GI Bill, had a cautious way of speaking, not much book culture. What hurts in all this is knowing that I probably would have condescended to someone like him at college, barely eight years after looking up to him as everything.   —PHILIP LOPATE, "Summer Camps"

■ **Exercise 3** Identify the topic sentences in the following paragraphs. If the main idea is implied, write out the implied topic sentence.

9 Ambivalence as a defining sensibility, widespread and full-blown, is something new. There is virtually nothing today about which thoughtful people—especially thoughtful younger people—do not feel mixed emotions. Every hankering, whether it's for a policy (like national health insurance), or a commodity (like microwave ovens), or a performer (like David Letterman), comes with disclaimers, a special codicil of qualifiers or qualms. —KURT ANDERSEN, *"Hot Mood"*

10 A TV set stood close to a wall in the small living room crowded with an assortment of chairs and tables. An aquarium crowded the mantelpiece of a fake fireplace. A lighted bulb inside the tank showed many colored fish swimming about in a haze of fish food. Some of it lay scattered on the edge of the shelf. The carpet underneath was sodden black. Old magazines and tabloids lay just about everywhere.
—BIENVENIDO SANTOS, "Immigration Blues"

11 Certainly the [U.S.] political problems, difficult and delicate though they may be, are not insoluble. Some, like the control or the liquidation of monopolies which stand in the way of individual initiative, have a long history in this country. Others, like the struggle to liberate individuals from the degrading fear of unemployment or old age or sickness, are less familiar—at least in the United States. Still others, like the overriding question of the relation between individual freedom and the intervention of the state, have a meaning for our generation which they did not have for generations before. But only a man who did not wish to find an answer to questions such as these would argue that no answer can be found.
—ARCHIBALD MacLEISH, "The Conquest of America"

■ **Exercise 4** Write a paragraph with a topic sentence at the beginning, another with the topic sentence at the end, and a third with the topic sentence at the beginning and restated at the end. Here are a few possible approaches.

1. Two reasons for . . .
2. An example of . . .
3. Two results of . . .
4. Fog can be defined as . . .

32b

Make paragraphs coherent by arranging ideas in a clear, logical order and by providing appropriate transitions.

A paragraph has coherence when the relationship among ideas is clear and the progression from one sentence to the next is easy for the reader to follow. To achieve coherence, arrange ideas in a clear, logical order. Also provide transitions between sentences (both within the paragraph and between paragraphs) by the effective use of pronouns, repetition, conjunctions, transitional phrases, and parallel structure.

ARRANGEMENT OF IDEAS

(1) Arrange ideas in a clear, logical order.

There are many ways to arrange ideas in a paragraph. One of the simplest is **chronological order**.

12   Standing in line at the unemployment office makes you feel very much the same as you did the first time you ever flunked a class or a test—as if you had a big red "F" for "Failure" printed across your forehead. I fantasize myself standing at the end of the line in a crisp and efficient blue suit, chin up, neat and straight as a corporate executive. As I move down the line I start to come unglued and a half hour later, when I finally reach the desk clerk, I am slouching and sallow in torn jeans, tennis shoes and a jacket from the Salvation Army, carrying my worldly belongings in a shopping bag and unable to speak.

—JAN HALVORSON, "How It Feels to Be Out of Work"

Descriptive passages are often arranged in **spatial order**. Starting from a single point of reference, the description can move from north to south, from near to distant, from left to right, and so on. Note the movement from the top of the plateau to the bottom of the gorge in paragraph 13, and from a broad to a close perspective in 14.

13   The highway, without warning, rolled off the plateau of green pastures and entered a wooded and rocky gorge; down, down, precipitously down to the Kentucky River. Along the north slope, man-high columns of ice clung to the limestone. The road dropped deeper until it crossed the river at Brooklyn Bridge. The gorge, hidden in the tableland and wholly unexpected, was the Palisades. At the bottom lay only enough ground for the river and a narrow strip of willow-rimmed floodplain.
                              —WILLIAM LEAST HEAT MOON, *Blue Highways*

14   Weasel! I'd never seen one wild before. He was ten inches long, thin as a curve, a muscled ribbon, brown as fruitwood, soft-furred, alert. His face was fierce, small and pointed as a lizard's; he would have made a good arrowhead. There was just a dot of chin, maybe two brown hairs' worth, and then the pure white fur began that spread down his underside. He had two black eyes I didn't see, any more than you see a window.   —ANNIE DILLARD,
                                        Teaching a Stone to Talk

Another useful arrangement is **order of importance** (climactic), from most important to least or from least to most. (See also **29c**). In paragraph 15 the author focuses on a hierarchy of intelligence, moving from lower to higher forms of life.

15   An ant cannot purposefully try anything new, and any ant that accidentally did so would be murdered by his colleagues. It is the ant colony as a whole that slowly learns over the ages. In contrast, even an earthworm has enough flexibility of brain to enable it to be taught to turn toward the left or right for food. Though rats are not able to reason

to any considerable degree, they can solve such problems as separating round objects from triangular ones when these have to do with health or appetite. Cats, with better brains, can be taught somewhat more, and young dogs a great deal. The higher apes can learn by insight as well as by trial and error. —GEORGE RUSSELL HARRISON, *What Man May Be*

Sometimes the movement within the paragraph is from **general to specific** or from **specific to general**. A paragraph may begin with a general statement or idea, which is then supported by particular details, as in paragraph 16, or it may begin with a striking detail or series of details and conclude with a summarizing statement, as in paragraph 17.

16   The *conventions* of a period are the inherited, invented, and prescribed formulas that the people who formed its culture generally understood. The traditional arrangement of areas and rooms in a temple or dwelling, the larger-than-life representations and rigid postures of gods and rulers, the appearance of a masked deity or hero to pronounce the prologue and epilogue of a Greek drama, the required fourteen lines of a sonnet, the repeated rhythmic patterns of dances, the way characters speak in rhymed meters in poetic drama and sing their lines in opera—all are conveniences that became conventions through their acceptance by a representative number of people whose commonly held values and attitudes formed a culture.
—WILLIAM FLEMING, *Arts and Ideas*

17   When we watch a person walk away from us, his image shrinks in size. But since we know for a fact that he is not shrinking, we make an unconscious correcting and "see" him as retaining his full stature. Past experience tells us what his true stature is with respect to our own. Any sane and dependable expectation of the future requires that he have the same stature when we next encounter him. Our perception is thus a prediction; it embraces the past and the future as well as the present.
—WARREN J. WITTREICH, "Visual Perception and Personality"

One common form of the general–specific pattern is **topic–restriction–illustration**, in which the writer announces the topic, restricts it, and illustrates the restricted topic. In paragraph 18, which is from an essay demonstrating how nature helps us to understand human beings, Jacob S. Bronowski announces the topic—the physical differences between man and other animals—restricts it in the first sentence to the differences between man and a particular animal, and then illustrates it with the act of vaulting.

18   Naturally there are physical differences between man and the other animals, even between man and the apes. In the act of vaulting, the athlete grasps his pole, for example, with an exact grip that no ape can quite match. Yet such differences are secondary by comparison with the overriding difference, which is that the athlete is an adult whose behavior is not driven by his immediate environment, as animal actions are. In themselves, his actions make no practical sense at all; they are an exercise that is not directed to the present. The athlete's mind is fixed ahead of him, building up his skill; and he vaults in imagination into the future.
—JACOB BRONOWSKI, "The Athlete and the Gazelle"

A variation of this pattern—**topic–restriction–illustration–topic**—restates the topic at the end of the paragraph.

In the **question–answer** pattern, the first sentence asks a question that the supporting sentences answer.

19   What's wrong with the student-union bookshop? Everything. It's interested in selling sweatshirts and college mugs rather than good books. Its staff often is incompetent and uncivil. The manager may not be intelligent enough even to order a sufficient number of copies of required textbooks for the beginning of a term. As for more lively books— why, there are masses of paperbacks, perhaps, that could be procured at any drugstore; there are a few shelves or racks of volumes labeled "Gift Books," usually lavishly illustrated and inordinately costly, intended as presents to fond

parents; but there are virtually no *book* books, of the sort that students might like to buy.

—RUSSELL KIRK, "From the Academy: Campus Bookshops"

Another common paragraph arrangement is the **problem–solution** pattern, in which the first sentence or two states the problem and the rest of the paragraph suggests the solution.

20   That many women would be happier not pursuing careers or intellectual adventures is only part of the truth. The whole truth is that many *people* would be. If society had the clear sight to assure men as well as women that there is no shame in preferring to stay non-competitively and non-aggressively at home, many masculine neuroses and ulcers would be avoided, and many children would enjoy the benefit of being brought up by a father with a talent for the job instead of by a mother with no talent for it but a sense of guilt about the lack. —BRIGID BROPHY, "Women"

Paragraphs 12 through 20 illustrate eight of the many possible types of arrangement within the paragraph. Any order or combination of orders is satisfactory as long as the sequence of ideas is logical and clear.

■ **Exercise 5** Identify the pattern of each of the following paragraphs (chronological, spatial, climactic, general to specific, specific to general, topic–restriction–illustration, question–answer, problem–solution). Be prepared to discuss how each paragraph follows the pattern you have identified.

21   Perhaps the most mystifying of the habits peculiar to whales is their "singing." Humpback whales are the most renowned for a wide range of tones, and whole herds often join together in "songs" composed of complete sequences, which, repeated, can last for hours. Some evenings, we listened to the humpbacks starting to make a few sounds, like musicians tuning their instruments. Then, one by one, they began to sing. Underwater canyons made the sounds echo, and it seemed as though we were in a cathedral listening to the faithful alternating verses of a psalm.

—JACQUES-YVES COUSTEAU, "Jonah's Complaint"

22   The so-called "Western Code" never really existed. Men bent on killing did so in the most efficient and expeditious way they knew. Jesse James was shot in the back by Bob Ford as he stood on a chair adjusting a picture. Ben Thompson was led into a trap in a theater and shot down with his friend King Fisher. Billy the Kid died as he entered a darkened room. Wild Bill Hickok was shot from behind while he was playing poker. In each case the victim had no chance to defend himself.   —JOSEPH G. ROSA,
"The Gunfighter"

23   We have an image of what a leader ought to be. We even recognize the physical signs: leaders may not necessarily be tall, but they must have bigger-than-life, commanding features—LBJ's nose and ear lobes, Ike's broad grin. A trademark also comes in handy: Lincoln's stovepipe hat, JFK's rocker. We expect our leaders to stand out a little, not to be like ordinary men. Half of President Ford's trouble lay in the fact that, if you closed your eyes for a moment, you couldn't remember his face, figure or clothes. A leader should have an unforgettable identity, instantly and permanently fixed in people's minds.
—MICHAEL KORDA, *"What Makes a Leader?"*

24   The humorous story is told gravely; the teller does his best to conceal the fact that he even dimly suspects that there is anything funny about it; but the teller of the comic story tells you beforehand that it is one of the funniest things he has ever heard, then tells it with eager delight, and is the first person to laugh when he gets through. And sometimes, if he has had good success, he is so glad and happy that he will repeat the "nub" of it and glance around from face to face, collecting applause, and then repeat it again. It is a pathetic thing to see.   —MARK TWAIN,
"How to Tell a Story"

25   The inflated whale lies on her side, washed by red waves of her own blood. Already the bright stain on the bright sea is huge and thick, as if it would never wash away. The blood spurting from the wounds is a deep mammalian

red, but on the surface of the sea it turns red red, as vivid as a dye, and the amount of it is awful. —PETER MATTHIESSEN, "The Killing of the Whale"

26   Who is to say, then, if there is any right path to the top, or even to say what the top consists of? Obviously the colleges don't have more than a partial answer—otherwise the young would not be so disaffected with an education that they consider vapid. Obviously business does not have the answer—otherwise the young would not be so scornful of its call to be an organization man. —WILLIAM ZINSSER, "The Right to Fail"

■ **Exercise 6** Using paragraphs 12 through 20 as models, write paragraphs following three of the arrangements described in this section (chronological, spatial, climactic, general to specific, specific to general, topic–restriction–illustration, question–answer, problem–solution). Use as possible topics the following: insects, football, desserts, sport shoes, or any other topics your instructor approves.

■ **Exercise 7** Examine paragraphs from your own writing in other projects you have had and find examples of three of the arrangements described in this section.

TRANSITIONS

The linking of sentences and paragraphs by transitional devices such as pronouns, repetition of key words or ideas, conjunctions and other transitional expressions, and parallel structures helps create a coherent paper (see also sections **26, 28**).

(2) Link sentences by using pronouns.

In paragraph 27 the writer links sentences by using the pronouns *their* and *they*. Although these same two pronouns are used repeatedly, their referent, "easy victims," is always clear.

27   Several movements characterized easy victims: their strides were either very long or very short; they moved awkwardly, raising their left legs with their left arms (instead of alternating them); on each step, they tended to lift their whole foot up and then place it down (less muggable sorts took steps in which their feet rocked from heel to toe). Overall, the people rated most muggable walked as if they were in conflict with themselves; they seemed to make each move in the most difficult way possible.

—CARIN RUBENSTEIN, "Body Language That Speaks to Muggers"

(3) Link sentences by repeating words, phrases, or ideas.

In paragraph 28, the repetition of the key word "wave" links the sentences. (The repetition also serves to provide emphasis: see **29e**.)

28   The weekend is over, and we drive down the country road from the cottage to the pier, passing out our last supply of waves. We wave at people walking and wave at people riding. We wave at people we know and wave at people who are strangers.   —ELLEN GOODMAN,

"Waving Good-Bye to the Country"

(4) Link sentences by using conjunctions and other transitional expressions.

Such expressions demonstrate the logical relationship between ideas. Notice the subtle changes in the relationship between two clauses linked by different conjunctions.

Mary laughed, and Bill frowned.
Mary laughed while Bill frowned.
Mary laughed because Bill frowned.
Mary laughed, so Bill frowned.
Mary laughed; later Bill frowned.

Here is a list of some frequently used transitional connectives arranged according to the kinds of relationships they establish.

1. *Alternative and addition:* or, nor, and, and then, moreover, further, furthermore, besides, likewise, also, too, again, in addition, even more important, next, first, second, third, in the first place, in the second place, finally, last.
2. *Comparison:* similarly, likewise, in like manner.
3. *Contrast:* but, yet, or, and yet, however, still, nevertheless, on the other hand, on the contrary, conversely, even so, notwithstanding, for all that, in contrast, at the same time, although this may be true, otherwise, nonetheless.
4. *Place:* here, beyond, nearby, opposite to, adjacent to, on the opposite side.
5. *Purpose:* to this end, for this purpose, with this object.
6. *Cause, result:* so, for, hence, therefore, accordingly, consequently, thus, thereupon, as a result, then, because.
7. *Summary, repetition, exemplification, intensification:* to sum up, in brief, on the whole, in sum, in short, as I have said, in other words, that is, to be sure, as has been noted, for example, for instance, in fact, indeed, to tell the truth, in any event.
8. *Time:* meanwhile, at length, soon, after a few days, in the meantime, afterward, later, now, then, in the past, while.

(5) Link sentences by using parallel structures.

Parallelism is the repetition of the sentence pattern or of other grammatical structures. See also **26**.

In paragraph 29, notice that the first three sentences are structured in the same way:

> When you're three years old . . . , that's expected.
> When you're six . . . , you deserve some credit. . . .
> When you're nine . . . , you should be applauded. . . .

Repeating this pattern emphasizes the close relationship of the ideas.

29   When you're three years old and stick mashed potatoes up your nose, that's expected. When you're six and make your bed but it looks like you're still in it, you deserve some credit for trying. When you're nine and prepare the family meal but the casserole looks worse than the kitchen, you should be applauded for your effort. But somewhere along the line, some responsible adult should say, "You're too old for this nonsense."
                                                                    —DAN KILEY,
The Peter Pan Syndrome: Men Who Have Never Grown Up

■ **Exercise 8**   Indicate the linking devices in the following paragraphs by circling the pronouns, underlining repeated words and phrases, bracketing conjunctions, double underlining transitional phrases, and placing parentheses around parallel structures. Prepare for a class discussion.

30   Electronic music is a new departure from orthodox, or generally accepted, music in that it is electrically originated or modified sound. This sound is the output of electric pianos, organs, synthesizers, saxophones, guitars, flutes, violins, trumpets, and many other instruments. It is the product of composers who use tape recorders and tape manipulation to distort, for better or worse, conventional sounds. Also, it is the sounds we hear in concerts and on records that use amplification to boost or alter the volume of instruments.
                    —MERRILL C. LEHRER, "The Electronic Music Revolution"

31   There are obvious advantages for the writers of allegorical tales like country music's to have a conventionalized geography to reinforce the message. But why does country music use *this* image of America? Why is country music so pleased with the South and so upset with the North? The answer to this question lies not in the actual geography of the United States, but in how country music's audience perceives the geography of the United States. It is not a question of what America is, but of what America means to these people. As a result, the question has to do with far

more than just a style of singing; it has to do with the attitudes of the millions of Americans who listen to country
music—attitudes about regional differences in American
society, about the role of the media as part of the American power structure, and about the value of progress in general. —BEN MARSH, "A Rose-Colored Map"

■ **Exercise 9**   Revise the sentences and add linking devices in the
following paragraph so the thought flows smoothly from one sentence to
the next.

Cable television sounds like a good deal at first. All available
local channels can be piped into a television set for a relatively low
cost per month. The reception is clear—a real bonus in fringe and
rural areas. Several channels for news and local access are in the
basic monthly fee. A cable connection to a second or third TV set
costs extra. In most places subscribers have to pay as much as
thirty dollars a month extra to get the channels like Home Box
Office and The Disney Channel. The movies change each month.
The pay-TV movie channels run the same films over and over during a month's time. Many of the films offered each month are box
office flops or reruns of old movies that can be viewed on regular
channels. Cable television isn't really a bargain.

(6) Link paragraphs with clear transitions.

Transitions between paragraphs are as important as transitions between sentences and are achieved by many of the
same devices—repetition of words or ideas, conjunctions
and other transitional expressions, and parallel structures.
Such devices are usually evident in the first sentence of a
paragraph.

You can repeat a word or idea from the last paragraph in
the first sentence of the new paragraph.

Psychologists call these toys—these furry animals and old,
cozy baby blankets—*"transitional objects"*; that is, objects
that help the child move back and forth between the exac-
tions of everyday life and the world of wish and dream.

Superstitions have some of the qualities of these *transitional objects*.   —MARGARET MEAD, "New Superstitions for Old"

No man was born to anything, except perhaps to a chance to show how far he could rise. Life was competition.

Yet along with *this feeling* had come a deep sense of belonging to a national community. —BRUCE CATTON,
"Grant and Lee: A Study in Contrasts"

You can use transitional words or phrases to connect paragraphs.

The decision was made to reduce the thickness of the paper and to provide different-sized bags to go with larger or smaller orders.

As a result, the supermarket chain's profits dropped further. —LEONARD SILK, "What Economics Can Do for You"

You can use parallel structures to demonstrate relationships between paragraphs.

32   I have a dream that one day on the red hills of Georgia the sons of former slaves and the sons of former slaveowners will be able to sit down together at the table of brotherhood.

33   I have a dream that one day even the state of Mississippi, a desert state sweltering with the heat of injustice and oppression, will be transformed into an oasis of freedom and justice.

34   I have a dream that my four little children will one day live in a nation where they will not be judged by the color of their skin but by the content of their character.
—MARTIN LUTHER KING, JR., "I Have a Dream" Speech

Sometimes a transitional paragraph serves as a bridge between two paragraphs. Ordinarily, such a paragraph is short (often consisting of only one sentence) because the writer intends it to be merely a signpost. Notice below that the first noun phrase in the transitional paragraph 36 echoes the preceding key idea and that the second noun phrase points to a fact to be explained next.

35   Indeed, instead of seeing evolution as a smooth process, many of today's life scientists and archaeologists are

studying the "theory of catastrophes" to explain "gaps" and "jumps" in the multiple branches of the evolutionary record. Others are studying small changes that may have been amplified through feedback into sudden structural transformations. Heated controversies divide the scientific community over every one of these issues.

36   But all such controversies are dwarfed by a single history-changing fact.

37   One day in 1953 at Cambridge in England a young biologist, James Watson, was sitting in the Eagle pub when his colleague, Francis Crick, ran excitedly in and announced to "everyone within hearing distance that we had found the secret of life." They had. Watson and Crick had unraveled the structure of DNA.

—ALVIN TOFFLER, *The Third Wave*

32c

Develop the paragraph with details and examples.

Many short paragraphs are adequately developed and supply enough information within the context of the essay to satisfy the reader. For example, the following paragraph, although only one sentence, contains considerable detail.

38   If environment refers to what's around us, then our environment also includes the awesome coast of Oregon, the sparkling desert nights in southern Arizona, the Everglades glowing red in the summer dawn, the waltzing wheatfields of Kansas, the New York City skyline at dusk, the luxurious cabin of a jet airliner, air-conditioned autos and broad turnpikes and winding parkways, the pretty clothes of American women, and the laughter of children.

—EDWIN A. ROBERTS, JR.,
"Struggling to Control Growing Trash Heaps"

Sometimes short paragraphs can be combined if they deal with the same idea. More often, however, short paragraphs need to be developed with more specific details or examples.

(1) Develop with specific details.

Notice how the series of details in the following example support the topic sentence (underlined).

39   Poised for that leap, the pole-vaulter is a capsule of human abilities; the grasp of the hand, the arch of the foot, the muscles of the shoulder and pelvis—the pole itself, in which energy is stored and released like a bow firing an arrow. The radical character in that complex is the sense of foresight, that is, the ability to fix an objective ahead and rigorously hold his attention on it. The athlete's performance unfolds a continuous plan; from one extreme to the other, it is the invention of the pole, the concentration of the mind at the moment before leaping, which give it the stamp of humanity.   —JACOB BRONOWSKI,
"The Athlete and the Gazelle"

Paragraph 40 uses details to explain why violence is both impractical and immoral.

40   Violence as a way of achieving racial justice is both impractical and immoral. It is impractical because it is a descending spiral ending in destruction for all. The old law of an eye for an eye leaves everybody blind. It is immoral because it seeks to humiliate the opponent rather than win his understanding; it seeks to annihilate rather than to convert. Violence is immoral because it thrives on hatred rather than love. It destroys community and makes brotherhood impossible. It leaves society in monologue rather than dialogue. Violence ends by defeating itself. It creates bitterness in the survivors and brutality in the destroyers. A voice echoes through time saying to every potential Peter, "Put up your sword." History is cluttered with the wreckage of nations that failed to follow this command.
—MARTIN LUTHER KING, JR.,
"Three Types of Resistance to Oppression"

(2) Develop with examples.

Use appropriate and specific examples to clarify your ideas. The following definition may be unclear without the italicized example.

> A euphemism is the substitution of a pleasant expression for an unpleasant one, *such as "passed away" for "died."*

You can use several closely related examples, as in paragraph 41, or one striking example, as in paragraph 42, to clarify your idea.

41   The letters were trivial in content. They began with criticism of the poem each had sent in the letter before, and proceeded into an endless banter, in which each related the music he had heard, daily episodes in his family, impressions of girls he found beautiful, reports of books he had read, poetic experiences in which worlds would be revealed from single words, and so on. Neither the twenty-year-old youth nor the fifteen-year-old boy tired of this habit.

> —MISHIMA YUKIO, "The Boy Who Wrote Poetry"

42   He was one of the greatest scientists the world has ever known, yet if I had to convey the essence of Albert Einstein in a single word, I would choose *simplicity*. Perhaps an anecdote will help. Once, caught in a downpour, he took off his hat and held it under his coat. Asked why, he explained, with admirable logic, that the rain would damage the hat, but his hair would be none the worse for its wetting. This knack for going instinctively to the heart of the matter was the secret of his major scientific discoveries—this and his extraordinary feeling for beauty.

> —BANESH HOFFMANN, "My Friend, Albert Einstein"

Details and examples clarify and explain your point.

■ **Exercise 10** Develop the following topic sentences with details and/or examples.

1. The biographies of famous people suggest that there are special characteristics that make such persons successful.
2. It was the filthiest room that I had ever seen.

3. My friend Bill was the soul of generosity.
4. I grew up in the friendliest neighborhood in the world.

■ **Exercise 11**   Select a paragraph from your own writing. Rewrite it adding details or an appropriate example.

32d

Use various strategies of paragraph development.

You can learn to write good paragraphs by studying the various techniques professional writers use to develop ideas. All the strategies for developing paragraphs discussed in the following pages are useful for developing whole compositions. (See also section **33**.)

The more you read, the more you will find that paragraphs are rarely developed by a single method; a combination is more common. For example, the formal definition may be developed through both classification and contrast. No one method, or no one combination, is better than another except insofar as it better suits your purpose. As you study the following illustrations of good paragraphs, notice how each main idea is developed.

(1) Narrate a series of events.

A narration is a discussion of a sequence of events, normally in the order in which they occur, that develops the point you are making. This form often uses time markers such as *then, later,* or *at a later date.* (Longer narratives often begin in the middle of a sequence of events and contain flashbacks to earlier events.) The narrative must be closely related to your main idea and must develop that idea in some way. Notice how Denis Waitley in paragraph 43 uses narrative to develop the idea in his topic sentence.

43 It's amazing how parents continue to pass their own hang-ups on to their children. It reminds me of the story about the young bride who cooked a ham for her new husband. Before putting it in the pan, she cut off both ends. When her husband asked her why she did that, she replied that her mother had always done it that way. At a later date, when they were having baked ham dinner at her mother's home, he asked her, casually, why she cut both ends off the ham. The mother shrugged and said she really didn't know, except that her mother had always done it that way. Finally, he asked the grandmother why she always cut the ends off the ham before she baked it. She looked at him suspiciously, replying, "Because my baking dish is too small!"
         —DENIS WAITLEY, *Seeds of Greatness*

(2) Describe to make a point.

Focus your description according to your purpose. In describing your car you would emphasize certain features to a prospective buyer, others to a mechanic who is going to repair it, and still others to a friend who wants to borrow it.

  Present descriptive details in a clear order—from near to far, from general to particular, from right to left, from top to bottom—thus providing an orderly scheme for the reader. In paragraph 44, Thomas Merton uses a near–far perspective, enabling the reader to share his experience of approaching the monastery that was to become his home. Notice also his use of metaphors ("a barrier and a defense against the world"), similes ("as grey as lead"), and personification ("The tires sang"). See figurative language in **20a(4)**

44 I looked at the rolling country, and at the pale ribbon of road in front of us, stretching out as grey as lead in the light of the moon. Then suddenly I saw a steeple that shone like silver in the moonlight, growing into sight from behind a

rounded knoll. The tires sang on the empty road, and, breathless, I looked at the monastery that was revealed before me as we came over the rise. At the end of an avenue of trees was a big rectangular block of buildings, all dark, with a church crowned by a tower and a steeple and a cross: and the steeple was as bright as platinum and the whole place was as quiet as midnight and lost in the all-absorbing silence and solitude of the fields. Behind the monastery was a dark curtain of woods, and over to the west was a wooded valley, and beyond that a rampart of wooded hills, a barrier and a defense against the world.

—THOMAS MERTON, *The Seven Storey Mountain*

Write descriptions that appeal to all of the senses, not just sight. Alice Walker in paragraph 45 makes her description of Mr. Sweet vivid by using the senses of touch, smell, and sound in addition to sight.

45   We never felt anything of Mr. Sweet's age when we played with him. We loved his wrinkles and would draw some on our brows to be like him, and his white hair was my special treasure and he knew it and would never come to visit us just after he had had his hair cut off at the barbershop. Once he came to our house for something, probably to see my father about fertilizer for his crops because, although he never paid the slightest attention to his crops, he liked to know what things would be best to use on them if he ever did. Anyhow, he had not come with his hair since he had just had it shaved off at the barbershop. He wore a huge straw hat to keep off the sun and also to keep his head away from me. But as soon as I saw him I ran up and demanded that he take me up and kiss me with his funny beard which smelled so strongly of tobacco. Looking forward to burying my small fingers into his woolly hair I threw away his hat only to find he had done something to his hair, that it was no longer there! I let out a squall which made my mother think that Mr. Sweet had finally dropped me in the well or something and from that day I've been wary of men in hats. However, not long after Mr. Sweet

showed up with his hair grown out and just as white and kinky and impenetrable as it ever was. —ALICE WALKER, "To Hell with Dying"

(3) Explain a process.

Process paragraphs, in explaining how something is done or made, often use both description and narration. You might describe the items used in the process and then narrate the steps in the process, following a chronological arrangement, as in paragraph 46.

46   The best of all scientific tricks with an egg is the well-known one in which air pressure forces a peeled hard-boiled egg into a glass milk bottle and then forces it out again undamaged. The mouth of the bottle must be only slightly smaller than the egg, and so you must be careful not to use too large an egg or too small a bottle. It is impossible to push the egg into the bottle. To get the egg through the mouth you must heat the air in the bottle. That is best done by standing the bottle in boiling water for a few minutes. Put the egg upright on the mouth and take the bottle off the stove. As the air in the bottle cools it contracts, creating a partial vacuum that draws the peeled egg inside. To get the egg out again invert the bottle so that the egg falls into the neck. Place the opening of the bottle against your mouth and blow vigorously. This will compress the air in the bottle. When you stop blowing, the air expands, pushing the egg through the neck of the bottle and into your waiting hands. —MARTIN GARDNER, "Mathematical Games"

(4) Show cause and effect.

A paragraph that explores causes raises the question of "why" and must answer that question to the satisfaction of the reader. (Make sure to avoid the fallacy of assuming that since one event precedes another it is necessarily the cause of that event [see **31c**, False cause].) Paragraph 47 provides several reasons why the dollar became the basis of American currency.

47 Why did the dollar, a Spanish monetary unit, become the basis of American currency rather than the British pound sterling, to which the Americans were accustomed? In part, it was a reaction against all things British. More important, there was more Spanish than British coin circulating in the colonies and states in the late eighteenth century. The British paid in trade goods for the American products they purchased, and they preferred British coin for what they sold to the colonies. Thus pounds tended to flow back to Great Britain. But the colonists had a favorable balance of trade with Spanish America—selling more than they bought—so Spanish coin was comparatively abundant.
                —JOSEPH CONLIN, *The American Past*

Paragraphs can also be developed by demonstrating effects, as in the following paragraph, which discusses the damage from acid rain.

48 What are these effects? What do acids do to lakes, streams, and other substances? Acids have different effects on different materials. In the case of statues, monuments, and stone buildings, acids simply break down the composition of minerals—slowly, for certain, but there is a definite breakdown. If you pour soda onto a hard crust of bread, the crust will hold up for awhile, but soon it will start to melt away and will eventually fall apart. Of course the presence of buffers combats the destruction but if, somehow, the acids become stronger (or the buffers weaker), the defense will be less powerful. More immediately noticeable effects can be seen in aquatic and terrestrial environments. Acids can leach essential nutrients from lakes, streams and soils. They can also increase the ability of toxic metals (lead and mercury, for example) to dissolve into a medium. When these metals are released into water, for example, they can cause pipes to corrode faster, fish to become contaminated and die, and plants to be destroyed. Whole habitats can be wiped out and have been. There are lakes in the Adiron-

dacks which have become completely barren of all life due to the devastation of acid rain. —KELLY SHEA, "Acid Rain"

(5) Compare and contrast to develop an idea.

A comparison points out similarities; a contrast points out differences. A comparison or contrast may be organized in either of two ways (or a combination of them), the choice depending on the writer's purpose. Writers often use both methods for the sake of variation. Daniel Boorstin uses the *unit-by-unit method* in paragraph 49, in which he gives a detailed history first of the term *discover* and then of the term *explore*. He switches in the next paragraph (50) to the *part-by-part method,* alternating between the definitions of *discoverer* and *explorer*.

49   Columbus was a discoverer and not an explorer. The crucial distinction between these two roles we can see in the origins of our English words. The etymology of the word "discover" is obvious. Its primary meaning is to uncover, or to disclose to view. The discoverer, then, is a *finder*. He shows us what he already knew was there. Columbus set out to "discover," to find, the westward oceanic route to Asia. Of course he knew the ocean, and he knew of Asia. He set out to find the way. The word "explore" has quite different connotations. Appropriately, too, it has a disputed etymology. Some say it comes from *ex* (out) and *plorare* (to cry out), on the analogy of "deplore." The better view appears to be that it comes from *ex (out) and plorare* (from *pluere*, to flow). Either etymology reminds us that the explorer is one who surprises (and so makes people cry out) or one who makes new knowledge flow out.

50   The discoverer simply uncovers, but the explorer opens. The discoverer concludes a search; he is a finder. The explorer begins a search; he is a seeker. And he opens the way for other seekers. The discoverer is the expert at what is known to be there. The explorer is willing to take chances. He is the adventurer who risks *un*certain paths to the *un*known. Every age is inclined to give its laurels to the

discoverers, those who finally arrive at the long-thought-inaccessible known destination. But posterity—the whole human community—owes its laurels to the happener-upon dark continents of the earth and of the mind. The courageous wanderer in worlds never known to be there is the explorer.   —DANIEL BOORSTIN, "The Exploring Spirit"

Two valuable kinds of comparisons are analogy and metaphor. A *metaphor* is a figure of speech (see **20a[4]**). An *analogy,* often used in argument, makes a point by comparing a complex or unfamiliar concept to a simple or familiar one or by comparing two familiar concepts that are not ordinarily thought to be similar. In paragraph 51, the writer draws an analogy between controlling one's own life and controlling the ball in a pinball machine.

51   A player is not powerless to control the ball's wild flight any more than man is powerless to control his own life. He may nudge the machine with hands, arms, or hips, jogging it just enough to change the angle of the ball's descent. And he is armed with "flippers" which can propel the ball back up the playfield, aiming at the targets with the richest pay-offs. But, just as man's boldest strokes and bravest ventures often boomerang, so an ill-timed flip can ricochet the ball straight down "death alley," and a too vigorous nudge will send the machine into "tilt." Winning pinball, like rewarding life, requires delicate touch, fine calibrations, careful discrimination between boldness and folly.

—ANTHONY LUKAS, "Pinball"

Avoid false analogies—assuming that because two things are alike in some ways they are alike in all ways (see **31c**, False analogy).

(6) Use classification and division for a purpose.

Classify objects and ideas by placing them in larger groups that share certain common characteristics. When you classify chocolate pudding as a dessert, you tell your reader that, like most desserts, it is probably sweet and high in calories. Divide by separating objects and ideas into parts that are smaller. A store manager might group books according to publisher for his own inventory or according to types—biography, science fiction, mystery, and so forth—for his customers.

Classification and *division* represent two different perspectives; ideas may be put into groups (classification) or split into subclasses (division) on the basis of a dividing principle. Apples may be divided on the basis of color for a table decoration or according to taste for eating. Classification and division often work together. In paragraph 52, thin people are classified according to the personality characteristics they display.

52   Caesar was right. Thin people need watching. I've been watching them for most of my adult life, and I don't like what I see. When these narrow fellows spring at me, I quiver to my toes. Thin people come in all personalities, most of them menacing. You've got your "together" thin person, your mechanical thin person, your condescending thin person, your tsk-tsk thin person, your efficiency-expert thin person. All of them are dangerous.
        —SUZANNE BRITT JORDAN, "That Lean and Hungry Look"

Analysis is a kind of division that breaks an object or idea into its elements. In paragraph 53, the author analyzes a factory trawler by breaking it into "four essential elements."

53   Common to all factory trawlers are four essential elements that set them apart from the generations of fishing vessels that preceded them. These are a stern ramp or slipway for the rapid recovery of nets from astern (rather than over the side), a sheltered belowdecks factory section with assembly-line machines to gut and fillet fish (as opposed to cleaning by hand on an exposed main deck), an ammonia or freon refrigerating plant for the quick freezing and frozen storage of fish (in place of heavy and space-consuming

chopped ice), and equipment to make fishmeal (to utilize both the factory leavings and trash or nonmarketable fish).

—WILLIAM W. WARNER,
Distant Water: The Fate of the North Atlantic Fisherman

(7) Formulate a definition.

Paragraphs of definition explain. A *formal* definition puts a concept into a class and then differentiates it from other members of the class.

TERM	CLASS	DIFFERENCE
A tornado is a	storm	characterized by a funnel shaped cloud.
A concerto is a	symphonic piece	performed by one or more solo instruments and orchestra.

The *difference* distinguishes the *term* from all other members of the *class*. Note that the definition

A *stool* is a piece of furniture used for sitting

does not distinguish the stool from other pieces of furniture such as a couch or a chair. If other differences (for instance, "used for seating one person," or "without arms or back") are used, the definition is improved. Putting the term in as small a class as possible makes the difference step easier. For example, distinguishing a lion from other members of the class of *wild animals* would be easier than distinguishing it from the larger class of all *animals*. Paragraph 54 defines volcanoes by putting them in a class ("landforms") and by distinguishing them ("built of molten material") from other members of that class. The definition is then clarified by examples.

54   Volcanos are landforms built of molten material that has spewed out onto the earth's surface. Such molten rock is called *lava*. Volcanos may be no larger than small hills, or thousands of feet high. All have a characteristic cone

shape. Some well-known mountains are actually volcanos.
Examples are Mt. Fuji (Japan), Mt. Lassen (California),
Mt. Hood (Oregon), Mt. Etna and Mt. Vesuvius (Italy),
and Paricutin (Mexico). The Hawaiian Islands are all immense volcanos whose summits rise above the ocean, and
these volcanos are still quite active.

—JOEL AREM. *Rocks and Minerals*

Definitions may be clarified and extended by example, as
in paragraph 54, or by details, synonyms, or etymology (the
history of the word). Synonyms are often only one or two
words enclosed in commas immediately following the term.

Sophomores, *second-year students*, derive their name from
two Greek words meaning "wise fool."

For an example of an extended definition developed by etymology, see paragraph 49.

COMBINING STRATEGIES

Most paragraphs are developed by a combination of methods. Some good paragraphs almost defy analysis. The important consideration is not that a specific method is used to
develop the paragraph, but that the development is clear,
complete, and appropriate. The strategies described in this
subsection (**32d**) allow you to explore options for developing
your ideas.

■ **Exercise 12** Prepare for a class discussion of the following paragraphs. Identify topic sentences or main ideas (**32a**), transitions (**32b**),
and methods of development (**32c** and **32d**).

55   Yet along with this feeling had come a deep sense of
belonging to a national community. The Westerner who
developed a farm, opened a shop or set up in business as a
trader, could hope to prosper only as his own community
prospered—and his community ran from the Atlantic to the
Pacific and from Canada down to Mexico. If the land was
settled, with towns and highways and accessible markets,

he could better himself. He saw his fate in terms of the nation's own destiny. As its horizons expanded, so did his. He had, in other words, an acute dollars-and-cents stake in the continued growth and development of his country.

—BRUCE CATTON, "Grant and Lee: A Study in Contrasts"

56   Alcatraz Island is covered with flowers now: orange and yellow nasturtiums, geraniums, sweet grass, blue iris, black-eyed Susans. Candytuft springs up through the cracked concrete in the exercise yard. Ice plant carpets the rusting catwalks. "WARNING! KEEP OFF! U.S. PROPERTY," the sign still reads, big and yellow and visible for perhaps a quarter of a mile, but since March 21, 1963, the day they took the last thirty or so men off the island and sent them to prisons less expensive to maintain, the warning has been only *pro forma,* the gun turrets empty, the cell blocks abandoned. It is not an unpleasant place to be, out there on Alcatraz with only the flowers and the wind and a bell buoy moaning and the tide surging through the Golden Gate, but to like a place like that you have to want a moat.

—JOAN DIDION, "Rock of Ages"

57   Both NASA and Columbus made not one but a series of voyages. NASA landed men on six different parts of the moon. Columbus made four voyages to different parts of what he remained convinced was the east coast of Asia. As a result both NASA and Columbus had to keep coming back to the Government with their hands out, pleading for refinancing. In each case the reply of the Government became, after a few years: "This is all very impressive, but what earthly good is it to anyone back home?" —TOM WOLFE, "Columbus and the Moon"

58   Sound has shaped the bodies of many beasts. Noise tapped away at the bullfrog until his ears became bigger than his eyes. Now he hears so well that at the slightest sound of danger he quickly plops to safety under a sunken leaf. The rabbit has long ears to hear the quiet "whoosh" of the owl's wings, while the grasshopper's ears are on the

base of his abdomen, the lowest point of his body, where he can detect the tread of a crow's foot or the stealthy approach of a shrew.   —JEAN GEORGE, "That Astounding Creator—Nature"

59   Just as I meant "shimmer" literally I mean "grammar" literally. Grammar is a piano I play by ear, since I seem to have been out of school the year the rules were mentioned. All I know about grammar is its infinite power. To shift the structure of a sentence alters the meaning of that sentence, as definitely and inflexibly as the position of a camera alters the meaning of the object photographed. Many people know about camera angles now, but not so many know about sentences. The arrangement of the words matters, and the arrangement you want can be found in the picture in your mind. The picture dictates the arrangement. The picture dictates whether this will be a sentence with or without clauses, a sentence that ends hard or a dying-fall sentence, long or short, active or passive. The picture tells you how to arrange the words and the arrangement of the words tells you, or tells me, what's going on in the picture. *Nota bene* [Note well].   —JOAN DIDION, "Why I Write"

■ **Exercise 13**   Write paragraphs using any of the strategies of development described in **32d**. Start with one of the following topic sentences.

1. A dog is the best friend a person can have.
2. Tying your shoe is more complicated than it looks.
3. High school courses are very different from college courses.
4. There are three kinds of friends who will help you out in an emergency.

33
THE WHOLE COMPOSITION

Learn to plan, draft, and revise your compositions effectively.

No writing takes place in a vacuum. The rhetorical situation—purpose, audience, and occasion—determines your tone and shapes your writing (**33a**). Whenever you write, you engage in a process of developing an appropriate topic (**33b**) for a certain audience. You will explore and gather information and focus the subject (**33c**), form a thesis (**33d**), and then develop an appropriate plan of organization (**33e**). You will probably revise several drafts before preparing a final version (**33f–33g**).

This process of planning, drafting, and revising is seldom as neat and straightforward as inexperienced writers may suppose. As you move through the process, you may need to engage in any of the activities several times. For example, you may need to go back and collect more ideas. Or you may write a draft only to discover that you have strayed from your main idea (or thesis). Such a discovery is not the catastrophe it may seem at first: writing is one of the best ways of clarifying your own views and gaining new insights. You may want to go back and change your thesis, or even throw it out and start with a new one. Whatever repetition of the steps in the process is necessary, the effort will be worthwhile if the result is a clear, coherent, unified composition.

As you read the following essay, notice how the author arouses your interest by developing his main idea through use of definition, examples, and specific details.

Appetite

Laurie Lee

One of the major pleasures in life is appetite, and one of our major duties should be to preserve it. Appetite is the keenness of living; it is one of the senses that tells you that you are still curious to exist, that you still have an edge on your longings and want to bite into the world and taste its multitudinous flavours and juices. 1

By appetite, of course, I don't mean just the lust for food, but any condition of unsatisfied desire, any burning in the blood that proves you want more than you've got and that you haven't yet used up your life. Wilde said he felt sorry for those who never got their heart's desire, but sorrier still for those who did. I got mine once only, and it nearly killed me, and I've always preferred wanting to having since. 2

For appetite, to me, is this state of wanting, which keeps one's expectations alive. I remember learning this lesson long ago as a child, when treats and orgies were few, and when I discovered that the greatest pitch of happiness was not in actually eating a toffee but in gazing at it beforehand. True, the first bite was delicious, but once the toffee was gone one was left with nothing, neither toffee nor lust. Besides, the whole toffeeness of toffees was imperceptibly diminished by the gross act of having eaten it. No, the best was in wanting it, in sitting and looking at it, when one tasted an inexhaustible treasure-house of flavours. 3

So, for me, one of the keenest pleasures of appetite remains in the wanting, not the satisfaction—in wanting a peach, or a whisky, or a particular texture or sound, or to be with a particular friend. For in this condition, of course, I know that the object of desire is always at its most flawlessly 4

perfect, which is why I would carry the preservation of appetite to the extent of deliberate fasting, simply because I think
that appetite is too good to lose, too precious to be
bludgeoned into insensibility by satiation and overdoing it.

For that matter, I don't really want three square meals a   **5**
day—I want one huge, delicious, orgiastic, table-groaning
blow-out, say every four days, and then not be too sure where
the next one is coming from. A day of fasting is not for me just
a puritanical device for denying oneself a pleasure, but rather
a way of anticipating a rarer moment of supreme indulgence.

Fasting is an act of homage to the majesty of appetite. So I   **6**
think we should arrange to give up our pleasures regularly—
our food, our friends, our lovers—in order to preserve their
intensity and the moment of coming back to them. For this is
the moment that renews and refreshes both oneself and the
thing one loves. Sailors and travellers enjoyed this once, and
so did hunters, I suppose. Part of the weariness of modern
life may be that we live too much on top of each other and are
entertained and fed too regularly. Once we were separated
by hunger both from our food and families, and then we
learned to value both. The men went off hunting, and the
dogs went with them; the women and children waved good-
bye. The cave was empty of men for days on end; nobody ate
or knew what to do. The women crouched by the fire, the wet
smoke in their eyes; the children wailed; everybody was hungry. Then one night there were shouts and the barking of
dogs from the hills, and the men came back loaded with
meat. This was the great reunion, and everybody gorged
themselves silly, and appetite came into its own; the long-
awaited meal became a feast to remember and an almost sa-
cred celebration of life. Now we go off to the office and come
home in the evenings to cheap chicken and frozen peas—
very nice, but too much of it, too easy and regular, served up
without effort or wanting. We eat, we are lucky, our faces are
shining with fat, but we don't know the pleasure of being
hungry any more.

Too much of anything—too much music, entertainment,   **7**
happy snacks, or time spent with one's friends—creates a
kind of impotence of living by which one can no longer hear,
or taste, or see, or love, or remember. Life is short and pre-

cious, and appetite is one of its guardians, and loss of appetite is a sort of death. So if we are to enjoy this short life, we should respect the divinity of appetite and keep it eager and not too much blunted.

It is a long time now since I knew that acute moment of **8** bliss that comes from putting parched lips to a cup of cold water. The springs are still there to be enjoyed—all one needs is the original thirst.

Essays like Lee's, so natural and seemingly effortless, are the result of hard work. His carefully chosen metaphor—appetite as something that makes you "want to bite into the world"—tells you immediately that he is talking about appetite, as he says, in the larger sense of "any condition of unsatisfied desire." He supports his thesis that "loss of appetite is a sort of death" by examples and details. Such carefully crafted writing does not come easily. Experienced writers wrestle with the same activities that inexperienced writers do: planning, drafting, and revising. For almost everyone, writing is a process of returning again and again to the various writing tasks, adjusting and fine-tuning until the result is a unified, coherent, and well-developed composition.

33a

Consider the purpose, audience, and occasion of your composition.

Considerations of *purpose, audience,* and *occasion* shape your writing in many ways. For example, a letter describing your summer job to a friend will differ from one directed to a prospective employer. Your subject is the same but your purpose, audience, and occasion are different. Such considerations are reflected in your *tone*—the attitude you take toward your subject.

PURPOSE

The clearer your purpose, the better your writing is likely to be. The purposes of nonfiction writing may be classified as expressive, expository, and persuasive. These purposes are often combined in an extended piece of writing.

Expressive writing emphasizes the writer's feelings and reactions to the world—to people, objects, events, and ideas. Some examples of expressive writing are journals and diaries, reminiscences, and, frequently, personal letters. The following example is a reminiscence.

> We went fishing the first morning. I felt the same damp moss covering the worms in the bait can, and saw the dragonfly alight on the tip of my rod as it hovered a few inches from the surface of the water. It was the arrival of this fly that convinced me beyond any doubt that everything was as it always had been, that the years were a mirage and there had been no years. The small waves were the same, chucking the rowboat under the chin as we fished at anchor, and the boat was the same boat, the same color green and the ribs broken in the same places, and under the floor-boards the same fresh-water leavings and débris—the dead helgramite, the wisps of moss, the rusty discarded fishhook, the dried blood from yesterday's catch. We stared silently at the tips of our rods, at the dragonflies that came and went. I lowered the tip of mine into the water, tentatively, pensively dislodging the fly, which darted two feet away, poised, darted two feet back, and came to rest again a little farther up the rod. There had been no years between the ducking of this dragonfly and the other one—the one that was part of memory. I looked at the boy, who was silently watching his fly, and it was my hands that held his rod, my eyes watching. I felt dizzy and didn't know which rod I was at the end of.
>
> —E. B. WHITE, "Once More to the Lake"

Expository writing focuses the reader's attention upon the objective world—the objects, the events, and the ideas themselves rather than upon the writer's feelings or attitudes about them. Some examples of expository writing are news accounts, encyclopedia articles, laboratory and scientific reports, textbooks, and articles in professional journals and other publications directed to specialized audiences. In the following paragraph, the writer discusses how our culture came to be concerned with age.

> This preoccupation with age came about because modern technological society radically changed the conditions of growing up and the entire human life cycle. As modern societies developed age-graded institutions, age came to matter in new ways: our birthdates came to determine when we must go to school and when we can leave school, when we can vote, or work full time, drive, marry, buy liquor, enter into contracts, run for public office, retire, and receive Social Security.
> —ARLENE SKOLNICK,
> *The Psychology of Human Development*

Persuasive writing is intended to influence the reader's attitudes and actions. Most writing is to some extent persuasive; even something as apparently straightforward as a résumé may be persuasive through the choice and arrangement of material. However, writing is usually called persuasive if it is clearly arguing for or against a position.

Persuasion depends on both rational and emotional appeals. The reader's perception of a writer's honesty, fairmindedness, and goodwill is as crucial as the writer's presentation of evidence and rational arguments. In turn, the writer needs to respond to a reader's concerns and doubts. In the following opening paragraph of his "Letter from Birmingham Jail," notice how Martin Luther King, Jr., establishes his own patience and good sense while confirming that his readers are men "of genuine good will."

MY DEAR FELLOW CLERGYMEN:
    While confined here in the Birmingham city jail, I came across your recent statement calling my present activities "unwise and untimely." Seldom do I pause to answer criticism of my work and ideas. If I sought to answer all the criticisms that cross my desk, my secretaries would have little

time for anything other than such correspondence in the course of the day, and I would have no time for constructive work. But since I feel that you are men of genuine good will and that your criticisms are sincerely set forth, I want to try to answer your statement in what I hope will be patient and reasonable terms.
—MARTIN LUTHER KING, JR., "Letter from Birmingham Jail"

Most writing combines all three purposes, but usually one intention predominates. You might write one essay expressing your personal encounter with poverty, another exposing the effects of poverty, and a third persuading readers to accept certain measures to eliminate poverty. You could also draw all of these together; for example, the persuasive paper might be more effective if it included a discussion of the effects of poverty together with your personal experience.

■ **Exercise 1**   Select two of the following subjects and explain how you could treat each (1) as expressive writing, (2) as expository writing, and (3) as persuasive writing.
a. word processors   b. nutrition   c. car trouble   d. job hunting

AUDIENCE

Always be aware of who will read your writing. Your understanding of your audience will determine your choice of words (diction), examples, and details. Audiences vary considerably, but there are at least two kinds that you can distinguish: specialized and general.

Specialized audiences

A specialized audience has considerable knowledge of the subject about which you are writing and a keen interest in it. For example, if your subject is a new skiing technique, a group of ski instructors would obviously constitute a specialized audience. So would readers of *Ski* magazine, though in writing for this audience you would allow for a greater variation in knowledge and interest. A specialized audience for one subject would be a general audience for another; the ski instructor, unless also a gifted chef, would probably constitute a general audience for an essay on cooking with a wok.

It is often easier to write for specialized audiences because you have a specific idea of how much and what kinds of information, as well as what methods of presentation, are called for. You can adjust your tone and the kind of language you use as you tailor your presentation to their expertise and attitudes. The following example from the *Annual Review of Astronomy and Astrophysics* is written for a specialized audience that understands mathematical notation and is familiar with the terminology.

> It is now generally believed that a cometary nucleus consists of some sort of conglomerate of ice and meteoric material, as was envisioned by Whipple (1950, 1951). As the comet nears the Sun, the ices are sublimated, and the resultant gas and released meteoric dust become available for forming the coma and tail. Reaction of the comet to the ejection of this material then provides an explanation for the nongravitational effects in the motions of comets. The prevalence of strong outward radial components of the nongravitational forces $(A_1 \approx 10|A_2|)$ is precisely to be expected from the icy-conglomerate model. The fact that there is any transverse component at all follows from the comet's rotation and a lag between the direction of maximum mass ejection and the subsolar meridian: $A_2 > 0$ corresponds to direct rotation of the comet, $A_2 < 0$ to retrograde rotation.
>
> —BRIAN G. MARSDEN, "Comets"

General audiences

Think of a general audience as a reader or readers not expert on your topic but presumably willing to read what you have to say about it. It is possible to identify certain characteristics even in a general audience so you can shape your presentation accordingly. For example, the audience for which your instructor usually wishes you to write is one made up of educated adults, intellectually alert and receptive to ideas, but with many different special interests of their own. This assumed audience is not very different from the one for which the articles in a general encyclopedia are written. Consider the following description from such an encyclopedia.

> A comet is a generally nebulous celestial body of small mass revolving around the Sun. Its appearance and brightness vary markedly with its distance from the Sun. A comet far from the Sun is very faint, appears starlike, and consists of a small body or group of bodies reflecting sunlight, called the nucleus. As the comet approaches the Sun, a nebulosity called the coma develops around the nucleus; with the nucleus it constitutes the head of the comet. The coma contains dust and gas released from the nucleus through the action of solar radiation. When close enough to the Sun, a tail may develop, sometimes very long and bright, directed away from the Sun. Such a comet shines partly by scattering of solar radiation on dust particles and partly by re-emission of the gas of absorbed solar radiation (through processes called resonance or fluorescence). —ENCYCLOPEDIA BRITANNICA

General audiences may be of quite different kinds. Think about the following passage from a fifth-grade science textbook. It describes a comet by using details (such as "flying frozen gravel pits") that appeal to ten-year-old readers and by using simple words in short, uncomplicated sentences.

> Comets may be no more than a few miles across. They are made of bits of frozen gas and dust. They can be thought of as flying frozen gravel pits. Much of a comet's matter changes to vapor when the comet travels near the sun. As the comet "head" absorbs the sun's energy, the gas of the comet expands. So the comet takes up more space. A "tail" is formed. The tail may be as much as 500 million miles long. The matter of a comet is spread very thin. —GEORGE MALLISON et al.,
> *Science: Understanding Your Environment*

When you are writing for a general audience, a useful technique is to imagine one specific reader whose background and expectations are typical; then adjust your choice of details and your tone accordingly.

Sometimes you may know little about a general audience. You can usually assume an audience of educated adults, but be careful when making assumptions about their sex, religion, politics, or special interests.

Multiple audiences

Often in work-related situations you will be writing one document—such as an application or a proposal—for a group of readers with different interests. In reading a proposal for a new city parking garage, for instance, the city treasurer is primarily concerned with cost, the ecologist with the environment, the general public with convenience, and the police department with safety. The writer of such a proposal must be aware of all these concerns.

■ **Exercise 2**   Choose a recent class or party and write a letter describing it to (1) a close friend, (2) a former teacher, and (3) a member of your family.

OCCASION

The rhetorical situation involves not only audience and purpose but also the occasion for which you are writing. A letter of condolence calls for a kind of writing different from a letter of congratulation. In the sentence below, Churchill sets forth his occasion, his purpose, and his audience.

> In the twenty-second month of the war against Nazism we meet here in this old Palace of St. James's, itself not unscarred by the fire of the enemy, in order to proclaim the high purposes and resolves of the lawful constitutional Governments of Europe whose countries have been overrun; and we meet here also to cheer the hopes of free men and free peoples throughout the world.
> —WINSTON CHURCHILL, "Until Victory Is Won"

TONE

Tone is a reflection of your attitude toward your subject and must be appropriate to your purpose, audience, and occasion, whether for a personal essay or a lab report. Although humor might well be suitable in a letter to a friend telling her of trouble with your new car, it would be inappropriate in a letter of complaint to the manufacturer. Notice how the tone of Chief Joseph's speech delivered in 1877 reflects the defeat and despair that he feels as his tribe surrenders to the U.S. Cavalry in their struggle to keep their lands.

> I am tired of fighting. Our chiefs are killed. Looking Glass is dead. Toohulsote is dead. The old men are all dead. It is the young men who say no and yes. He who led the young men is dead. It is cold and we have no blankets. The little children are freezing to death. My people, some of them, have run away to the hills and have no blankets, no food. No one knows where they are—perhaps they are freezing to death. I want to have time to look for my children and see how many of them I can find. Maybe I shall find them among the dead. Hear me, my chiefs, I am tired. My heart is sad and sick. From where the sun stands I will fight no more forever.
> —CHIEF JOSEPH of the Nez Percé, "I Am Tired of Fighting"

■ **Exercise 3** Write a letter to three different audiences about a college or university problem: a humorous letter to a friend, a serious letter to a family member, and a letter of complaint to the administration.

33b

Find an appropriate subject.

If you are assigned a subject to write about or if your situation clearly dictates a subject—as in most business writing, for example—you can move directly to a consideration of your audience (pages 362–65), of the particular aspect of the subject you will emphasize (**33c**), and of the ways you might organize your discussion (**33e**). Especially in college writing, however, you will sometimes be expected to choose a subject for yourself. Remember to consider your purpose, audience, and occasion when searching for an appropriate subject.

Often the best subject may be one drawn from your own experience—your personal knowledge, interests, and beliefs. Do you play a musical instrument? Climb mountains? Like to travel? Do you have a job? What classes are you taking? Can you think of a particular place that is important to you? An interesting character you have met? Something unusual about your family? What ambitions do you have for yourself? What strong convictions do you hold? When you are free to choose a subject, you can write an interesting paper on almost anything you care about.

Sometimes you will need to choose a subject outside your own experience because you want to extend your knowledge of a subject or because your instructor has assigned it. If you have to write a term paper for a microbiology course, you may be free to write on any aspect of that discipline that interests you, but the instructor making the assignment wants a paper demonstrating your command of information, not your personal feelings about or experiences with microbes. Just as with writing about personal experience, however, you should take some trouble to find a subject that interests you. You can often find a subject by looking in your textbook, particularly in the sections listing suggestions for further reading and study. You can go through your lecture notes, examine books and articles in the library, look through the subject catalog, or refer to encyclopedias. Sometimes talking to other students or to your instructor will help you find a subject.

■ **Exercise 4**

1. Choose a personal experience that might be an appropriate subject to write about. How was the experience meaningful to you? What reasons can you think of for sharing this experience with others?
2. Select a controversial subject that interests you. What are the issues involved?
3. Write a short composition on any of the subjects that you selected.

33c

Explore and focus the subject.

When you have a subject in mind—whether it is one assigned by an instructor, one dictated by some other writing situation, or one you have chosen for yourself—you will need to explore all the possible ways to develop it. You will also need to follow certain leads while eliminating others as you direct and focus your ideas.

(1) Explore your subject.

Writers use many different methods to explore a subject. Some especially useful methods are listing, questioning, applying different perspectives, and surveying the possible development strategies. Use whatever methods seem to be productive for you. Different methods may work best for different subjects; if you run out of ideas using one method, switch to another. Sometimes, especially for an assigned subject remote from your own interests and knowledge, you may need to try several methods.

Listing One way to gather ideas about your writing topic is to make an informal list. Jot down any ideas that come to you while you are thinking about your subject. Don't worry if the ideas come without any kind of order, and don't worry about the form in which you write them down; grammar, spelling, and diction are not concerns at this stage. Devote as much time to making your list as necessary—perhaps five minutes, perhaps an entire evening. The point is to collect as many ideas as you can.

If you were thinking about writing about personal computers, you might make a list like the one on the next page. This one took a student about five minutes.

reasons people want personal computers
playing games
keeping track of money
helping to organize daily tasks
what should you look for when you choose one
size and what price
what do you want it to do for you
what kinds of programs are available for it
cost of programs
variety of programs
ease of use—programs and computer
any gadgets to attach—like printers, disk drives
what about monitors—color, monochrome
what kind of storage is best
what do you have to know before you can use one
do you need to know math
where can you learn
any hidden costs—higher electrical bills, repairs, etc.
do they break frequently
where do you get them fixed
where should you buy one
keeping records—addresses, Christmas cards, spending
    habits, taxes

This list may appear chaotic, but earlier items suggest later ones, and a review of the whole list may suggest ones that need to be added. As you look through the list you will find some ideas that are closely related and might be grouped together; out of this seeming chaos, order and direction will begin to emerge.

Questioning   Explore a subject by asking yourself questions. The journalists' questions *who? what? when? where? how?* and *why?* are easy to use and can help you discover ideas about any subject. Using journalists' questions to explore the subject of personal computers could lead you to think about *how* computers affect people, *what* they are and *what* kinds are available, *when* and *how* they were developed, *where* they are used or *who* uses them, *why* people want personal computers, *how* computers work or *how* to decide which one to buy.

Applying perspectives Sometimes it is helpful to consider a subject in three quite different ways—as static, dynamic, and relative. A *static* perspective would focus your attention on what a personal computer is. You might define it, describe its physical characteristics, analyze its parts or its main uses, or give examples of personal computers.

The *dynamic* perspective focuses on action and change. Thus you might examine the history or development of the computer, its workings or the processes involved in using it, and changes of all sorts resulting from its use.

The *relative* perspective focuses on relationships, on systems. You might examine relationships of the computer to other things and to people. You can view the personal computer as a system in itself or as a part of a larger system of information management. You can also analyze it in relation to other kinds of computers, such as mainframe computers, or to other kinds of information management tools, such as library catalogs.

Strategies for development Strategies for development, which are more fully discussed in **32d**, are natural thinking processes that are especially useful for generating ideas about a subject. Remember that purpose, audience, and occasion, as well as the subject, must be considered when selecting a guiding strategy. Often the strategy emerges as you brainstorm or draft; do not impose an inappropriate strategy. Here are some questions that you might ask yourself.

Narration What was your first experience with a computer? When did you write your first paper on a computer?
Process How does a computer work? How do you use a computer?

Cause and Effect   Why were computers developed? Why do you use one? What effect have computers had on grocery stores and other merchandising businesses? What effects have computers had on you?

Description   What does a computer keyboard look like? How can you describe the monitor? The disk drive? The direction manual?

Definition   What is a personal computer? A mainframe? A word processor? What are some of the common computer terms? Can you define them?

Classification and Division   What classes do computers belong to? Communication technologies? Writing aids? Calculators? Artificial intelligence? How can you divide computers into subclasses? According to use (business and personal)? According to price? According to size?

Example   How do computers save time? Give an example. What advantages do lap-top computers have over desktop personal computers? Give an example.

Comparison and Contrast   How are computers like typewriters? How are they different? How is computer memory like your own memory? How is it different?

Often whole compositions are guided by one or more of these strategies. The following introduction suggests a comparison–contrast essay.

> Americans have a sense of space, not of place. Go to an American home in exurbia, and almost the first thing you do is drift toward the picture window. How curious that the first compliment you pay your host inside the house is to say how lovely it is outside his house! He is pleased that you should admire his vistas. The distant horizon is not merely a line separating earth from sky, it is a symbol of the future. The American is not rooted in his place, however lovely: his eyes are drawn by the expanding space to a point on the horizon, which is his future.
>
> —YI-FU TUAN, "American Space, Chinese Place"

In the following introduction, Desmond Morris suggests the overall organization of a classification–division essay. In the essay itself, however, he also uses definition, narration, and description to develop his discussion of the three kinds of territory he names in the opening.

> A territory is a defended space. In the broadest sense, there are three kinds of human territory: tribal, family and personal. —DESMOND MORRIS, "Territorial Behavior"

(2) Limit and focus your subject.

Exploring the subject will suggest not only productive strategies for development but also a direction and focus for your writing. Some ideas will seem worth pursuing; others will seem inappropriate for your purpose, audience, or occasion. You will find yourself discarding ideas even as you develop new ones. A simple analogy will help explain. When you want a picture of a landscape, you cannot photograph all that your eye can take in. You must focus on just part of that landscape. Then as you aim your camera, you look through the viewfinder to make sure the subject is correctly framed and in focus. At this point you may wish to move in closer and focus on one part of the scene or to change your angle, using light and shadow to emphasize some features of the landscape over others. You can think of your writing in the same way—focusing and directing your ideas just as you focus and direct the lens of your camera—moving from a general subject to a more specific one.

For example, "personal computers" is too large and general a subject to make a good writing topic. However, some of the items that appear on the list about the home computer in **33c(1)** can be grouped to form a writing topic that might be manageable. Items about cost can be grouped, as can items about programs, about things the computer can do, or about learning to use the computer. Conceivably, an essay focusing on any one of these groups—eliminating all the other, irrelevant items—might be both workable and interesting.

However, chances are that still more focusing will be required. Suppose you have narrowed "personal computers" to "learning to use a personal computer." This is still a very big topic, one on which sizable books are written. For a short paper you would do better to focus on, for example, the ways such knowledge can be acquired. You might examine the relative merits of college courses, training sessions given by dealers, and self-instruction through reading manuals and other publications. Or you could focus your paper on the specific kinds of knowledge that are needed: how to turn the computer on and off, how to use disk drives, how to save information you have put into the computer, and so forth. The exact focus you finally choose will be determined by your purpose, your audience, and the time and space available.

■ **Exercise 5** Taking one of the subjects from Exercise 4, explore it by using the journalists' questions (who? what? when? where? how? and why?) Next explore it using the three perspectives: What is it? How does it change? What is it related to (part of, different from, or like)? Finally, explore the subject by surveying development strategies. How would you limit your subject? What would you focus on?

33d

Formulate a focused, directed thesis.

A thesis statement contains a single idea, clearly focused and specifically stated, which grows out of your exploration of a subject. A thesis statement is basically a *claim* statement (see **31b**)—that is, it indicates what you claim to be true or interesting or valuable about your subject.

You will probably try out several thesis statements as you explore your subject. Rather than starting with a preconceived thesis that you must then rationalize, let it develop out of your thinking and discovery process (see **33c**).

However, your goal should be a claim that is not self-evident or too broad or too specific to interest your reader.

A thesis statement serves a number of purposes: it helps you keep your writing on target and tells your reader your subject, your point of view, and in some cases your plan of development. Note how the thesis below does all of these.

> The effects of drugs on the individual involved are disastrous, but the social, economic, and personal effects on that person's close associates can be equally serious.

In the next thesis the author divides the subject of discipline into three kinds for an expository essay.

> A child, in growing up, may meet and learn from three different kinds of disciplines. —JOHN HOLT, "Kinds of Discipline"

The thesis in a persuasive essay usually carries a strong point of view—an argumentative edge.

> The arms race must stop.
> —HANS BETHE, "The Nuclear Freeze"

In some cases a thesis may be stated in one sentence, but in others it may be two sentences or even a paragraph, as in this essay on American women, written by Pearl Buck after her many years in China.

> It seems to me that women are very badly treated in America. A few of them know it, more of them dimly suspect it, and most of them, though they know they ought to be glad they live in a Christian country where women are given an education, do not feel as happy in their lonely hearts as they wish they did. The reason for this unhappiness is a secret sense of failure, and this sense of failure comes from a feeling of inferiority, and the feeling of inferiority comes from a realization that actually women are not much respected in America. —PEARL BUCK, "America's Medieval Women"

A good thesis statement will help you maintain unity and will guide many decisions about what details to include.

Sometimes you have information about your subject that is interesting but does not really help you make your point. When you are tempted to include such material simply because it is interesting, looking at your thesis statement can help you decide to leave it out. You can also use the thesis to guide your search for additional information that you may need to make your point.

As you write, refer to your thesis statement from time to time to see if you have drifted away from your main idea. However, do not hesitate to change your thesis if you find a more productive path, one you would rather pursue. Make whatever adjustments you need to insure a unified essay.

A thesis statement is often a declarative sentence with a single main clause—that is, either a simple or complex sentence. If your thesis statement announces two or more co-ordinate ideas, as a compound sentence does, be sure you are not in danger of having your paper lose direction and focus. If you wish to sharpen the thesis statement by adding information that qualifies or supports it, subordinate such material to the main idea.

Beware of vague qualifiers such as *interesting*, *important*, and *unusual*. Often such words signal that you have chosen a subject that does not interest you much; you would do better to rethink your subject to come up with something you care about. In a thesis statement such as "My education has been very unusual" the vague word *unusual* may indicate that the idea itself is trivial and unproductive and that the writer needs to find a more congenial subject. On the other hand, this kind of vague thesis may disguise an idea of real interest that simply needs to be made specific: "Unlike most people, I received my high school education from my parents on a boat." Sometimes thesis statements containing vague words can be made more effective by simply replacing the bland words with other, more meaningful ones. The following examples show ways to focus, clarify, and sharpen vague thesis statements.

VAGUE	Rock collecting can be an interesting hobby.
BETTER	Rock collecting fills empty time, satisfies a yen for beauty, and brings in a little extra cash.
VAGUE	I have trouble making decisions.
BETTER	Making decisions is difficult for me, especially when money is involved, and most of all when such decisions affect other people.
VAGUE	Summer is an interesting season.
BETTER	Summer is the rich growing season.

Thesis statements appear most often in the first paragraph although you may put them anywhere that suits your purpose—occasionally even in the conclusion. The advantage, however, of putting the thesis statement in the introductory paragraph is that your reader knows from the beginning what you are writing about and where the essay is going. If the thesis statement begins the introductory paragraph, the rest of the sentences in the paragraph usually support or clarify it with more specific information.

> Clutter is the disease of American writing. We are a society strangling in unnecessary words, circular constructions, pompous frills and meaningless jargon.
> —WILLIAM ZINSSER, *On Writing Well*

> In many ways a pool is the best place to do real swimming. Free water tends to be too tempestuous, while in a pool it is tamed and imprisoned; the challenge has been filtered out of it along with the bacteria.
> —JOHN KNOWLES, "Everybody's Sport"

Sometimes an essay has no explicit thesis statement. This is especially common in writing that is primarily narrative or descriptive. Sometimes, even in the kinds of writing where a thesis is most often explicitly stated (persuasive and expressive), there may be special reasons for leaving the thesis statement out. Yet even when your thesis is implied, your readers should be able to sense a clear direction and focus in your paper. You can make sure that they will by writing a thesis statement for your own use and then testing each paragraph to make sure it is relevant to the thesis. What is important is to think about your thesis even if you never intend your readers to see it.

■ **Exercise 6**   Write a focused thesis for one of the subjects you listed in Exercise 4.

33e

Choose an appropriate method or combination of methods for arranging ideas.

Most writers need a working plan to direct their ideas and to keep their writing on course. Some follow a formal arrangement pattern; others use informal written lists or formal topic or sentence outlines. Such plans are especially helpful for full-length papers and for writing under pressure.

INFORMAL WORKING PLANS

An informal working plan need be little more than an ordered list that grows out of a collection of ideas like those used to explore subjects (see **33c**) and suggests a way of organizing your information. A student who wrote a paper on automobile drivers made the following list while exploring the subject.

> bad drivers
> create havoc
> irresponsible drivers
> speeding in school zones
> changing lanes
> driving without lights
> driving on left side of road

forgets turn signals
automobile telephones
drunk drivers
absent-minded drivers
driving too slowly
driving too fast
speeding
speed limits
eating while driving
stubborn drivers
angry drivers
drivers' tests

When starting to write about automobile drivers, the student examined the list and noticed that it was primarily concerned with two things: types of bad drivers and bad driving habits. She then started grouping the bad driving habits under types of bad drivers and wound up with the following thesis statement and informal list:

Thesis: In my years of driving, I have encountered several kinds of automobile drivers who tend to create havoc on the road.

1. Irresponsible drivers
2. Stubborn drivers
3. Absent-minded drivers

When you make a list such as this, ideas often overlap. Some are general; some are specific. They appear in no particular order. But you have the beginning of a plan. Examine your list carefully to see if any items are repeated and if any particular plan suggests itself.

Working from this list, she then grouped bad driving habits under the appropriate type of driver and thought of driving habits to add to the new list. Notice that she abandoned some items while focusing and narrowing. Such an informal listing can help her not only organize but also think of new ideas.

OUTLINES

Outlines often grow out of working plan lists. A structured outline uses indention and numbers to indicate various levels of subordination. Thus it is a kind of graphic scheme of the logic of your paper. The main points form the major headings, and the supporting ideas for each point form the subheadings.

> Thesis
>   I. Major idea
>   A. Supporting idea
>   1. Example or illustration for supporting idea
>   2. Example or illustration for supporting idea
>   a. Detail for example or illustration
>   b. Detail for example or illustration
>   B. Supporting idea
>   II. Major idea

A decimal system is also commonly used.

> Thesis
>   1. Major idea
>   1.1. Supporting idea
>   1.2. Supporting idea
>   2. Major idea
>   2.1. Supporting idea
>   2.2. Supporting idea

The types of outlines most commonly used are the topic outline and the sentence outline. The headings in a *topic outline* are expressed in grammatically parallel phrases, and those in a *sentence outline* are in complete but not necessarily parallel sentences. A topic outline has the advantage of brevity and highlights the logical flow of your paper; a sentence outline forces you to think through your ideas more thoroughly. The major headings in the sentence outline can serve as topic sentences. Regardless of what type of outline you choose, you will need enough major headings to develop your subject fully within the boundaries established by your thesis. The following outlines were developed from the student paper beginning on page 393.

Topic Outline

Thesis: In my years of driving, I have become aware of three types of drivers who tend to create havoc on the road and have learned to guard against them.
Introduction: The hazardous types of drivers
  I. Irresponsible drivers
      A. Unaccountable to other drivers
      B. Dangerous to other drivers
      C. Defense: Keep a distance
  II. Stubborn drivers
      A. Determined
      B. Unsafe
      C. Defense: Don't argue
  III. Absent-minded drivers
      A. Heedless of surroundings
      B. Unaware of their driving
      C. Defense: Be ready to use the horn
Conclusion: Development of awareness of other drivers in order to drive defensively.

Sentence Outline

Thesis Statement: In my years of driving, I have become aware of three types of drivers who tend to create havoc on the road and have learned to guard against them.
Introduction: There are three types of hazardous drivers on the road.
  I. Irresponsible drivers refuse to be accountable for the welfare of others.
      A. They speed through school zones.
      B. They change lanes heedlessly.
      C. I have learned to keep a safe distance.

II. Stubborn drivers insist on having their own way.
   A. They drive in the left lane, forcing others to pass on the right.
   B. They drive slowly, not allowing others to pass.
   C. I don't try to argue with stubborn drivers.
III. Absent-minded drivers are heedless of their surroundings and do not have their minds on what they are doing.
   A. They are oblivious of other cars.
   B. They do not use turn signals.
   C. They change lanes, ignoring other cars.
   D. I try to be ready to alert them by honking my horn.
Conclusion: I have developed an awareness of other drivers and have learned to drive defensively.

Even if you do not use an outline as a planning aid, you may use it profitably in revision. Notice that the topic outline highlights a problem that plagues this student throughout the writing of her paper. Her categories are overlapping: the stubborn and absent-minded drivers are irresponsible, and all three types of drivers are unsafe (II.B) and dangerous to other drivers (I.B). If you have difficulty outlining your draft, it may have organizational problems.

Also use outlines to summarize main ideas of lectures and reading materials or to communicate ideas to other persons in a brief and readily accessible form.

CLASSICAL ARRANGEMENT

You may follow a classical arrangement when your primary purpose is expository or persuasive:

Introduction   Announce the subject, set the tone, and gain the reader's attention and interest.
Background   Provide any background information that the reader may need.
Definition of Terms and Issues   Define technical terms. Stipulate meanings for ambiguous terms. Make clear the

particular meaning that will be used throughout the context of the composition.

Development or Proof Develop thesis. This is the body of your paper containing well-developed paragraphs that support the thesis.

Refutation After you have presented your own ideas, try to predict and answer the disagreements or questions that your reader might have.

Conclusion Summarize the main points of your paper, leaving your reader well-disposed toward what you have said. You may repeat the thesis, setting it in a wider context, or urge your reader to action or reconsideration of an accepted viewpoint.

You may not need to include all of these parts, and, depending on the rhetorical situation, you may choose to emphasize certain ones more than others. An expository composition will emphasize background and definition, whereas a persuasive paper will focus on the proof and refutation. The only parts that are necessary are the introduction, the development, and the conclusion. This formal pattern can serve as a guide as you organize and arrange your ideas.

33f

Write the first draft.

As you write the first draft of your composition, keep your plan in mind, but put your ideas on paper quickly without much concern for matters such as spelling, punctuation, and usage. Although these elements are very important in the final draft, they do not matter in the first draft. If you realize you have veered from your plan, you may find it helpful to stop drafting and reread what you have written to reorient yourself. If you find yourself stuck, not knowing where to go next, referring to your plan should help you discover how to continue. When you complete your draft, set it aside for a time, several days if possible.

Some writers find that they work best by writing chunks or blocks of their essay without worrying about the order in which the chunks will finally appear. For example, if writing the introduction is difficult for you, try starting with one of the supporting ideas you feel sure of, and draft that idea through to a stopping point. You may find that when you actually are writing, your thinking processes will operate more efficiently. If that happens, you can move on to any part of the composition you think will be easy to write next—another supporting idea paragraph, even the introduction or conclusion. What is important is to begin writing and to write as quickly as you can. One word of caution: if you find that writing in chunks works best for you, you will later need to give special care to insuring that you have clear transitions.

(1) Write effective introductions.

An effective introduction arouses the reader's interest and indicates the subject and tone of the composition (see **33a**). Introductions have no set length; they can be as brief as one sentence or as long as a paragraph or more. Although introductions appear first in the essay, experienced writers may compose them at any time during the writing process— even after they have drafted the rest of the paper. Notice how the author of the following introduction indicates his subject (gluttony) and his tone (humorous).

> How do things stand with you and the seven deadly sins? Here is my scorecard: Sloth I fight—to a draw. I surrendered to Pride long ago. Anger I tend to give in to so often that it makes me angry. Lust I'd rather not discuss. I haven't thus far done well enough in the world to claim Avarice as anything more than a theoretical sin. I appear to be making some headway against Envy, though I realize that it's touch and go.

Of the seven deadly sins, the only one that has a continuing interest for me is Gluttony. But "continuing interest" is a euphemism; by it I mean that Gluttony is the last deadly sin that excites me in a big way—so much so that, though I am prepared to admit that Gluttony can be deadly, I am not all that prepared to say it is a sin. As soon as I pop this chocolate-chip cookie in my mouth, I shall attempt to explain what I mean. —ARISTIDES, "A Fat Man Struggles to Get Out"

You can arouse your reader's interest by writing your introduction in a number of ways:

1. Start with an interesting fact or unusual detail that catches the reader's attention.

   Twenty-eight percent of the occupations that will be available to children born in 1976 were not in existence when those children were born.

2. Use an arresting statement to lure the reader into continuing.

   During the Gold Rush of 1849 and the years that followed, San Francisco attracted more than any city's fair share of eccentrics. But among all the deluded and affected that spilled through the Golden Gate in those early days, one man rose to become perhaps the most successful eccentric in American history: Norton I, Emperor of the United States and Protector of Mexico.

   —JOAN PARKER, "Emperor Norton I"

3. Engage the reader's attention with an anecdote.

   It was hard to call it science when physician Peter Hackett dangled upside down on a sheer rock face 8,000 feet above his next stopping place. And it was hard to call it science when medical researcher Chris Pizzo misplaced his ice ax, grabbed a flimsy aluminum tent pole and marched toward the summit of Everest in a glorious quest for data. But science it was when the 1981 American Medical Research Expedition to Everest transformed the mountain into the highest research laboratory on Earth.

   —ERIC PERLMAN, "For a Breath of Thin Air"

4. Begin with a question that the composition will answer.

What do they do at the computer at all hours of the day or night? They design and play complex games; they delve into the computer's memory bank for obscure tidbits of information; like ham radio operators, they communicate with hackers in other areas who are plugged into the same system. They even do their everyday chores by computer, typing term papers and getting neat printouts. One hacker takes his terminal home with him every school vacation so he can keep in touch with other hackers. And at Stanford University, even the candy machine is hooked up to a computer, programmed by the students to dispense candy on credit to those who know the password.
—DINA INGBER, "Computer Addicts"

5. Start with an appropriate quotation.

"All students study for the revolution, not just for grades," declared Liu Shu-min in a quiet yet firm voice. "They usually do not think about how high their grades are but just about what their real knowledge is—for without real knowledge one cannot join the construction of the motherland!" Liu Shu-min, a lively girl of seventeen, with eyes at once smiling and serious and long dark pigtails which swing just below her shoulders, is the third oldest of the five Liu children. —RUTH SIDEL, "The Liu Family"

6. Open with an illustration.

Autobiography is only to be trusted when it reveals something disgraceful. A man who gives a good account of himself is probably lying, since any life when viewed from the inside is simply a series of defeats. However, even the most flagrantly dishonest book (Frank Harris's autobiographical writings are an example) can without intending it give a true picture of its author. Dali's recently published *Life* comes under this heading. Some of the incidents in it are flatly incredible, others have been rearranged and romanticised, and not merely the humiliation but the persistent *ordinariness* of everyday life has been

cut out. Dali is even by his own diagnosis narcissistic, and his autobiography is simply a strip-tease act conducted in pink limelight. But as a record of fantasy, of the perversion of instinct that has been made possible by the machine age, it has great value. —GEORGE ORWELL,
"Benefit of Clergy: Some Notes on Salvador Dali"

7. Simply begin with general information as background about the subject and then focus specifically upon the thesis.

It has just occurred to me that there are young people growing up today who have never had the experience of using a fountain pen. All they know is a ballpoint. I haven't used a fountain pen for many years myself, but I remember what it was like.
—RICHARD ARMOUR, "Fountain of My Youth"

8. Simply state your thesis.

Even today, when the American landscape is becoming more and more homogeneous, there is really no such thing as an all-American style of dress. A shopping center in Maine may superficially resemble one in Georgia or California, but the shoppers in it will look different, because the diverse histories of these states have left their mark on costume.
—ALISON LURIE, "American Regional Costume"

Use definitions only when necessary; avoid such phrases as "Webster's defines *hate* as. . . . " Present yourself positively whenever possible by explaining your experience or knowledge on your subject. Establish your credibility and goodwill.

(2) Write effective conclusions.

The conclusion often summarizes the main points and may also encourage the reader to action or further thought on the subject. A composition should not merely stop; it should finish. Some suggestions follow:

1. You might conclude with a rephrasing of the thesis.

   Hard as it is for many of us to believe, women are not really superior to men in intelligence or humanity—they are only equal.
   —ANNIE ROIPHE, "Confessions of a Female Chauvinist Sow"

2. Direct the reader's attention to larger issues.

   That night I thought hard and long. Could not this simple gambit of Joad's be extended to include other aspects of the game—to include all games? For me, it was the birth of gamesmanship.
   —STEPHEN POTTER, *Gamesmanship*

3. Encourage your readers to change their attitudes or to alter their actions, as in the following example.

   Consuming less, conserving more, they (the poor) are the good citizens of this country, but not by their own choice. They are patriots by necessity, because the expensive choices have already been made, and those of us still naive to the power of their witness would be well—would do mortally well—to fear their rebuke.
   —BARBARA BROWN, "All the Poor Patriots"

4. Conclude with a summary of the main points covered.

   All our giving carries with it messages about ourselves, our feelings about those to whom we give, how we see them as people and how we phrase the ties of relationship. Christmas giving, in which love and hope and trust play such an intrinsic part, can be an annual way of telling our children that we think of each of them as a person, as we also hope they will come to think of us.
   —MARGARET MEAD and RHODA METRAUX,
   "The Gift of Autonomy"

5. Clinch or stress the importance of the central idea by referring in some way to the introduction, as Russell Baker does in the next example.

   INTRODUCTION   I read *The National Enquirer* when I want to feel exhilarated about life's possibilities. It tells me of a world where miracles still occur. In the world of *The National Enquirer,* UFOs flash over the Bermuda Triangle, cancer cures are imminent, ancient film stars at last find love that is for keeps. Reached on The Other Side by spiritualists, Clark Gable urges America to keep its chin up. Of all possible worlds, I like the world of *The National Enquirer* best. . . .

CONCLUSION   So I whoop with glee when a new edition of *The National Enquirer* hits the newsstands and step into the world where Gable can cheer me up from The Other Side.

—RUSSELL BAKER, "Magazine Rack"

Finally, in very short essays where all the points can easily be kept in mind, a conclusion is often unnecessary.

(3) Choose an appropriate title.

The title is the reader's first impression and, like the introduction, fits the subject and tone of the paper. Sometimes the title announces the subject simply and directly: "Grant and Lee," or "Civil Disobedience." Often a title uses alliteration to reflect the writer's humorous approach, as in Witchel's "A Pepsi Person in the Perrier Generation," or a twisted cliché, as in Cullen Murphy's "The Right Wrong Stuff." A good title may also arouse the reader's curiosity by asking a question, as does Maurice Shadbolt's "Who Killed the Bog Men of Denmark? And Why?"

A good way to begin developing a title is to try condensing your thesis statement without becoming too vague or general. Reread your introduction and conclusion and examine key words and phrases for possible titles. Try to work in some indication of what your attitude and approach are.

■ **Exercise 7**   Select two of the example introductions in this section and write possible conclusions. Select two of the conclusions and write possible introductions. What do the titles of the essays from which the example paragraphs are taken suggest about the tone of the essay?

33g
Revise and edit.

In one way or another you revise throughout the writing process. For example, even in the earliest planning stages, as you consider a possible subject and then discard it in favor of another, you are revising. Similarly, after choosing a subject, if you decide to change your focus to emphasize some new aspect of it, you are revising. And of course you are revising when, as you draft your paper, you realize that a sentence or a paragraph you have just written does not belong where it is and you pause to strike it out or move it to an earlier or later place in the paper. But once you have finished a draft, you should set it aside for a time (at least overnight) so that you will be able to see it freshly and objectively, and then you should revise it carefully and systematically as a whole. In scheduling your work, allow plenty of time for multiple drafts and revising.

REVISING

Consider the essay *as a whole* before you turn to the individual matters because, as you revise paragraphs or reorganize the essay, you often change or eliminate smaller elements—sentences, words, punctuation, mechanics, and so forth. Check to be sure that you have stuck to your purpose and your subject and that you have not lost sight of your audience anywhere in the essay.

Examine *paragraphs*. Make sure that every paragraph is unified, coherent, and well developed, and that sentences are related to the paragraph's central idea and presented in the most effective order. Check that transitions between paragraphs and between sentences are effective.

Next, look at *sentences*. If your sentences are choppy or unconnected, consider combining some of them. Rework long, overly complicated sentences. Avoid similar grammatical structures. For example, if your essay contains many sentences that begin with prepositional phrases, try to rework some of those into other patterns. Avoid needless shifts in grammatical structures, tone, style, or point of view.

Examine your *diction*. Check to make sure that your choice of words is appropriate for your audience and occasion and that you have defined technical and unfamiliar words. Avoid vague words, such as *area, interesting,* or *unusual,* where more precise words would be more effective. Watch for clauses and sentences in the passive voice. The active voice usually, though by no means always, makes your writing more direct and forceful. Cut any nonessential words, phrases, and sentences to make your writing tighter and more emphatic. Make sure sentences are grammatically correct.

The following checklist can help you revise.

Reviser's Checklist

The essay as a whole

1. Does the whole essay stick to the purpose (see **33a**) and the subject (see **33b**)?
2. Have you kept your audience clearly in mind? Is the tone appropriate and consistent? See **33a**. Do any terms require definition?
3. Is the focus consistent (see **33c[2]**)? Do the ideas in the essay show clear relationships to the central idea, or thesis?
4. Is the central idea or thesis sharply conceived? Does your thesis statement (if one is appropriate) clearly suggest the position and approach you are taking? See **33d**.
5. Have you chosen an effective method or combination of methods of development? See **33e**.

6. Is the reasoning sound in the essay as a whole and in individual paragraphs and sentences? See **31**.
7. Will the introduction arouse the reader's interest? Does it indicate what the paper is about? See **33f(1)**.
8. Does the essay come to a satisfying close? See **33f(2)**.

Paragraphs

1. Are all the paragraphs unified? Are there any ideas in any paragraph that do not belong? See **32a**.
2. Is each paragraph coherent? Are sentences within each paragraph in a natural and effective order? Are the sentences connected by repetition of key words or ideas, by pronoun reference, by parallel structure, or by transitional expressions? See **32b**.
3. Is the progression between paragraphs easy and natural? Are there clear transitions where needed? See **32b(6)**.
4. Is each paragraph adequately developed? See **32c**.

Sentences and diction

1. Have you used subordination and coordination to relate ideas effectively? See **24**.
2. Are there misplaced sentence parts or dangling modifiers? See **25**.
3. Do you find any faulty parallelism? See **26**.
4. Are there any needless shifts in grammatical structures, in tone or style, or in viewpoint? See **27**.
5. Does each pronoun refer clearly to its antecedent? See **28**.
6. Are ideas given appropriate emphasis within the sentence? See **29**.
7. Are the sentences varied in length? In type? See **30**.

8. Are there any fragments? Comma splices or fused sentences? See **2** and **3**.
9. Do all verbs agree with their subjects? Pronouns with their antecedents? See **6**.
10. Have you used the appropriate form of the verb? See **7**.
11. Are any words overused? Imprecise? Vague? See **20**.
12. Have all unnecessary words and phrases been eliminated? See **21**. Have any necessary words been omitted? See **22**.
13. Is your vocabulary appropriate for the audience and occasion? See **33a**.
14. Have you avoided or defined all technical words that are unfamiliar to the audience?

EDITING AND PROOFREADING

Before preparing your final draft, check spelling and punctuation and proofread for typos. A carefully edited paper that is easy to read will make your ideas more acceptable.

Editing Checklist

Punctuation, spelling, mechanics

1. Are commas (see **12**) and semicolons (see **14**) used where required by the sentence structure? Have superfluous commas been removed (see **13**)?
2. Is any end punctuation omitted? See **17**.
3. Are apostrophes (see **15**) and quotation marks (see **16**) placed correctly?
4. Are all words spelled correctly? See **18**.
5. Are capitals (see **9**), italics (see **10**), and abbreviations (see **11**) used correctly?

6. Is your manuscript in an acceptable form? Have all words been divided correctly at the ends of lines? See **8**.

7. Does your manuscript present a neat, professional appearance?

AN ESSAY UNDERGOING REVISION

Following are two drafts of an essay by Ruth Vanderhoek, the first marked with her notes for revision. Compare the drafts and observe all the ways that she has made the final version more effective than the first. Many of the revisions were made in response to the suggestions from the instructor that follow the first draft.

Hazardous Driving
on the road,
In my ten years ~~of driving~~ I have encounter~ed~ all
^but the three   *the most*
kinds of ~~automobile~~ drivers,₍who~ ~~tend to~~ create~
and danger
havoc ~~on the road. Four of these~~ are₎ the
^   *i*
irrespons₍able ~~driver~~, the stubborn ~~driver~~, and the
absent—minded drivers₎ ~~and the drunk drivers. These~~
~~drivers are the ones we so often encounter when we~~
were
~~are driving.~~ If we ~~are~~ aware of which one of these
^   *were*
~~four types of drivers~~ we ~~are~~ meeting₎ ~~on the road~~ we
might be able to   ^ *c*
~~can~~ adjust our own driving a₍cordingly.
i
First₎ there is the irrespons₍able driver₍;
who ^   *s*   ^
~~Irresponsible is to~~ refuse₎ to be accountable for
^
the welfare of others₍. ~~therefore~~ ţhis kind of
^
driver will speed through a school zone unconcerned

about the safety of the children walking. On the

highway, ~~he is the driver who will~~ they move over into

the lane with another car ~~in it~~ without caring

~~weather~~ whether there is space, ~~in that lane.~~ Rather than

considering ~~the welfare of the~~ other driver~~s~~, ~~he~~ they

simply ~~moves into the other lane and~~ expects the

other car~~s~~ to ~~move~~ go somewhere else.

~~Being irresponsible in driving~~ Such drivers can be

dangerous. Speeding through a school zone ~~when~~

~~children are walking~~ could be tragic if a child

suddenly darted out into the street. ~~Being irresponsible~~

~~when~~ changing lanes without looking ~~is dangerous, because it~~ may

cause ~~the~~ an other driver~~s~~ to swerve into the ditch.

Such matters do not seem to bother the

irresponsible driver, who simply moves into another

car's territory and ~~doesn't~~ isn't concern~~ed~~ ~~himself~~ with

what that driver has to do to get out of ~~his~~ the way. (Insert 2)

Then we have the stubborn driver~~s~~ who are ~~Stubborness~~

~~is being~~ determined to have their own way. ~~in will or purpose and this is~~

~~exactly what stubborn drivers are. The kind of~~

~~drivers who~~ They insist on staying in the left lane

regardless ~~of how slow they may be going and~~

~~regardless~~ of how many drivers honk their hor~~n~~s or

flash their ~~car~~ lights. ~~There may be~~ a line of cars

(Insert 1) I have learned to keep a safe distance from these
drivers, allowing them plenty of room to move around.

...may be passing them on the right, but they refuse to move over. They are quite aware of what they are doing and actually enjoy being stubborn.

Stubbornness can create havoc on the road. An unsafe driving practice. Driving slowly in the left lane forces other drivers to pass on the right. If there is heavy traffic, then cars going at highway speeds are too close together. All of these dangers would be eliminated if the stubborn driver would simply pull over to the right, so that traffic could continue moving at normal highway speeds. Instead, stubborn drivers insist on having their own way and doing their own thing, regardless of other drivers. I know that there is nothing to be gained from arguing with stubborn drivers, so I have learned just to sit back and let them have their way.

The third type are the absent-minded drivers who are heedless of their surroundings and blithely drive down the road, oblivious of all other cars and traffic conditions. They cause accidents not because they are irresponsible

or stubborn
~~their driving~~, but because they just don't have
(Insert 3)
their minds on what they are doing. They have their

minds on other things and are not aware of the

problems they are creating (Insert 4)

~~As we can see,~~ all of the *se* ~~above~~ drivers ~~can be~~ *are*
menace
a, ~~menase~~ on the streets and make driving dangerous.
although there are also many courteous and safe drivers,
~~Each of these drivers displaies a personality in~~
you never really know which type of driver is in the
~~his driving that does not make one a responsible~~
car behind you, beside you, or ahead of you. The best
~~courteous driver. There are, no doubt, other,~~
solution is to drive as though all drivers were
~~dangersous driving personalities, but these three~~
irresponsible, stubborn, or absent-minded. In that
~~have been some of the most obvious ones that I have~~
case, the best policy when you get behind the wheel is
~~encountered during my years of driving.~~
not just to drive carefully but also to drive defensively.

(Insert 3) *They drive, slowly in the left lane,* ~~down the highway at a slow~~
~~speed~~ *totally unaware of the line of traffic*
behind them. They change lanes without looking
to see if a car is there, but, unlike stubborn drivers,
they're just not conscious of where they are or what
they are doing. They turn corners without
signaling and go through stop signs and red lights
simply because they are absent-minded.

(Insert 4) *Over the years, I have learned to keep my hand*
near the horn in case I have to use it and to drive as
though every car I meet has an absent-minded driver.

INSTRUCTOR'S COMMENTS

In your first paragraph you mention drunk drivers and adjusting our own driving to these dangerous drivers. Either follow up on these ideas or omit them (**33c**). Your development is good for the irresponsible and the stubborn drivers, but you need more details and examples for your discussion of the absent-minded driver (**32**). Are your categories overlapping? (See **33c**.) Watch wordiness (**21**), unnecessary repetition (**21**), and your use of the generic *he* (**6**). Try to make your introduction, conclusion, and title more interesting (see **33f**). Check spelling and punctuation, especially the use of the semicolon (**14**).

REVISED ESSAY

Hazardous Driving

In my ten years on the road, I have encountered all kinds of drivers, but the three who create the most havoc and danger are the irresponsible, the stubborn, and the absent—minded drivers. If we were aware of which one of these we were meeting, we might be able to adjust our own driving accordingly.

First, there is the irresponsible driver, who refuses to be accountable for the welfare of others. This kind of driver will speed through a school zone unconcerned about the safety of the children walking. On the highway, they move over into the lane with another car without caring whether there is space. Rather than considering other drivers, they simply expect other cars to go somewhere else.

Such drivers can be dangerous. Speeding through a school zone when children are walking could be tragic if a child suddenly darted out into the street. Changing lanes without looking may cause another driver to swerve into the ditch. Such matters do not seem to bother the irresponsible driver, who simply moves into another car's territory and isn't concerned with what that driver has to do to get out of the way. I have learned to keep a safe distance from these drivers, allowing them plenty of room to move around.

Then we have the stubborn drivers, who are determined to have things their own way. They insist on staying in the left lane regardless of how many drivers honk their horns or flash their lights. A line of cars may be passing them on the right, but they refuse to move over. They are quite aware of what they are doing and actually enjoy being stubborn.

Stubbornness can create havoc on the road. Driving slowly in the left lane forces other drivers to pass on the right, an unsafe driving practice. If there is heavy traffic, cars going at highway speeds back up behind them and are too close together. All of these dangers would be eliminated if the stubborn driver would simply pull over to the right, so that traffic could continue moving at normal speeds. Instead, stubborn drivers insist on having their own way and doing their own thing, regardless of other drivers. I know that there is nothing to be gained from arguing with stubborn drivers, so I have learned just to sit back and let them have their way.

The third type are the absent—minded drivers who are heedless of their surroundings and blithely drive down the road, oblivious of all other cars and traffic conditions. They cause accidents not because they are irresponsible or stubborn but because they just don't have their minds on what they are doing. They drive slowly in the left lane, totally unaware of the line of traffic behind them. They change lanes without looking to see if a car is there, but, unlike stubborn drivers, they're just not conscious of where they are or what they are doing. They turn corners without signaling and go through stop signs and red lights simply because they are absent—minded. They have their minds on other things and are not aware of the problems they are creating. Over the years, I have learned to keep my hand near the horn in case I have to use it and to drive as though every car I meet has an absent—minded driver.

All of these drivers are a menace on the road and make driving dangerous. Although there are also many courteous and safe drivers, you never really know which type of driver is in the car behind you, beside you, or ahead of you. The best solution is to drive as though all drivers were irresponsible, stubborn, or absent—minded. In that case, the best policy when you get behind the wheel is not just to drive carefully but also to drive defensively.

INSTRUCTOR'S COMMENTS

> This is a big improvement. The organization is good, although your categories still overlap. Your writing would be livelier if you used more specific details (**32c**) and showed each driver in action rather than telling me about them (**32d**).

Notice that the writer corrected the spelling and punctuation errors on her own, although she failed to respond to the comment about the overlapping categories. The final essay is not a perfect composition, as the instructor's comments indicate, but it is a great improvement over the original version. The instructor gives suggestions for the student to use in writing her next draft and later papers.

■ **Exercise 8**

1. Rewrite the above composition stressing the seriousness of the problem by drawing attention to the menace of bad drivers. Use more details and show, instead of tell, as the instructor suggests.
2. Rewrite the above composition as a humorous essay. Start by renaming the categories.

WRITING UNDER PRESSURE

33h

Write well-organized answers to essay tests; write effective in-class essays.

Frequently in college you will be required to write clearly and correctly in a brief time and under pressure—for example, when you write compositions in class and when you take essay examinations.

(1) Write clear, concise, well-organized answers on essay tests.

When you write an answer to an essay question, you are conveying information, but you also are proving to your audience—the examiner—that you have mastered the information and can work with it. In other words, your purpose is both informative and persuasive. There are several things you can do in preparing for and taking an essay examination to insure that you do the best job you can.

Prepare ahead of time.

Perhaps the best way to get ready for an essay examination is to prepare yourself from the first day of class. Try to decide what is most important about the material you have been learning and pay attention to indications that your instructor considers certain material especially important. As you assimilate facts and concepts, attempt to work out questions that your instructor is likely to ask. Then plan how you would answer such questions.

Read instructions and questions carefully.

First read the whole examination and underline specific directions (i.e., "Answer either A or B"). Then read the question that you are answering. If there are alternatives, choose quickly and stick to your choice. Most questions are carefully worded and contain specific instructions about *how* as well as *what* you are to answer. Always answer exactly the question asked without digressing. Furthermore, if you are asked to define or identify, do not evaluate. Instead, give clear, concise, and accurate definitions or identifications. If you are asked to explain, you must demonstrate that you have a depth of understanding about the subject. If you are asked to evaluate, you must decide what is important and then measure what you plan to say against that yardstick. If you are asked to compare and contrast, you will need to have a thorough knowledge of at least two subjects, and you will need to show efficiently how they are similar and/or different.

Plan your time.

Although you will be working under pressure, take a few minutes to make a time schedule based on the value assigned to each question, or divide the time that you have by the number of questions. Allow some time to revise and proofread. If you are running out of time, outline the answers that you do not have time to write completely.

Plan your answer.

Jot down the main points you intend to make as you think through how you plan to respond. This list of main points can serve as a working plan to help you stay on target.

State main points clearly.

Make your main points stand out from the rest of the essay by identifying them in some way. For instance, you can use transitional expressions such as *first, second, third;* you can underline each main point; or you can create headings to guide the reader.

Support generalizations.

Be sure you support any generalizations that you make with specific details, examples, and illustrations. Write with assurance to help convince the instructor that you have a thorough knowledge of the subject. Make sure your answers are complete; do not write one- or two-sentence answers unless it is clearly specified that you should. Do not, however, pad your answers in an effort to make the instructor think you know more than you do. A clearly stated, concise, emphatic, and complete answer, though somewhat brief, will impress a reader much more than a fuzzy, shotgun-style answer that is much longer.

Stick to the question.

Sometimes you may know more about a related question than you do about the question asked. Do not wander from the question asked to answer a question you think you could handle better. Similarly, make sure that you follow your thesis as you answer the question and do not include material that is irrelevant.

Revise and proofread.

Finally, save a few minutes to reread your answer. Make whatever corrections and revisions you think are necessary. It is much better to cross out a paragraph that is irrelevant (and to replace it with a relevant one if time permits) than to allow it to stand. Similarly, consider whether your sentences are clear and correct. Check sentence structure, spelling, and punctuation; clarify any illegible scribbles.

(2) Write well-organized, clear in-class essays.

Writing an in-class essay is much like writing any other essay except that you are usually given the topic and required to produce the finished essay during one class period. Consequently, make the best possible use of your time. Take a few minutes at the beginning to consider your main idea or thesis, and jot down a short working outline or make a mental plan. Write on every other line so you have room to make revisions or changes. Be sure to reserve a few minutes at the end for revision and proofreading.

As you draft the essay, keeping your plan in mind will help you stay on the track. Pace yourself so you can cover all your major points. Don't forget transitions. It is just as important to support your generalizations and to stick to the point in an in-class essay as in an essay test or in an essay you write at home.

In the time you have saved for revision and proofreading, check your essay for unity and coherence. Strike out any unrelated matter and make any needed insertions. Unless you are instructed to do so, it is best not to use your revising time to make a clean copy of the essay. Make your revisions as neatly and clearly as possible. Proofread carefully.

■ **Exercise 9**   Revise one of the in-class compositions that you wrote in this class or one of the answers that you wrote for an essay examination in another course.

■ **Exercise 10**   Outline the following composition. Read it carefully in preparation for a class discussion of (1) its thesis; (2) its purpose and audience; (3) the arrangement and development of its main points; (4) the introduction, conclusion, and title.

The "Miracle" of Technofix

Somehow this nation has become caught in what I call the mire of "technofix": the belief, reinforced in us by the highest corporate and political forces, that all our current crises can be solved, or at least significantly eased, by the application of modern high technology. In the words of former Atomic Energy Commission chairman Glenn Seaborg: "We must pursue the idea that it is more science, better science, more wisely applied that is going to free us from [our] predicaments."

Energy crisis? Try synfuels. Never mind that they will require billions—eventually trillions—of dollars transferred out of the public coffers into the energy companies' pockets, or that nobody has yet fully explored, much less solved, the problems of environmental damage, pollution, hazardous-waste disposal and occupational dangers their production will create. Never mind—it's technofix.

Food for the hungry world? Try the "Green Revolution." Never mind that such farming is far more energy- and chemical-intensive than any other method known, and therefore generally too expensive for the poor countries that are supposed to benefit from it, or that its principle of monoculture over crop diversity places whole regions, even whole countries, at the risk of a single breed of disease or pest. Never mind—it's scientific.

Diseases? Try wonder drugs. Never mind that few of the thousands of drugs introduced every year have ever been fully tested for long-range effects, or that they are vastly overprescribed and overused, or that nearly half of them prove to be totally ineffective in treating the ailments they are administered for and half of the rest produce unintended side effects. Never mind—it's progress.

And progress, God help us all, may be our most important product.
—KIRKPATRICK SALE

34
THE RESEARCH
PAPER

Learn how to acquire information and how to write a research paper.

Although writing a research paper usually takes much more time than writing essays based on what you already know, the process involves many of the same skills. The distinctive feature of a research assignment is that it requires you to develop a subject in depth by drawing upon outside resources and acknowledging these sources properly. Improving your ability to work with sources may subsequently help you with other writing assignments as well, since you may need to obtain information from sources even when you are not specifically required to do research.

You may begin a research assignment with a question that you want to answer or with a tentative *thesis* (**33d**). If you begin with a thesis, you may need to revise it if your research findings do not support it (see also **31a**). As you proceed, you will need to decide whether the *purpose* (**33a**) of your paper will be chiefly expository (to report, analyze, or explain) or persuasive (to prove a point). Your *audience*

(**33a**) may or may not be an expert on your subject (this will depend on the assignment), but you may safely envision a reader who is intelligent, fair-minded, and interested in finding out what you have to say. Because any sign of bias can undermine your credibility as a researcher, your *tone* (**27d** and **33a**) should be objective.

A word of caution: scheduling your time is especially important because the research paper is usually assigned several weeks before it is due, and the temptation to procrastinate is strong. Make sure to allow enough time for the long process of choosing a subject, preparing a preliminary bibliography, reading extensively, taking notes, outlining, drafting, and revising. Keep your schedule flexible, however. As you write your paper, you may need to return to a part of the research process that you thought you had already completed. For example, when drafting your essay, you may discover that you need additional information, and when you consult the sources you have already acquired, you may then discover that you need to return to the library for further research.

34a

Choose a subject for a research paper and limit it appropriately. See also **33b** and **33c**.

Occasionally, you may be assigned a specific topic. If so, you are ready to begin your search for sources (**34b**). Often, however, choosing a subject will be up to you. An inquiring mind is the best equipment you can bring to this task: choose a subject that interests you and is appropriate for your audience. If you are stuck for an idea, consider some of the resources mentioned in **33b**. You might also try scanning the subjects covered in the *Library of Congress Subject Headings* (see page 410) or in an index like the *Readers'*

Guide (see page 412), keeping alert for headings that interest you.

Once you have a subject in mind, the exploration methods discussed in **33c**—listing, questioning, considering perspectives, surveying development strategies—will almost certainly help you find an interesting focus. Limiting is especially important with the research paper, since one of your main objectives is to show your ability to treat a subject in some depth within the constraints of time and (usually) a specified length. One basic test of any subject you may have in mind is the amount of pertinent material in the library. If you find dozens of relevant sources, you should probably narrow the subject to one with a more manageable scope. On the other hand, if you can find only two or three sources, chances are that your subject is too narrow and needs to be made more inclusive. Because the best research papers usually draw upon different kinds of material, you should also reconsider any topic that would force you to rely exclusively upon one type of source. A paper based only on newspaper articles, for example, could easily lack depth, and research drawn exclusively from books might overlook the most current information in the field.

■ **Exercise 1** Consider the following subjects for an eight-page research paper. If any seem too broad, suggest a narrower focus—for example, "The Second World War" can be limited to "The Bombing of Pearl Harbor." If any seem too narrow, suggest a broader focus—for example, "Raising Soybeans in the Soviet Union" can be expanded to "Problems in Soviet Agriculture." Consider which subjects would be most appropriate for an audience consisting of a college English teacher and which have the broadest appeal for a general audience. Eliminate any subject for which you would be unable to obtain a range of reliable sources.

censorship
breeding pandas in zoos
drug abuse in professional wrestling
Shakespeare's attitude toward women

flying saucers
Leonardo da Vinci
the Japanese economy
U.S. immigration policy

34b

Learn to find the sources you need and to prepare a working bibliography.

College and university libraries are organized to make research as efficient as possible. Most provide a map or diagram—either printed for handing out or posted on the wall—to show you where various kinds of materials are located. Reference books, encyclopedias, and indexes—materials that cannot usually be checked out of the library—are located in the *reference collection.* Other books are located in the *stacks* or at the *reserve desk* and may be checked out for a specified length of time. If your library has a closed-stack policy, you request the books you need by call number from the *circulation desk.* You can find the call number in the *main catalog.* If the stacks are open, however, you may find it useful to browse among the books shelved near those you have located through the catalog. *Periodicals* (magazines, journals, newspapers) are usually stored in a special section of the library. Also bear in mind that many colleges participate in interlibrary loan programs, which are arrangements among local or regional college libraries for the exchange of books. You may also be entitled to use the facilities of other college libraries in your area. If you have difficulty locating or using any research materials, do not hesitate to ask a *reference librarian* for help.

(1) Learn to find books and periodicals.

BOOKS

The first place to look is usually the *main catalog.* This may be in a card catalog or on a computer. The main catalog lists all books owned by the college or university and shows whether a book is in the general library or in a special collection in another building.

A card catalog consists of cards arranged alphabetically in drawers. For each book, cards are filed alphabetically in at least three ways: by author, by title, and by subject or subjects. Author and title cards are usually filed in the same cabinet, while subject cards are often filed separately.

Many libraries have now computerized their catalogs to save space and make research more efficient. By pressing a few keys at typewriter-like terminals (located in the library and often elsewhere on campus), users have instant access to the same information previously available in a card catalog. Like a card catalog, a computerized catalog is designed to identify books by author, title, or subject. Some programs also allow researchers to locate sources by supplying the computer with other information, such as a book's call number or a key word that may appear in the title.

Visually, there may be a slight difference between the format of a catalog card and its equivalent on a computer screen. (See the illustrations on pages 410–11.) But whether you use a card catalog or a computer catalog, you will be provided with essentially the same information: author, title, place of publication, publisher, date of publication, the length and size of the book, and any special features such as a bibliography. You will also be given the book's call number, which tells you exactly where the book is located in the library.

If your library provides you with access to both a card catalog and a computer catalog, check with a librarian to see if they are both current. Libraries that have computerized their catalogs may have stopped including new acquisitions in their card catalogs, and libraries that have only recently computerized their catalogs may not yet have their entire collections on-line.

A catalog card

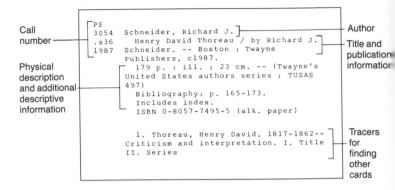

Call number ⎯
```
PS
3054    Schneider, Richard J.
.s36      Henry David Thoreau / by Richard J.
1987    Schneider. -- Boston : Twayne
          Publishers, c1987.
```
Author

Title and publication information

Physical description and additional descriptive information ⎯
```
      179 p. : ill. ; 23 cm. -- (Twayne's
United States authors series ; TUSAS
497)
      Bibliography: p. 165-173.
      Includes index.
      ISBN 0-8057-7495-5 (alk. paper)
```

```
      1. Thoreau, Henry David, 1817-1862--
Criticism and interpretation. I. Title
II. Series
```
Tracers for finding other cards

This example is an author card. Cards filed by title and by subject will have the same information under different headings.

An entry from a computer catalog

In addition to providing all the data found on the printed card, a computerized catalog entry often (see page 411) reveals the location and status of the book—information that can save a researcher time when looking for a book that has been moved to a special collection or checked out by someone else. The following entry concludes with instructions for how to continue searching for other sources. Libraries use a number of different systems for computerizing catalogs, so expect to encounter variations on this example.

Library of Congress subject headings   If your library uses Library of Congress numbers for cataloging books, there is an easy way to find out quickly what books your library has in your subject area. First, look for your subject in the *Library of Congress Subject Headings.* If your subject is one

```
PUBLIC CATALOG                                    Searching:UWSP


PUBLIC CATALOG                                    Searching:UWSP

  Schneider, Richard J.
   Henry David Thoreau / by Richard J. Schneider.
  Boston : Twayne Publishers, c1987.
     179 p. : ill. ; 23 cm.
     Twayne's United States authors series ; TUSAS 497

     Includes index.
     Bibliography: p. 165-173.

   Thoreau, Henry David, - 1817-1862 - Criticism and
      interpretation.
   Twayne's United States authors series ; TUSAS 497


LOCATION       CALL#/VOL/NO/COPY          STATUS

STACKS         PS3054 .S36 1987             Available


(END) Press RETURN to continue or /ES to start a new search:
```

indexed by that catalog, you will find a specific catalog number for books on your subject as well as cross-references to related subject areas that may help you sharpen your focus. If you find a number indexed, write it down; then find that number in your library's own *shelf list*, which lists all the books in the library by call number. The first part of a call number indicates the subject of a book (for example, the PS in PS3054 stands for American literature). Therefore, when you look up the call number of only one book, you should find adjacent to it the call numbers of other books the library owns on that subject.

PERIODICALS

Since periodicals (magazines, journals, newspapers) are published frequently, and much more quickly than books, they often contain the most recent information on your subject. A variety of the periodical indexes (usually located in the reference section of the library) do for articles what the main catalog does for books. You may need to consult a number of indexes to find the information you need, since each index includes many publications not listed in the others.

Indexes for general interest periodicals If articles on your subject may have appeared in popular or general interest magazines or in newspapers, you might want to consult the *Readers' Guide to Periodical Literature*, published from 1900 to the present, and a newspaper index, the best known of which is the *New York Times Index*, published since 1913.

Anxiety

Cross-references {
  See also
  Fear
  Stage fright
  Worry
}

Articles on topic {
Anxiety and panic; their cause and treatment. S. M. Fishman and D. V. Sheehan. il *Psychol Today* 19:26-30+ Ap '85

"Anxiety peptide" found in brain [diazepam binding inhibitor acts through benzodiazepine receptor; work of Alessandro Guidotti and others] J. L. Marx. il *Science* 227:934 F 22 '85

Childhood: the age of anxiety [views of M. B. Rothenberg] M. Abrams. *Harpers Bazaar* 118:128+ Ag '85

The fight against fear. G. Walker. *Ladies Home J* 102:147-51 Mr '85

From panic to anxiety [research on MAO inhibitors and beta blockers by Michael Leibowitz] J. Fischman. *Psychol Today* 19:8 Mr '85

Heavy dose of caffeine brews clues to panic disorder. B. Bower. *Sci News* 127:199 Mr 30 '85

⟶ Mettle testing [test anxiety] A. McGrath. *Forbes* 136:236+ N 4 '85
}

The front pages of each issue of the *Readers' Guide* provide an example of a sample entry as well as a key to abbreviations. The example above (from the search Sharon Johnson conducted for her paper on test anxiety, reprinted on pages 489–503) shows that the November 4, 1985, issue of *Forbes* magazine contains an article on test anxiety by A. McGrath. The subject of the essay is revealed in brackets after the title, because the title does not make the subject clear. (Note that several of the other entries in this column do not provide this explanation.) The volume number of this issue is 136, and the article begins on page 236. The plus sign (+) means that the article continues later in the magazine.

Many college and university libraries now provide access to the *Readers' Guide* on a CD-ROM disk that is used with a computer. This disk, which is updated regularly, covers several years' worth of information otherwise found in a number of separate, bound volumes.

Like the *Readers' Guide*, the *New York Times Index* arranges authors and subjects in alphabetical order. Entries include a brief summary of the contents and an abbreviation that reveals the article's length.

Article summary { Article on special programs being created by school districts around nation to encourage involvement of parents in their children's education; photo; drawing (special section, Education Life) (L), N 9,XII,18:2 ⌐

A long article   November 9 issue (in year of volume consulted)   Section, page, and column numbers

The *New York Times Index* is widely available in bound volumes published annually. Depending upon the resources of your library, you may also be able to search for information in the *New York Times* (and in other newspapers like the *Christian Science Monitor* and the *Wall Street Journal*) with a CD-ROM disk or through an on-line database search.

For older articles of general interest, you can consult *Poole's Index*, 1802–1907, or *Nineteenth Century Readers' Guide*, 1890–99.

Indexes for special interest periodicals Virtually every specialized field has its own periodicals, which usually provide much more detailed information than can be found in magazines or newspapers designed for the general public. When conducting research in college, you should be familiar with the indexes that cover periodicals within various professions. Some of the most useful ones are listed below.

Applied Science and Technology Index. 1958–.
Art Index. 1929–.
Biological and Agricultural Index. 1946–.
Business Periodicals Index. 1958–.
Education Index. 1929–.
General Science Index. 1978–.
Humanities Index. 1974–.
Index to Legal Periodicals. 1908–.
Music Index. 1949–.
Public Affairs Information Service (Bulletin). 1915–.
Social Sciences Index. 1974–.

These indexes are organized like the *Readers' Guide.* (Consult the front of any volume for a key to the abbreviations used in individual entries.) A similar format is also used by the *MLA Bibliography,* which is essential for doing research in literature. The *MLA Bibliography* includes books as well as periodicals, and each volume is subdivided into separate sections covering research on the literature of different languages and time periods. Like most indexes to special interest periodicals, the *MLA Bibliography* can be consulted in printed volumes, through an on-line data-base search, or through access to a CD-ROM disk covering several years.

For additional research in periodicals, see also the monthly catalog for *United States Government Publications,* 1895–, and abstracting services such as *Chemical Abstracts,* 1907–; *Historical Abstracts,* 1955–; *Psychological Abstracts,* 1927–.

REFERENCE BOOKS

When doing research, you may need to consult a variety of reference works. For example, you will almost certainly need to consult a dictionary (see **19a**). For a detailed list of reference books and a short description of each, consult *Guide to Reference Books,* by Eugene P. Sheehy, and *American Reference Books Annual (ARBA),* edited by Boydan S. Wynar. A few of the most important reference books are listed on the following pages, with abbreviated bibliographical information. Note that these are sources for *reference*: refer to them for help, but do not rely upon any of them as a principal source for a research paper in college.

General encyclopedias

Collier's Encyclopedia. 24 vols. 1988.
Encyclopedia Americana. Int. ed. 30 vols. 1989.
Encyclopaedia Britannica. 32 vols. 1988.

Special dictionaries and encyclopedias

Adams, James T. *Dictionary of American History.* Rev. ed. 8 vols. 1983.
Encyclopedia of American Foreign Policy. Ed. Alexander DeConde. 3 vols. 1978.
Encyclopedia of Philosophy. Ed. Paul Edwards et al. 4 vols. 1973.
Encyclopedia of Psychology. Ed. Raymond J. Corsini. 3 vols. 1984.
Encyclopedia of Religion. Ed. Mircea Eliade. 16 vols. 1987.
Encyclopedia of World Art. 15 vols. 1959–68. Supp. 1983, 1987.
International Encyclopedia of Higher Education. Ed. Asa K. Knowles. 10 vols. 1977.
International Encyclopedia of the Social Sciences. Ed. D. E. Sills. 17 vols. 1968. Supplements.

McGraw-Hill Encyclopedia of Science and Technology. 15 vols. 6th ed. 1987. Yearbooks.

The New Grove Dictionary of Music and Musicians. Ed. Stanley Sadie. 20 vols. 1980.

Biography

Contemporary Authors. 1962–.

Current Biography. 1940–.

Dictionary of American Biography. 16 vols. and index. 1927–80. Supplements.

Dictionary of National Biography (British). 22 vols. 1882–1953. Rpt. 1981. Supplements.

Dictionary of Scientific Biography. 16 vols. 1970–80.

Webster's New Biographical Dictionary. 1983.

Who's Who in America. 1899–. (See also Marquis *Who's Who Publications: Index to All Books,* revised annually.)

Literature

Benét, William Rose. *The Reader's Encyclopedia.* 3rd ed. 1987.

Drabble, Margaret. *The Oxford Companion to English Literature.* 5th ed. 1987.

Cambridge History of English Literature. 15 vols. 1907–33.

Elliott, Emory, et al. *Columbia Literary History of the United States.* 1988.

Hart, James D. *The Oxford Companion to American Literature.* 5th ed. 1983.

Harvey, Sir Paul. *The Oxford Companion to Classical Literature.* 2nd ed. 1937. Rpt. 1980.

Holman, C. Hugh, and William Harmon. *Handbook to Literature.* 5th ed. 1986.

Klein, Leonard G. *Encyclopedia of World Literature in the 20th Century.* 2nd ed. 4 vols. 1981–84.

New Cambridge Bibliography of English Literature. 5 vols. 1969–77.

Patterson, Margaret C. *Literary Research Guide.* 2nd ed.
2nd rev. ptg. 1984.

Smith, Horatio. *Columbia Dictionary of Modern European Literature.* 2nd ed. 1980.

Spiller, Robert E., et al. *Literary History of the United States.* 4th ed. 2 vols. 1974.

(2) Learn to use nonprint sources.

Depending upon your topic, you may want to supplement your reading with other types of research. The most common alternative to library research is to conduct a personal interview. The faculty members of your college, business and professional people, and even relatives and friends may make appropriate subjects for an interview if they have relevant firsthand experience with the subject you are researching. You should schedule the interview in advance and ask permission to use a tape recorder if you plan to use one. For the interview itself, you should prepare a list of questions, avoiding any that could be answered with a simple yes or no. Begin with questions that are broad enough to give people room to reveal their own special interests; then follow up with more specific questions. Be prepared to depart from your list of planned questions whenever your subject says something of particular interest that would be useful to pursue. Since the best questions are usually asked by well-informed interviewers, you should usually consider an interview only after you have done some reading on your subject.

Your own experience may also be appropriate for some assignments, but you should check with your instructor to make sure the material you have in mind is acceptable. (For an example of personal experience included within a research paper, see pages 489–503.)

(3) Evaluate your sources.

When doing research, one important consideration always is the reliability of the source. What are the author's credentials? Do others speak of the writer or speaker as an authority? Do you find evidence that the author is competent and well informed, not prejudiced in any way? Is the work recent enough to provide up-to-date information? Does it include a bibliography, and is there documentation to support important points? The *Book Review Digest,* which contains convenient summaries of critical opinion on a book, may help you decide which sources in your bibliography are most dependable. You should also consider the reputation of the publisher of a book or that of a journal in which an article has appeared. For example, university presses usually demand a high standard of scholarship, and an article published in an academic journal (as opposed to a popular magazine) has usually been reviewed by experts before publication. Be alert for bias that may be built into a source, even if it is not obvious when you are reading: an article on malpractice suits published in the *Journal of the American Medical Association* is likely to be sympathetic to physicians.

(4) Prepare a working bibliography.

A working, or preliminary, bibliography contains information (titles, authors, dates, and so on) about the materials you think you might use. Write down the most promising sources you can find. Often the books you consult will have helpful bibliographies. Draw upon them, but do not use them exclusively; otherwise the research will no longer be your own, and you will miss other sources. Put each on a separate index card (preferably 3 × 5 inches) so you can readily drop or add a card and can arrange the list alphabetically without recopying it. Follow consistently the bibliographical form you are instructed to use. Using the specified style from the start will save you valuable time later, when you must compile a formal list of works cited to appear at the end of your paper. Be sure to note the call number for books in case you need to recheck a book after you have returned it or want to see if there are similar books shelved near it.

The style illustrated by the sample bibliography cards below follows the guidelines of the Modern Language Association (MLA). See pages 438–47 for examples of entries you are likely to need for a bibliography in MLA style.

■ **Exercise 2**   Select a subject that would be suitable for a research paper. Then check the availability of materials. (If you cannot find enough books, periodicals, and so on, try another subject.) As you skim through the information, perhaps beginning with an encyclopedia, single out facets that you would like to investigate further. Finally, focus the subject so you can develop it into a paper of the assigned length.

Bibliography cards

Yardley, Jonathan. "Ten Books That Shaped the American Character." *American Heritage* April/May 1985: 24–31.

Bridgman, Richard. *Dark Thoreau.* Lincoln: U. of Neb. P. 1982.

PS
3054
.B7
1982

■ **Exercise 3** Prepare a working bibliography for the subject you have chosen for Exercise 2. Make sure your working bibliography includes both books and articles. Since you are likely to discard some of the sources when you begin to look more closely at them, include enough sources here so you will not find later that you need to start your search over again.

34c

Take notes on your sources.

As you read your sources, learn how to find and evaluate useful passages with a minimum of time and effort. Seldom will a whole book, or even a whole article, be of use as subject matter for any given research paper. You will find that you must turn to many books and articles, rejecting most of them altogether and using from others only a section here and there. You cannot always take the time to read each book completely. Use the table of contents and the index of a book, and learn to skim the pages until you find the passages you need. When you find them, read critically. Ask yourself if you agree with what you are reading and if the material raises any unanswered questions.

As you take notes, use a system that will help you to organize them. One of the best ways to take notes is on cards of uniform size, preferably 4 × 6 inches. (Many researchers use larger cards for notes than for bibliographical references because notes often require more room than references. Different sizes of cards also help a writer to keep the cards' functions separate.)

Each card must show the author's name (and title if your bibliography contains more than one work by that author), including the exact page(s) from which the information is drawn. (See the sample note card on page 421.) Put no more than a single note, however brief, on each card. Then put a heading of two or three key words on the top of each card. Filling out your note cards this way will allow you to

Note card

Measuring Test Anxiety
(*Davies* 53)

*Traditional means of measuring TA may not
be accurate. People may exaggerate or be
influenced by other factors like time of day.
"Clearly, the tests are inadequate...."*

Source (from Davies, page 53)

The accuracy of the above tests, as with all self-report measures, is generally influenced by such factors as honesty and the desire to create a favourable impression or to be seen in a "good light." Even when people try to be honest, however, the answers they give may not be objectively true. Neurotic people, for example, have a tendency to exaggerate their defects. They complain about aches and pains and about sleep problems to an objectively excessive degree. Generally, they tend to be more self-deprecative than people of a calmer and more stable disposition. Scores on self-report measures are also influenced by such factors as the personality of the tester, the time of day, experience of previous tests and temporary moodswings. In a review of self-report instruments to assess trait anxiety, Tryon (1980) . . . concludes by saying that the tests are easily "fakeable." Clearly, the tests are inadequate by themselves except when used for research purposes with large groups of people. (Don Davies, *Maximizing Examination Performance*, New York: Nichols, 1986.)

arrange your cards easily as you prepare to write your paper.

Be careful to write down accurate bibliographic information about every source from which you take notes. Scrupulous care now can prevent a multitude of problems later on—such as being forced to abandon important information because you lost track of exactly where it came from. When you discover a useful passage that you think you may later quote, take it down verbatim—that is, copy every word, every capital letter, and every mark of punctuation exactly as it is in the original. Be especially careful to put quotation marks around any words you take directly from a source; failure to do so on a note card may lead to unintended plagiarism when you draft your paper. See **34e**.

Another way to take notes is to use photocopies of short excerpts from materials you think you may quote directly. On a photocopy you can mark quotable material and jot down your own ideas as you study the source. Make sure you document the source on the photocopy.

Photocopied source with notes (from "Thoreau" by James Russell Lowell, page 199)

I have just been renewing my recollection of Mr. Thoreau's writings, and have read through his six volumes in the order of their production. I shall try to give an adequate report of their impression upon me both as critic and as mere reader. He seems to me to have been a man with <u>so high a conceit</u> of *!* himself that <u>he accepted without questioning</u>, and insisted on our accepting, <u>his defects and weaknesses</u> of character as virtues and powers peculiar to himself. Was he indolent, he finds none of the activities which attract or employ the rest of mankind worthy of him. <u>Was he wanting</u> in the qualities that <u>make success</u>, <u>it is success that is contemptible</u>, and not himself that lacks persistency and purpose. <u>Was he poor, money was an unmixed</u> evil. Did his life seem a selfish one, he condemns doing good as one of the weakest of superstitions. To be of use was with him the most killing bait of the wily tempter Uselessness. <u>He had no faculty of generalization</u>

is this fair?

(Lowell 199)

422

34d
Make a working plan or outline.

After completing a working bibliography and taking notes on your subject, make a working plan for your paper. Do not feel that you must adhere rigidly to this plan, though. No plan or outline should be regarded as complete until the research paper has been finished. As you write the paper, you will probably revise your original plan frequently, adding points, changing points, and perhaps dropping points you had originally intended to cover.

It is sometimes useful, especially if your paper is long or complicated, to have a detailed outline before you actually begin to write. If you work best with a formal outline, decide whether to use a topic outline or a sentence outline. A topic outline presents information in parallel phrases or single words (see pages 378 and 450–51). A sentence outline presents the same ideas in declarative statements (see pages 378–79). If your instructor has asked you to submit a formal outline of your paper before you begin to draft, prepare a topic or sentence outline as you are directed.

When you have finished drafting your paper, a good way to check your organization is to correlate the ideas in your text with those in an outline and to make any needed revisions. Also check the form of your outline: see **33e**.

34e
Use sources responsibly.

When you write a paper, you should realize that you have several options for including material from other writers. You can quote their exact words, paraphrase them, or summarize them. Whatever option you choose, make sure that you use sources responsibly. Words or ideas taken from other writers should not be distorted in any way, and credit should be given whenever appropriate.

▲ Note: The documentation style of the Modern Language Association is used in the following examples of quotation, paraphrase, and summary. For additional information on documentation, see **34f** and **34g**.

(1) Plagiarism

You must acknowledge all material quoted, paraphrased, or summarized from any published or unpublished work. Failing to cite a source, deliberately or accidentally, is plagiarism—presenting as your own work the words or ideas of another. As the *MLA Handbook* (New York: MLA, 1988) states,

> The most blatant form of plagiarism is to repeat as your own someone else's sentences, more or less verbatim. . . .
> Other forms of plagiarism include repeating someone else's . . . apt phrase without appropriate acknowledgment, paraphrasing another person's argument as your own, and presenting another's line of thinking as though it were your own. (22–23)

After you have done a good deal of reading about a given subject, you will be able to distinguish between common knowledge in that field and the distinctive ideas or interpretations of specific writers. When you use the ideas or information that these writers provide, be sure to cite the exact source of the material used.

NOT In *Walden*, Thoreau argued that a man is rich in proportion to the number of things which he can afford to let alone. [undocumented copying]

BUT In *Walden*, Thoreau argued that "a man is rich in proportion to the number of things which he can afford to let alone" (166). [Quotation marks enclose copied words, and the number in parentheses refers the reader to the exact page in the source.]

NOT   Academic competition can weaken the motivation of students who are not evenly matched in ability. [an undocumented idea from the work of another writer]

BUT   Academic competition can weaken the motivation of students who are not evenly matched in ability (Davies 27).

OR   According to Don Davies, academic competition can weaken motivation "if an individual is either being continually outclassed or is surpassing the other students with ease" (27).

If you are in doubt about whether you need to cite a source, the best policy is to cite it.

(2) Direct quotations

A quotation should contribute an idea to your paper. Select quotations only if they are important and make them an integral part of your text. (For examples of ways this can be done, see pages 455, 461, 495.) Quote accurately. Enclose every quoted passage in quotation marks. Any quotation (except well-known or proverbial passages) of the words of another person should be placed in quotation marks or, if longer than four lines, set off as an indented block (see **16a**). Exact sources should be cited.

Thoreau argued in <u>Walden</u> that "men have become the

tools of their tools" (132). [Quotation marks enclose copied words, and internal documentation indicates the source.]

If a source may be unfamiliar to your audience, identify the author to establish his or her authority in your first reference to this source:

Don Davies, a British psychologist, argues that

traditional methods of measuring test anxiety are

"inadequate . . . except when used for research

purposes with large groups of people" (53).

For examples of the use and the documentation of direct quotations, see the sample research papers on pages 453–79 and 489–503.

When you write your research paper, keep a few guidelines in mind: direct quotations must be accurate in all details. Pay close attention to form, punctuation, and spacing: see **16a**. Use ellipsis points appropriately to indicate omissions: see **17i**. But do not use ellipsis points before quotations that are clearly only parts of sentences. Use brackets (**17g**) to surround any word or phrase that you add within a quotation to clarify its meaning.

▲ Note: Too many quotations in a paper can convey the impression that you have little to say for yourself.

(3) Paraphrase

A paraphrase is a restatement of a source in about the same number of words. Paraphrasing enables you to demonstrate that you have understood your reading; it also enables you to help your audience understand the results of your reading. The most common reason for paraphrasing is to restate difficult material more simply.

Your restatement of someone else's words should honor two important principles: your version should be almost entirely in your own words, and your words should accurately convey the content of the original passage. If you simply change a few words in a passage, you have not adequately restated it. As you compare the source below with the paraphrase that follows, notice differences in sentence structure as well as word choice.

Source (from *Walden* by Henry David Thoreau, page 109)

> Most men, even in this comparatively free country, through mere ignorance and mistake, are so occupied with the factitious cares and superfluously coarse labors of life that its finer fruits cannot be plucked by them.

Paraphrase

```
Thoreau argued that most people miss some of the

best pleasures in life because they make the

mistake of working unnecessarily hard and worrying

about unimportant problems (109).
```

In this example, the page reference establishes where the paraphrase ends; the introductory "Thoreau argued" establishes where it begins. When you paraphrase, make sure that your audience will be able to tell whether you are paraphrasing a single sentence or more. As a general rule, begin paraphrases with a phrase that indicates you are about to restate another writer's words.

Paraphrase whenever doing so will make your sources clearer or your paper flow more smoothly; quote when you want to retain the beauty or clarity of someone else's words. (When writing about *Walden*, for example, it would be hard to improve upon a line such as "The mass of men lead lives of quiet desperation.") For further examples of the use and documentation of paraphrases, see pages 452 and 470.

▲ Note: If you simply change a few words in a passage, you have not adequately restated it. You may be charged with plagiarism if the wording of your version follows the original too closely, even if you provide a page reference to the source you used. A page reference after an inadequate paraphrase would acknowledge the source of your idea but not the extent of your debt to another writer's language.

(4) Summary

A summary is a concise restatement (shorter than the original source). An essential skill for writing research papers, summarizing enables writers to report the work of others without getting bogged down in unnecessary detail. Paraphrase when you want to restate a passage so that it is easier to understand or fits more smoothly into your paper; summarize whenever you can save space by condensing a passage (or, in some cases, an entire work).

Source (from *Maximizing Examination Performance* by Davies, page 27)

> Competition during study and practice sessions can be an incentive and a useful motivational technique provided it is used wisely and is closely related to the needs of individuals. Moderate competition between students provides interest and enjoyment, but it can be disastrous and destroy morale if too much importance is attached to the results. Motivation will also be weakened if an individual is either being continually outclassed or is surpassing the other students with ease. Competition between low-skilled people tends to disrupt performance but for highly skilled people performance tends to be enhanced.

Summary

According to Don Davies, competition can hurt

students if the results are emphasized too much.

But moderate competition can help improve both the

motivation and performance of highly skilled

students who are evenly matched (27).

▲ Note: When you are summarizing, you may find it useful to retain a key phrase from your source but if you do so, put quotation marks around the words in question.

■ **Exercise 4**   Carefully read paragraphs 3 (page 324), 11 (page 328), and 16 (page 331) in section **32**. First paraphrase one of these paragraphs; then write a summary of the same paragraph. Unless you are quoting directly, avoid using the same sentence patterns as the source. To convey the source's ideas exactly, choose your words carefully.

34f

Draft and revise a research paper with MLA style documentation.

As you draft a research paper, remember that it is *your* paper. Using the headings on your note cards (see page 420), arrange your notes in the order of your working plan or outline, and then use the notes as the basis of your paper. Make sure to write the paper in your own words and your own style. Integrate your source material—paraphrases, summaries, quotations—with your own statements rather than making the paper a patchwork of other people's comments.

(1) Parenthetical citations

Give proper credit by citing your sources. Traditionally, such citations took the form of notes numbered consecutively throughout the paper and placed either at the bottoms of the appropriate pages (footnotes) or all together at the end of the paper (endnotes). Although some writers still use a note system (see pages 480–82), the Modern Language Association (MLA) recommends placing citations directly in the text, in parentheses. These parenthetical citations refer the reader to a list of works cited at the end of the paper. The advantage of this system is that it is easy for both writers and readers to use. The MLA suggests reserving the numbered note system for cases in which the writer needs to make supplementary or explanatory comments about given references. (The numbers are inserted in the appropriate places in the text, and the notes are gathered at the end of the paper [see page 475].)

The basic elements of the parenthetical citation are the author's last name and the page number of the material used in the source. (If your bibliography includes more than one work by the same author, parenthetical documentation within the essay should also include a shortened version of the appropriate title and, if necessary, a volume number.) However, it is not necessary to repeat any information that is already clearly provided. In other words, the author's name can be omitted from the parenthetical citation if it is identified in the text of the paper, shortly before the material being cited. As you study the following examples, observe that common sense determines the information that must be included in a parenthetical citation and that this system is easy to use. (The first example is taken from the research paper on pages 453–79 so you can see how a citation refers readers to a source listed alphabetically in the list of works cited at the end of the paper.)

A work by one author

```
Henry David Thoreau's now-famous account of his

two-year sojourn at Walden Pond has successfully

weathered the storms of controversy, survived the

doldrums of uninterest, and emerged as one of "ten

books that shaped America" (Yardley 24).
```

In this citation, the author's name is included within the parentheses because it is not mentioned in the text. Since only one work by Yardley is included in the list of works cited (on page 479), there is no need to use a title in the parentheses. However, a page number is included because the reference is to a specific passage.

Notice how the citation changes if the text includes more information about the source:

```
According to Yardley, Thoreau's Walden is one of

the "ten books that shaped America" (24).
```

A work by two or three authors

```
During the 1960s, economic failure was widely

blamed for social alienation and political

extremism (Aiken, Ferman, and Sheppard 114—16).
```

Provide the last name of each author, punctuating as you would for items in a series. Commas are not necessary in a citation involving only two authors, for example: (Meltzer and Harding 237). (See page 479 for the corresponding bibliographic entry for this example.)

A work by more than three authors

If you are citing a source by more than three authors, supply the name of the first author and follow the name with *et al.*, the Latin abbreviation for *et alii*, meaning "and others." (Follow this same convention when supplying the corresponding bibliographic entry.)

```
The rise of the American public school system has

been attributed, at least in part, to the lack of

other "authoritative institutions" (Bailyn et al.

513).
```

A multivolume work

When you cite material from a multivolume work, include the volume number (followed by a colon and a space) before the page number.

As Katherine Raine has argued, "true poetry begins
where human personality ends" (2: 247).

▲ Note: If your list of works cited includes only one volume
of a multivolume work, then you do not need to include the
volume number within the parenthetical citation.

More than one work by the same author

When your list of works cited includes more than one work
by the same author, your parenthetical citations should include a shortened title revealing which of the author's
works is being cited in a particular instance.

According to John Kenneth Galbraith, 17% of the
American work force was unemployed as late as 1939
(<u>Uncertainty</u> 221). Many historians have argued that
the Depression was ended by the Second World War.
But after the war, "it would be a deliberate
purpose of government to . . . ensure full
employment" (Galbraith, <u>Economics</u> 251).

This passage cites two different books by John Kenneth
Galbraith, *The Age of Uncertainty* and *Economics in Perspective*. The author's name is not necessary in the first
citation since it is mentioned in the text; it is included in
the second citation because Galbraith's name is not mentioned in this sentence or the preceding sentence.

You can often avoid cumbersome references by including
information in the text that might otherwise have to appear
parenthetically: "In *Economics in Perspective*, John Kenneth Galbraith argues that government interest in ensuring
full employment began after the Second World War (251)."

▲ Note: A comma separates the author's name from the shortened title when both are provided in parentheses.

Works by different authors with the same last name

Occasionally your list of works cited will contain sources by two authors with the same last name—for example, K. Patricia Cross and Wilbur Cross. In such cases, you must use the first name as well as the last.

```
Educator Wilbur Cross has suggested that the

situation of the mature student has excited

considerable interest in academic circles (8-9).

Other commentators explore the ways that academe

can serve these students (K. Patricia Cross 32, 41).
```

▲ Note: In these references to more than one page, "8–9" identifies continuous pages and "32, 41" indicates that the reference is to two separate pages.

An indirect source

Although you should try to consult original sources whenever possible, you may want to include a quotation that one of your sources quoted from a work you have not read. In this situation, use the following form:

```
The critic Susan Hardy Aikens has argued on behalf

of what she calls "canonical multiplicity" (qtd. in

Mayers 677).
```

A reader turning to the list of works cited should find a bibliographic entry for Mayers (which was the source consulted) but not for Aikens (because the quotation was obtained secondhand).

Poetry, drama, and the Bible

When you refer to poetry, drama, and the Bible, you must often give numbers of lines, acts, and scenes, or of chapters and verses, rather than page numbers. This practice enables a reader to consult an edition other than the one you are using. Nonetheless, your list of works cited should still identify your edition.

Act, scene, and line numbers (all Arabic) are separated by periods with no space before or after them. MLA suggests that biblical chapters and verses be treated similarly, although some writers prefer to use colons instead of periods in scriptural references. In all cases, the progression is from larger to smaller units.

The following example illustrates a typical citation of lines of poetry.

```
Emily Dickinson concludes "I'm Nobody! Who Are

You?" with a characteristically bittersweet

stanza:

          How dreary to be somebody!

          How public, like a frog

          To tell your name the livelong June

          To an admiring bog!  (5-8)
```

The following citation shows that Hamlet's "To be, or not to be" soliloquy appears in act 3, scene 1, lines 56–89 of *Hamlet*.

```
In Hamlet Shakespeare presents the most famous

soliloquy in the history of the theater: "To be, or

not to be . . ."  (3.1.56-89).
```

For additional examples, see section **35**. The following reference to the Bible indicates that the account of creation in Genesis extends from chapter 1, verse 1, through chapter 2, verse 22.

```
The Old Testament creation story (Gen. 1.1—2.22),

told with remarkable economy, culminates in the

arrival of Eve.
```

▲ Note: Names of books of the Bible are neither underlined (italicized) nor enclosed in quotation marks, and abbreviation is desirable.

Punctuation and mechanics

Commas are used to separate authors' names and titles (Galbraith, *Economics*) and to indicate interruptions in a sequence of pages or lines (44, 47). Hyphens are used to indicate continuous sequences of pages (44–47) and lines (1–4). Colons separate volume and page numbers (Raine 2: 247). A space follows the colon. Periods separate acts, scenes, and lines in drama (3.1.56–89) and chapters and verses in the Bible (Gen. 1.1).

Citations should, wherever possible, appear just before punctuation in the text of the paper.

```
Wilbur Cross speaks of adult learners who "range

in age from the mid—twenties to the upper sixties,

and vary in background from nurses, teachers,

business people and government employees to truck

drivers, police officers and 'just ordinary family

people'" (116), whereas K. Patricia Cross views
```

```
adult learners as a class of students dispropor-

tionately young, white, and affluent (45).
```

Wilbur Cross's citation falls just before a comma; K. Patricia Cross's just before a period. However, in a sentence such as the following, the citations should follow the authors' names to keep the references separate.

```
Wilbur Cross (116) and K. Patricia Cross (45) speak

of different kinds of adult learners.
```

When a quotation is more than four lines long, set it off from the text by indenting ten spaces from the left margin. The citation, in this case, follows the final punctuation.

```
As J. W. Krutch, a Thoreau biographer, puts it:

          If "Simplify" is the one word which sums

          up his [Thoreau's] teaching, it also sums

          up . . . what his own contemporaries were

          not doing and what we have . . . tended

          not to do. They lived in an age of

          increasing complexity and great hope; we

          in an age of . . . growing despair. (2)
```

▲ Note: Single quotation marks become double quotation marks in an extract. (See **16a**.)

(2) List of works cited

When you are ready to make the final revision of your paper, you will know which sources from your working bibliography you have actually used and cited in your paper.

Now eliminate the bibliography cards for the works that you do not cite, and arrange the remaining cards in alphabetical order by authors' last names. You are now ready to prepare the list of works cited that will conclude your paper. As you make your final revision, you will be checking your citations against this list to ensure that they are complete and correct.

In MLA style the list of works cited is arranged alphabetically by author and is double-spaced throughout. The first line of each entry is flush with the left margin; subsequent lines are indented to leave five spaces. If you use more than one work by the same author, list the works alphabetically by title. Give the author's name with the first title, but substitute three hyphens for the name in subsequent entries. (Other documentation styles handle this list differently and have different names for it. See **34g** and **34h**.)

Thomas, Lewis. <u>The Lives of a Cell: Notes of</u>

   <u>a Biology Watcher</u>. New York: Viking, 1975.

   <u>The Medusa and the Snail: More Notes of</u>

   <u>a Biology Watcher</u>. New York: Viking, 1979.

Bibliographical entries often consist of only three units, which are separated by periods:

Toffler, Alvin. <u>The Third Wave</u>. New York: Morrow,

   1980.

1. *Who is the author?* Give the last name first. Your final list of works cited will be arranged alphabetically by authors' last names.
2. *What is the title?* Underline (italicize) the title of a book, and capitalize it in accordance with **9c**. Always include the book's subtitle.

3. *Where and when was it published?* Include the place of publication, the publisher, and the latest copyright date as shown on the copyright page. Give a shortened form of the publisher's name as long as it is clear.

Some entries, however, require more than three units and must be given special treatment. As you study the following MLA style entries, which cover most of the problems you are likely to encounter, observe both the punctuation and the arrangement of information. See also pages 447–49 for a list of abbreviations that are permissible in bibliographies, notes, and tables.

▲ Note: The MLA style favors Arabic numbers throughout, except when citing pages that are identified by Roman numerals within the source itself.

SAMPLE BIBLIOGRAPHICAL ENTRIES

Books

One author

Reynolds, David. <u>Beneath the American Renaissance:</u>

<u>The Subversive Imagination in the Age of</u>

<u>Emerson and Melville</u>. New York: Knopf, 1988.

Notice that a colon is placed before the subtitle and that the underlining of the complete title is continuous.

▲ Note: Although you should always provide the full title of a book, you should shorten the publisher's name (in this instance, Alfred A. Knopf) as much as possible while still identifying it clearly.

Two authors

Barlett, Donald L., and James B. Steele.

> Forevermore: Nuclear Waste in America. New

> York: Norton, 1985.

Three authors

Aiken, Michael, Lewis A. Ferman, and Harold L.

> Sheppard. Economic Failure, Alienation, and

> Extremism. Ann Arbor: U of Michigan P, 1968.

▲ **Note:** Abbreviations (without periods) are used for "university" and "press" for books published by universities.

More than three authors

Bailyn, Bernard, et al. The Great Republic: A

> History of the American People. Lexington:

> Heath, 1977.

Corporate author

American Red Cross. Standard First Aid and

> Personal Safety. 2nd ed. Garden City:

> Doubleday, 1979.

Edition after the first

Grout, Donald Jay. A History of Western Music.

> 3rd ed. New York: Norton, 1980.

Editors

Zigler, Edward F., and Meryl Frank, eds. <u>The</u>

    <u>Parental Leave Crisis</u>. New Haven: Yale UP,

    1988.

Work from an anthology

Hollander, John. "Wordsworth and the Music of

    Sound." <u>New Perspectives on Coleridge and</u>

    <u>Wordsworth</u>. Ed. Geoffrey H. Hartman. New

    York: Columbia UP, 1972. 41–84.

Use this form for an article or essay that was first published in an anthology; use it also for a story, poem, or play reprinted in an anthology. For an article or essay that was published elsewhere before being included in an anthology, use the following form:

Welty, Eudora. "The Eye of the Story." <u>Yale Review</u>

    55 (1966): 265–74. Rpt. in <u>Katherine Anne</u>

    <u>Porter: A Collection of Critical Essays</u>. Ed.

    Robert Penn Warren. Englewood Cliffs:

    Prentice, 1979. 72–80.

Report where the essay first appeared and then show where you read it. Use the abbreviation "Rpt." for "reprinted."

Translation

Laborit, Henri. <u>Decoding the Human Message</u>. Trans.

Stephen Bodington and Alison Wilson. New York:

St. Martin's, 1977.

Reprint

Massie, Robert K. <u>Peter the Great: His Life and</u>

<u>World</u>. 1980. New York: Ballantine, 1986.

The original hardcover edition was published six years earlier than this paperback version.

A work in more than one volume

Odell, George C. D. <u>Annals of the New York Stage</u>.

15 vols. New York: Columbia UP, 1927–49.

This multivolume work was published over a period of
years.

▲ Note: Cite the total number of volumes in a work when
you have used more than one volume. If you use only one
volume, include that volume number (preceded by the
abbreviation *Vol.*) after the title and include the number of
volumes in the complete work at the end of the entry.

A work in a series

Bebout, John E., and Ronald J. Grele. <u>Where Cities</u>

<u>Meet: The Urbanization of New Jersey</u>. New

Jersey Historical Ser. 22. Princeton: Van

Nostrand, 1964.

Provide the name of the series and the number designating the work's place in the series.

An introduction, foreword, or afterword

Grumbach, Doris. Foreword. <u>My Antonia</u>. By Willa

    Cather. Boston: Houghton, 1988. vii—xxix.

Magazines and newspapers

Weekly magazine or newspaper

Boswell, Robert. "The Good Man." <u>New Yorker</u>

    3 Oct. 1988: 36—39.

Queenan, Joe. "The Ridiculous to the

    Sublime." <u>Barrons</u> 17 Oct. 1988: 40—41.

▲ Note: As a rule, the names of months (except May, June, and July) are abbreviated. Volume numbers are unnecessary because specific dates are given.

Monthly magazine

Koretz, Jane F., and George H. Handleman. "How the

    Human Eye Focuses." <u>Scientific American</u> July

    1988: 92—99.

▲ Note: Sometimes a magazine article is printed on pages that are separated by other articles; for example, the first part appears on pages 137–39, the last on pages 188–203. In such a case, give only the first page number followed by a plus sign: 137+.

Journal: Continuous pagination

```
Himmelfarb, Gertrude.  "Manners into Morals: What

    the Victorians Knew."  American Scholar 57

    (1988): 223-32.
```

Citing a specific issue (e.g., Spring 1988) is not necessary when a journal's pages are numbered continuously throughout the year.

Journal: Separate pagination

```
Chomsky, Carol.  "Stages in Language Development

    and Reading Exposure."  Harvard Educational

    Review 42.2 (1972): 1-33.
```

When the pages of each issue are numbered separately, put a period after the volume number and add the issue number.

Daily newspaper

```
Duetsch, Claudia H.  "Taking the Reins from a

    Legend."  New York Times 30 Oct. 1988, natl.

    ed., sec. 3: 6-7.
```

When it is not part of the newspaper's name, the city's name should be given in brackets after the title. If a specific edition is not named on the masthead, put a colon after the date and then provide the page reference. Column numbers are not used, but you should specify the section. If sections are lettered rather than numbered, include the section letter next to the page number as it appears in the newspaper (A1 or 1A).

Editorial

```
"False Negatives."  Editorial.  Wall Street Journal

     8 Nov. 1988, midwest ed.: A14.
```

Begin the citation with the author's name if the editorial is signed.

Book review

```
Gates, David.  "The Trouble with Charlie."  Rev. of

     Dickens: A Biography, by Fred Kaplan.

     Newsweek 7 Nov. 1988: 120—21.
```

Encyclopedias and almanacs

```
Hopkinson, Ralph G.  "Electric Lighting."

     Encyclopedia Americana.  1985 ed.
```

Full publication information is not necessary for a well-known reference work organized alphabetically. For sources that are somewhat remote or difficult to find, you should reveal more about the source:

```
Dreyer, Edward L.  "Inner Mongolia."  Encyclopedia

     of Asian History.  Ed. Ainslee T. Embree.  4

     vols. New York: Scribner's, 1988.
```

Pamphlets and bulletins

<u>Safety Data Sheet: Kitchen Machines</u>.   Pamphlet 690.

Chicago: Natl. Restaurant Assn., 1970.

Titles of pamphlets are italicized (underlined).

United States.   Bur. of Labor Statistics.

<u>Tomorrow's Manpower Needs</u>.   Washington: GPO,

1973.

Notice the sequence for a government publication: government, agency, title—each followed by a period and two spaces. The publisher in this example is the Government Printing Office.

Nonprint sources

Motion picture

<u>Fatal Attraction</u>.   Dir. Adrian Lyne.   Paramount,

1987.

Radio or television program

<u>At Your Service</u>.   Writ. and prod. by Jim

White.   KMOX, St. Louis.   24 May 1985.

Williams, Tennessee.   <u>Cat on a Hot Tin Roof</u>.   Dir.

Jack Hofsiss.   American Playhouse.   PBS.

KCET, Los Angeles.   24 June 1985.

Stage play

Ghosts. By Henrik Ibsen. Dir. Stuart Vaughan.

Roundabout Theatre, New York. 23 Oct. 1988.

Recording

Springsteen, Bruce. "Badlands." Darkness on the

Edge of Town. Columbia, JC 35318, 1978.

Provide album title, publisher, catalog number, and copyright date.

Computer software

Button, Jim. PC File III. Vers. 4.0. Computer

software. ButtonWare, 1986. PC–DOS 2.0,

128KB, disk.

Provide author, title, version number, descriptive label, · distributor, and copyright date. Add other pertinent information at the end of the entry, including the operating system and units of memory necessary for running the program.

Lecture

Holborn, David. Class lecture. English 200.

University of Wisconsin, Stevens Point. 21

Nov. 1988.

Provide a descriptive label for an untitled lecture, use the title if available, and give the date and location.

Interview

```
Dorgan, Ruth.   Personal interview.   14 Aug. 1989.
```

For samples of citations of other nonprint sources—such as games, filmstrips, microscope slides, and transparencies—consult Eugene B. Fleischer's *A Style Manual for Citing Microform and Nonprint Media* (Chicago: American Library Association, 1978).

COMMON ABBREVIATIONS

Below is a list of abbreviations commonly used in documenting research papers.

abr.	abridged, abridgment
Acad.	Academy
anon.	anonymous
app.	appendix
Apr.	April
Assn.	Association
Aug.	August
biog.	biography, biographer, biographical
bk., bks.	book, books
bull.	bulletin
c.	*circa*, "about" (for example, "c. 1966")
cf.	compare
ch., chs.	chapter, chapters
col., cols.	column, columns
Coll.	College
comp.	compiled by, compiler
Cong. Rec.	*Congressional Record*
cont.	contents, continued

DAB	*Dictionary of American Biography*
Dec.	December
dept.	department.
dir.	directed by, director
diss.	dissertation
div.	division
DNB	*Dictionary of National Biography*
ed., eds.	edition(s) OR editor(s)
enl.	enlarged (as in "rev. and enl. ed.")
et al.	*et alii,* "and others"
Feb.	February
fig.	figure
fwd.	foreword, foreword by
gen. ed.	general editor
govt.	government
GPO	Government Printing Office
HR	House of Representatives
illus.	illustrated by, illustrator, illustration
inc.	incorporated; including
Inst.	Institute, Institution
intl.	international
introd.	[author of] introduction, introduced by
Jan.	January
jour.	journal
l., ll.	line, lines
mag.	magazine
Mar.	March
ms., mss.	manuscript, manuscripts
n, nn	note, notes (used immediately after page number: 6n3)
natl.	national
n.d.	no date [of publication]
no., nos.	number [of issue], numbers
Nov.	November
n.p.	no place [of publication]; no publisher
n. pag.	no pagination
Oct.	October
P	Press (used in documentation; see "UP")

p., pp.	page, pages (omitted before page numbers unless reference would be unclear)
pref.	preface, preface by
pseud.	pseudonym
pt., pts.	part, parts
rept.	reported by, report
rev.	revision, revised, revised by OR review, reviewed by
rpt.	reprinted, reprint
sec., secs.	section, sections
Sept.	September
ser.	series
sic	thus, so
Soc.	Society
supp.	supplement
trans.	translated by, translator, translation
U	University (used in documentation; see "UP")
UP	University Press (used in documentation: Wesleyan UP)
vol., vols.	volume, volumes (omitted before volume numbers unless reference would be unclear)

(3) Final revisions and proofreading

After writing and carefully documenting the first draft of your paper, make needed revisions. To make your writing as clear and effective as possible, you will probably need to rewrite some sentences and strike out or add others. Use the Reviser's Checklist on pages 390–92. (You may wish to review pages 389–93 of section **33**.) Refer to **8b** and especially to the sample research papers on pages 453–79 and 489–503 as you put your paper in final form. Even when writing final copy, you will probably continue to make changes in word choice and to correct occasional errors in spelling, mechanics, or grammar. Type or write legibly. Proofread your final revision before handing it in.

Some instructors ask their students to submit outlines, notes, and drafts along with the final paper. Other instructors require a title page and a final outline along with the text of the paper. A title page usually gives the title of the paper, the author, the name of the course and its section number, the instructor's name, and the date—all attractively centered on the page: see the example on page 489. The MLA recommends using no title page and giving the identification on the first page before the title of the paper: see page 453.

When submitted with the text of a research paper, the final outline serves as a table of contents. In this case, a title page is advisable. (For a sample title page that can be modified for an MLA style paper, see page 489 and the comment on page 488.)

The following sample is a topic outline. (If your instructor specifies a sentence outline, see the sample on pages 378–79.) Some instructors ask students to make the introduction and conclusion numbered headings. Other instructors require an outline only of the main discussion and suggest that references to introduction and conclusion be omitted from the outline.

```
                          Outline

Thesis:   The popularity of Walden ebbs and flows in
          relation to political and economic
          factors.

Introduction:   Brief overview of changing responses
                to Walden emphasizing current status.
```

   I. The initial reaction to <u>Walden</u>
       A. Regarded as a nature book, not philosophy
       B. Compared to Defoe's <u>Robinson Crusoe</u>
       C. Created false expectations for readers
  II. The second half of the nineteenth century
       A. America's rapid industrialization
       B. Thoreau's social criticism
       C. Lowell's review of <u>Walden</u>
 III. The first half of the twentieth century
       A. Renewal of interest in Thoreau
       B. Rise of <u>Walden</u>'s status in 1940s
  IV. The second half of the twentieth century
       A. Popularity of <u>Walden</u> in 1960s
       B. Status of <u>Walden</u> today

Conclusion: <u>Walden</u> may be regarded as a
              masterpiece today, but its future
              status cannot be predicted.

SAMPLE RESEARCH PAPER

A sample research paper follows, the format of which may
serve as a model for an MLA-style paper of your own. The
left-hand pages contain passages from sources, some note
cards, and comments on content and form.

■ **Exercise 5**   Prepare for a class discussion of the following research
paper. Does the paper have a clear thesis? Where is it first introduced?
How well is the paper organized? Could it be organized another way?
How well has the source material been included? Does the author include ideas of his own or does he simply report the views of others?

COMMENTS

1. The identification, double-spaced, begins one inch from the top of the page and flush with the left margin. A double-spaced line precedes the centered title of the paper. A margin of about one inch is provided at the left, right, and bottom.

2. Double-space between the title from the first line of the text. (A title consisting of two or more lines is double-spaced, and each line is centered.)

3. All pages (including the first page) are numbered with Arabic numerals in the upper right-hand corner, about one-half inch from the top. The page number is preceded by the student author's last name. Notice that no period follows the page numbers.

4. The first citation is to a book by two authors; the list of works cited at the end of the paper reveals that Meltzer and Harding's book was published in 1962. Because Kelley wanted to use material from this source, but realized it was no longer current, he supplements it with a note providing additional information (see page 475). Study the note card reproduced below, and consider how he has paraphrased his source.

Walden's publication history
(Meltzer and Harding 237)
     Since 1862, _Walden_ "has never been out of print and has appeared in at least one hundred and fifty different editions, many of the individual editions selling up in the hundreds of thousands of copies. There are probably more copies of it in print than any other American literary work of nonfiction that appeared in the nineteenth century. It has been translated into Czechoslovakian, Danish, Dutch, Finnish, French, German, Greek, Hebrew, Italian, Japanese, Norse, Portuguese, Russian, Sanskrit, Spanish, and Swedish."

Dennis Kelley

Professor Young

English 199

3 November 1988

The Changing Response to <u>Walden</u>

Since 1854, when <u>Walden</u> was launched upon the **1**
literary waters, it has proven to be a sturdy,
seaworthy craft. Over one hundred and fifty
editions have been issued, and the book has been
translated into at least sixteen foreign languages
(Meltzer and Harding 237).[1] Henry David Thoreau's
now-famous account of his two-year sojourn at
Walden Pond has successfully weathered the storms
of controversy, survived the doldrums of
uninterest, and emerged as one of "ten books that
shaped America" (Yardley 24).

Through the years, the direction of the **2**
political wind and the strength of the economic
tide determined whether <u>Walden</u>'s sails were hoisted
by the book's proponents or furled and stowed by
its detractors. It has not always been clear
sailing for <u>Walden</u>.

The early reviews of the book were less than **3**
spectacular. Many critics seemed confused by
Thoreau's wide-ranging choice of topics and the
seeming lack of structure in the work. <u>Walden</u> was
reviewed by some critics as a simple nature study
and by others as a serious work of social

COMMENTS

1. The "Review" citation shows an example of how to credit an anonymous work by providing an abbreviated title. The comma that separates the two page references reveals that the material cited in this sentence comes from two separate pages in the same source.
2. The citation to Krutch includes a shortened version of a title because the list of works cited includes more than one work by Krutch.
3. Study the note card reprinted below and observe how Kelley paraphrases his material in his final paper to avoid a quotation that requires clarification in several brackets.

Early reviews
(Scharnhorst)
"... they [Thoreau's editors] placed a large classified ad for _Walden_ in five successive early August issues of the Boston [Transcript] paper and in three issues of the [N.Y.] _Post_, they placed an identical advertisement in... two issues of the [N.Y.] _Tribune_."

(117)

philosophy, but rarely was it read as a synthesis
of both. Seeking a convenient slot in which to
file <u>Walden</u>, an anonymous reviewer, writing one
month after the book's publication, praised
Thoreau's descriptions of nature for their
"Defoe—like accuracy and reality" while he
considered the author's philosophizing "strikingly
original, [but] sometimes merely eccentric and odd"
("Review" 5, 7). This short review was one of
several that linked <u>Walden</u> to the work of Daniel
Defoe, the author of <u>Robinson Crusoe</u>.[2]

This link created false expectations among   **4**
readers. Those who bought Thoreau's latest work
looking for a tale of adventure like <u>Robinson
Crusoe</u> or a nature study were often disappointed to
find that, while accurate and realistic
descriptions of nature were certainly one of the
book's strongest features, a casual reader had to
sift through many pages of Thoreau's unorthodox
philosophy to find them. Interest in the book
lagged. Though <u>Walden</u>'s publisher ran large
classified ads for the book in three influential
newspapers in Boston and New York (Scharnhorst
117), only two thousand copies were sold during
Thoreau's lifetime (Krutch, <u>Thoreau</u> 103). <u>Walden</u>
appeared to be dead in the water. The overwhelming
problem Thoreau faced was not with his style or
structure in <u>Walden</u>, but that when the book was

COMMENT

1. Although Kelley had two note cards from Graebner, Fite, and White, he used only one in the paper. Writers must be willing to discard some of their notes. Avoid the temptation to include more material than you need just because you have it at hand.

Industrial Expansion
(Graebner)

"In 1859, America's 140,433 industrial establishments produced some $2 billion worth of products; in 1914, 275,791 estab. turned out products valued at more than $24 billion." (447)

Begins with Thoreau's death / ends at WWI

Expansion
(Graebner)

"In 1860, the U.S. had 30,626 miles of railroads. By 1914, the United States boasted a rail network of 252,105 miles..." (449)

Thoreau's hate affair w/ railroads

published, the ideas he expressed about work and
machines were at odds with the prevailing economic
attitudes in the United States. <u>Walden</u> was
published at the wrong time.

In the 1850s, the U.S. was entering the **5**
industrial age, and as factories increased
production, farming slowly began to fade from its
role as the most important factor in the American
economy. The Puritan work ethic, with its emphasis
on hard work as a means by which to acquire wealth
and material possessions, formed the bedrock of the
American business philosophy, especially in
Thoreau's New England--the old Puritan stomping
grounds, where the factories first flourished.
Following this philosophy, industry prospered,
proliferating at an amazing rate. In 1859,
American factories produced products worth about
$2 billion; by 1914, the number of factories in the
U.S. had nearly doubled and produced manufactured
goods worth over $24 billion (Graebner, Fite, and
White 447).

It was onto this turbulent ocean of industrial **6**
progress that Thoreau launched <u>Walden</u> with a call
for "Simplicity, simplicity, simplicity!"
(173). Thoreau's message is stridently opposed to
the dehumanizing expansion of American industry
where a factory laborer "has no time to be anything
but a machine" (109). Beyond all else, <u>Walden</u>

COMMENTS

1. The ellipses at the end of the citation from Gabriel reveal that what reads here as a complete sentence continued further in the original source.
2. Study the following excerpt from the first draft of this essay and evaluate the changes Kelley made to what would become paragraphs 6 and 7.

~~Thoreau was alarmed   Alarmed by factories and,~~

~~for Thoreau, machines were gadgets which made life~~

s   *Once inside a*
~~so complicated that they made living difficult;~~

~~factory~~ *As the factory gates close behind him* *american*
~~they were burdens.~~ *The* self-reliant ~~individual is~~

to Thoreau   *one mindless automaton at the controls*
becomes only a memory, ~~one machine controlling~~ of a

And for Thoreau, machines were
machine. ~~another~~ "gadgets that made life so

complicated that they made living difficult; they

were burdens which men carried on their backs

              Above all else, (*self-reliancy*)
. . . ." (Gabriel 49). ~~Walden champions the~~

the worth of)   ~~He also~~ *at the same time*
individual ~~and~~ rejects the Puritan work ethic

~~solely~~   *out of hand*
~~Work for the sake of acquiring material~~

          runs
~~possessions ran counter to Thoreau's philosophy, as~~

does   ~~still popular~~
~~did the promise Yankee belief that a man's~~

          Puritan
~~occupation a popular belief that a man was is~~

~~defined by his occupation.~~

~~The accumulation of material possessions runs~~

~~counter to Thoreau's ascetic philosophy as does the~~

~~notion that~~

champions the worth of the individual. Once the factory gates close behind him, the once self-reliant American becomes only a memory, according to Thoreau. Factories turned men and women into mindless automatons running the controls of machines or "gadgets that made life so complicated that they made living difficult . . ." (Gabriel 49).

Thoreau also rejected the Puritan work   **7** ethic. He believed a man is not defined by the type or amount of work he does, nor by the amount of wealth he accumulates. To Thoreau, a man's thoughts are much more important than his occupation, and he believed it was necessary to forsake the pursuit of money in order to gain a wealth of knowledge instead. In <u>Walden</u>, Thoreau expounded an ascetic philosophy that argued that "a man is rich in proportion to the number of things which he can afford to let alone" (166). During the rapid industrial expansion following the Civil War, when the country was beginning to flex its commercial muscles, Thoreau's plea for a simpler, more natural life was sure to draw fire from supporters of big business. In 1865, James Russell Lowell's cannonade very nearly blew <u>Walden</u> out of the water.

Lowell was unquestionably the most well-known   **8** and respected literary critic of his generation.

COMMENTS

1. An endnote provides additional information about James Russell Lowell.
2. The long citation to page 206 of Lowell's essay is set off as a block because it is more than four typed lines.
3. Observe how Kelley used the following notes selectively.

Lowell's review / 1865   PRO-INDUSTRY
  (Lowell)

" Mr. Thoreau seems to me to insist in public on
going back to flint and steel, when there is a
match-box in his pocket which he knows very
well how to use at a pinch." (202)

" To seek to be a natural implies a consciousness
that forbids all naturalness forever." (205)

Lowell's review / 1865
  (Lowell)

" I look upon a great deal of the modern
sentimentalism about nature as a mark
of disease.... To a man of wholesome
constitution the wilderness is well enough
for a mood or a vacation, but not for
a habit of life." (205)

His pronouncements carried great weight. The
critic was also pleased by America's growing
wealth, and he had little patience for naysayers
like Thoreau.[3] In a scathing attack on <u>Walden</u>
published shortly after Thoreau's death, Lowell
almost destroyed the book and its author's
reputation for the next forty years. Lowell
charged that while Thoreau

> studied with respectful attention the
> minks and woodchucks, his neighbors, he
> looked with utter contempt on the august
> drama of destiny of which his country was
> the scene, and on which the curtain had
> already risen. (206)

Lowell branded Thoreau a curmudgeon who hid   9
out in the woods and tried to ignore inevitable,
desirable industrial progress. In an America
sailing rapidly forward, <u>Walden</u> had dropped anchor
and refused to go with the tide. To Lowell, who
referred to Thoreau's love of nature as a "disease"
(205), it seemed ridiculous that Thoreau should
"insist in public on going back to flint and steel,
when there is a match—box in his pocket . . ."
(202). He also charged that Thoreau was
contemptuous of money and success only because the
author was poor and unsuccessful (199). The
critic's salvos were so successful in damaging
<u>Walden</u> that until the eve of World War I, the book

COMMENTS

1. The first sentence in paragraph 10 establishes a link between World War I and the economic history provided on page 3 of the essay.
2. The citation in paragraph 10 is only to a page reference, since the text clearly reveals that Thoreau is the author and the list of works cited includes only one work by Thoreau.

was regarded as an eccentric nature study by a
minor writer.

World War I may well have been the culmination **10**
of nineteenth-century industrialism and economic
competition. The outbreak of the war ushered in an
era of unequaled sophistication in the production
of weapons. Industrial technology, one of
Thoreau's greatest concerns, was geared to produce
not products for the betterment of mankind but
submarines, machine guns, tanks, long-range
artillery, mustard gas, and airplanes. Factories
concentrated on developing more effective means for
armies to destroy each other. Within this lethal
storm, concerned readers and critics began to take
a more careful look at Thoreau's belief in
simplicity and his message that "men have become
the tools of their tools" (132). <u>Walden</u> was
re-evaluated, and, to a nation entangled in the
complex web of world politics, Thoreau's philosophy
began to make more sense.

Early twentieth-century readers identified **11**
with Thoreau's concerns of the 1840s and 1850s.
Portions of <u>Walden</u> had been written during the
Mexican War and in the years immediately preceding
the Civil.War. Thoreau faced many of the same
problems and fears that Americans faced in
1917. He had spoken out against the unchecked
proliferation of machines and progress solely for

COMMENT

1. The transition from paragraph 11 to paragraph 12
   gave Kelley difficulty, since he wanted to move
   ahead over twenty years in his survey of criticism.
   (See the following excerpt from his rough draft, and
   don't get discouraged if you encounter a similar
   problem in your own writing: getting stuck is a perfectly normal part of the writing process.) Note how
   Kelley solved his problem by linking "protestor"
   (paragraph 11) to "protest" (paragraph 12).

If the aftermath of WWI left ready to ~~return~~

to normalcy after wholesale slaughter then ~~WW II~~ *late 1940s*

with development shadow of A—Bomb.

~~The aftermath of the Second World War~~

~~The dropping~~

~~The destruction of Hiroshima and Nagasaki~~

~~ushered in~~

~~Twenty years later, the~~

In the ~~aftermath~~ *beginning* of the Second World War

twenty ~~six~~ years ~~later provided a perfect~~ *after the armistice*

ending the First World War   *seem to*

~~environment for Thoreau's "less is more" philosophy~~

~~proved~~ ~~that although~~ ~~Walden~~ was again being read, *warning*

~~its message~~ ~~Walden's~~   Thoreau's ~~contention~~ ~~in the~~

~~pages of~~ *all* that ~~every~~ human*s* *have* ~~"are conscious of"~~ "an

animal in us, which awakes in proportion as our

Kelley 7

the sake of progress. In 1917, thoughtful
Americans could see the result of technology out of
control. Mark Van Doren, whose work on Thoreau
helped spark the critical re-evaluation of <u>Walden</u>
during this period, believed that Thoreau was still
valuable as a protestor and as a spokesman for
anyone concerned about the limitations of
materialism (125-27).

Since World War I, there have been many world   **12**
events to protest, and Thoreau's reputation
continued to improve in difficult times. The early
1940s proved a high point in Thoreau's
reputation. <u>Walden</u> was finally being read as a
well-organized book, rather than as a series of
seemingly unrelated chapters, and was thought to be
"the firmest product in our literature"
(Matthiessen 173). This claim was made in 1941,
the year the United States entered World War II.
The death and destruction of that horrible war
added further credence to Thoreau's contention that
all humans have "an animal in us, which awakens in
proportion as our higher nature slumbers" (267).
Who would have thought that European railroads
would be used to transport millions of victims to
their deaths in concentration camps or that a bomb
would be manufactured that could destroy an entire
city? It would not have surprised Thoreau that
technology had produced the ultimate weapon.

COMMENTS

1. Kelley identifies Krutch in case his audience is unfamiliar with this source. The citation clearly reveals which of the two works by Krutch in the list of works cited is being quoted in this instance.
2. A bracketed interpolation within the long quotation is used to clarify a reference that might not be clear out of context.
3. Note that the period comes *before* the parenthetical reference in indented quotations although it normally is placed after the parenthetical reference. (See page 436.)

Thoreau's contemporaries failed to heed his warning
about technology, but so, it seems, have
twentieth-century Americans. We admire <u>Walden</u> but
do not follow its advice. As J. W. Krutch, a
Thoreau biographer, puts it:

> If "Simplify" is the one word which sums
> up his [Thoreau's] teaching, it also sums
> up better than any other could what his
> own contemporaries were not doing and
> what we have, increasingly, tended not to
> do. They lived in an age of increasing
> complexity and great hope; we in an age
> of . . . growing despair. (Introduction 2)

This sense of growing despair reached its peak **13**
in the 1960s. Americans faced the constant threat
of nuclear annihilation, a controversial war in
Vietnam that divided the nation, and a growing
concern with the pollution of the environment. In
<u>Walden</u>, concerned Americans found a voice that
addressed each of these issues, even from the
distance of over one hundred years. Thoreau's
message seemed as fresh and revolutionary as the
day it was written, and at least eleven major books
were written about Thoreau and his work during this
decade (Schneider 166–70).

If a person felt estranged from society, out **14**
of touch with a world dominated by a technocracy,
Thoreau's philosophy allowed that person to follow

COMMENT

1. The quotation from Stanley Edgar Hyman illustrates how to cite a quotation that was not obtained from its original source. Hyman is identified in the text as the author of the quotation, but there is no reference to Hyman in the list of works cited. The parenthetical citation reveals that Schneider (who is in the list of works cited) had quoted Hyman. When you take a quotation secondhand, there is always a possibility that it has been misquoted. This format protects you from being held accountable for someone else's error. (See the source below.)

Source (from Richard J. Schneider's *Henry David Thoreau*, page 61)

These motifs of morning and light merge quite smoothly with traditional Christian symbols of resurrection, so that by the conclusion of the book Thoreau is no longer the comic outsider or the outcast prophet-preacher, but rather a welcome herald announcing a familiar concept of rebirth in familiar language. As spring arrives, Thoreau tells us that "Walden was dead and is alive again" (311). The spring light suggests that "all things must live in such a light. O Death, where was thy sting? O Grave, where was thy victory, then?" (317). In such a mood and in such light, even the ugliest truths, such as the dead horse decaying on the path to the pond, could seem beautiful. This grand confidence in rebirth makes *Walden,* as Stanley Edgar Hyman says, "a vast rebirth ritual, the purest and most complete in our literature."[29] Thus by finally adapting the village's religious vocabulary to his own ideas, Thoreau is symbolically reintegrated into the village, which he hopes has by now taken his advice and at least started to wake up.

the lead of <u>Walden</u>'s author and drop out of
society. In one of his most quoted lines from
<u>Walden</u>, Thoreau wrote, "If a man does not keep pace
with his companions, perhaps it is because he hears
a different drummer. Let him step to the music he
hears . . ." (345). Thousands of Americans embraced
this maxim during the 1960s and started a
counterculture that followed Thoreau's philosophy
very closely.

For example, Thoreau gave hope and support to **15**
those protesting America's involvement in the war
in Southeast Asia (Schneider 143). Patriotism is
given short shrift in <u>Walden</u>, since Thoreau
believed that self-respect and love of oneself is
much more important than the love of one's
country. He rejected the notion that people
refusing to take part in a war were cowards by
indicating that perhaps they were only protecting
what they considered most valuable, themselves.
After all, he reasoned, "A living dog is better
than a dead lion" (345).

But the appeal of <u>Walden</u> is not limited to war **16**
protestors. One of the most inspiring aspects of
this book is the way it teaches us to treasure the
Earth and respect its capacity for renewal; as
Stanley Edgar Hyman observed, <u>Walden</u> is "a vast
rebirth ritual" (qtd. in Schneider 61). One
hundred years before ecology became a popular

COMMENTS

1. The quotation from Yardley is not set apart by indention because it does not exceed four full lines.
2. The citation from Gold at the bottom of the page combines quotation with paraphrase. The phrase "in order to preserve" enabled Kelley to include key phrases from his source without using a second ellipsis and a bracketed interpolation. (Compare "Conservationists have been fighting developers . . . over how to manage growth . . . [in order to preserve] the quality of life.")

Kelley 10

cause, Thoreau eloquently advocated the
preservation of natural resources. In a country
grown concerned with industrial pollution, toxic
waste dumping, and the slaughter of endangered
species of animals, Thoreau's conception of a
"living earth" (332) struck a responsive chord that
continues to reverberate.

Walden found its widest, most receptive **17**
audience in the 1960s probably because, as Jonathan
Yardley, Pulitzer Prize—winning critic from the
Washington Post, believes, "From the libertarians
to the civil rights marches, the right wing to the
vegetarians, almost every organized (and
disorganized) American ism has found something to
its taste in Walden . . ." (27). Once scorned by
J. R. Lowell as a crackpot who was out of step with
contemporary issues, Thoreau found a receptive
audience over a hundred years later. For a
generation that questioned the value of material
wealth, emphasized the importance of the
individual, and showed great concern for a fragile
environment, Walden became a self—help manual.

Walden remains popular today because Thoreau's **18**
concerns are still very much our concerns. A
recent news story in the New York Times is evidence
of this. In Thoreau's New England, the article
states, "Conservationists have been fighting
developers . . . over how to manage growth" in order

COMMENTS

1. The concluding paragraph includes the essay's thesis: "Surveying the critical response to *Walden* reveals that the reputation of this work changes from one generation to another depending, at least in part, on political and economic factors."
2. The conclusion includes an example of the extended metaphor (to a ship) that Kelley has used throughout the paper as a way of unifying it.
3. Consider two lines that the paper concluded with in earlier drafts. The last line of the first draft was "*Walden* is still underway and making good time into the future." In a later draft, the last line became "But whether it is admired or condemned, *Walden* seems likely to endure." Why do you think these lines were dropped in favor of the concluding sentences that appear in the final draft?

to preserve "the quality of life" (Gold 2).
Thoreau would be right in the middle of the debate,
squarely on the conservationist side.

    Thoreau was a revolutionary, and **19**
revolutionaries are not always popular. In later
times of war, Thoreau's voice has sounded the
loudest and has been heard by Americans yearning
for a simpler, more natural way of life. In times
of peace and prosperity, Thoreau may not be
listened to as much as he deserves. Surveying the
critical response to <u>Walden</u> reveals that the
reputation of this work changes from one generation
to another depending, at least in part, on
political and economic factors. While <u>Walden</u> now
seems widely recognized as a masterpiece of
American literature, and safely anchored within the
harbor of critical opinion, its future status
cannot be predicted. What happens to <u>Walden</u> will
depend upon what happens to our country.

COMMENTS

1. Three endnotes provide supplementary information that is not directly related to the thesis but that might be of interest to readers.
2. The second note ends by directing readers to a source that will support claims Kelley has made about *Walden*'s critical reception in the nineteenth century.
3. The parenthetical reference to Howe in the third note does not contain a page reference, meaning that the citation is to the entire work (in this case an article in a reference work).

Notes

[1]According to the 1987–88 edition of <u>Books in Print</u>, twenty-one editions are currently in print in the United States.

[2]Thoreau was far from being deserted on an island as was Robinson Crusoe. His cabin on Walden Pond was only a couple of miles from the center of Concord, Massachusetts, and a railroad track and a main road ran very near the site. He walked to town almost every day. For representative nineteenth-century reviews of <u>Walden</u>, see Glick (3–150).

[3]James Russell Lowell came from a prominent New England family. An active Republican, he eventually became American ambassador to Great Britain (Howe).

COMMENTS

1. All (and only) works cited as sources in the paper should be included in the list of works cited.
2. Alphabetization: Initial articles (A, An, The) are ignored in alphabetizing. An anonymous source is alphabetized under the first important word in the title. For example, "Review of *Walden*" comes between Meltzer and Scharnhorst. Works with more than one author are alphabetized under the name of whichever writer is listed first in the source itself.
3. Punctuation: Observe the use and placement of periods and commas, especially in relation to parentheses and quotation marks. A colon separates a title from a subtitle and the place of publication from the publisher's name. A colon also precedes page numbers of articles from periodicals.
4. For Graebner, Fite, and White, only one volume (the second) of a two-volume work was cited. This entry reveals which volume was used and how many volumes there were altogether.
5. For Howe, which is an article in an alphabetized reference work, page numbers are not required. Full publication data is supplied for readers who may be unfamiliar with this source.
6. When listing two or more works by the same author (see the Krutch entry), type three hyphens in the space where you would repeat the author's name and insert the period that regularly follows the name.

Works Cited

Gabriel, Ralph H. The Course of American
    Democratic Thought. 2nd ed. New York:
    Ronald, 1956.

Glick, Wendell, ed. The Recognition of Henry David
    Thoreau. Ann Arbor: U of Michigan P, 1969.

Gold, Allan R. "New England Debates More Rules to
    Make the Best of Its Progress." New York
    Times 23 Oct. 1988, natl. ed., sec. 4: 2.

Graebner, Norman, Gilbert C. Fite, and Philip L.
    White. A History of the American People. 2nd
    ed. Vol. 2. New York: McGraw, 1975. 2 vols.

Krutch, Joseph W. Henry David Thoreau. New York:
    Sloane, 1948.

---. Introduction. Walden and Other Writings. By
    Henry David Thoreau. New York: Bantam, 1962.
    1–23.

Howe, M. A. DeWolfe. "James Russell Lowell."
    Dictionary of American Biography.
    Ed. Dumas Malone. 16 vols. New York:
    Scribner's, 1933.

Lowell, James Russell. "Thoreau." North American
    Review 101 (1865): 597–608. Rpt. in My Study
    Windows. 1871. Boston: Houghton, 1913. 193–
    209.

Matthiessen, F. O. American Renaissance: Art and
    Expression in the Age of Emerson and
    Whitman. London: Oxford UP, 1941.

COMMENTS

1. For an article or an essay reprinted in an anthology (see "Review of Walden" entry), give the original publication data for the essay followed by "Rpt. in" and the publication data for the anthology.
2. For a work in a series (see the Schneider entry), identify the series and the number by which the work is listed in the series.
3. When an author's work has been edited by someone else, provide the editor's name, preceded by "Ed." between the title and the city of publication. (See the Thoreau entry.)

Annotation

Your instructor may ask you for an annotated bibliography at some point. This bibliography with notes can be either descriptive or evaluative. *Descriptive* annotation briefly summarizes the contents of a source; *evaluative* annotation appraises the value of a source. Here is an example of an entry in an evaluative bibliography:

```
Van Doren, Mark. Henry David Thoreau: A
     Critical Study. 1916. New York:
     Russell, 1961. An important scholar
     during the early twentieth century, Van
     Doren now seems dated because of his
     prose style. (He praises Thoreau for
     having "an antidotal flavor.") But his
     book is useful in establishing where
     Thoreau's reputation stood in the early
     twentieth century.
```

Kelley 14

Meltzer, Milton, and Walter Harding. <u>A Thoreau Profile</u>. New York: Crowell, 1962.

"Review of <u>Walden</u>." <u>Graham's Magazine</u> 45 (1854): 298–300. Rpt. in <u>The Recognition of Henry David Thoreau</u>. Ed. Wendell Glick. Ann Arbor: U of Michigan P, 1969.

Scharnhorst, Gary. "James T. Fields and Early Notices of <u>Walden</u>." <u>New England Quarterly</u> 55 (1982): 114–17.

Schneider, Richard J. <u>Henry David Thoreau</u>. Twayne's United States Authors Ser. 497. Boston: Twayne, 1987.

Thoreau, Henry David. <u>Walden and Other Writings</u>. Ed. Joseph W. Krutch. New York: Bantam, 1962.

Van Doren, Mark. <u>Henry David Thoreau: A Critical Study</u>. 1916. New York: Russell, 1961.

Yardley, Jonathan. "Ten Books That Shaped the American Character." <u>American Heritage</u> Apr.– May, 1985: 24–31.

FOOTNOTES AND ENDNOTES
FOR DOCUMENTATION

Although parenthetical documentation has been recommended by the Modern Language Association since 1984 (and by the influential *Chicago Manual of Style,* 13th edition, since 1982), some disciplines in the humanities still use either footnotes or endnotes for documentation. We provide the information here in case you are instructed to follow the note style of documentation.

Both footnotes and endnotes require that a superscript (raised) number be placed wherever documentation is necessary. The number should be as near as possible to whatever it refers to, following the punctuation (such as quotation marks, a comma, or a period) that appears at the end of the direct or indirect quotation.

Footnotes should be single-spaced four lines below the last line of text on the same page where the documentation is necessary. (Double-space between footnotes if more than one appears on any one page.) Endnotes should be double-spaced on a separate page headed *Notes.* The following model notes use sources in the list of works cited on pages 477–79 so you can see the differences between note and bibliographic form. (They are arranged here in a pattern designed for your convenience, so the numbers do not correspond to the order in which these sources were actually cited in the paper on *Walden.*)

A book by one author

[1] Joseph W. Krutch, <u>Henry David Thoreau</u> (New York: Sloane, 1948) 103.

Indent five spaces, then give the note number (without punctuation) followed by a space. Additional lines in a note should be flush with the left margin. Note that an abbreviation for "page" is not used before the page number at the end of the note.

A book by more than one author

[2] Milton Meltzer and Walter Harding, <u>A Thoreau Profile</u> (New York: Crowell, 1962) 237.

If the book has more than two authors, use commas to separate the authors' names.

A book in a series

[3] Richard J. Schneider, <u>Henry David Thoreau</u>, Twayne's United States Authors Ser. 497 (Boston: Twayne, 1987) 166–70.

A multivolume work

[4] Norman Graebner, Gilbert C. Fite, and Philip L. White, <u>A History of the American People</u>, 2nd ed., vol. 2 (New York: McGraw, 1975) 447.

Edition numbers should be specified after the title only for the second and subsequent or revised editions.

An anthology

[5] Wendell Glick, ed., <u>The Recognition of Henry David Thoreau</u> (Ann Arbor: U of Michigan P, 1969) 3–150.

A work in an anthology

[6] "Review of Walden" (1854), rpt. in <u>The Recognition of Henry David Thoreau</u>, ed. Wendell Glick (Ann Arbor: U of Michigan P, 1969) 5, 7.

This example begins with an anonymous article. Begin with the author's name when available.

An introduction, preface, foreword, or afterword

⁷ Joseph W. Krutch, introduction, <u>Walden and
Other Writings</u>, by Henry David Thoreau (New York:
Bantam, 1962) 2.

An article from a newspaper

⁸ Allan R. Gold, "New England Debates More
Rules to Make the Best of Its Progress," <u>New York
Times</u> 23 Oct. 1988, natl. ed., sec. 4: 2.

When sections are lettered, put the letter next to the page
number as it appears in the newspaper (natl. ed.: A12.).

An article from a magazine

⁹ Jonathan Yardley, "Ten Books That Shaped the
American Character," <u>American Heritage</u> Apr.–May
1985: 24.

Issues of this magazine cover two months. For other magazines, report the date as given but abbreviate all months
except May, June, and July, and put the day before the
month for weekly magazines (*Reader's Digest* Nov. 1989;
New Yorker 6 June 1988).

An article from a journal with continuous pagination

¹⁰ Gary Scharnhorst, "James T. Fields and
Early Notices of <u>Walden</u>," <u>New England Quarterly</u> 55
(1982): 117.

For an article in a scholarly journal that begins every issue
with page 1, put a period after the volume number and
then give the issue number.

34g

Draft and revise a research paper using APA style documentation.

Text Citations in APA style

The documentation style recommended by the American Psychological Association (APA) is widely used for writing in the social sciences. In APA style, the basic elements of a parenthetical citation in the text are the author's last name, the year of publication, and the page number if the reference is to a specific passage in the source. If the author's name is mentioned in the text of the paper, give the date alone or the date and the page number within the parentheses. In the following examples, note the details of punctuation and the treatment of the page number.

A work by one author

```
One writer has stated, "Prisons can be divided into

specific social groups organized by type of crime"

(Liptz, 1979, p. 235).
```

OR

```
Liptz has stated, "Prisons can be divided into

specific social groups organized by type of crime"

(1979, p. 235).
```

OR

```
Liptz (1979) has stated, "Prisons can be divided

into specific social groups organized by type of

crime" (p. 235).
```

▲ Note: APA style, unlike MLA style, requires the abbreviation *p.* (or *pp.* for "pages") before the page reference. Use commas to separate the author's name from the date and the date from the page reference.

A work by two authors

```
There is evidence that students in second and third
grade respond favorably to guidance from elementary
school students in higher grades (Bowman & Myrick,
1987).
```

▲ **Note:** The ampersand (&) is used to separate the authors' names.

A work by more than two authors

```
One recent study has shown that people who fear
failure are not susceptible to hypnosis
(Manganello, Carlson, Zarillo, & Teeven, 1985).
```

Cite all the authors in the first reference, but in subsequent references give only the last name of the first author followed by "et al." ("Manganello et al." in this case). If a work has more than six authors, provide only the last name of the first author followed by "et al.," even in the first citation.

Anonymous works

Use a shortened version of the title to identify an anonymous work:

```
Chronic insomnia usually requires medical
intervention ("Sleep," 1987).
```

In this case, the author has cited a short article identified in the bibliography as "Sleep disorders: What can be done about them."

Two or more works within the same parentheses

```
Much animal experimentation may be both unnecessary

and cruel (Mayo, 1983; Singer, 1975).
```

Use a semicolon to separate different studies, and arrange the studies in alphabetical order.

References in APA style

In APA style, the alphabetical list of works cited is called "References." Make the first line of each entry flush with the left margin, and indent subsequent lines three spaces. The reference entries below follow the style of the 1983 edition of the APA *Publication Manual.* Observe all details of indention, spacing, and mechanics.

Book by one author

```
Liptz, A. (1979).  Prisons as social structures.

   Los Angeles: Scholarly Press.
```

Give the author's last name and use initials for first and middle names. (If two authors have the same last name and initials, spell out their first names and list the references in the alphabetical order of their first names.) Put the date in parentheses, followed by a period. Capitalize only the first word and any proper name in a book title and subtitle. Give only enough of the publisher's name so that it can be identified clearly.

Book by two or more authors

```
Klein, D. F., & Wender, P. H. (1981).  Mind, mood,

   and medicine: A guide to the new biological

   psychiatry.  New York: Farrar.
```

Article in an edited book

```
Gardner, W. I. (1970).  Use of behavior therapy
```

```
with the mentally retarded.   In F. J.

Menolascino (Ed.), Psychiatric approaches to

mental retardation (pp. 250—275).   New York:

Basic.
```

Capitalize only the first word and any proper nouns in article titles, and do not put quotation marks around the title. (If the article has a subtitle, put a colon after the title, and capitalize the first word in the subtitle.) For an article in an edited book, provide both the title of the article and the title of the book in which it appears. Identify who edited the book and give the complete pages of the article.

Article in a journal with continuous pagination

```
Faulstich, M. E.   (1984).   Effects upon social

perceptions of the insanity plea.   Psychological

Reports, 55, 183—187.
```

▲ Note: The titles of journals are capitalized differently from article or book titles. Underline the volume number so it will be distinct from the page reference (which is not preceded by an abbreviation).

Article in a journal paginated separately

```
Graham, L. R.   (1978).   Concerns about science and

attempts to regulate inquiry.   Daedalus, 107(2),

1—21.
```

Insert the issue number within parentheses immediately after the volume number.

Article in a monthly magazine

```
Kahn, R. E.   (1987, October).   Networks for
```

advanced computing. <u>Scientific American</u>,

pp. 136–143.

For a weekly magazine, provide the exact date of issue: (1989, January 12).

Article in a newspaper

Ingersoll, B. (1988, December 2). FDA asked to

ban sales of quinine over the counter. <u>Wall</u>

<u>Street Journal</u>, p. A12.

For an anonymous article, place the article title where the author's name would normally appear, and alphabetize by the first important word in the title.

A government document

Department of Energy. (1987) <u>Energy security</u>

(DOE/S–0057). Washington, DC: U.S. Government

Printing Office.

Treat the issuing agency as a corporate author when no author is specified. Include a document or contract number (but not a library's call number) if either number is printed on or in the document.

▲ Note: If you use more than one work by the same author, list the works in order of publication date, earliest first. Repeat the author's name for each entry.

SAMPLE RESEARCH PAPER

For additional examples of APA style documentation, see the following student essay and the commentary on it printed on the left-hand pages.

COMMENT

1. The title page should include the title, the author's full
   name, the course in which the paper is being submitted,
   the name of the instructor who is teaching the course,
   and the date the essay is submitted. The APA *Publication Manual* requires that a shortened version of the
   title, identified as "Running head" appear centered near
   the bottom of the title page. This heading is then used
   in the upper right-hand corner of every page, including
   the title page—which is counted as page 1. This format
   allows a reader to remove the title page and evaluate the
   paper without being influenced by prior knowledge of
   the author. (If you use this model for an MLA paper, do
   not number the title page and do not include a running
   head.)

Treatment for Test Anxiety

Sharon Johnson

Psychology 101, Section 7

Professor Marquez

May 4, 1989

Running head: TEST ANXIETY

COMMENTS

1. An abstract is a short summary of a paper. The APA requires that an abstract be supplied on the second page of any essay that is to be submitted for publication. Check with your instructor to see if an abstract is required for your own assignment.

2. Sharon Johnson draws upon personal experience in her opening paragraph to catch the interest of her audience. But she introduces her topic by the end of paragraph 1.

3. Paragraph 2 (report page 4) includes a citation to a specific page, a citation to an entire work, and a citation to several studies that reached the same conclusion. The data reported in this paragraph establish the purpose for the paper by demonstrating that test anxiety is a widespread problem.

4. Paragraph 3 (report page 5) defines "test anxiety" by showing how it differs from nervousness.

5. Paragraph 4 (report pages 5–6) surveys early research in this field and offers an explanation for disappointing results.

Abstract

The cause—and—effect relationship between test anxiety and poor academic performance now seems well established. Although some researchers question whether reducing test anxiety will necessarily lead to higher grades, the most recent research in this field suggests that the grades of test—anxious students are raised when such students are provided with therapy that combines relaxation training and tutoring to improve study skills.

Treatment for Test Anxiety

Although my younger sister is very smart, she   **1** had trouble in school for many years. She would carefully do her homework and usually seem to have mastered her assignments when my parents or I helped her to review. Unfortunately, whenever Stacey had to take a test, she would freeze up and seem to forget everything she knew. Since her grades were based mostly upon her tests, she usually received low grades that did not reflect how much she really knew. Everyone in the family could see that Stacey was nervous about taking tests, and we kept telling her to try to relax. What we did not realize was that Stacey was

suffering from a condition called "test anxiety," a
psychological syndrome that has been the subject of
much research since the early 1950s when an
important study on college students was conducted
at Yale University (Mandler & Sarason, 1952).

Research reveals that my sister's problem is   **2**
not unusual. It has been estimated that "4—5
million children in elementary and secondary
schools experience strong debilitating evaluation
anxiety" and that another 5 million experience
"significant anxiety" (Hill & Wigfield, 1984,
p. 110); moreover, as much as 25% of college
students may suffer from this condition (McGrath,
1985; Wilson & Rotter, 1986). Although there is
evidence that females may be more vulnerable than
males to test anxiety (Couch, Garber, & Turner,
1983; Furst, Tennenbaum, & Weingarten, 1985;
Hembree, 1988), the problem is widespread within
both sexes, and it can be found at all levels of
intelligence. One recent study suggests that
students of Asian background may be especially
likely to suffer from test anxiety because they
come from cultures that emphasize the importance of
scholastic excellence (Dion & Toner, 1988), but
most research reports that test anxiety is not
limited to students of any particular race or
culture.

Test anxiety should not be confused with **3**
simple nervousness. A student may be nervous
before a test but then be able to successfully
concentrate on taking the test once it is under
way; this same student may be relaxed before
another exam in a subject he or she enjoys. In
some cases, a little anxiety can even be helpful,
since some students are motivated to excel when
they are concerned about performance. In other
cases, anxiety may be appropriate if a student has
neglected assignments and has no real hope of
passing an examination on material that has gone
unread. A student with test anxiety, on the other
hand, is likely to be dominated by negative
feelings (including anger, guilt, and frustration)
before almost <u>any</u> exam, and these feelings will
subsequently interfere with performance once the
test has begun. Students suffering from test
anxiety thus lose the ability to concentrate on
problem solving. Instead of concentrating on the
exam before them, they are usually distracted
by other concerns such as how poorly they are
doing and what other people will think of them
if they fail.

Early research in this field demonstrated that **4**
students who scored high in tests designed to
measure test anxiety consistently did poorly in
test situations (Mandler & Sarason, 1952). But the

COMMENTS

1. Paragraph 5 includes evidence that will support Johnson's argument. Note that she was careful to avoid relying too heavily on Zitzow (which, as the reference list reveals, was a short article). When introducing the Hembree study, Johnson was careful to include background information that would enable her audience to recognize the value of this source.

2. Paragraph 6 (report page 7) includes a second citation to a source with more than two authors.

3. Paragraphs 7–10 (report pages 8–10) include recommendations for treatment. Note how paragraphs 9 and 10 begin with concessions likely to reassure a skeptical audience.

4. Note that the long quotation—a quotation of more than 40 words—in paragraph 8 (report page 9) is indented five spaces only, per APA style.

tests used to measure student anxiety may not be
entirely accurate. Some students may exaggerate
their defects (Davies, 1986), and the tests
themselves may be biased (Couch et al.,
1983). Faulty methods of measuring test anxiety
may account for the disappointing results of much
research in this field: many researchers have
reported successful reduction of student anxiety
levels without noting a corresponding improvement
in academic achievement (Lent, Lopez, & Romano,
1983; Ricketts & Galloway, 1984).

Evidence suggests, however, that there is hope **5**
for students who suffer from test anxiety. In one
study, "grade improvements were noted for over 70%
of participants in identified courses . . ."
(Zitzow, 1983, p. 565). Although a single study is
insufficient to prove anything conclusively, a
recent, exhaustive study is highly persuasive.
Reviewing the results of 562 separate studies on
test anxiety (including 369 journal articles and
148 doctoral dissertations) and subjecting them to
statistical analysis, a mathematician has
concluded, "Contrary to prior perceptions, improved
test performance and grade point average (GPA)
consistently accompany TA reduction" (Hembree,
1988, p. 47). According to this study, early
researchers failed to detect significant academic

improvement because many of them based their observations on sample groups that were too small. Drawing the results of many studies together reveals that treatment for test anxiety improves students' test scores by an average of 6 points on a 100-point scale (p. 73). This may seem like a small improvement for a student who is failing a course, but a 6-point improvement can be significant in some cases. More importantly, even a 6-point improvement helps to prove that there is a cause-and-effect relationship between test anxiety and academic performance. If this is the case, then improved methods of treatment may produce greater academic improvement in the future.

For treatment to be effective, counselors need **6** to realize that test anxiety is a complex state involving two factors: "worry," which involves thinking about negative possibilities; and "emotionality," which describes the perception of such physiological phenomena as accelerated heart beat and sweating (Furst et al., 1985). Irwin G. Sarason, one of this country's foremost experts on test anxiety, has concluded that "worry" has an especially significant impact upon academic performance (1985). Taking this research into account, it would seem that therapy that does not address the problem of worry is unlikely to help

students do better on tests.   A test-anxious
student needs something more than soft music and
deep-breathing exercises.

   The best results seem to be achieved by   **7**
counseling programs that provide students with more
than one type of help.   Many test-anxious students
devote insufficient time to studying because they
spend so much time worrying (Davies, 1986) or
because they have given up in frustration.   Such
students often need specific help in learning good
study habits in addition to receiving therapy to
reduce anxiety.   Several experts recommend that
treatment for test anxiety be accompanied by a
tutoring program in study skills (Lent et al.,
1983; Wilson & Rotter, 1986; Zitzow, 1983).
Tutoring alone, however, is not likely to provide
much help for someone suffering from test anxiety:
"Study skills training is . . . not effective unless
another treatment style is also present" (Hembree,
1988, p. 73).

   One problem in the treatment of test anxiety   **8**
is that individual students respond very
differently to the same situation: "The same test
that seems to maximize the performance of low
anxious examinees results in relatively poor
performance by moderately anxious examinees"
(Rocklin & Thompson, 1985, p. 371).   A possible

solution to this problem would be to devise
different tests for students with different degrees
of anxiety. Another possibility would be to put
students into testing groups determined by anxiety
levels. According to I. G. Sarason,

> A highly test-anxious college student might
> simply become more tense before, during, and
> after tests by virtue of contacts with
> completely confident, effective, and seemingly
> worry-free models. On the other hand,
> opportunity to observe and perhaps interact
> with other students who are mildly fearful of
> tests but who are not immobilized by them . . .
> might have decidedly therapeutic results.
> (1972, p. 396)

Reorganizing classes to group together **9**
students of similar anxiety levels may not be
feasible, however, since this would require
elaborate organization and registration
procedures. (This method might be considered,
however, when planning for special tests, like the
SATs, that are of particular importance and are
independent of course work.) Within a classroom
situation, teachers can help reduce anxiety levels
by providing students in advance with clear
instructions regarding the nature of upcoming tests
and how to prepare for them (Davies, 1986).

Teachers should also realize that anxiety
levels in general increase when students are
undergoing a stressful life event such as the
transition from junior to senior high school or
from high school to college. Additional support
for students during these times has been shown to
be beneficial (Bloom, 1985). One type of support
that should be considered is to reduce test time
pressure by allowing students sufficient time to
complete tests (Hill & Wigfield, 1984).

It would be a mistake, however, to assume that **10**
the responsibility for treating test anxiety rests
within the schools. Many schools do not have the
resources to undertake any new special programs,
and many teachers are so overworked that it would
be unrealistic to expect them to give troubled
students the individualized attention they may
need. Parents should be alert to the problem of
test anxiety and take the initiative in seeking
therapeutic help for any child who seems regularly
immobilized by tests. And college students should
be prepared to seek such help for themselves if
they are certain that anxiety--rather than lack
of preparation--causes them to do poorly on
tests.

I now know that simply telling someone with **11**
test anxiety to "try to relax"--as my parents and I

COMMENTS

1. The conclusion, with its reference to "my sister," establishes a link with the introduction.
2. The reference list is organized alphabetically and begins on a new page. The last name is always given first, and initials are provided for first and middle names. The date of publication is always given parenthetically, immediately after the author's name.
3. Observe the use of periods and commas and the unusual capitalization in book and article titles (but not in journal titles). Underline book titles, journal titles, and volume numbers for periodicals. If citing material from more than one work by the same author, repeat the author's name (as in the Sarason, I. G., entry) before each work.

used to tell my sister—is about as useful as telling someone with severe depression to "try to cheer up." Whatever the cause that triggers it, someone suffering from anxiety needs trained, professional help. Students with test anxiety are no exception, and they need to know that help is available. Although the evidence is not conclusive, and more research needs to be done, what we know about test anxiety suggests that it can be treated effectively: treatment that combines therapy with tutoring is likely to improve students' self-concepts and lead to higher scores on tests.

References

Bloom, B. L. (1985). Stressful life event theory and research: Implications for primary prevention (DHHS Publication No. ADM 85-1385). Rockville, MD: National Institute of Mental Health.

Couch, J. V., Garber, T. B., & Turner, W. E. (1983). Facilitating and debilitating test anxiety and academic achievement. Psychological Record, 33, 237-244.

Test Anxiety

13

Davies, D. (1986). <u>Maximizing examination performance</u>. New York: Nichols.

Dion, K. L., & Toner, B. B. (1988). Ethnic differences in test anxiety. <u>Journal of Social Psychology</u>, <u>128</u>, 165–172.

Furst, D., Tennenbaum, G., & Weingarten G. (1985). Test anxiety, sex, and exam type. <u>Psychological Reports</u>, <u>56</u>, 663–668.

Hembree, R. (1988). Correlates, causes, effects, and treatment of test anxiety. <u>Review of Educational Research</u>, <u>58</u>, 47–77.

Hill, K. T., & Wigfield, A. (1984). Test anxiety: A major educational problem and what can be done about it. <u>Elementary School Journal</u>, <u>85</u>, 105–126.

Lent, R. W., Lopez, F. G., & Romano, J. L. (1983). A program for reducing test anxiety with academically underprepared students. <u>Journal of College Student Personnel</u>, <u>24</u>, 265–266.

Mandler, G., & Sarason, S. (1952). Some correlates of test anxiety. <u>Journal of Abnormal and Social Psychology</u>, <u>47</u>, 561–565.

McGrath, A. (1985, November 4). Mettle testing. <u>Forbes</u>, pp. 236–239.

Ricketts, M. S., & Galloway, R. E. (1984). Effects of three different one-hour single-session

Test Anxiety

14

treatments for test anxiety. <u>Psychological Reports</u>, <u>54</u>, 115–120.

Rocklin, T., & Thompson, J. M. (1985). Interactive effects of test anxiety, test difficulty, and feedback. <u>Journal of Educational Psychology</u>, <u>77</u>, 368–372.

Sarason, I. G. (1972). Experimental approaches to test anxiety: Attention and the uses of information. In C. D. Spielberger (Ed.). <u>Anxiety: Current trends in theory and research</u> (Vol. 2, pp. 381–403). New York: Academic.

Sarason, I. G. (1985). Cognitive processes, anxiety and the treatment of anxiety disorders. In A. H. Tuma & J. Maser (Eds.). <u>Anxiety and anxiety disorders</u> (pp. 87–107). Hillsdale, NJ: Erlbaum.

Wilson, N., & Rotter J. C. (1986). Anxiety management training and study skills counseling for students on self-esteem and test anxiety and performance. <u>School Counselor</u>, <u>34</u>, 18–31.

Zitzow, D. (1983). Test anxiety: A trimodal strategy. <u>Journal of College Student Personnel</u>, <u>24</u>, 564–565.

■ **Exercise 6**   Compose a topic outline for Sharon Johnson's research paper on test anxiety.

■ **Exercise 7**

Drawing upon the bibliographical information on pages 483–87, change the following MLA style citations to APA style:
(Yardley 24)
("Review" 5, 7)
(Graebner, Fite, and White 447)
(Krutch, *Thoreau* 103)
(Howe)

34h
Vary your documentation style according to discipline.

Each department of a college or a university ordinarily suggests a particular style for bibliographies and citations. Use the style your instructor specifies. Instructors in the sciences, business, economics, and so forth may recommend a documentation form from one of the style books listed below. If you are asked to use one of these manuals, study it carefully, and make sure your bibliography and notes correspond exactly to the examples it provides.

STYLE BOOKS AND MANUALS

American Chemical Society. *American Chemical Society Style Guide and Handbook.* Washington: American Chemical Soc., 1985.

American Institute of Physics. Publications Board. *Style Manual for Guidance in the Preparation of Papers.* 3rd ed. New York: American Inst. of Physics, 1978.

American Mathematical Society. *A Manual for Authors of Mathematical Papers.* 7th ed. Providence: American Mathematical Soc., 1980.

American Psychological Association. *Publication Manual of the American Psychological Association.* 3rd ed. Washington: American Psychological Assn., 1983.

Associated Press. *The Associated Press Stylebook.* Dayton: Lorenz, 1980.

The Chicago Manual of Style. 13th ed. Chicago: U of Chicago P, 1982.

Council of Biology Editors. Style Manual Committee. *CBE Style Manual: A Guide for Authors, Editors, and Publishers in the Biological Sciences.* 5th ed. Bethesda: Council of Biology Editors, 1983.

Harvard Law Review: *A Uniform System of Citation.* 13th ed. Cambridge: Harvard Law Review Assn., 1981.

Turabian, Kate L. *A Manual for Writers of Term Papers, Theses, and Dissertations.* 4th ed. Chicago: U of Chicago P, 1973.

United States. Government Printing Office. *Style Manual.* Rev. ed. Washington: GPO, 1973.

35
WRITING FOR SPECIAL PURPOSES

Write effective papers about fiction, poetry, and drama; write effective letters, résumés, memos, and reports.

You may be asked during one of your courses to read and analyze a work of literature and to write a paper about it. This exercise requires the kind of analytical skills necessary for any close reading and the kind of writing skills that involve exploration, development, and organization with an awareness of audience, purpose, and occasion. Its purpose is primarily persuasive as you attempt to support your viewpoint. Like all writing, it involves careful attention to the conventions of usage. Writing about literature is the focus of **35a**.

Business writing is the focus of **35b**. Whether it takes the form of a letter, memo, résumé, or formal report, business writing generally combines informative and persuasive aims (see **33a**): it gives necessary information and, at the same time, is designed to win a favorable response from the reader. Additionally, such documents—which sometimes have legal implications—often become important records for the company or organization and so should be objective, clear, and concise.

35a

Learn to read literature and write effective papers about fiction, poetry, and drama.

The research paper about literature requires you to go beyond your own reading of a work to critical analyses (see **34b**). This discussion covers the kind of writing about literature that draws from the work itself for support of your own interpretation, analysis, or evaluation.

Writing about literature is like writing about other subjects inasmuch as you state a thesis and support it. Like all writing in specialized fields, literature has its own vocabulary that is used in talking and writing about it. In learning this vocabulary you are not just learning a list of terms and definitions. You are grasping concepts that will help you to read and understand literature and to write about it as well. This section provides only the most basic guidelines for such concepts; ask your instructor for further help in reading and writing about literature.

(1) Use the principles of all good writing.

Consider the rhetorical situation: your audience, your purpose, and the occasion (**33a**). In addition to your instructor, envision an intelligent, educated general audience that has read the work. Your purpose, as mentioned earlier, is mainly to persuade since you are arguing for your own perspective or viewpoint. Finally, observe the conventions suggested by the occasion of your instructor's assignment.

Explore, limit, and focus your subject (see **33c**) as you read and write, and formulate a directed thesis statement that can be supported from the work itself (see **33d**). Reread the work to find ways to develop your thesis. Plan how you will arrange your ideas. Papers about literature often follow the arrangement of the work itself. For example, you might trace a certain character as he or she develops throughout a short story.

In your introduction (**33f**) state the name of the work, the author, and your thesis. You might also include a one- or two-sentence summary of the plot or story line, some background information on the author, or the historical context of the work. Make your conclusion brief, but you might also restate your thesis, evaluate the significance of the work for you as well as for a larger community, and analyze the success of the work in accomplishing its purpose (see **33f**).

As you write, new ideas may occur to you, or you may wish to go back to parts of the work to find support for a point. Be prepared to reread the work and revise and rewrite your paper. Finally, prepare a clean, neat manuscript for submission to your instructor (**8**).

(2) Read and reread with care.

Reading literature requires active participation and engagement with the work rather than the passive involvement of watching television. Read the work with such matters as plot, characters, and setting in mind.

First, analyze *how* the poem or story means what it says. What techniques has the author used? How might a story use setting or characters to express its meaning? How might a poem use metaphor to communicate its theme? How might a play use dialogue?

Second, read to discover *what* the work means to you. What is its theme? Every poem, story, and drama has one or more themes—that is, general truths that it attempts to communicate through the medium of its component parts: its plot, characters, and setting (the time and place of the action). Not all readers agree on what a poem or story means. New interpretations may change or enrich older interpretations. But any interpretation must be supported with such evidence as short quotations or references to acts or events in the work itself.

Third, evaluate *how well* the work accomplishes its purpose in communicating its meaning. Do not confuse this question with whether or not you liked the work. Your reaction is, of course, important, but even more important is your analysis of why you liked or disliked it. Did it move you? Did it offer new insights? Or did you detect specific flaws in its plot or characterization?

As you read, take notes and jot down ideas. Trust your own first reactions. What characters do you admire? Why? Does the setting help the story along? How? Can you find reasons for your reactions within the work itself? Work toward a tentative thesis (see **33c** and **33d**) that will enable other readers to share your response. As you develop an idea for a thesis, reread with that focus in mind, looking for evidence to support your tentative thesis. If you can't find such support, you may have to alter or abandon your thesis.

(3) Analyze, interpret, and evaluate.

There are different ways of reading and writing about literature. Look at a work by analyzing it, interpreting it, and evaluating it. A short paper may do only one of these, or a longer paper may do all three.

Analyze (see **32d[6]**) a work of literature by breaking it into its parts and examining how such parts as setting, characters, and plot combine to form the whole. How do the parts interact? For example, in her paper on King Lear (beginning on page 531), Susan Ferk demonstrates how the characters in the subplot comment on and intensify the main plot and theme.

Interpret a work by asking what it means—what its theme is. Support your interpretation by referring to elements in the work itself. For example, in her paper on Frankenstein (page 517), Susan Suehring shows how Frankenstein's quest for knowledge and Walton's journey exemplify Shelley's theme. In poetry, this kind of paper is often called an *explication*. You might choose to concentrate on how one element, such as sound, develops the theme. For example, the "s" sounds in William Wordsworth's "A Slumber Did My Spirit Seal" reinforce the hushed feeling of sleep and death in the poem.

Evaluate a work by asking how successful the author is in communicating the meaning to the reader. In his paper "The Tulips," James Dalgetty points out the many metaphors and images that reinforce the difference between the drugged, deathlike figure in the hospital bed and the bright, vital tulips. Finally, ask yourself if the work is of value to you? Does it reflect or enlighten your own experience? Would it reflect the experience of others? Would others also find it valuable? Are the subject and the theme worth writing about?

(4) Choose a subject and develop it.

Your instructor may give you a specific subject, such as a comparison of two characters in *The Color Purple*, or a more general subject, such as characterization in *The Color Purple*. You must form a thesis for both assignments, but the second requires you to narrow the subject.

If you are asked to select your own subject, your first step is to determine the author's purpose. What is he or she trying to say to you? What is the theme? Then ask yourself what techniques the author uses to accomplish that purpose.

Try some of the methods suggested in **33c** to explore your subject. List ideas and topics that occur to you after that first reading. Then reread the work with the list in mind to see if any of the topics seem supportable.

Question as you read and apply perspectives (**33c**). Think of a character as *static* by describing her as she appears at one point in the work, or think of her as *dynamic* by analyzing how or why she changes. Finally, think of her as *relative* to other characters, to the setting, or to other elements in the work.

Also, apply strategies of development (**32d**). *Define and classify* a play as a comedy or a tragedy, or *describe* a setting that contributes to a work's meaning. Determine *cause-and-effect* relationships: Why, for example, does an important character marry the wrong man? *Compare and contrast* two characters or two poems on a similar subject.

(5) Writing about fiction

Although the events have not happened and the characters may never have existed, fiction expresses a general truth about the human condition through such components as setting, character, and plot. Before you start to write, ask yourself what the author is trying to say in the work. In the following short story, Grace Paley examines the human desire to escape reality through the main character who retreats to an unreal world and lives vicariously.

Wants

Grace Paley

I saw my ex-husband in the street. I was sitting on the steps of the new library.   **1**

Hello, my life, I said. We had once been married for twenty-seven years, so I felt justified.   **2**

He said, What? What life? No life of mine.   **3**

I said, O.K. I don't argue when there's real disagreement. I got up and went into the library to see how much I owed them.   **4**

The librarian said $32 even and you've owed it for eighteen years. I didn't deny anything. Because I don't understand how time passes. I have had those books. I have often thought of them. The library is only two blocks away.   **5**

My ex-husband followed me to the Books Returned desk. **6**
He interrupted the librarian, who had more to tell. In many ways, he said, as I look back, I attribute the dissolution of our marriage to the fact that you never invited the Bertrams to dinner.

That's possible, I said. But really, if you remember: first, **7**
my father was sick that Friday, then the children were born, then I had those Tuesday-night meetings, then the war began. Then we didn't seem to know them any more. But you're right. I should have had them to dinner.

I gave the librarian a check for $32. Immediately she **8**
trusted me, put my past behind her, wiped the record clean, which is just what most other municipal and/or state bureaucracies will *not* do.

I checked out the two Edith Wharton books I had just **9**
returned because I'd read them so long ago and they are more apropos now than ever. They were *The House of Mirth* and *The Children,* which is about how life in the United States in New York changed in twenty-seven years fifty years ago.

A nice thing I do remember is breakfast, my ex-husband **10**
said. I was surprised. All we ever had was coffee. Then I remembered there was a hole in the back of the kitchen closet which opened into the apartment next door. There, they always ate sugar-cured smoked bacon. It gave us a very grand feeling about breakfast, but we never got stuffed and sluggish.

That was when we were poor, I said. **11**

When were we ever rich? he asked. **12**

Oh, as time went on, as our responsibilities increased, we **13**
didn't go in need. You took adequate financial care, I reminded him. The children went to camp four weeks a year and in decent ponchos with sleeping bags and boots, just like everyone else. They looked very nice. Our place was warm in winter, and we had nice red pillows and things.

I wanted a sailboat, he said. But you didn't want anything. **14**

Don't be bitter, I said. It's never too late. **15**

No, he said with a great deal of bitterness. I may get a **16**
sailboat. As a matter of fact I have money down on an eighteen-foot two-rigger. I'm doing well this year and can

look forward to better. But as for you, it's too late. You'll always want nothing.

He had had a habit throughout the twenty-seven years of **17** making a narrow remark which, like a plumber's snake, could work its way through the ear down the throat, halfway to my heart. He would then disappear, leaving me choking with equipment. What I mean is, I sat down on the library steps and he went away.

I looked through *The House of Mirth*, but lost interest. I **18** felt extremely accused. Now, it's true, I'm short of requests and absolute requirements. But I do want *something.*

I want, for instance, to be a different person. I want to be **19** the woman who brings these two books back in two weeks. I want to be the effective citizen who changes the school system and addresses the Board of Estimate on the troubles of this dear urban center.

I *had* promised my children to end the war before they **20** grew up.

I wanted to have been married forever to one person, my **21** ex-husband or my present one. Either has enough character for a whole life, which as it turns out is really not such a long time. You couldn't exhaust either man's qualities or get under the rock of his reasons in one short life.

Just this morning I looked out the window to watch the **22** street for a while and saw that the little sycamores the city had dreamily planted a couple of years before the kids were born had come that day to the prime of their lives.

Well! I decided to bring those two books back to the li- **23** brary. Which proves that when a person or an event comes along to jolt or appraise me I *can* take some appropriate action, although I am better known for my hospitable remarks.

The elements of setting, plot, characters, point of view, and tone all combine to reinforce Paley's theme.

Setting *Setting* involves time—not only historical time, but also the length of time covered by the action. It also involves place—not only the physical setting but also the atmosphere created by the author. The time sequence in Grace Paley's short story is brief—a chance meeting between a wife and her ex-husband. The library setting represents the unreal world of books, of fictional characters and settings, to which the wife escapes. At the end, the scene of "the little sycamores" represents a significant shift in the character's outlook, from the unreal world of fiction to the real world of the growing trees outside her window. Setting can be a determinant of action and character.

Plot   The series of events that make up the story is the *plot*. The plot of "Wants" is simple: a brief encounter between a woman and her ex-husband, the paying of a fine, a short conversation, a contemplation, and the returning of books to the library. Usually such events are arranged to produce a climax—the high point of the action toward which the plot builds and out of which the conclusion or solution evolves. The climax in this story comes with the husband's remark "You'll always want nothing," which makes the main character painfully aware of her tendency to avoid life, to live through her books, and to enjoy her breakfast only through the smells of the bacon cooking in the next apartment. This plot reveals the inner conflict within the wife and leads to the conclusion when she sees the growing sycamores for the first time in years and decides to return the books to the library. The nature and resolution of the conflicts often reveal the theme. Such conflicts can exist between characters; between characters and an opposing force, such as an institution or circumstances; and between different feelings within a single character as in this short story.

Characters   The *characters* carry the plot forward and include a main character, called a protagonist, who is often in conflict with another character or institution or with herself, as in "Wants." In this story she is also in conflict with her husband's desire to embrace life. Where she liked the ponchos, sleeping bags, boots, and the warm apartment, he longed for a sailboat—to strike out and to live life. You might choose to compare two characters in a story or to analyze one character's development on the basis of his or her actions or conversation. Support your thesis by referring to a description by the author-narrator or by what other characters say to or about him or her.

Point of view The position from which the action is observed—the person through whose eyes the events are seen, the narrator who tells the story—is the *point of view*. The first-person narrator is a character within the work who tells the story, but who may or may not be credible. Grace Paley relates the events from the point of view of the main character who sees only her own actions and thoughts. The third-person narrator is not a character within the story and may be omniscient—that is, all-knowing. This narrator may know all or only some of the thoughts or actions of the characters. Such narrators are not always consistent throughout an entire work. But it is important to explore why such an inconsistency exists.

Tone *Tone* is the narrator's attitude toward the events and characters in the story or even, in some circumstances, toward the readers. In writing about the narrator, tone is an important aspect. The tone of the narrator in "Wants" is naive and innocent, and she seems unaware of her own motivations. She is neither introspective nor reflective except in the most superficial kind of way. This tone emphasizes her detachment from the real world. You might analyze why the author uses a particular narrative technique and tone to make the theme clear to the reader.

Symbolism A common characteristic of fiction, *symbolism* is used in all literature. A symbol is an object, usually concrete, that stands for something else, usually abstract. In writing about a particular symbol, first determine what it stands for. Then trace the incidents in the story that reinforce that idea. In Grace Paley's story, the books symbolize her escape from reality in the same way that the hole in the back of the kitchen closet symbolizes her "grand feeling" about breakfast without ever having to suffer the consequences of feeling "stuffed and sluggish." In avoiding the real breakfast, she is avoiding the real world. The books, especially *The Children,* and the "little sycamores" are additional symbols that reinforce the author's theme.

As you read and write, ask yourself the following questions: What is the theme? How does the author use setting, plot, characters, and symbolism to support the meaning? Who is telling the story? What is the tone of the narrator? Who is the protagonist? How is his or her character developed? How does one character compare with another? What symbols does the author use?

In the following paper, the student compares two characters from a longer piece of fiction—a novel, *Frankenstein,* by Mary Shelley.

SAMPLE STUDENT PAPER ABOUT FICTION

Susan Suehring

Professor Rose

English 212

30 April 1989

Themes in <u>Frankenstein</u>

Romantic authors often wrote about subjects **1**
like the search for knowledge and the desire to
know the unknown. In her book <u>Frankenstein</u>,
Mary W. Shelley deals with these desires and
their consequences. This theme is present early
in the book as we are introduced to Robert Walton
and learn of his forthcoming exploration into
the Arctic. When Walton later meets Victor
Frankenstein, the friendship they develop and the
similarities and differences between the two men
prepare the reader to analyze their unusual
search for knowledge and their journeys into the
unknown.

Shelley advances the idea that man has a **2**
strong desire to attain the unattainable and
shows us that sometimes that desire can have
serious results. Although both men feel driven to
succeed and have noble goals--Walton's exploration
of regions of the Arctic and Frankenstein's
desire to give life back to the dead--Walton seems

better prepared mentally and emotionally. While
Walton is impatient to begin his journey, he
still takes six years to make preparations and
ready himself for the hardships he realizes he
will encounter. Frankenstein, on the other hand,
appears to plunge blindly forward. He has spent
many years studying his craft, but upon discovery
of the secret of life he blunders on, never
giving thought to what his creation will be like
and what his responsibilities toward it will
be. As the reader discovers later in the novel,
his failure to consider these questions causes
him his worst grief.

Chapters 2 and 4 of the novel concentrate on **3**
Frankenstein's quest for knowledge and his
accomplishments at school. We learn of his early
delights at finding the internal cause of things.
"Curiosity, earnest research to learn the hidden
laws of nature, gladness akin to rapture, as they
were unfolded to me, are among the earliest
sensations I can remember" (22). In his search
for truth, Frankenstein comes across the works of
authors currently ridiculed by modern scientists.
Just as Frankenstein studies works that are
scorned, he later creates a monster that he and
others abhor. Thus persons may unconsciously
protect themselves by denying knowledge that will
lead them to answers they cannot handle.

Shelley's point is that Frankenstein spends **4**
too much time learning and that he carries his
search into the unknown too far. We learn from
Frankenstein himself that, as his understanding
at school increases, "I . . . soon became so
ardent and eager that the stars often disappeared
in the light of morning whilst I was yet engaged
in my laboratory" (35). His success at school
seems to drive him onward. What end can there be
for a man who conquers knowledge and then goes in
search of more? "A mind of moderate capacity
which closely pursues one study must infallibly
arrive at great proficiency in that study,"
according to Frankenstein (36).

The result of Frankenstein's efforts is, of **5**
course, the creation of the monster whose unhappy
life is related throughout the remaining
chapters. Walton likewise encounters problems as
he ventures northward: men die in the bitter
cold, and the ship becomes entrapped by sheets of
floating ice. Unlike Frankenstein, however,
Walton realizes that he must end his journey
before its completion, since it is possible that
he and his crew will die. The crew threatens
mutiny if Walton tries to go north. Even so,
Walton shows that he has learned from
Frankenstein's experience and decides not to
pursue his voyage.

    Shelley shows us that at the end of   **6**
Frankenstein's life, he finally acknowledges the
disastrous results of his search for ultimate
knowledge. He tells Walton, "Learn from me, if
not by my precepts, at least by my example, how
dangerous is the acquirement of knowledge and how
much happier that man is who believes his native
town to be the world, than he who aspires to
become greater than his nature will allow" (38).

Work Cited

Shelley, Mary W. <u>Frankenstein</u>. 1818. New York:
    Bantam, 1981.

In this paper, Susan Suehring compares two characters'
search for knowledge and the consequences of those
searches—represented by Walton's Arctic exploration and
Frankenstein's desire to restore life to the dead. In paragraph 2, she points out similarities and then moves to differences between the two characters in their approaches to
their symbolic journeys. In paragraphs 3 and 4, she traces
Frankenstein's drive for knowledge and concludes with the
difference between Walton and Frankenstein's reactions to
the problems that they encounter, thus emphasizing Shelley's theme that acquiring knowledge has its dangers.
Suehring traces the development of this theme throughout
the novel by comparing and contrasting the two main characters and their searches.

■ **Exercise 1** In one sentence, write the thesis of this paper. This is
basically a comparison paper (see **32d[5]**). How does the author set up

the comparison? List five references to the text that support the points she is making. What symbols does she suggest that Shelley uses? Be prepared to discuss your answers in class.

(6) Writing about poetry

Poetry shares many of the components of fiction. It too may contain a narrator with a point of view, and dramatic monologues and narrative poems may have plot, setting, and characters. Like all literature, poetry uses symbols. But poetry is primarily characterized by voice and tone and its concentrated use of connotative diction, imagery, figures of speech, symbols, sound, and rhythm. Before starting to write a paper about a poem, try to capture the literal meaning of the poem in a sentence or two; then analyze how the poet transfers that meaning to the reader through the use of the following poetic devices.

Voice The speaker in the poem—the persona—is referred to as the *voice*. The first-person "I" in the poem is not necessarily the poet. Listen to the tone of the voice in a poem just as you do in conversation. Is it angry, joyful, melancholy, or fearful? What elements in the poem reinforce that impression? In Dylan Thomas's "Do Not Go Gentle into That Good Night," the tone of the voice, reinforced by diction and imagery, is one of rage and resistance against the inevitability of death.

Diction The term *diction* means "choice of words," and the words in poetry connote meanings beyond the obvious denotative ones (see **20a[2]**). As you read, check definitions and derivations of key words in your dictionary to find meanings beyond the obvious ones. How do such definitions and derivations reinforce the meaning of the poem?

Imagery The *imagery* in a poem is a word or phrase describing a sensory experience that reminds us of a feeling we have had. Notice the images in the following lines from the poem "Meeting at Night" by Robert Browning about a lover journeying to meet his sweetheart.

> Then a mile of warm sea-scented beach;
> Three fields to cross till a farm appears;
> A tap at the pane, the quick sharp scratch
> And a blue spurt of a lighted match,
> And a voice less loud, through its joys and fears,
> Than the two hearts beating each to each!

The feeling, the smell, and the sound of the beach; the sounds of the tap at the window, the scratch of a match being lighted, the whispers, and the hearts beating; and the sight of the two lovers in the match light, embracing—all give us the image of a young man, his senses fine-tuned with excitement and anticipation, traveling at night to his sweetheart's home where they meet in secret.

Figures of speech　The words or phrases that depart from the expected thought or word arrangement, to emphasize a point or to gain the reader's attention, are known as *figures of speech*. Metaphor, simile, and personification are common in poetry (see **20a**). The richness of such figures, although fully felt, is often subtle and difficult to identify. Sir Walter Raleigh uses simile and metaphor in this tightly woven couplet (a pair of rhyming or rhythmic lines):

> Our graves that hide us from the searching sun
> Are like drawn curtains when the play is done.

The above simile equates life with the sun and death with darkness, closure, endings, and separation, while the metaphor equates life with a drama. All of this is suggested in just two lines. As you read a poem, identify the figures of speech and then describe how they enrich the meaning by what they suggest.

Sound　*Sound* is an important element in poetry. *Alliteration* is the repetition of initial consonants, *assonance* is the repetition of vowel sounds in a succession of words, and *rhyme* is the repetition of similar sounds either at the end of lines or within a line (internal rhyme). When you encounter such repetitions, examine and analyze their connection to each other and to the meaning of a line or a stanza or a poem. For instance, notice how the repetition of the "w" and the "s" sounds in the following lines from Elinor Wylie's "Velvet Shoes" sound like the soft whisper of walking in a snowstorm.

> Let us walk in the white snow
> In a soundless space;

We are sensitive to sound in poetry because as we read poetry we unconsciously hear it.

Rhythm The regular occurrence of accent or stress that we hear in poetry is known as *rhythm*, and the rhythm is commonly arranged in patterns called *meters*. Such meters depend on the recurrence of stressed and unstressed syllables in units commonly called *feet*. The most common metrical foot in English is the *iambic*, which consists of an unstressed syllable followed by a stressed one (procéed). A second common foot is the *trochaic*, a stressed foot followed by an unstressed one (fífty). Less common are the three-syllable *anapestic* (overcóme) and the *dactylic* (páragraph). A series of feet make up a line to form a regular rhythm, as exemplified in the following lines from Coleridge's "Frost at Midnight."

> The Frost performs its secret ministry,
> Unhelped by any wind. The owlet's cry
> Came loud—and hark, again! loud as before.

Note the changes in rhythm and their significance—the ways in which rhythm conveys meaning. In the second line there is a pause (caesura), marked by the ending of the sentence, which adds special emphasis to the intrusion of the owlet's cry.

As you read and write, ask yourself the following questions: What is the meaning of the poem? How does the poet use diction? What words have strong connotations or multiple meanings? What images can you identify? What figures of speech does the poet use? How do these advance the meaning? How does the poet use sound, rhythm, and rhyme to reinforce the meaning?

The following is a student paper about a poem, "Tulips," by Sylvia Plath. The first-person narrator is in the hospital, and the tulips in her room intrude on her drugged state.

SAMPLE STUDENT PAPER ABOUT POETRY

James Dalgetty

Professor Anderson

English 2

15 March 1988

The Tulips

The angry, intractable image of life in her **1**
otherwise antiseptic plastic existence, the
tulips push disturbing images of the potency of
life into Sylvia Plath's opiate-induced,
trancelike existence. Seeming more alive than
the author herself, the imagery associated with
the tulips becomes stronger and more vital than
the images of the author. This constant struggle
between the tulips and self-image allows us to
enter the disturbing world of her nonexistence.
In order to understand the power of "Tulips,"
consider the pattern of the imagery, the power
of the specific metaphors, and the dichotomy
between the emotions of the author and the
emotions of the tulips.

The emotions of the tulips precipitate our **2**
journey into the author's confined, trancelike
existence. "The tulips are too excitable, it is
winter here" (1). This first line illustrates
both the powerful emotions of the personified
tulips and the author's lack of emotion about her

Dalgetty 2

world. From this initial metaphor we then get a spatial introduction into her fixed world. The first eighteen lines are a description of her hospital stay, confined to a bed with her head propped up "like an eye between two white lids that will not shut" (9). This narrative gives a disturbing picture of the poet, the metaphors associating her with images of a dazed nonexistence. She pictures herself as: "white," "winter," "peaceful," "nobody," and "a pebble." All of these images translate into a picture of a body with no name or identity; she is just there for the ride.

Line 18 starts a tone of active involvement **3** in her experience; however, again this is a disturbing portrait of a "lost soul." This is the story of cutting ties with the past and present, a distinct set of images promoting a loss of identity and disassociation. The author pictures herself as: "lost," "drowned," "nun," "pure," "empty," "dazed," "dead," and finally "I have no face" (48). Lines 25 through 35 further reinforce these images with a strong association of drowning and then seem to indicate death as a favorable set of affairs.

Into this "pleasant" state of oblivion the **4** tulips rear their heads. Their "excitable," glaring intrusion becomes more real and alive than anything in the author's private

Dalgetty 3

limbo. Their color is too alive: "The tulips
are too red in the first place, they hurt me"
(36). The tulips become "like an awful baby,"
wrapped in white swaddlings (38). They float in
her daze but try to "weigh me down" (40) like
"lead sinkers" (42) in an attempt to bring her
back down to earth and reality.

After their introduction, the tulips seem to **5**
personify strong emotions of hunger and life
force. Lines 46 and 47 describe the contrast
between the author's self—image and the
ever—growing personality of the tulips. "And I
see myself, flat, ridiculous, a cut paper
shadow / Between the eye of the sun and the eyes
of the tulips." Line 47 also illustrates the
complete projection of identity and personality
to the tulips; by equating the sun and the tulips
as "eyes," the author endows them with the same
image that she gives herself in line 9.

The projection now complete, the tulips   **6**
assume an almost "dangerous" (58) character to
the author. The tulips disturb, anger, and
generate fear in her soul. They force her
attention to the real world of life and beauty
and strong emotion. "They concentrate my
attention, that was happy / Playing and resting
without committing itself" (55, 56). The tulips
fill her nonexistence like a "loud noise"
(52). Their presence fills the air, which "snags

Dalgetty 4

and eddies round" them like "a river." The power
of their life force even penetrates the walls
(57). The final image is perhaps the most
potent: the tulips open their collective maw like
"dangerous animals," threatening to swallow the
author's safe oblivion and force her to face life
and reality.

As a most disturbing portrait of a woman who **7**
is so lost that briefly blooming flowers emote
more tenacious life force than does the author,
the complex series of images that comprise
"Tulips" is both sinister and compelling. It
is an entrance into a frightening world of
self—induced oblivion and nonexistence, with the
compelling portraits of the short—lived flowers
assuming more life, character, and tenacity than
the portrait of the author herself.

Dalgetty 5

Work Cited

Plath, Sylvia. "Tulips." The Collected Poems of

Sylvia Plath. Comp. Ted Hughes. New York:

Harper, 1981. 160—62.

In this paper James Dalgetty compares the images and
metaphors associated with the author or persona and those
associated with the tulips. He follows the order of the poem
itself, tracing these images throughout and supporting his

comments with appropriate quotations from the poem. For example, Dalgetty supports his point about the contrast between the author's image and the "ever-growing personality of the tulips" by a line from the poem: "And I see myself, flat, ridiculous, a cut paper shadow / Between the eye of the sun and the eyes of the tulips."

■ **Exercise 2**   In a single sentence, state the literal meaning of the following Shakespearean poem. Who is the persona? Find three images that the poet uses to convey that meaning. Be prepared to discuss your answers in class.

Sonnet 73

That time of year thou mayst in me behold
When yellow leaves, or none, or few, do hang
Upon those boughs which shake against the cold,
Bare ruined choirs, where late the sweet birds sang.
In me thou see'st the twilight of such day
As after sunset fadeth in the west;
Which by and by black night doth take away,
Death's second self, that seals up all in rest.
In me thou see'st the glowing of such fire,
That on the ashes of his youth doth lie,
As the deathbed whereon it must expire,
Consumed with that which it was nourished by.
This thou perceiv'st which makes thy love more strong,
To love that well which thou must leave ere long.

William Shakespeare

(7) Writing about drama

Although it is written to be filmed or performed on a stage, drama is also meant to be read, which is probably the way that you will encounter it in your course work. In a live performance, the director and the actors imprint the play with their own interpretations; in a book or script, you have only the printed word. Drama has many of the same elements as fiction and poetry, but they are presented differently.

Dialogue *Dialogue* is the medium through which we see action and characterization in reading a play. Examine dialogue to discover inner thoughts, motives, and internal conflicts, as well as relationships.

Characters Often identified briefly in a list at the beginning of the play, the *characters* are developed largely through what they say and what is said about them and to them. In Ibsen's "A Doll's House," Nora's growth from a child to a mature woman can be traced through her gestures and her speech. In writing about drama, you might compare characters or analyze their development and the significance of that development through their dialogue and their actions.

Plot *Plot* in drama is similar to plot in fiction and is marked by climax and conflict. Although there may be time lapses between scenes, the story line must be developed within the more narrow time and place constraints of the play. Subplots similar to the one outlined in the sample student paper that follows may reinforce the theme of the main plot. In a paper you might examine how dialogue, characterizations, and stage directions for gesture and movement further the action.

As you read and write ask yourself the following questions: What is the theme of the play? How does the dialogue move the action and support the meaning? How are the characters depicted through dialogue? through their gestures? through their actions?

The following student paper outlines the significance of the subplot in *King Lear* as intensifying the main plot and lending universality to the play.

SAMPLE STUDENT PAPER ABOUT DRAMA

Susan K. Ferk

Professor Dorgan

English 211

15 October 1989

The Subplot as Commentary in <u>King Lear</u>

To a careless eye, the subplot involving   **1**
Gloucester, Edgar, and Edmund in Shakespeare's
<u>King Lear</u> may appear to be trivial, unnecessary,
and a simple restatement of the theme of the main
story. After close examination, however, it is
clear that Shakespeare has skillfully introduced
a second set of characters whose actions comment
on and intensify the main plot and theme.

The first scene of <u>King Lear</u> sets up   **2**
comparison and contrast between Lear and
Gloucester. Gloucester jokes about his bastard
son while Lear angrily banishes his favorite
daughter. By the end of the second scene, we
realize how important their children are to both
men and yet how little they really know
them. Both are easily deceived: Lear by Goneril
and Regan, who convince him of their love with
flowery words, and Gloucester, who is convinced
by very little evidence of Edgar's plot against
his life. The audience is set up to accept Lear

Ferk 2

and Gloucester as old fools. Neither man takes
responsibility for what has happened. Gloucester
says "these late eclipses" (1.2.102) have brought
about these changes, and Lear blames Cordelia for
her losses. Neither realizes or acknowledges that
his own foolishness has brought about these
events.

Gloucester, however, does comment on Lear's **3**
actions in scene 2. He is amazed that the king
has limited his power so suddenly. When Edmund
suggests that "sons at perfect age, and fathers
declined, the father should be as ward to the
son, and the son manage his revenue" (1.2.72–
74), Gloucester is enraged by what he thinks are
Edgar's words. He calls Edgar unnatural, and
since this is exactly the action taken by Lear
with his daughters, we can assume that he thinks
Lear's act was unnatural also.

At Goneril's palace Lear foreshadows **4**
Gloucester's fate when he says "Old fond eyes,
beweep this cause again, I'll pluck ye out"
(1.4.305–06). In the same way that Lear fears
for his eyes because of Goneril, so does
Gloucester lose his eyes because of Edmund. At
the end of act 1, Lear foreshadows his own
destiny, "Oh, let me not be mad, not mad, sweet
heaven!" (1.5.43).

Shakespeare brings together the two plots in **5**
act 2 scene 2 when Regan, Cornwall, Gloucester,

and Edmund meet at Gloucester's castle.
Cornwall's offer of employment to Edmund made on
the pretense of his royal service seems logical
to the audience who knows the similarities of
their true natures. It is interesting to note
that Gloucester calls Edmund his "loyal and
natural boy" (2.1.91), while Lear names Goneril a
"degenerate bastard" (1.4.252).

   Lear arrives at the castle and is outraged **6**
when Cornwall and Regan do not meet him.
However, Lear decides that perhaps Cornwall is
ill and unable to come. Likewise, throughout the
remainder of act 2 Lear tries to imagine that
Regan and Cornwall love and respect him, and he
makes excuses for them when their actions do not
conform to his expectations. Lear has more at
stake here than Regan's love. If she proves as
evil as Goneril (and she proves even more so),
then Lear cannot deny that he was wrong in
supposing these two daughters more loving than
his banished Cordelia. Lear soon acknowledges
that the disease of his daughters is in his own
blood. The realization of his errors and his loss
of power and Cordelia drive him to the madness
seen in act 3.

   Gloucester and Lear meet in scene 4 of act 3 **7**
in the midst of a raging storm, Lear's madness,
and Gloucester's despair. Gloucester has not
suffered the worst, but his words begin to echo

those of Lear in earlier scenes. He says "Thou
sayest the King grows mad: I'll tell thee,
friend, I am almost mad myself" (166—67).
Gloucester helps the king into the hovel and
cares for him like a child, similar to the way
Edgar later helps Gloucester after his eyes are
plucked out.

Death begins in act 3 scene 7. A servant   **8**
dies defending Gloucester, and Cornwall is
fatally wounded. In the confusion, Gloucester
realizes his mistakes and his former
blindness. After losing his sight, he can now
see. When he is turned out, his wanderings in
the country remind us of Lear in the storm. Lear
likewise in his despair now has learned to see.

Gloucester and Lear share many similarities   **9**
at this point. Both men at the height of their
afflictions desire the company of Tom o'Bedlam,
who represents wise man. They also acquire a
sense of justice and care for less fortunate
men. Lear looks after his fool in the storm, and
Gloucester calls for clothes for Tom. Their
similarities intensify the pain and change in
each man. Also, Shakespeare's use of a king and
a nobleman both suffering from their foolishness
emphasizes the universality of man's
suffering. On the other hand, they do not suffer
in the same way. Gloucester does not lose his
mind, and Lear does not try suicide.

In the end, the story comes full   **10**
circle. Edgar tells Gloucester his identity and
asks his father's forgiveness, thus causing
Gloucester's heart to break "'twixt two extremes
of passion, joy and grief" (5.3.236). Lear also
dies, with Cordelia in his arms, trying so hard
to believe her alive that it strains his heart as
well. These men have learned much, but as in
real life, wisdom in old age and recognizing
one's children for what they are do not always
bring peace and happiness. The dismal final
scenes of this play in which almost everyone dies
serve to emphasize Shakespeare's intent to show
two unfortunate characters who suffer from
foolishness and Fortune's wheel.

Work Cited

Shakespeare, William. The Tragedy of King

    Lear. The Folger Library General Reader's

    Shakespeare. New York: Washington

    Square—Pocket, 1957.

Susan Ferk supports her thesis by comparing and contrasting the characters of Lear and Gloucester as they move
through the play. In act 1, the plots are separate, but she
points out how in act 2 they move together and proceed along parallel lines, crossing only occasionally. She
traces this progression throughout the play, following the

characters' actions and dialogue while emphasizing the significance of each plot in reinforcing and intensifying the other.

■ **Exercise 3** Select a recent film or television dramatization. In one sentence identify the theme. How do the plot and characters support that theme? Be prepared to discuss your answers in class.

(8) Use proper form in writing about literature.

See **34** for the conventions for a research paper. There are, in addition, certain special conventions for writing about literature.

Tense Use the present tense when referring to literature, since the author is communicating to a present reader in the present time.

Sherwood Anderson lets the boy speak for himself.

Documentation Check with your instructor about the reference format he or she prefers. Ordinarily, you will be writing about a work from a book used in the course. In such cases you usually do not need to give the source and publication information of the book. However, you should indicate if you are using another edition or anthology. One way of doing so is to use the MLA form for works cited, as explained in section **34f**, although in this case your bibliography might consist of only a single work. See the examples on pages 520, 528, and 535.

An alternative way of providing this information is by acknowledging the first quotation in an explanatory note at the end of the paper (see below and pages 474–75) and then giving all subsequent references to the work in the body of the paper.

[1]D. H. Lawrence, "Tickets, Please," The Norton Anthology of Short Fiction, ed. R. V.

Cassill (New York: Norton, 1986) 834. All

subsequent references to this work will be by page

number within the text.

If you use the note form, you may not need a works cited list to repeat the bibliographical information.

Whichever format you use, recall from **34f** that references to short stories and novels are by page number; references to poetry are by line number; and references to plays are usually by act, scene, and line numbers. The information in parentheses should be placed in the text directly after the quotation, and the period or comma follows the quotation marks and the parentheses (see **16e**).

Plot   Do not retell the plot. Refer to it only as necessary to support or clarify your thesis. Provide a brief summary of the plot, in two or three lines, only if you have reason to suspect that your audience may be unfamiliar with the work you are discussing, but do not take valuable space to describe the plot in great detail.

Poetry   For *poems and verse plays,* type quotations of fewer than three lines within your text and insert a slash with a space on each side to separate the lines.

> "Does the road wind uphill all the way?"/"Yes, to the very end"—Christina Rosetti opens her poem "Uphill" with this two-line question and answer.

Quotations of more than three lines should be indented ten spaces from the left margin with double-spacing between lines (see page 434).

Author references   Use the full name in your first reference to the author of a work and only the last name in all subsequent references. Treat male and female authors the same: Dickens and Cather, not Dickens and Miss Cather.

35b
Write effective letters, résumés, memos, and reports.

(1) Write effective letters and résumés; use an acceptable format.

A knowledge of how to write business letters, application letters, and résumés can be useful to you not only in job-related situations but in your college and personal life as well. The three main formats for business letters—full block, modified block, and indented—can be used for any kind of business letter.

FORMAT

Business letters are usually typed on only one side of white, unlined, $8\frac{1}{2} \times 11$ inch paper. Standard business envelopes measure about $3\frac{1}{2} \times 6\frac{1}{2}$ inches or 4×10 inches. (Letterhead stationery and envelopes vary in both size and color.)

Check to see if your company or organization has a policy about letter format. Most companies use either full block or modified block for regular correspondence, though an indented format is often used for personal business correspondence such as thank-you notes, congratulations, and the like.

A business letter has six parts: (1) heading, (2) inside address, (3) salutation, (4) body, (5) closing, which consists of the complimentary close and signature, and (6) added notations.

The *heading* gives the writer's full address and the date. If letterhead stationery is used, the date is typed beneath it flush left, flush right, or centered, depending on your format. If plain stationery is used, the address of the writer followed by the date is placed toward the top of the page—the distance from the top arranged so that the body of the letter will be attractively centered on the page—flush with the left- or right-hand margin, as in the letter on page 543. Notice that the heading has no end punctuation.

The *inside address,* typed two to six lines below the heading, gives the name and full address of the recipient. Use the postal abbreviation for the state name.

The *salutation* (or greeting) is written flush with the left margin, two spaces below the inside address, and is followed by a colon.

When the surname of the addressee is known, it is used in the salutation of a business letter, as in the following examples.

Dear Dr. Davis:	Dear Mayor Rodriguez:
Dear Ms. Joseph:	Dear Mrs. Greissman:

▲ Note: Use *Miss* or *Mrs.* if the woman you are addressing has indicated a preference. Otherwise, use *Ms.,* which is always appropriate and which most women accept.

In letters to organizations, or to persons whose name and sex are unknown, omit the salutation or use one such as the following:

Dear Sir or Madam:	Dear Mobil Oil:
Dear Subscription Manager:	Dear Registrar:

For the appropriate forms of salutations and addresses in letters to government officials, military personnel, and so on, check an etiquette book or the front or back of your college dictionary.

The *body* of the letter should follow the principles of good writing. Typewritten letters are usually single-spaced, with double-spacing between paragraphs. The first sentence of each paragraph should begin flush with the left margin (in full block or modified block) or should be indented five to ten spaces (in indented format). The subject matter should be organized so that the reader can grasp immediately what is wanted, and the style should be clear and direct. Do not use stilted or abbreviated phrasing:

| NOT | The aforementioned letter | BUT | Your letter |
| NOT | Please send it to me ASAP. | BUT | Please send it to me as soon as possible. |

The *closing* is typed flush with the left-hand margin in full-block style. In modified-block and indented style, it is typed to the right of the letter, in alignment with the heading. Here are the parts of the closing:

Complimentary close   This conventional ending is typed, after a double space, below the last paragraph of the body of the letter. Among the endings commonly used in business letters are the following:

FORMAL	LESS FORMAL
Very truly yours,	Sincerely,
Sincerely yours,	Cordially,

Typed name   The writer's full name is typed three or four lines below the closing.

Title of sender   This line, following the typed name, indicates the sender's position, if he or she is acting in an official capacity.

> Manager, Employee Relations
> Chairperson, Search Committee

Signature   The letter is signed between the complimentary close and the typed name.

Notations are typed two lines below the title of the sender, flush with the left margin. They indicate, among other things, whether anything is enclosed with or attached to the letter (*enclosure* or *enc.*, *attachment* or *att.*), to whom copies of the letter have been sent (*cc: AAW, PTN*), and the initials of the sender and the typist (*DM/cll*).

Model business letter

LETTERHEAD
CONTAINING
RETURN
ADDRESS

MIRACLE MILE COMMUNITY LEAGUE

1992 South Cochran Avenue   Los Angeles, CA 90036

February 1, 1990

Dr. Nathan T. Swift
Community Health Center
1101 Figueroa Street   **INSIDE ADDRESS**
Los Angeles, CA   90027

Dear Dr. Swift: **SALUTATION**

We have completed our study of the nutrition
education program being conducted by the Community
Health Center. The findings are encouraging.
However, we believe that awareness training for the
staff, a few schedule changes, and greater
involvement of the parents could significantly
improve the program.

Our final report, available by March 1, will   **BODY**
explain these recommendations more fully. Angel
Chavez, our Vice President for Management
Development, will be happy to work with you if you
would like his assistance.

We look forward to hearing from you soon.

Sincerely,   **Complimentary close**

Dorothy Muir

                        Signature   **CLOSING**

Dorothy Muir   **Typed name**
Director   **Title**

DM/ewl   **NOTATION**

Business envelopes The address that appears on the envelope is identical to the inside address of the letter. The return address regularly gives the full name and address of the writer.

Model addressed envelope

```
Diane Bellows
1830 Lexington Avenue
Louisville, KY  40227


              Mr. Aaron Navik
              Personnel Manager
              Echo Electronics
              627 East 3rd Street
              Louisville, KY  40223
```

APPLICATION LETTERS AND RÉSUMÉS

Application letters and résumés are essential parts of applying for a job. In both documents, your main concern is to emphasize your strong points, to present yourself in the best light so a prospective employer will grant you an interview. Usually written to draw the reader's attention to the résumé, the letter of application should indicate the job you want and state your qualifications briefly. In the last paragraph you should say when you are available for an interview. The résumé (page 546) that accompanies the letter of application gives more information about you than your letter can. Ordinarily, your letter should be no longer than one typed page, nor (unless you have worked for a long time and have held many positions) should your résumé.

Model application letter

1830 Lexington Avenue
Louisville, KY   40227
June 8, 1990

Mr. Aaron Navik
Personnel Manager
Echo Electronics
627 East 3rd Street
Louisville, KY   40223

Dear Mr. Navik:

Please consider me for the position of Assistant
Director of Employee Benefits in the Personnel Division
of Echo Electronics.

As you can see from my résumé, my major was
Business Administration with an emphasis in personnel
management. Whenever possible, I have found jobs and
campus activities that would give me experience
in dealing with people. As an assistant in the
Admissions Office, I dealt with students, parents,
alumni, and faculty. The position required both a
knowledge of university regulations and an
understanding of other people.

As an administrative intern with Echo last
summer, I learned about the management of a company
at first hand and gained a firmer grasp of the contri-
bution personnel management makes to the overall
objectives of the company. Participants in the intern
program were required to write a paper analyzing the
company where we were placed. If you are interested,
I will be happy to send you a copy of my paper.

I would very much like to put my interests and my
training to work for Echo Electronics, and I am
available for an interview at your convenience.

Sincerely,

Diane Bellows

Diane Bellows

enc.

A résumé is a list of a person's qualifications for a job and is enclosed with a letter of application. It is made up of four categories of information:

1. Personal data: name, mailing address, telephone number
2. Educational background
3. Work experience
4. References

Make your résumé look professional. Like the letter of application, the résumé is a form of persuasion designed to emphasize your qualifications for a job and to get you an interview. Since there is usually more than one applicant for every job, your résumé should make the most of your qualifications. Consider devising a résumé especially tailored to each job you apply for so you can present your qualifications in the strongest light. After reading all the letters and résumés received, a potential employer usually decides to interview only the best-qualified candidates.

Writing a résumé requires the same planning and attention to detail that writing a paper does. First, make a list of the jobs you have had, the activities and clubs you have been part of, and the offices you have held. Amplify these items by adding dates, job titles and responsibilities, and a brief statement about what you learned from each of them. Arrange these items with the most recent first. Activities that may not seem relevant to the job you want can often be explained to show that you learned important things from them. See the following tips on writing a résumé and the sample résumé on page 546.

TIPS ON RÉSUMÉ WRITING

1. Don't forget to include your name, address, and telephone number; unless relevant to the job, personal data such as age and marital status are better left out.

2. Mention your degree, college or university, and pertinent areas of special training.

3. Think about career goals, but generally reserve mention of them for the application letter or interview (and even then make sure they enhance your appeal as a candidate). Your interest should be to match your qualifications to the employer's goals.

4. Even if an advertisement asks you to state a salary requirement, any mention of salary should usually be deferred until the interview.

5. Whenever possible, make evident any relationship between jobs you have had and the job you are seeking.

6. Use an acceptable format and make sure the résumé is neat, orderly, and correct to show that you are an efficient, well-organized, thoughtful person.

You may find it helpful to consult one of the following books for further information on application letters, résumés, and interviews:

Angel, Juvenal L. *The Complete Resume Book and Job-Getter's Guide*. 3rd ed. New York: Pocket, 1990.

Bolles, Richard N. *What Color Is Your Parachute? A Practical Manual for Job-Hunters and Career-Changers*. Berkeley: Ten Speed, annual.

Petras, Kathryn, and Ross Petras. *The Only Job Hunting Guide You'll Ever Need*. New York: Poseidon, 1989.

Smith, Michael H. *The Resume Writer's Handbook*. 2nd ed. New York: Harper & Row, 1987.

Model résumé

Diane Bellows
1830 Lexington Avenue
Louisville, KY   40227
(502) 689–3137

EDUCATION   University of Louisville, B.A., 1989
Major: Business Administration with
emphasis in personnel management
Minor: Economics with emphasis in
corporate finance

EXPERIENCE

College   <u>Orientation</u> <u>Leader</u>, University Admissions
Office, 1987–89. Met with prospective
students and their parents, conducted tours
of campus, answered questions, wrote reports
for each orientation meeting.

<u>Academic</u> <u>Committee</u>, Alpha Phi Sorority,
1987–89. Organized study halls and tutoring
services for disadvantaged students.

<u>Advertising</u> <u>Manager</u>, university yearbook,
1988. Secured advertising that made the
yearbook self–supporting; wrote monthly
progress report.

Summers   <u>Intern</u>, <u>Echo</u> <u>Electronics</u>, June 1988.
Learned about pension plans, health care
benefits, employee associations, and work
regulations as they affect employee relations and personnel management.

<u>Volunteer</u>, Arthur Schneider's
School Board re–election campaign, 1987.
Wrote press releases, campaign brochures,
direct mailers; did research on teacher
competence.

REFERENCES   Placement Office
University of Louisville
Louisville, KY   40222
(502) 744–3219

(2) Write effective memos.

Generally, memos are used for communicating a variety of information within an organization—directives on policy or procedures, requests and responses to requests for information, trip reports and monthly action summaries, and informal reports such as field reports or lab reports. While the length of the memo varies according to its purpose, the basic format is relatively standardized, though companies often have specially printed forms for the first page. Usually, memos identify the person or persons to whom the memo is addressed in the first line, the person who wrote the memo in the second line, the date in the third line, and the subject of the memo in the fourth line.

To:	J. Karl Meyer, Senior Engineer
From:	Lee Dawson, Project Director
Date:	September 20, 1989
Subject:	4.5 oz. Dacron Load Test Results

If the memo is long, it sometimes begins with a *statement of the purpose*, and then gives a *summary* of the discussion. This summary helps a manager or executive, who may receive thirty or forty or more memos a day, decide which ones to read carefully and which to skim. The *discussion* is the main part of the memo. If it is more than a page long, it may benefit from the use of headings to highlight the main parts. If appropriate, the memo closes with *recommendations* for action to be taken. Clearly state in this part of the memo who is to do what and when it is to be done.

The tone of a memo can be friendly and casual, informal, or formal depending on its purpose and audience. Naturally, if you are a trainee, you would probably use a relatively formal tone in a memo addressed to your supervisor, but memos you address to co-workers you know well can often be casual. Whatever the tone, however, the memo should be clear, concise, and correct. Notice the format and the tone of the sample memo. It was sent by an executive to the people he supervises. The tone is formal but not stilted, and it is clear and concise.

Model memo

INTERNAL MEMO

To: All Field Personnel

From: R. W. Morgan
           Vice President, Field Operations

Date: October 6, 1989

Subject: PICCOLO 386 SOFTWARE DIRECTORY

The latest issue of the PICCOLO 386 SOFTWARE
DIRECTORY is attached. It lists DOS—based
software products that are on the market now for
people with 80386 microcomputer systems such as
the Piccolo 386.

We are trying to list only those products that we
have seen demonstrated on the 386 or that a vendor,
dealer, or distributor claims will run on the 386;
but we make no guarantees.

Please note: Inclusion in the directory does not
imply that Piccolo endorses the products or
suppliers or recommends them in preference to
others not listed. Further, Piccolo does not
warrant that these products are compatible with
Piccolo systems. The buyer is solely responsible
for determining application and suitability.

Although this directory can be copied for
distribution to others, it is a temporary listing
intended primarily for your own use. In late
November it will be revised and published in
booklet form as a stock item.

Approximately 250 vendors have already been
contacted for information on software products that
might be appropriate in the directory. A Software
Vendor Listing Form is included in the back of the
directory for additional vendors to whom you may
wish to give copies.

(3) Write effective reports.

Formal reports differ from informal memo reports in length and tone and in the addition of such elements as a letter of transmittal, title page, abstract, executive summary, table of contents, glossary, and appendix (although not all reports include each of these elements). Writing a formal report often requires many of the same skills and basic techniques as writing a research paper (see section **34**). Many organizations have a format guide for formal reports; in the absence of such a guide, you might begin by studying several successful reports from the company files.

An *abstract* is a brief summary of the material in the report, usually in language similar to that of the report (whether technical or nontechnical). The abstract enables prospective readers to determine whether the report will be useful and whether they need to read all of it or only parts of it. If a report intended for technical personnel will also be read by nontechnical management, it often includes an *executive summary*, in nontechnical language, in addition to an abstract.

A *table of contents* provides a guide to the structure of the report and makes finding exact sections of the report easier for readers. If you have used effective and accurate headings in the body of your report, the simplest way to create a table of contents is to list them.

A *glossary* is an alphabetical list that defines terms used in the report. Using a glossary lets you continue your discussion without having to stop to define terms. Generally, a glossary appears at the end of a report, but it may also be placed after the table of contents.

An *appendix* contains information that is relevant to the report but is too detailed or extensive to be included in the discussion. For example, an appendix might contain supplementary data, tables, maps, diagrams, or a list of references. An appendix usually appears last.

You may find it helpful to consult one of the following books for further information on letters, memos, and reports.

Brusaw, C. T., G. J. Alred, and W. E. Oliu. *Handbook of Technical Writing*. 3rd ed. New York: St. Martin's, 1987.

Damerst, William A. *Clear Technical Reports*. 2nd ed. San Diego: Harcourt, 1982.

MacGregor, A. J. *Graphics Simplified: How to Plan and Prepare Effective Charts, Graphs, Illustrations, and Other Visual Aids*. Toronto: U of Toronto P, 1979.

Mathes, J. C., and D. W. Stevenson. *Designing Technical Reports*. Indianapolis: Bobbs, 1976.

■ **Exercise 4**

1. Prepare a résumé, and then write a letter of application for a position you are qualified to fill.
2. Write a letter to a former teacher to express appreciation for recommending you for a summer job.
3. In a letter, call the attention of your representative in city government to repairs needed on neighborhood streets.
4. Write a letter to a national record company complaining about the technical quality of a record you ordered from them.

GLOSSARY OF GRAMMATICAL AND RHETORICAL TERMS

This glossary presents brief explanations of frequently used grammatical terms. Consult the index for references to further discussion of most of the terms and for a number of terms not listed.

absolute phrase   A grammatically unconnected part of a sentence—generally a noun or pronoun followed by a participle (and all the words associated with it). Some absolute phrases have the meaning (but not the structure) of an adverb clause. See **24a** and **30b(4)**. See also **phrase** and **sentence modifier**.

> We will have a cookout, **weather permitting**.   [noun + present participle]
> COMPARE   We will have a cookout *if the weather permits.*   [adverb clause: subordinator (*if*) + subject + predicate]
>
> **The national anthem sung for the last time**, the old stadium was closed.   [noun + past participle with modifier]
> COMPARE   *After the national anthem had been sung for the last time,* the old stadium was closed.   [adverb clause]
>
> The two of us worked on the homecoming float—**Tom in the morning and I at night**.   [Note the use of *I,* the subjective case.]
> COMPARE   *Tom worked in the morning, and I worked at night.*

abstract noun   Abstract words express qualities, concepts, and emotions that cannot be perceived through the senses: truth, justice, fear, future. See **20a(3)**.

acronym A word formed by combining the initial letters of a series of words: NASA—National Aeronautics and Space Administration.

active voice The form of a transitive verb indicating that its subject performs the action the verb denotes: Emily *sliced* the ham. See **7**, **29d**. See also **passive voice**, **verb**, and **voice**.

adjective A part of speech modifying a noun or a pronoun. Limiting adjectives restrict the meaning of the words they modify: *that* cheese, *its* roots. Descriptive adjectives usually have degrees of comparison: *newer* car, *green* shirt. Proper adjectives are derived from proper nouns: *Roman* candle. See **4b**, **9a(3)**, and **12c(2)**. See also **comparative**, **comparison** and **predicate adjective**.

adjective clause A subordinate clause used as an adjective: people *who bite their fingernails*. An adjective clause may be restrictive. See **12d(1)** and **25a(1)**. See also **clause**.

adverb A part of speech modifying a verb, an adjective or another adverb: *slowly* ate, *too* tall, left *very quietly*. An adverb may also modify a verbal, a phrase or clause, or the rest of the sentence: *Naturally* [sentence modifier], the villain succeeds at first by *completely* outwitting [gerund] the hero.

adverb clause A subordinate clause used as an adverb. An adverb clause may indicate time, place, cause, condition, concession, comparison, purpose, or result: *Although he is usually quiet* [concession], everyone listens to him *when he speaks* [time], *because he makes good suggestions* [cause]. See **12b** and **30b(1)**. See also **clause** and **conditional clause**.

adverbial conjunction See **conjunctive adverb**.

agreement The correspondence in number and person of a subject and verb [*a boy asks, boys ask*] or in number and gender of a pronoun and its antecedent [*the woman herself, the man himself*]. See section **6**.

allusion A brief, unexplained reference to a work or to a person, place, event, or thing that the writer expects the reader to be familiar with. See also **20a(4)**.

ambiguity   The capability of being understood in two or more different ways: "Reading alone comforts me" could mean "*Reading by myself* comforts me" or "*Only reading* comforts me."

analogy   The features of something familiar (and often concrete) are used to explain something unfamiliar (and often abstract), or similarities between things that are not usually associated.

analysis   A separation of a whole into its constituent parts.

analytical reading   A reader's active engagement by the writer's ideas and how the ideas are expressed; paying attention to content and form.

antecedent   A word or a word group that a pronoun refers to. The antecedent may follow (but usually precedes) the pronoun: Like their trainers, *pets* can be polite or rude. [The pronoun *their* precedes the antecedent *pets*.] See **6b** and section **28**.

antonym   A word that means the opposite of another: *follow* is the antonym for *lead*.

appeal   The means of persuasion in argumentative writing; appeal relies upon reason, authority, and/or emotion.

appositive   A noun or noun phrase placed next to or very near another noun or noun phrase to identify, explain, or supplement its meaning. Appositives may be restrictive. See **12d(1)**, **24a**, **30b(4)**, and **30c(3)**.

argument   A kind of writing that uses various rhetorical strategies and appeals to convince the reader of the truth or falsity of some proposition or thesis. See also **appeal** and **thesis**.

article   *The*, *a*, or *an* used as adjectives before nouns: *the* cups, *a* cup, *an* extra cup. *The* is a definite article. *A* (used before consonant sounds) and *an* (used before vowel sounds) are indefinite articles. See **9f**.

audience   In writing, the reader or readers for whom the writing is intended. See **33a**.

auxiliary   A form of *be*, *have*, or *do* (or a modal, such as *will*, *should*) used with a verb: *is* seeing, *did* see, *will be* seeing, *have* seen, *should* see, *had been* seen. An auxiliary, or helping verb, regularly indicates tense but may also indicate voice, mood, person, number. See **6a** and section **7**. Modal auxiliaries—*will, would, shall, should, may, might, must, can, could*—do not take such inflectional endings as *-s*, *-ing*.

brainstorming A way of finding ideas for writing by listing ideas as they occur in a session of intensive thinking about a general subject.

case The form or position of a noun or pronoun that shows its use or relationship to other words in a sentence. The three cases in English are the *subjective* (or nominative), the *possessive* (or genitive), and the *objective* (sometimes called the accusative). See section **5** and **15a**.

cause and effect A rhetorical strategy by which a writer seeks to explain why something happened or what the results of a particular event or condition were or will be. See **32d(4)**.

chronological order The arrangement of events in a time sequence (usually the order in which they occurred).

classification and division A rhetorical strategy in which a writer sorts elements into categories (*classification*) or breaks down a topic into its constituent parts, showing how they are related (*division*). See **32d(6)**.

clause A sequence of related words within a sentence. A clause has both a subject and a predicate and functions either as an independent unit (*main clause*) or as a dependent unit (*subordinate clause*, used as an adverb, an adjective, or a noun). See section **24**. See also **sentence**.

> I saw the moon. It was glowing brightly.   [sentences]
> **I saw the moon**, for **it was glowing brightly**.   [main clauses connected by a coordinating conjunction]
> I saw the moon, **which was glowing brightly**.   [adjective clause]
> I saw the moon **because it was glowing brightly**.   [adverb clause]
> I saw **that the moon was glowing brightly**.   [noun clause—direct object]

cliché An expression that may once have been fresh and effective but that has become trite and worn out with overuse. See **20c**.

coherence The principle that all the parts of a piece of writing should stick together, one sentence leading to the next, each idea evolving from the previous one. See also **32b**.

collective noun A noun singular in form that denotes a group: *flock, jury, band, public, committee.* See **6a(7)**.

colloquial expression Found mainly in writing that strives for the informal effect of speech: "He's *grumpy*" is a colloquial expression describing an irritable person.

common gender A term applied to words that can refer to either sex (*parent, instructor, salesperson, people, anyone*). See also **6b(1)**.

common noun A noun referring to any or all members of a class or group (*woman, city, apples, holidays*) rather than to a specific member (*Susan Anthony, Las Vegas, Winesap, New Year's Day*).

comparative, comparison Inflection or modification of an adjective or adverb to indicate degrees in quality, quantity, or manner. The three degrees are *positive* (*good/well, high, active*), *comparative* (*better, higher, more/less active*), and *superlative* (*best, highest, most/least active*). See **4c**.

comparison and contrast A rhetorical strategy in which the writer examines similarities and/or differences between two ideas or objects. See **32d(5)**.

complement A word or words used to complete the sense of a verb. Although the term may refer to a direct or an indirect object, it usually refers to a subject complement, an object complement, or the complement of a verbal like *be*. See **1b**.

complete predicate A simple predicate (a verb or verb phrase) with any objects, complements, or modifiers: We *ate the fresh homemade pie before the salad.* See also **predicate**.

complete subject A simple subject (a noun or noun clause) with any modifiers: *Everyone at the picnic* liked the pie. See also **subject**.

complex sentence   A sentence containing one main clause and at least one subordinate clause: My neighbor noticed a stranger [main clause] who looked suspicious [subordinate clause]. See section **24** and **30c(1)**. See also **clause**.

compound-complex sentence   A sentence containing at least two main clauses and one or more subordinate clauses: When the lights went out [subordinate clause], there was no flashlight at hand [main clause], so we sat outside and gazed at the stars [main clause]. See **clause**.

compound predicate   Two or more predicates having the same subject: Clara Barton *nursed the injured during the Civil War* and *founded the American Red Cross later*. See **2a** and **30c(2)**. See also **predicate**.

compound sentence   A sentence containing at least two main clauses and no subordinate clause: The water supply was dwindling [main clause], so rationing became mandatory [main clause]. See **12a** and **14a**. See also **clause**.

compound subject   Two or more subjects of the same verb: *Women, men,* and *children* call the crisis center.

conclusion   A sentence or paragraph that brings a piece of writing to a satisfying close, usually by summarizing, restating, evaluating, asking a question, or encouraging the reader to continue thinking about the topic. See **33f(2)**.

concrete, concrete noun   Concrete words refer to things that can be experienced through the senses: *cologne, sunset, onions, thorns.* Concrete words make writing clear, vivid, and lively.

conditional clause   An adverb clause (beginning with such conjunctions as *if, unless, whether, provided*) expressing a real, imagined, or nonfactual condition: *If she does a good job,* then I will pay her. See **7c**.

conjugation   A set or table of the inflected forms of a verb that indicate tense, person, number, voice, and mood. See section **7**.

conjunction   A part of speech (such as *and* or *although*) used to connect words, phrases, clauses, or sentences. *Coordinating con-*

junctions (*and, but, or, nor, for, so, yet*) connect and relate words and word groups of equal grammatical rank: Color-blind people can usually see blue, *but* they may confuse red with green *or* with yellow. See section **26**. See also **correlatives**.

Subordinating conjunctions (such as *although, if, when*—see list on page 39) mark a dependent clause and connect it with a main clause: *When* Frank sulks, he acts *as if* he were deaf. See section **24**.

conjunctive adverb A word (*however, therefore, nevertheless*—see the list on page 39) that serves not only as an adverb but also as a connective. See **3b**, **14a**, and **32b(4)**.

connective A word or phrase that links and relates words, phrases, clauses, or sentences (*and, although, otherwise, finally, on the contrary, which, not only . . . but also*). Conjunctions, conjunctive adverbs, transitional expressions, relative pronouns, and correlatives function as connectives. See also **32b(4)**.

connotation The suggested or implied meaning of a word through the associations it evokes in the reader's mind. See **20a(2)**. See also **denotation**.

construction A grammatical unit (a phrase, clause, or sentence) or the arrangement of related words in a grammatical unit.

context The surrounding information that helps to give a particular word, sentence, or paragraph its meaning: *cabinet* means "a group of leaders" in a political context, "a place for storage" in a building context. Context also refers to circumstances surrounding the composition of a piece of writing—the occasion, the audience, and what the writer and reader already understand about the topic. See also **33a**.

contrast See **comparison and contrast**.

controlling idea The central idea of a paragraph or essay, often expressed in the paragraph's *topic sentence* or the essay's *thesis statement*. See also **32a**.

coordinating conjunction One of seven connectives: *and, but, for, or, nor, so, yet*. See **1c**, **12a**, and sections **24** and **26**. See also **conjunction**.

Glossary of Grammatical and Rhetorical Terms

coordination The use of grammatically equivalent constructions to link ideas, usually (but not always) those of equal weight. See **12c**, **24b**, and section **26**.

correlatives One of five pairs of connectives: *both . . . and; either . . . or; neither . . . nor; not only . . . but also; whether . . . or.* Correlatives link equivalent constructions: *both* Jane *and* Fred; *not only* in Peru *but also* in Mexico. See **26c**.

dangling modifier A modifier that modifies nothing in a sentence and does not clearly refer to another word or word group in the sentence. Not a dangler, an absolute phrase modifies the rest of the sentence. See **25b**.

declension A set or table of inflected forms of nouns or pronouns. See the examples on pages 51–52.

deduction Reasoning that begins with a generalization (*premise*), relates a specific fact to that generalization, and forms a conclusion that fits both. See section **31b**. See also **induction**.

definition A brief explanation of the meaning of a word, as in a dictionary. Also, an extended piece of writing, employing a variety of rhetorical strategies, to explain what something is or means. See **32d(7)**.

degree See **comparative, comparison**.

demonstratives Four words that point out (*this, that, these, those*): **Those** are as good as **these**. [pronouns] **Those** curtains have never been cleaned. [adjective]

denotation The literal meaning of a word as commonly defined. See **20a(1)**. See also **connotation**.

dependent clause A subordinate clause. See **clause**.

description A rhetorical strategy using details perceivable by the senses to portray a scene, object, performance, and so on. See **32d(2)**.

details Bits of specific information such as facts, sensory data, or examples that clarify and explain.

determiner A word (such as *a, an, the, my, their*) that signals the approach of a noun: **the** newly mown *hay*.

development The elaboration of an idea through organized discussion filled with examples, details, and other information. See **32c**.

dialects Regional or cultural varieties of a language, distinguished by vocabulary, pronunciation, and/or syntax: British English, American English, Black English. See **19d**.

dialogue A reproduction in writing of conversation by two or more people, real or fictional. See **9e**, **16a**, **19b**.

diction The writer's choice of exact, idiomatic, and fresh words, as well as appropriate levels of usage. See **19a** and section **20**.

direct address A name or descriptive term (set off by commas) designating the one (or ones) spoken to: Don't forget, **backseat passengers**, to use those seatbelts.

direct object A noun (or noun clause) naming *whom* or *what* after a transitive active verb: Emily sliced the *ham*. See **1b**. See also **object**.

direct quotation A repetition of the exact spoken or written words of others: *"Where an opinion is general,"* writes Jane Austen, *"it is usually correct."* See **16a** and **34e**.

double negative The nonstandard combination of two negatives and having a negative meaning: We ca*n't* do *nothing* about the weather. See **4e**.

draft, drafting A working version of a piece of writing. The process of setting ideas down in writing so they may be revised and edited. See **33f** and **33g**.

edited American English Expected in most college writing, this formal style observes established rules of spelling, punctuation, mechanics, grammar, and sentence structure.

editing Reworking a piece of writing for clarity and sense and to conform to established rules of spelling, punctuation, mechanics, grammar, and sentence structure.

elliptical construction A construction in which words are omitted but clearly understood: The curtains are newer than the carpet [is].

emphasis Special weight or importance given to a word, sentence, or paragraph by a variety of techniques. It may also mean stress applied to one or more syllables in a word. See also section **29.**

essay A brief piece of nonfiction writing on a single subject in which a writer typically states the thesis in the introduction, develops several points in support of that thesis, and concludes.

evidence Facts, statistics, examples, testimony, sensory details, and so on that support generalizations.

example Refers to any fact, anecdote, or the like that is used to illustrate an idea. See **32c.**

expletive A signal of a transformation in the structure of a sentence without changing the meaning. The expletive *there* shifts the order of subject and verb in a sentence: *There* were only a few ballet tickets left. [Compare: Only a few ballet tickets were left.] The expletive *it* transforms the main clause into a subordinate clause: *It* is obvious that they do not like us. [Compare: Obviously, they do not like us.]

expository writing Writing whose chief aim is to clarify, explain, or evaluate a subject—to inform or instruct the reader. See **33a.**

expressive writing A form of writing that emphasizes the writer's own feelings and reactions to a topic. See **33a.**

fallacy A false argument or incorrect reasoning. See **31c.**

faulty predication The use of a predicate that does not logically belong with a given subject: One superstition is a black cat. [The verb should be *has to do with*.]

figurative language The use of words in an imaginative rather than a literal sense. See **20a(4).**

finite verb A verb form that can function as the only verb in the predicate of a sentence: They *ate* a can of pork and beans. Verb forms classified as gerunds, infinitives, or participles cannot. See **predicate**; contrast **verbal**.

focus The narrowing of a subject to a manageable size; also the sharpening of the writer's view of the subject. See **33c** and **33d.**

free writing   A way of finding a writing topic by composing for a specified length of time without stopping to reflect, reread, or check for or correct errors.

function words   Words (such as prepositions, conjunctions, auxiliaries, and articles) that indicate the functions of other words (**vocabulary words**) in a sentence and the grammatical relationships between them.

gender   The grammatical distinction that labels nouns or pronouns as masculine, feminine, or neuter. In English, grammatical gender usually corresponds with natural gender.

general/specific, generalization   *General* words are all-embracing, indefinite, sweeping in scope: *food. Specific* words are precise, explicit, limited in scope: *spaghetti carbonara.* The same is true of *general* and *specific* ideas. A *generalization* is vague and may be untrue.

gerund   A verbal (nonfinite verb) that ends in *-ing* and functions as a noun. Gerunds may take objects, complements, or modifiers: *Borrowing* money is a mistake. [The gerund phrase—*borrowing* and its object, *money*—serves as the subject of the sentence.] A noun or pronoun serving as the subject of the gerund takes the possessive case: *His* [*or Richard's*] *borrowing* money is a mistake.

grammar   The system of rules by which words are pronounced and arranged into the structures meaningful in a language.

helping verb   See **auxiliary**.

homonyms   Words that are spelled differently but sound alike. See **18b**.

hyperbole   Overstatement for effect. See **20a(4)**.

imperative   See **mood**.

indefinites   The article *a* or *an* (*a* cigar, *an* idea) as well as pronouns (*anybody, everyone*) and adjectives (*any* book, *few* friends, *several* pages) that do not specify distinct limits. See **6a(1)** and **6b(1)**.

independent clause   A main clause: see **clause**.

indicative   See **mood**.

indirect object   A word (or words) naming the one (or ones) indirectly affected by the action of the verb: Emily sliced *me* some ham. See also **object**.

indirect question   A question phrased as a statement, usually a subordinate clause: We can ask *whether Milton's blindness was the result of glaucoma,* but we cannot be sure. See also **27c**.

indirect quotation   A report of the written or spoken words of another without using the exact words of the speaker or writer: The registrar said *that the bank returned my check for my tuition.* See also **direct quotation**.

induction   Reasoning that begins with evidence and interprets it to form a conclusion. See **31a**. See also **deduction**.

infinitive   A verbal (nonfinite verb) used chiefly as a noun, less frequently as an adjective or an adverb. The infinitive is usually made up of the word *to* plus the present form of a verb (called the *stem* of the infinitive). Infinitives may have subjects, objects, complements, or modifiers: Hal wanted *to open* the present. [*Present* is the object of the infinitive *to open;* the whole infinitive phrase is the object of the verb *wanted.*]

inflection   A change in the form of a vocabulary or lexical word to show a specific meaning or grammatical relationship to another word or group of words: verb—*grasp, grasps, grasped;* noun—*cat, cats, cat's, cats';* pronoun—*I, me, my, mine, we, us, our, ours;* adjective—*light, lighter, lightest;* adverb—*carefully, more carefully, most carefully.*

informative writing   See **expository writing**.

intensifier   A modifier used for emphasis: *very* boring, *certainly* pleased. See also **qualifier**.

intensive/reflexive pronoun   The *-self* pronouns (such as *myself, himself, themselves*). The *intensive* is used for emphasis: The teenagers *themselves* had the best idea. The *reflexive* is used as an object of a verb, verbal, or preposition: He blames *himself;* she bought a present for *herself.* An intensive or reflexive pronoun always refers to another noun or pronoun in the same sentence that denotes the same individual or individuals.

interjection   A word (one of the eight parts of speech) expressing a simple exclamation: *Whew! Ouch!* When used in sentences, mild interjections are set off by commas. See **17c**.

interrogatives   Words like *which, whose,* or *why* used to ask a question: *Which* did he choose? [pronoun] *Whose* car is it? [adjective] *Why* are treasury bills a good investment. [adverb]

intransitive verb   A verb (such as *appear* or *belong*) that does not take an object. See **verb**.

introduction   The beginning of an essay, often a single paragraph, that engages the reader's interest and indicates, usually by stating the thesis, what the essay is about. See **33f(1)**.

inversion   A change in the usual word order of a sentence: In the middle of the lake is a small island. See **29f**.

irony   A deliberate inconsistency between what is stated and what is meant. Irony may be verbal or situational. See **20a(4)**.

irregular verb   A verb not inflected in the usual way—that is, by the addition of *-d* or *-ed* to the present form (or the stem of the infinitive). There are five common types of irregular verbs classified according to how they indicate past tense and past participle: vowel changes (*swim, swam, swum*); *-en* added (*beat, beat, beaten*); vowel shortens (*feel, felt, felt—ee* becomes *e*); *-d* changes to *-t* (send, sent, sent); no change (set, set, set).

jargon   Technical slang, appropriate as a shortcut to communication when the audience is knowledgeable of the topic and the terms; it should be avoided in writing that is intended for a more general kind of reader. See **19g**.

linking verbs   A verb that relates the subject complement to the subject. Words commonly used as linking verbs are *become, seem, appear, feel, look, taste, smell, sound,* and forms of the verb *be:* She *is* a pharmacist. The music *sounds* brassy. See **1b, 4b,** and **5f**.

logic   The presentation of ideas that shows a clear, predictable, and structured relationship among those ideas. See sections **23** and **31**.

main clause   An independent clause: When I explored the Black Hills, *I found many rocks to add to my collection.* See **1d, 12a,** and **14a**. See also **clause**.

mechanics The correct use of capitals, italics, abbreviations, acronyms, and numbers; includes the fine points of manuscript form.

metaphor An imaginative comparison between dissimilar things without using *like* or *as*. See **20a(4)**.

misplaced modifier A modifier in an awkward position—usually, far away from what it modifies: I heard how to make catsup flow out of the bottle *on the radio*. [Place the modifier after the verb *heard*.] Sometimes a misplaced modifier confuses the reader because it could qualify either of two words: To do one's best *sometimes* is not enough. [Place the adverb after the verb.] See **25a**.

mixed construction A garbled sentence that is the result of an unintentional shift from one grammatical pattern to another. See **23c**.

modal auxiliary An auxiliary verb (not conjugated) that shows ability (*can, could*); permission or possibility (*may, might*); determination, promise, or intention (*shall, should; will, would*); obligation (*ought*); or necessity (*must*).

modifier A word or word group that describes, limits, or qualifies another: a *true* statement, walked *slowly*, yards *filled with rocks*, the horse *that jumped the fence*. See sections **4** and **25**.

mood The way a speaker or writer regards an assertion—that is, as a declarative statement or a question (*indicative* mood); as a command or request (*imperative*); or as a supposition, hypothesis, recommendation, or condition contrary to fact (*subjunctive*). Verb forms indicate mood. See **1d**, **7c**, and **7d**.

narration A rhetorical strategy that recounts a sequence of events, usually in chronological order (but occasionally in some other order). See **32d(1)**.

nominative See **case**.

nonfinite verb A verb form (verbal) used as a noun, an adjective, or an adverb. A nonfinite verb cannot stand as the only verb in a sentence. See **1b** and **2a**. See also **verbal**.

nonrestrictive   Nonessential to the identification of the word or words referred to. A word or word group is nonrestrictive (parenthetical) when it is not necessary to the meaning of the sentence and can be omitted: My best friend, *Pauline*, understands me. See **12d**.

noun   A part of speech that names a person, place, thing, idea, animal. quality, or action: *Mary, America, apples, justice, goose, strength, departure.* A noun usually changes form to indicate the plural and the possessive case, as in *man, men; man's, men's.*

TYPES OF NOUNS

COMMON	a **man**, the **cities**, some **trout** [general classes]
PROPER	**Mr. Ford**, in **Boston**, the **Forum** [capitalized, specific names]
COLLECTIVE	a **flock**, the **jury**, my **family** [groups]
CONCRETE	an **egg**, the **bus**, his **ear**, two **trees** [tangibles]
ABSTRACT	**honor, jealousy, pity, hatred** [ideas, qualities]
COUNT	one **dime**, ten **dollars**, a **job**, many **times** [singular or plural—often preceded by adjectivals telling how many]
MASS	much **money**, more **work**, less **time** [singular in meaning—often preceded by adjectivals telling how much]

FUNCTIONS OF NOUNS

SUBJECT OF FINITE VERB   **Dogs** barked.

OBJECT OF FINITE VERB OR OF PREPOSITION   He gave **Jane** the **key** to the **house**.

SUBJECT COMPLEMENT (PREDICATE NOUN)   She is a **nurse**.

OBJECT COMPLEMENT   They named him **Jonathan**.

SUBJECT OF NONFINITE VERB   I want **Ed** to be here.

OBJECT OF NONFINITE VERB   I prefer to drive a **truck**.

APPOSITIVE   Moses, a **prophet**, saw the promised land.

ADVERBIAL   **Yesterday** they went **home**.

ADJECTIVAL   The **mountain** laurel is the **state** flower of Connecticut and Pennsylvania.

DIRECT ADDRESS   What do you think, **Angela**?

KEY WORD OF ABSOLUTE PHRASE   The **food** being cold, no one really enjoyed the meal.

noun clause   A subordinate clause used as a noun. See **clause**.

> **Whoever comes** will be welcome.   [subject]
> I hope **that he will recover**.   [direct object]
> I will give **whoever comes first** the best seat.   [indirect object]
> Spend it for **whatever seems best**.   [object of a preposition]
> This is **what you need**.   [subject complement]
> I loved it, **whatever it was**.   [appositive]
> **Whoever you are**, show yourself!   [direct address]

number   The inflectional form of a word that includes singular (one) or plural (more than one): *river–rivers, this–those, he sees– they see*. See section **6** and **18e**.

object   A noun or noun substitute governed by a transitive active verb, by a nonfinite verb, or by a preposition.

A *direct object*, or the *object of a finite verb*, is any noun or noun substitute that answers the question, *What?* or *whom?* after a transitive active verb. A direct object frequently receives, or is in some way affected by, the action of the verb: William raked *leaves. What* did he say? A direct object may be converted into a subject with a passive verb. See **voice**.

An *object of a nonfinite verb* is any noun or its equivalent that follows and completes the meaning of a participle, a gerund, or an infinitive: Washing a *car* takes time, He likes to wear a *tie*.

An *indirect object* is any noun or noun substitute that states *to whom* or *for whom* (or *to what* or *for what*) something is done. An indirect object ordinarily precedes a direct object: He bought *her* a watch. I gave the *floor* a second coat of varnish. It is usually possible to substitute a prepositional phrase beginning with *to* or *for* for the indirect object: He bought a watch *for her*.

An *object of a preposition* is any noun or noun substitute that a preposition relates to another word or word group: Cedars grow tall in these *hills*. [*Hills* is the object of *in*.]

object complement   A word that helps to complete the meaning of such verbs as *make, paint, elect, name*. An object complement refers to or modifies the direct object: They painted the cellar door *blue*. See **1b**, **4b**. See also **complement**.

objective   See **case**.

paradox   A seemingly contradictory statement that may actually be true. See **20a(4)**.

paragraph   Usually a group of related sentences unified by a single idea or purpose but occasionally as brief as a single sentence (or even a single word or phrase). The central, or controlling, idea of a paragraph is often explicitly stated in a *topic sentence*. A paragraph is physically defined by the indention of its first line.

parallelism   The use of corresponding grammatically equal elements in sentences and paragraphs. It aids the flow of a sentence, making it read smoothly, and also emphasizes the relationship of the ideas in the parallel elements. See also section **26**.

parenthetical element   Nonessential matter (such as an aside or interpolation) usually set off by commas but often by dashes or parentheses to mark pauses and intonation. A word, phrase, clause, or sentence may be parenthetical: *Granted,* over eighty million people, *according to that estimate*, did watch one episode. See **12d**, **17e**, and **17f**.

participle   A verb form that may function as part of a verb phrase (was *laughing,* had *finished*) or as a modifier (a *finished* product; the players, *laughing* at their mistakes).

The *present participle* ends in -*ing* (the form also used for verbal nouns: see **gerund**). The past participle of regular verbs ends in -*d* or -*ed*; for past-participle forms of irregular verbs, see **7a**. See also **irregular verb**.

Functioning as modifiers in *participial phrases*, participles may take objects, complements, and modifiers: The prisoner *carrying* **the heaviest load** toppled forward. [The participle *carrying* takes the object *load;* the whole participial phrase modifies *prisoner.*] See **25b(1)**.

particle   A word like *across, away, down, for, in, off, out, up, with* combined with a verb to form idiomatic usages where the combination has the force of a single-word verb: He *cut* me *off* without a cent.

parts of speech   The classes into which words may be grouped according to their form changes and their grammatical relationships. The traditional parts of speech are *verbs, nouns, pronouns,* *adjectives, adverbs, prepositions, conjunctions,* and *interjections.* Each of these is discussed separately in this glossary. See also **1c**.

passive voice   The form of the verb which shows that its subject is not the agent performing the action to which the verb refers but rather receives that action: The ham *was sliced* by Emily. See section **7** and **29d**. See also **active voice**.

perfect tenses   The tenses formed by the addition of a form of *have* and showing complex time relationships in completing the action of the verb (the present perfect—*have/has eaten; the past perfect—had eaten;* and the future perfect—*will have eaten*).

person   Changes in the form of pronouns and verbs denoting or indicating whether one is speaking (*I am*—first person), is spoken to (*you are*—second person), or spoken about (*it is* —third person). In the present tense, a verb changes its form to agree grammatically with a third-person singular subject (*I eat, a bird eats*). See **6a** and **27b**.

personal pronoun   Any one of a group of pronouns—*I, you, he, she, it,* and their inflected forms—referring to the one (or ones) speaking, spoken to, or spoken about. See section **5**.

personification   The attributing of human characteristics to nonhuman things (animals, objects, ideas): That night wind was breathing across me through the spokes of the wheel.

—WALLACE STEGNER

persuasive writing   A form of writing intended chiefly to change the reader's opinions or attitudes or to arouse the reader to action. See also **33a**.

phrasal verb   A unit consisting of a verb plus one or two uninflected words like *after, in, up, off,* or *out* (see **particle**) and having the force of a single-word verb: We *ran out on* them.

phrase   A sequence of grammatically related words without a subject and a predicate. See **2a** and **30c(4)**.

NOUN PHRASE   A **young stranger** stepped forward.
VERB PHRASE   All day long they **had been worrying**.
PREPOSITIONAL PHRASE   **By seven o'clock** the lines stretched **from the box office to the corner**.

GERUND PHRASE   **Building a sun deck** can be fun.
INFINITIVE PHRASE   Do you want **to use your time that way?**
PARTICIPIAL PHRASE   My friends **traveling in Italy** felt the earthquake.
APPOSITIVE PHRASE   I introduced her to Bob, **my roommate**.
ABSOLUTE PHRASE   **The game over**, we shook hands.

plagiarism   The use of another writer's words or ideas without acknowledging the source. Akin to theft, plagiarism has serious consequences and should be avoided at all cost.

planning   The part of the writing process involving the discovery and organization of ideas. See **33c–33e**.

point of view   The vantage point from which the subject is viewed, as in **description** (see **32d[1–2]**). See also **27e**. It also refers to the stance a writer takes—objective or impartial (third person), directive (second person), or personal (first person).

positive   See **comparison**.

possessive   See **case**.

predicate   A basic grammatical division of a sentence. A predicate is the part of the sentence comprising what is said about the subject. The *complete predicate* consists of the main verb and its auxiliaries (the *simple predicate*) and any complements and modifiers: We **used** *a patriotic theme for our homecoming parade that year*. [*Used* is the simple predicate; *used* and all the words that follow make up the complete predicate.]

predicate adjective   The adjective used as a subject complement: The bread tastes *sweet*. See **1c** and **4b**. See also **linking verb**.

predicate noun   A noun used as a subject complement: Bromides are *sedatives*. See **1c** and **5f**. See also **linking verb**.

predication   See **faulty predication**.

prefix   An added syllable or group of syllables (such as *in-*, *dis-*, *un-*, *pro-*) placed before a word to form a new word: *disposed–indisposed*.

Glossary of Grammatical and Rhetorical Terms

premise   Generally, an assumption—a proposition—on which an argument or explanation is based. In logic, premises are either major (general) or minor (specific); when combined correctly, they lead to a conclusion. See **31b**. Also see **syllogism**.

preposition   A part of speech that links and relates a noun or noun substitute to another word in the sentence: The paintings hung *in* the hall. [The preposition *in* connects and relates *hall* (its object) to the verb *hung*.] See page 15 for a list of words commonly used as prepositions.

prepositional phrase   A *preposition* with its object and any modifiers: *in the hall, between you and me, for the new van.*

prewriting   Another term for the planning part of the writing process.

principal parts   The forms of any verb from which the various tenses are derived: the present (*take, laugh*); the past (*took, laughed*); and the past participle (*taken, laughed*). See **7a**.

process, process writing   See **writing process**.

process analysis   A rhetorical strategy that writers use to instruct the reader in performing a procedure or to explain how something occurs. See **32d(3)**.

progressive verb   A verb phrase consisting of a present participle (ending in *-ing*) used with a form of *be* and denoting continuous action. See the top of page 74.

pronoun   A part of speech that takes the position of nouns and functions as nouns do. See sections **5** and **28**, **6b**. See also **noun** and the separate entries for the types of pronouns listed below.

PERSONAL	**She** and **I** will see him in St. Paul.
RELATIVE	Leslie is the one **who** likes to bowl.
INDEFINITE	**Each** of you should help **someone**.
INTENSIVE	**I myself** saw the crash.
REFLEXIVE	Roy blames **himself**.
DEMONSTRATIVE	**Those** are riper than **these**.
INTERROGATIVE	**Who** are they? **What** is right?

proper adjective   An adjective (such as *Scottish*) derived from a proper noun (*Scotland*). See **9a(3)**.

proper noun   A noun (written with a capital letter) referring to a particular or specific member of a class or group (*John Adams,*

Wyoming, November, God) rather than to any member or all members (*man, state, months, gods*). See **9a**.

purpose A writer's reason for writing. The purpose for nonfiction writing may be predominantly expressive, expository, or persuasive, though all three aims are likely to be present in some measure. See also **expository writing, expressive writing**, and **persuasive writing, 33a**.

qualifier Any modifier, descriptive or limiting: *Sometimes* children are *too* selfish to share. Frequently, however, the term refers only to those modifiers that restrict or intensify the meaning of other words. See also **intensifier**.

quotation See **direct quotation**.

reciprocal pronoun One of two compound pronouns expressing an interchangeable or mutual action or relationship: *each other* or *one another*.

redundant Needlessly repetitious, unnecessary.

reflexive pronoun See **intensive/reflexive pronoun**.

regular verb A verb that forms its past tense and past participle by adding -*d* or -*ed* to the present form (or the stem of the infinitive): *love, loved; laugh, laughed.* See **7a**.

relative clause An adjective clause introduced by a relative pronoun: the suits *that they wore*.

relative pronoun One of a small group of noun substitutes (*who, whom, whose, that, which, what, whoever, whomever, whichever, whatever*) used to introduce subordinate clauses: He has a son **who** *is a genius*. [adjective clause introduced by the relative pronoun *who*] OR **Whoever** *wins the prize* must have talent. [noun clause introduced by the relative pronoun *whoever*] See **5b**, **5c**, and **6a(5)**.

restrictive Essential to the identification of the word or words referred to. A word, phrase, or clause is restrictive (and therefore necessary) when its meaning limits the word referred to by imposing conditions on or by confining the word to a particular group or to a specific item or individual: Every drug *condemned by doctors* should be taken off the market. [The restrictive phrase *condemned by doctors* imposes conditions upon—restricts—the meaning of "every drug."] See **12d**.

revision   Part of the writing process. Writers revise by rereading and rethinking a piece of writing to see where they need to add, delete, move, replace, reshape, and even completely recast ideas.

rhetoric   The art of using language effectively. Rhetoric involves the writer's **purpose (33a)**, the consideration of **audience (33a)**, the discovery and exploration of a subject (**33b** and **33c**), its arrangement and organization (**33e**), the style and tone in which it is expressed (**33a**), and the form in which it is delivered (**33a** and section **8**).

sentence   A grammatically independent unit of expression. A simple sentence contains a subject and a predicate. Sentences are classified according to structure (simple, complex, compound, and compound-complex) and purpose (declaratory, interrogatory, imperative, exclamatory). See section **1**.

sentence modifier   An adverb or adverb substitute that modifies the rest of the sentence, not a specific word or word group in it: *All things considered*, Middle America is a good place to live. OR *Yes*, the plane arrived on time.

sexist language   Language that arbitrarily excludes one sex or the other or that arbitrarily assigns stereotypical roles to one or the other sex: A secretary should keep *her* desk tidy. [Compare: Secretar*ies* should keep *their* desks tidy.]

simile   The comparison of two dissimilar things using *like* or *as*.

simple tenses   The tenses that refer to present, past, and future time.

slang   An arbitrary use of language, often peculiar to specific groups or cultures and often considered unacceptable—sometimes even tasteless or obscene. Occasionally, slang can be effective if the writer carefully considers purpose and audience. See also **19c**.

space order   A concept often used to organize descriptive passages. Details are arranged according to how they are encountered as the observer's eye moves vertically, horizontally, from far to near, and so forth. See also **32d(2)**.

style An author's individual choice and arrangement of words, sentence structures, and ideas as well as less definable characteristics such as rhythm and euphony. To a limited extent, style can be thought of as the written expression of a writer's personality and quality of thought.

subject A basic grammatical division of a sentence. The subject is a noun or noun substitute about which something is asserted or asked in the predicate. It usually precedes the predicate. (Imperative sentences have subjects that are implied, not stated.) The *complete subject* consists of the *simple subject* and the words associated with it: *The dog locked in the hot car* needed air. [simple subject—*dog*; complete subject—*the dog locked in the hot car*]

subject complement A word (or words) that completes the meaning of a linking verb and that modifies or refers to the subject: The old car looked *shabby*. [predicate adjective] The old car was an *eyesore*. [predicate noun] See **1c**, **4b**, **5f**. See also **linking verb**.

subjective See **case**.

subjunctive See **7c**. See also **mood**.

subordinate clause A dependent clause: Her cough vanished *after she had quit smoking*. See **clause**.

subordinating conjunction, subordinator A connective (such as *although*, *if*, or *when*) that marks the beginning of a subordinate (dependent) clause: see page 22. See also **conjunction**.

subordination The use of dependent structures (phrases, subordinate clauses) lower in grammatical rank than independent ones (simple sentences, main clauses). See section **24**.

suffix An added sound, syllable, or group of syllables placed after a word to form a new word, to change the meaning of a word, or to indicate grammatical function: *play, plays, player, playful, playfulness*.

superlative See **comparison**.

syllogism A three-part form of deductive reasoning. See **31b**.

syntax Sentence structure; the grammatical arrangement of words, phrases, clauses.

Glossary of Grammatical and Rhetorical Terms

tense The form of the verb that denotes time. Inflection of single-word verbs (*pay, paid*) and the use of auxiliaries (*am paid, was paid, will pay*) indicate tense. See section **7**.

thesis The central point or idea of an essay. It is one of the main ways an essay is unified (see **unity**). A clearly focused and specific thesis statement helps the writer make all the other elements of the essay work together to accomplish the writer's purpose. See also **33d**.

tone Often conveyed through diction and sentence structure. Tone reflects a writer's attitude toward the subject and the audience and affects the reader's response to the piece of writing.

topic sentence States the central thought of a paragraph and, though very often appearing at the beginning, may appear anywhere in it.

transitions Relate ideas and provide coherence by linking sentences, paragraphs, and larger units of writing. Transitions may be special expressions (words or phrases such as *moreover, first, nevertheless, for example,* and so on) or structural features a writer uses such as parallelism or repetition of key words and phrases. When they link larger units of writing, they may take the form of sentences or even brief paragraphs. See **32b**.

understatement Intentional underemphasis for effect, usually ironic. See **20a**.

unity All the elements in an essay contribute to developing a single idea or thesis. A paragraph is unified when each sentence contributes to developing a central thought. See also **32a** and **33d**.

validity Having to do with the structure rather than the truth of a deductive argument. An argument has validity when the premises of a syllogism are correctly related to form a conclusion. See also **31b**.

verb A part of speech denoting action, occurrence, or existence (state of being). Inflections indicate tense (and sometimes person and number) and mood of a verb: see **inflection**, **mood**, **voice**, and section **7**.

A *transitive* verb requires an object to complete its meaning. Transitive verbs can usually be changed from the active to the passive voice (see **object** and **voice**): Sid *hung* a wreath on his door. [direct object—*wreath*]

An *intransitive* verb (such as *go* or *sit*) does not have an object to complete its meaning. Linking verbs, which take subject complements, are intransitive: She *has been waiting* patiently for hours.

The same verb may be transitive in one sentence and intransitive in another: Dee *reads* novels. [direct object—*novels*] Dee *reads* well.

verbal   A nonfinite verb used as a noun, an adjective, or an adverb. Infinitives, participles, and gerunds are verbals. Verbals (like finite verbs) may take objects, complements, modifiers, and sometimes subjects: Mr. Nelson went *to see his daughter*. [*To see,* an infinitive, functions as an adverb modifying the verb *went*. The object of the infinitive is *daughter.*] See also **nonfinite verb** and **gerund, infinitive, participle.**

verb phrase   See **phrase.**

vocabulary (lexical) words   Nouns, verbs, and most modifiers—those words found in vocabulary-building lists. See also **function words.**

voice   The form of a transitive verb that indicates whether or not the subject performs the action denoted by the verb. A verb with a direct object is in the *active voice*. When the direct object is converted into a subject, the verb is in the *passive voice*. A passive verb is always a verb phrase consisting of a form of the verb *be* (or sometimes *get*) followed by a past participle. See also **7, 29d.**

ACTIVE   Priscilla **chose** John.   The subject (*Priscilla*) acts.]
PASSIVE   John **was chosen** by Priscilla.   [The subject (*John*) does not act.]

Speakers and writers often omit the *by*-phrase after a passive verb, especially when the performer of the action is not known or is not the focus of attention: Those flowers *were picked* yesterday. We just heard that a new secretary *was hired*.

word order   The arrangement of words in sentences. Because of lost inflections, modern English depends heavily on word order to convey meaning.

Nancy gave Henry $14,000.   Henry gave Nancy $14,000.
Tony had built a garage.   Tony had a garage built.

writing process   The various activities of planning (gathering, shaping, and organizing information), drafting (setting down ideas in sentences and paragraphs to form a composition), revising (rethinking, reshaping, and reordering ideas), editing (checking for clear, effective, grammatically correct sentences), and proofreading (checking for correct spelling, mechanics, and manuscript form). The writing process determines no set sequence of these activities but allows writers to return to any activity as necessary.

INDEX

Boldface numbers refer to rules; other numbers refer to pages.

A

a, an. See also *article.*
  before common nouns, **9f:** 110
  before consonant sound, **19j:** 212
abbreviations, **11:** 117–20
  BA, MD, etc., **11a:** 117–18
  capitalization of, 104
  capitalized names, **9a:** 107; **11e:** 120
  courses of study, **11d:** 119
  end-of-line, not divided, **8d:** 97
  in bibliographies, etc., 447–49
  Jr., Sr., **11a:** 117
  Latin, list of, 120
  lists of, 118, 447–49
  Mr., Dr., Prof., etc., **11a:** 117–18
  Ms., usc of, **35b:** 539
  plurals of, **15c:** 155
  postal, **11b:** 118–19
  punctuation of, **17a:** 166
  redundant use of, **11a:** 118
  states, months, etc., **11b:** 118–19
  Street, Mount, etc., **11c:** 119
  units of measurement, **11b:** 118
  volume, chapter, page, **11d:** 119
  with dates or figures, 120
above, 212
absolute phrase, 551
  and subordination, **24a:** 263
  commas with, **12d:** 139
  for variety, **30b:** 304
  introductory, **12b:** 131
  used as adverb, 120

absolutes, comparison of, 47
abstract diction, **20a:** 231–32, 551
abstract words, 551
abstracts
  in APA style paper, 491
  in reports, **35b:** 549
accept. See *except, accept.*
accidently, accidentally, 212
accusative. See *objective* case.
acronyms
  defined, 552
  end-of-line, not divided, **8d:** 97
  first-time use of, **11e:** 121
  full capitals for, **9a:** 107
active voice, 552
  and emphasis, **29d:** 295
  changed to passive, 7, 76–77
  tense forms, 7, 74–76
ad, 213
addresses
  commas with, **12d:** 137
  inside and outside, **35b:** 538, 539, 541
  numbers in, **11f:** 122
ad hominem fallacy, **31c:** 319
adjective clause, 552
  and subordination, **24a:** 263
  placement of, **25a:** 270–71
  punctuation of, **12d:** 134–35
adjective phrase
  and subordination, **24a:** 263
  punctuation of, **12d:** 134–36
  recognition of, 20

Index

adjective-forming suffixes, 14, 42–43
adjectives, 552
  and adverbs, **4:** 42–50
  and subordination, **24a:** 263
  as complements, **4b:** 44–45
  clauses used as, 23
  comparison of, **4c:** 46–48
  compound, hyphen with, **18f:** 195
  coordinate, **12c:** 133–34
  hyphenated, **18f:** 195
  nouns used as, **4d:** 48–49
  participles used as, 45, 78, 520
  phrases used as, 20
  proper, **9a:** 107
  recognition of, 14
adverb clause, 23–24, 552
  and subordination, **24a:** 263
  dangling, **25b:** 273
  elliptical, 24, 273
  for variety, **30b:** 303
  punctuation with, **12b:** 130
adverb phrases, 20, **24a:** 263
adverbial conjunction. See *conjunctive adverbs.*
adverbs, 14, 552
  and adjectives, **4:** 42–50
  and subordination, **24a:** 263
  clauses used as, 24
  comparison of, **4c:** 46–48
  conjunctive, list of, 39
  ending in *-ly*, 42–43, **18f:** 196
  for variety, **30b:** 303
  misused as complements, **4b:** 44
  phrases used as, 20
  recognition of, 14
  with two forms, 3
affect, effect, 213
aggravate, 213
agreement, defined, 552
agreement, pronoun-antecedent, **6b:** 68–70
  and sexism in language, 68–69
  antecedents joined by *and, or,* 69
  collective nouns, 70
  person, each, etc., 68
agreement, subject-verb, **6a:** 61–67
  and tense, 61,
  anyone, each, etc., 65

  collective nouns, 65
  each, or *every* with subject, 63, 65
  intervening words, 62–63
  inverted word order, 64
  measles, physics, etc., 66
  quantity-denoting phrases, 65
  some, none, all, etc., 65
  subjects joined by *and,* 63
  subjects joined by *or, nor,* 63–64
  there + verb + subject, 64
  title of a work, 66
  who, which, that, 64
  with predicate noun, 66
  word referred to as word, 66
a half a, 213
ahold of, 213
ain't, 213
airplanes, names of, **10c:** 114
all, verb agreement with, **6a:** 65
all-, hyphen with, **18f:** 197
alliteration, misuse of, **19h:** 211
allusion, 552
allusion, illusion, 213
almanacs, in "Works Cited," 444
alot, 213
alphabetization, 437, 476
already, all ready, 213
alright, 213
altogether, all together, 213
a.m., p.m., 122, 214
ambiguity, 553
ambiguous reference, **28a:** 286
American and British spelling, 180–81
among, between, 214
amount of, number of, 214
ampersand (&), **11d:** 120
analogy, 553
analogy, false, **31c:** 319. See also *comparison and contrast.*
analysis, as development strategy, 351–52, 553
analytical reading, 509, 553
and
  antecedents joined by, **6b:** 69
  as coordinating conjunction, 16
  as transitional word, **32b:** 337
  beginning sentences, **30b:** 303–04
  excessive use of, **24b:** 264–65

misuse of comma with, **13b:** 142
parallel elements with, 274
punctuation with, **12a:** 127–28; **12c:** 133
spelled out, 120
subjects joined by, **6a:** 63
unstressed, **18a:** 181
and etc., 214
and/or, 214
and which, and who, 214
anecdote, 373–74
annotation of source, 478
answering test questions, **33h:** 400–03
antecedent, 553
ambiguous reference to, **28a:** 286
anyone, person, etc., as, **6b:** 68
collective noun as, **6b:** 70
compound, **6b:** 69
implied, **28c:** 287
modifier as, **28b:** 286–87
of *who, which, that,* **6a:** 65
pronoun agreement with, **6b:** 68–70
reference of pronoun to, **28:** 285–89
remote, **28b:** 286–87
whole clause, etc., as, **28c:** 287
anthology, in "Works Cited," 440–41, 481
anticlimax, 294
antonyms, **19a:** 201–03, 553
a number, the number, 214
any, verb agreement with, **6a:** 65
anyone
anyone, any one, everyone, every one,
214
pronoun agreement with, **6b:** 68
verb agreement with, **6a:** 65
anyways, anywheres, 214
APA style of documentation, 483–87
parenthetical citations, 483–85
reference list, 485–87
model research paper, 489–503
apostrophe, **15:** 152–56
misuse of, **15d:** 155
to form possessives, **15a:** 152–54
to indicate plurals, **15c:** 155
to mark omissions, **15b:** 154
appeal, 553
appended element, **12d:** 138
appendix, in a report, 549
"Appetite," 357–59

application letter, 542–43
appositives, 553
and subordination, **24a:** 283
case of pronouns in, **5:** 53; **5a:** 54
for variety, **30b:** 304; **30c:** 306
in definitions, 259
misused as sentence, **2a:** 31
punctuation of, **12d:** 136
archaic words, **19f:** 210
argument, 553. See also *logical thinking.*
arrangement of ideas
classical, 381–82
in composition, **33e:** 377–82
in paragraph, **32b:** 329–35
in sentence, for emphasis, **29a–29c:**
291–94
article (*a, an,* or *the*)
defined, 553
in titles, **9c:** 108; **10a:** 112–13
omission of, **22a:** 248–49
repetition of, 248, **26b:** 277
articles. See *magazines, newspapers.*
as
case of pronoun after, **5b:** 55–56
usage, 215
as far as, 215
as if clauses, **7c:** 87
as to, 215
at, 215
audience, 553
analysis of, **33a:** 362–65
and diction, **19b–19d:** 207–10; **19g:**
210–11
and tone, **33c:** 366
types of, 362–65
authors, names of
in bibliographies, 437–38, 485–87
in citations, **34e:** 431–34, 483–84
auxiliaries, 553
and tense, 82
list of, **7:** 73
omission of, **22b:** 249
awful, awfully, 215
awhile, a while, 215

B

back of, 215
backwards, 215

Index

bad, badly, 215
balanced sentence, **29g:** 298
bandwagon fallacy, **31c:** 319
barely, with negative, **4e:** 49–50
be
    as auxiliary, 4, 73
    as linking verb, 76–77
    forms and uses of, 73–74
    in subjunctive, **7c:** 86
    unemphatic use of, **29d:** 295–96
because, after *reason is*, **23e:** 258–59
begging the question, **31c:** 320
beginning of paper, **33f:** 383–86
beginning of sentence
    capital for, **9e:** 107
    important words at, **29a:** 291–92
    number at, spelled out, **11f:** 123
    subject-first, overuse, **30b:** 303–04
being as, being that, 215
beside, besides, 216
besides, **3b:** 39; **32b:** 337
better, had better, 216
between. See *among, between*.
bias, prejudice, 216
Bible
    capitalization of, **9a:** 106
    colon in references to, **17d:** 169
    in citations, MLA style, 435–37
    no italics for, **10a:** 113
bibliographies
    abbreviations used in, 447–49
    annotated, 478
    APA "References," **34g:** 485–87
    cards for, 419–20
    in sample research papers, 477, 479,
        501, 503
    MLA "Works Cited," **34f:** 436–47
    preliminary or working, 419–20
body of business letter, 539
book review, in "Works Cited," 444
books
    among library resources, 408–11
    capitals for titles of, **9c:** 108
    in APA "References," 485–86
    in citations, 438–47, 480–81, 485–86
    in MLA "Works Cited," 438–47
    italics for titles of, **10a:** 112–13
borrow off, borrow from, 216
both . . . and, parallelism with, **26c:** 278

bottom line, 216
brackets, uses of, **17g:** 173–74
brainstorming, 554
bring, 216
British and American spelling, 180
broad reference, **28c:** 287
bulletins, in "Works Cited," 445
bunch, 216
business writing, **35b:** 481–500. See also
    letters; memos; reports; résumés.
    format, 538
    model envelope, 542
    model letter, 541–43
    model memo, 548
    model résumé, 546
but
    as coordination conjunction, 14
    as preposition, 13
    as transitional word, **32b:** 337
    beginning sentences, **30b:** 303–04
    excessive use of, **24b:** 264–65
    in contrasted element, **12d:** 137
    linking main clauses, **12a:** 127–28
but what, 216

C

call numbers, in library, 408–11
can, may, 216
can't hardly, can't scarcely, 216
capitalization, **9:** 104–12
    abbreviations and acronyms, **9a:** 107
    after a colon, **17d:** 169
    beginning of sentence, **9e:** 109
    calendar designations, **9a:** 106
    companies, agencies, etc., **9a:** 106
    derivatives, **9a:** 107
    dictionary as guide to, 104
    for emphasis, 107
    geographical names, **9a:** 105
    historical periods, etc., **9a:** 106
    holy books, holy days, **9a:** 106
    I and *O*, **9d:** 109
    in quoted speech, **9e:** 109
    in series of questions, 167
    languages, **9a:** 105
    peoples, **9a:** 105
    personifications, **9a:** 106–07
    pronouns referring to Deity, 106
    proper names, **9a:** 105–07

religions and adherents, **9a:** 106
seasons, **9a:** 106
style sheet for, 110
Supreme Being, **9a:** 106
titles of books, etc., **9c:** 108
titles of persons, **9b:** 107–08
trademarks, **9a:** 105
unnecessary, 109–10
card catalog, in library, 399–401
caret, for insertions, **8e:** 96
case, **5:** 51–60, 554
    after *than* or *as*, **5b:** 55–56
    before gerund, **5b:** 58–59
    forms, 51–52, 152
    in compound constructions, **5a:** 53–54
    objective, uses of, 53
    of appositives, 53, 54
    of subject complements, **5f:** 59
    possessive, uses of, 53, 145–47
    subjective, uses of, 52
    who as subject of clause, **5b:** 55
    who or *whom* with *he says*, **5b:** 55
    whom for objects, **5c:** 57
    whose, of which, 52
    with infinitives, **5e:** 59
cassettes, titles of, **10a:** 107
catalogs, library, 408–11
cause and effect, as development strategy,
    347–48, 371, 554
censor, censure, 216
center about, center around, 216
central idea. See *thesis statement; topic
    sentence.*
characters, 514, 530
checklists,
    Editing, **33g:** 392–93
    Reviser's, **33g:** 390–92
chronological order, 329, 344–45, 347, 554
circular reasoning, **31c:** 320
citations
    in APA style, 483–87
    in footnote or endnote style, 480–81
    in MLA style, 438–47
classification and division, as development
    strategy, **32d:** 350–52, 371, 554
clauses, defined and classified, 21–25, 554.
    See also *main clauses; subordinate
    clauses.*
clichés, **20c:** 236–37, 555

climax, order of, **29c:** 294
clipped forms, **11:** 121; **17a:** 166
closing of business letter, 540, 541
cognates, 203, 555
coherence of paragraphs, **32b:** 319–30, 555
collective noun, 555
    pronoun agreement with, **6b:** 70
    verb agreement with, **6a:** 65–66
colloquial usage, **19b:** 208, 212, 555
colon
    after salutation, **35a:** 539
    before clause or sentence, **17d:** 169
    before explanation or summary, **17d:** 169
    before quotation, **17d:** 169
    before series, **17d:** 169
    between title and subtitle, **17d:** 169–70
    in citations, **34f:** 435
    in scriptural references, **17d:** 169
    in time references, **17d:** 169
    superfluous, **17d:** 170
    with quotation marks, **16e:** 163
combining sentences
    to eliminate wordiness, **21b:** 243–45
    to subordinate ideas, **24a:** 262–63
    to vary sentence length, **30a:** 301–02
comma, **12:** 126–40
    after adverb clause, **12b:** 129–30
    after introductory phrase, **12b:** 130–31
    after *yes* or *no*, **12b:** 131
    and emphasis, 173
    before *and, but*, etc., linking main
        clauses, **12a:** 127–29
    before tag questions, **3a:** 37
    between main clauses, 36, 147
    for special emphasis, 128, 133
    in citations, **34f:** 435
    misuse of, as splice, **3:** 34–41
    superfluous, **13:** 141–44
    to mark omissions, **21d:** 246; **22a:** 249
    to prevent misreading, **12e:** 139
    with absolute phrases, **12d:** 139
    with conjunctive adverb, 147
    with coordinate adjectives, **12c:** 133
    with contrasted elements, **12d:** 137
    with direct address, **12d:** 139
    with geographical names, **12d:** 137
    with items in dates, addresses, **12d:** 137
    with items in series, **12c:** 132–33
    with mild interjections, **12d:** 139

Index

comma (*continued*)
with nonrestrictive elements, **12d:** 134–39
with parenthetical elements, **12d:** 138
with quotation marks, **16e:** 163
comma splice or fault, **3:** 34–41
before *however*, etc., **3b:** 38–39
in divided quotations, **3c:** 40
without conjunction, **3a:** 35–36
command. See *imperative sentence.*
common gender, 555
common noun, **9f:** 109–10, 555
comparative degree, **4c:** 46–47, 555
compare to, compare with, 217
comparison, 555
completion of, **22c:** 251
degrees of, 46–48, 558
double, **4c:** 47–48
forms of modifiers in, **4c:** 46–47
metaphor as, 233–34
of absolutes, **4c:** 47
other in, **4c:** 47; **22c:** 251
parallel elements in, 274
simile as, 233–34
comparison and contrast, 555
as development strategy, 349–50, 371
in balanced sentence, **29g:** 298
complementary, complimentary, 217
complements, 555
adjectives as, **4b:** 44–45
and subject-verb agreement, **6a:** 66
complete subjects and predicates, 555
complex sentence, 25, **30c:** 306, 556
complimentary close, 484
composition (the whole), **33:** 356–401. See also *paragraphs; research paper; business writing.*
arrangement of ideas, **33e:** 377–82
classical, 381–82
formal outlines, 379–81
informal plans, 377–78
audience, **33b:** 362–65
choice of subject, **33c:** 366–73
conclusion, **33f:** 388
development strategies, 371
exploring the subject, **33c:** 366–73
focusing the subject, **33d:** 373–76
introduction, **33f:** 383–86
logical thinking in, **31:** 312–21
perspectives, 362–63, **33c:** 370
purpose, **33a:** 360–62
revision, **33g:** 389–400
checklist, 390–92
of draft, sample, 393–400
word processing and, **8:** 101–03
thesis statement, **33d:** 373–77
title, **33f:** 388
tone of, **33c:** 366
writing drafts of, **33f:** 382–88
compound-complex sentence, 24, 556
compound constructions
case of pronoun in, **5a:** 53–55
parallel elements in, 274
compound predicate, **1a:** 3, 556
for variety, **30c:** 306
part of, as fragment, **2a:** 31
punctuation of, **12a:** 128
compound sentence, 25, 556
compound subject, 6, 556
compound words, 195
hyphenation of, **18f:** 195–97
possessive of, **15a:** 153
computers. See *word processor.*
computer catalog in library, 408–11
computer search for periodicals, 409–11
conciseness, **21:** 240–45
conclusion, 556
of composition, **33f:** 386–88
in deductive reasoning, **31b:** 314–15
in inductive argument, **31a:** 312–14
in Toulmin method, **31b:** 315–18
concrete words, **20a:** 231–33, 556
conditional clause, **7c:** 87–88, 556
conjugation, **7:** 74–76, 556
conjunctions, 16, 556–57
as transitional words, **32d:** 336–37
beginning sentences, **30b:** 303–04
coordinating, recognition of, 16
correlative, parallelism with, **26c:** 278–79
omission of, **22a:** 249–50
repetition of, **26b:** 277
subordinating, lists of, 16, 21–22
conjunctive adverbs, 557
beginning a sentence, **30b:** 303–04
between main clauses, **3b:** 38–39; **14a:** 146–47

list of, 39
position of, 39, 146–47
connectives, 557
connotation, **20a:** 229–31, 557
conscious, conscience, 217
consensus of opinion, 217
consequently, **3b:** 39; **32b:** 337
construction, 557
context, 557
continual, continuous, 217
contractions
  and possessive pronouns, **18b:** 182
  apostrophe in **15b:** 154
  appropriate use of, **19b:** 208
contrast. See *comparison and contrast.*
contrasted elements
  and subordination, **24a:** 266
  comma with, **12d:** 137
  parallel elements in, 274
controlling idea, 557
coordinate adjectives, **12c:** 133
coordinating conjunctions, 16, 557
  beginning sentences, **30b:** 303–04
  fixed position of, 39
  in titles, **9c:** 108
  linking main clauses, **12a:** 127–29
  parallel elements with, 278–79
  superfluous comma with, **13b:** 142
coordination, 558
  and subordination, **24:** 261–68
  excessive or faulty, **24a:** 263–65, 266
  ineffective, **24b:** 260–62
  parallel elements and, 278
correlatives, 16, **26c:** 273–74, 558
could of, 217
count nouns, 517
couple, couple of, 217

D

-d, -ed, 71–72, 75
dangling modifiers, 72, 78, **25b:** 272–73,
    558
  elliptical, 273
  gerund or infinitive in, 272–73
  participial phrases, 272
dash, **17e:** 171–72
  after introductory list, **17e:** 172
  for emphasis or clarity, **17e:** 171
  overuse of, **17e:** 172
  to mark sudden break, **17e:** 171
  to set off parenthetical element, **17e:** 171
  with quotation marks, **16e:** 164
data, number of, **6a:** 65–66
database services, 414–15
dates
  abbreviations with, **11:** 118–20
  commas with, **12d:** 134, 137–38
  numbers in, **11:** 122
days of week
  capitalization of, **9a:** 106
  spelled out, **11b:** 118
decimals, figures for, **11f:** 123
declarative sentence
  as sentence type, 26
  containing questions, **17b:** 167
  period with, **17a:** 166
declension, 558
deduction, 314–15, 558
definition, 558
  as development strategy, 352–53, 369
  faulty, **23e:** 258–60
  formal and informal, 258–60
  in dictionary, 201, 258
  precision in, **23e:** 259–60
  quotation marks or italics for, 162
degrees, academic, **11a:** 117–18; **12b:** 136
Deity, pronouns referring to, 106
demonstratives, 558
denotation, **20a:** 228–29, 558
dependent clauses. See *subordinate
    clauses.*
description, **32d:** 345–47; **33c:** 371, 558
descriptive adjective. See *adjective.*
detail, excessive, **23b:** 255–56
details, in development, **32c:** 341–42, 558
determiner, 14, 558
development, **32d:** 344–55, 559. See also
    paragraphs.
dialect, **19d:** 209–10, 559
dialogue, 559
  capitalization in, **9e:** 109
  in drama, 529
  informal words in, **19b:** 207–08
  paragraphing of, **16a:** 158–59
  quotation marks for, **16a:** 158
diction, **19–22:** 198–252, 559. See also
    words, choice of.

Index

dictionaries, **19a:** 199–207
  abbreviations shown in, 166
  antonyms in, 201–02
  biographical, 416–17
  capitalization shown in, 104
  college, list of, 198
  definition in, 201, 259
  etymology shown in, 202–06
  grammatical information in, 200
  list of, special, 199
  list of, unabridged, 198
  pronunciation shown in, 200
  sample entries from, 201–02
  special usage labels, 201
  spelling, authority for, 178–81, 200
  syllabication shown in, 200
  synonyms in, 201
  thesaurus and, 201
different from, 217
differ from, differ than, 217
direct address, **12d:** 139, 559
direct discourse, **27c:** 282
direct object, 6–7, 8–10, 559
direct quotations, 559
  capitalization in **9e:** 109
  colon before, **17d:** 169
  divided, **3c:** 40; **9e:** 109
  in note-taking, 426–27
  in research paper, 420–21
  indention of, **16a:** 157
  interpolations in, **17g:** 173–74
  omissions in, **17i:** 175–77
  poetry as, **16a:** 160–61
  prose as, **16a:** 159–60
  quotation marks with, **16a:** 157–59
  within quotations, 157–58
discourse, shift in, **27c:** 282
disinterested, uninterested, 217
disks, titles of, **10a:** 112–13
divided quotations, **3c:** 40
division, end-of-line, **8d:** 95–97
do, as auxiliary, 73
documented paper. See *research paper.*
don't, 218
double comparison, **4c:** 47–48
double negative, **21a:** 241, 559
double subject, **21a:** 241
draft, 559. See also *composition, the whole.*

drama
  in citations, **34f:** 434
  in "Works Cited," **34f:** 440
  writing about, 529–36
due to, 218
dynamic perspective, 370

E

each
  as antecedent, **6b:** 68
  as subject, **6a:** 63, 65
  with compound subject, **6a:** 63
-ed, -d, 71–72, 75
edited American English, 212, 559
editing, 559
  Checklist, **33g:** 392–93
  with word processor, 91, 101–03
editorials, in "Works Cited," 444
effect. See *affect, effect.*
effect and cause, in development, **32d:**
     347–49, 371
ei/ie, in spelling, **18e:** 188–89
either, number of
  as antecedent, **6b:** 68
  as subject, **6a:** 65
either . . . or
  parallel elements with, **26c:** 278
  subjects joined by, **6a:** 63–64
either/or fallacy, **31c:** 319
-elect, hyphen with, **18f:** 197
ellipsis points, **17i:** 175–78
  to indicate pause, 177
  to mark omissions, 175–77
elliptical constructions, 559
  after *as* or *than*, **5b:** 55–56
  dangling, **25b:** 273
  use of, to avoid repetition, **21d:** 244–45
emigrate from, immigrate to, 218
eminent, imminent, 218
emphasis, **29:** 289–97, 560
  active and passive voice, **29d:** 295
  balanced sentence, **29g:** 298
  capitalization for, 107
  climactic order, **29c:** 294–95
  colon for, **17d:** 168–69
  comma for, 128, 133
  coordination and, **24b:** 264–65

dash for, **17e:** 171
exclamation point, **17c:** 168
inverted word order, **29f:** 297
italics for, **10e:** 114–15
parentheses and, 173
periodic sentence, **29b:** 292–93
repetition for, **29c:** 296–97
semicolon for, **14b:** 148–49
short sentence, **29h:** 298
subordination and, **29b:** 292–93
verbs for *be, have,* **29d:** 295–96
word placement and, **29a:** 291–92
encyclopedias
in "Works Cited," 444
lists of, 415–16
end marks, **17a–17c:** 165–68
ending of paper, **33f:** 386–88
endnote style, 480–82
English language, development of, **19a:**
    202–06
enthuse, 218
envelope, sample addressed, **35b:** 542
equivocation, **31c:** 320
-er, -est, **4c:** 46–47
-es, -s, **6:** 62; **18d:** 186–88
essay, **33h:** 400–04, 560. See also
    composition.
et al., 433, 448
etc., 218. See also *and etc.*
etymology, 202–06
euphemisms, **20c:** 236–37
evaluating sources, **34c:** 418–19
even, position of, **25a:** 269–70
every, before subject, **6a:** 63
everyday, every day, **18b:** 182
everyone, everybody. See *anyone,
    any one.*
    as antecedent, **6b:** 68
    as subject, **6a:** 65
evidence, 560
    in deductive reasoning, **31b:** 314–15
    in inductive reasoning, **31a:** 312–14
    in persuasive writing, **33a:** 361
    misuse of, **31c:** 318–20
ex-, hyphen with, **18f:** 197
exactness, **20:** 227–39. See also *words,
    choice of.*
examination, essay, **33h:** 400–04

examples, 560
    as development strategy, **32c:** 343
    in definitions, 352–53
except, accept, 218
exclamation point
    uses of, **17c:** 168
    with quotation marks, **16e:** 164
exclamatory sentence, 26
expansion of simple sentence, **1d:** 17
expect, 218
expletive, defined, 560
explicit, implicit, 218, 360–61
expository writing, 560
expressive writing, 360, 560

F

fallacy, **31c:** 318–21, 560
    ad hominem, 319
    bandwagon, 319
    begging the question, 320
    circular reasoning, 320
    either . . . or, 319
    equivocation, 320
    false analogy, 319
    false cause, 320
    hasty generalization, 319
    non sequitur, 318
    oversimplification, 320
    post hoc, 320
    red herring, 319
    slippery slope, 320
false analogy, 319
false premise, **31b:** 314–15
family relationship, words denoting,
    9b: 108
fantastic, 219
farther, further, 219
faulty predication, **23d:** 257–58, 560
fewer, less, 219
fiction, writing about, **35a:** 511–20
figurative language, 560
    effective use of, **20a:** 233–35
    mixed metaphors, **23c:** 256
figure, 219
figures (numerals). See also *numbers.*
    abbreviations with, **11f:** 121–22
    for enumeration, **17f:** 172

Index

figures (numerals). *(continued)*
 for numbers, **11f:** 122–23
 forming the plural of, **15c:** 155
 in outlines, **33e:** 379
 omissions in, **15b:** 154
 when to italicize, **10d:** 114
figures of speech, 233–35
films, titles of, **10a:** 112–13. See also
  motion pictures.
finite verb, defined, 560
fixing to, 219
focusing the subject, **33c:** 368–73, 560
footnote style, 480–82
for
 as conjunction, 16
 as preposition, 14–15
 as transitional word, **32b:** 337
foreign spellings, retention of, 188
foreign words, italicized, **10b:** 113–14
form changes. See *inflection.*
formal definition, 257, 352–53
formal English, **19b:** 207–08
formal outlines, 379–81
formats for business letters, **35b:** 538–41
former, 219
fractions
 hyphen with, 196
 use of figures for, **11f:** 123
fragment, sentence, **2:** 28–33
 appropriate use of, 29–30
 phrase as, **2a:** 30–31
 recognition of, 29–30
 revision of, 28–29
 subordinate clause, as, **2b:** 31–32
free writing, 383, 561
function words, 11, 561
further. See *farther, further.*
fused sentence, **3:** 34–35
future and future perfect tenses, **7b:** 83

G

gender
 and agreement, 62–68
 common, defined, 561
general audience, 63, 363
general words, **20a:** 228–33, 561
generalization, 561
 as major premise, 314–15

effective use of, 232
 hasty, **31c:** 319
 in essay test, 402
genitive case. See *possessive case.*
geographical names
 capitalization of, **9a:** 105
 commas with, **12d:** 137–38
 use of apostrophe with, 154, 158
gerund, 561
 in dangling phrase, **25b:** 272
 possessive before, **5d:** 58–59
 tense forms of, 77
gerund phrase, 18
glossary, in a report, **35b:** 549
Glossary, Usage, **19i:** 212–26
Glossary of Grammatical and Rhetorical
  Terms, 551–76
go, goes, 219
good, for *well,* **4a:** 43, 219
government agencies, **9a:** 106; **11:** 120–21
grammar, 561
great, 219

H

hackneyed phrases, **20c:** 236–39
had drank, had drunk, 219
had of, had have, 219
had ought, hadn't ought, 220
half, verb agreement with, **6a:** 65
half a, a half, a half a, 220
handwritten paper
 legibility of, **8c:** 93
 manuscript form, **8a–8b:** 90–93
hanged, hung, 220
hardly
 position of, **25a:** 269–70
 with negative, **4e:** 49
hasty generalization, **31c:** 319
have, unemphatic, **29d:** 295–96
heading of business letter, **35b:** 538–39
headings of formal outline, **33e:** 379–81
helping verbs. See *auxiliaries.*
hence, **3b:** 39; **32b:** 337
hisself, 220
historical documents, periods, events,
 9a: 106
historical present, **7b:** 82
holidays, holy days, **9a:** 106

homonyms, 561
hopefully, 220
however, **3b:** 39; **32b:** 337
hyperbole, 234, 561
hyphen, hyphenation
    before capital, **18f:** 197
    in citations, 435
    in compound words, **18f:** 195
    in series, **18f:** 195
    in titles, **9c:** 108
    not used after *-ly*, **18f:** 196
    to avoid ambiguity, **18f:** 196
    to mark word division, **8d:** 96
    with figures or letters, **18f:** 196
    with page numbers, 435
    with prefixes, **18f:** 196
    with spelled-out numbers, **18f:** 196
    with suffix *-elect*, **18f:** 197

I

I, capitalized, **9d:** 109
identification on a paper, **8b:** 94
    in APA style, 488, 489
    in MLA style, 452, 453
idiomatic expressions, **20b:** 235–36
idioms, 236
ie/ei, in spelling, **18e:** 188–89
if clause, **7c:** 87
illiteracies, **19e:** 210
illusion. See allusion, illusion.
image, imagery, 233, 521–22
*immigrate. See emigrate from, immi-
    grate to.*
imminent. See eminent, imminent.
imperative, 76. See also *mood.*
imperative sentence, 5–6, 26
implicit. See explicit, implicit.
imply, infer, 220
in to, into, **18b:** 182
Inc., Ltd., 120
incidently, 220
include, 220
inclusive language, **6b:** 66–68
incomplete comparisons, **22c:** 251–52
incomplete constructions, **22:** 248–52
incomplete sentence, **2:** 28–33. See also
    fragment.
indeed, **3b:** 39; **32b:** 337

indefinites, 561
    and agreement, **6a:** 65; **6b:** 68
    possessive case of, **15a:** 152–53
indention
    for paragraphs, 322
    for quotations, **16a:** 158–59
    in APA "References," 485
    in MLA "Works Cited," 437
    in outlines, 379
independent clauses. See *main clauses.*
indexes to periodicals, 412–15
indicative, 76. See *mood.*
indirect discourse, **27c:** 282
indirect object, 7, 9–12, 562
indirect question, **17b:** 167, 562
indirect quotation, 157–58, 562
individual ownership, **15a:** 153–54
Indo-European languages, 203
induction, reasoning by, **31a:** 312–14,
    562
in fact, 220
infinitive, 562
    and repetition of *to*, **26b:** 277
    in titles, **9c:** 108
    objective case with, **5e:** 59
    split, **25a:** 271
    tense forms of, 74–76, **7b:** 82–84
infinitive phrases
    as modifiers, 20–21
    as nouns, 18–19
    dangling, **25b:** 272
    for variety, **30b:** 303
inflected forms, in dictionary, 201
inflection, 562
informal English, **19b:** 208, 212
informative writing. See *expository
    writing.*
input, 220
in regards to, with regards to, 220
insertions
    in quoted matter, **17g:** 173–74
    in revision of paper, **8e:** 99
inside address, 539
instead, **3b:** 39
institutions, names of, **9a:** 106
intensifiers (*so, such, too*), **22d:** 252,
    562
intensive/reflexive pronoun, 562

Index

interjections, 16–17, 563
  commas with, **12b:** 131; **12d:** 138–39
  exclamation points with, **17c:** 168
interrogative sentence, 26
interrogatives, 563
interview, in "Works Cited," 447
into, in to, 182
intransitive verb, 563
introduction, **33f:** 383–86, 563
introductory phrases
  for variety, **30b:** 303–04
  punctuation of, 129–32
introductory series or list
  dash after, **17e:** 172
  for variety, **30b:** 304
inversion, 563
  agreement and, **6a:** 64
  for emphasis, **29f:** 297
irony, **20a:** 235, 563
irregardless, 220
irregular verb, 72–74, 563
is when, is where, **23e:** 258–59
it, awkward use of, **28d:** 288–90
italics (underlining)
  for book titles, etc., **10a:** 112–13
  for emphasis, **10e:** 115
  for foreign words, **10b:** 113–14
  for names of ships, etc., **10c:** 114
  for titles of works of art, **10c:** 114
  for words, etc., as such, **10d:** 114
  overuse or misuse of, **10e:** 115
its, it's, **15d:** 155; **18b:** 183, 220
-ize, 221

J

jargon, **19g:** 210–11, 563
joint possession, **15a:** 154
journals. See *periodicals.*
just, position of, **25a:** 269

K

key idea, repetition of, **32b:** 336
kind, sort, 221
kind of, kind of a, 221

L

languages, capitalization of, **9a:** 105
later, latter, 221
Latin abbreviations, 120

lay, lie, 81–82, 221
learn, 221
leave, 221
lectures, in "Works Cited," 446–47
legibility, **8c:** 93
less. See *fewer, less.*
let's us, 221
letters, business, **35b:** 538–44
  addresses on envelopes, 542
  formats of, 538–41
  of application, 542–43
  parts of, 538–40
letters of alphabet
  for enumeration, **17f:** 172
  italics for, **10d:** 114
  plural form of, **15c:** 155
let's you and me, **5a:** 54
lexical words, 12
liable, likely, 221
library, finding materials in, 408–20
Library of Congress Subject Headings, 411
lie, lay, **7a:** 81–82. See also *lay, lie.*
like, 221
likewise, **3b:** 39; **32b:** 337
limiting adjective. See *adjective.*
limiting the subject, **33b:** 366–67; **34a:**
      406–07
linking verbs, 14, **4b:** 45, 563
list or series, introductory, **17e:** 172; **30b:**
      304
list-making, in planning paper, **33c:** 368–69
literary present, 83
literary work from anthology, 440
literature
  papers about, **35a:** 507–37
  reference books on, 417
localisms, **19d:** 209
logic and logical thinking, **31:** 312–21, 563.
      See also *fallacies.*
  deduction, **31b:** 314–15
  induction, **31a:** 312–14
  mistakes in, **31c:** 318–20
  syllogism, 314
  Toulmin method, 315–17
look, complement with, **4b:** 44–45
loose sentences
  and emphasis, **29b:** 292–93
  revision of, for variety, **30c:** 306–07
lose, loose, 221

lots, 222
Ltd., Inc., 120
-ly
  as suffix of modifiers, **4:** 43
  hyphen not used after, **18f:** 196
  retention of final *l* with, **18d:** 187

M

magazines. See *periodicals.*
main clauses
  defined, 24, 25, 563
  linked by *and, but,* etc., **12a:** 127–29
  linked by *however, for example,* **3b:** 38;
    14a: 146–47
  overuse of, **24b:** 264–65
  recognition of, 24–25
  semicolon between, **14a:** 145–47
  use of colon before, **17d:** 168–69
man, woman, person, **6b:** 68
manuscript form, **8:** 92–103
  handwritten, **8a:** 92–93
  identification, **8b:** 94
  indention, **8b:** 94
  legibility, **8c:** 95
  margins, **8b:** 93
  paging, **8b:** 94
  punctuation, **8b:** 94
  quoted lines, **8b:** 94; **16a:** 159–61
  revision of, **8e:** 97–98
  title, **8b:** 94
  typewritten, **8b:** 93; **8c:** 95
  word division, **8d:** 95–97
  See also *research paper.*
margins of manuscript, **8b:** 93
markers, 4, 22
mass noun, 565
may be, maybe, 222
me and, 222
measurement, units of, **11b:** 118
mechanics
  defined, 564
  in citations, **34f:** 435–36
media, verb agreement with, **6a:**
    65
memos, business, **35b:** 547–48
merely, position of, **25a:** 269
metaphorical words, 233–34
metaphors
  defined, 564

  effective use of, **20a:** 233–34
  mixed, **23c:** 256
Middle English, 204–05
might could, 222
mild interjection, **12d:** 139
"The Miracle of Technofix," 404
misplaced modifier, defined, 564
misplaced parts, **25a:** 269–71
  clauses and phrases, 270
  single-word modifiers, 269
  split infinitives, 271
  squinting modifiers, 271
misspelling, **18:** 180–97. See also *spelling.*
mixed constructions, 564
mixed metaphors, **23c:** 256
MLA documentation
  list of "Works Cited," 436–47
  notes, 474–75
  parenthetical citation, 429–36
modal auxiliaries, 564
mode. See *mood.*
Modern English, vocabulary of, 205–06
modifiers
  adjectives and adverbs, **4:** 42–50
  and subordination, **24a:** 262–64
  as antecedents, **28b:** 286
  clauses as, 23–4
  coordinate, **12c:** 137
  dangling, **25b:** 272–73
  defined, 564
  hyphenated, **18f:** 195
  misplaced, **25a:** 269–71
  nonrestrictive, **12d:** 134–36
  nouns as, **4d:** 48–49
  phrases as, 20–21
  placement of, **25a:** 270
  restrictive, **12d:** 134–35
  squinting, **25a:** 271
  used as complements, 44–45
months, capitalization of, **9a:** 106
mood
  defined, 564
  indicated in conjugation, 75–76
  indicative and imperative, **7:** 76
  shift in, **7d:** 88
  subjunctive, **7c:** 86–88
morale, moral, 222
moreover, **3b:** 39; **32b:** 337
most, 222

Index

motion pictures
    in "Works Cited," 445
    italics for titles of, **10a:** 112–13
Miss, Mrs., Ms., in letter, 539
Mr., Dr., etc., **11a:** 117–18
much, 222
multiple audiences, 365
multivolume work, 441
musical works, titles of
    italics for, **10a:** 112–13
    quotation marks for, **16b:** 161
myself, 222

N

names
    capitalization of, **9a:** 105–07
    plural forms of, **18d:** 187
    possessive forms of, **15a:** 152–54
    titles with, **9b:** 107–08; **11a:** 117–18
narration, 564
nauseous, 222
nearly, position of, **25a:** 269
negative, double, 49–50, **21a:** 241
neither
    as antecedent, **6b:** 68
    as subject, **6a:** 65
neither . . . nor
    as correlatives, 16
    linking antecedents, **6b:** 69
    linking subjects, **6a:** 63–64
    parallelism with, **26c:** 278
nevertheless, **3b:** 39; **32b:** 337
newspapers
    in APA "References," 487
    in MLA "Works Cited," 443
    italics for titles of, **10a:** 112–13
    See also *periodicals*.
nicknames, capitalized, **9a:** 105
no
    in double negative, **4e:** 49
    in indirect discourse, quotation marks
        with, **16d:** 162
    introductory, comma after, 130
no . . . nor, 222
nobody, no body, **18b:** 182
nominative. See *subjective case*.
none, verb agreement with, **6a:** 65
nonetheless, **3b:** 39; **32b:** 337

nonfinite verb, defined, 564
nonprint sources, 445–47
nonrestrictive
    defined, 565
    elements, **12d:** 134–36
non sequitur, **31c:** 318
nonstandard English, **19e:** 210
nor
    antecedents linked by, **6b:** 69
    as coordinating conjunction, 16
    as transitional word, **32b:** 337
    main clauses linked by, **12a:** 127–28
    subjects joined by, **6a:** 63–64
    word order with, 34–36
not . . . but, **12d:** 135
not . . . no/none/nothing, 222
not only . . . but also, parallelism with,
        26c: 278
notations, in letters, **35b:** 540
note cards, 420–22, 452, 456, 460
notes
    endnotes or footnotes, 480–82
    in MLA style, 474–75
note-taking
    evaluation of sources, 418
    on cards, 420–21
    on photocopies, 422
    paraphrasing in, 426–27
    quoting directly in, 425–26
    summary in, 428
noun clause
    defined, 17, 566
    recognition of, 22–23
noun-forming suffixes, 13
noun phrase, 18–21
nouns
    as adjectives, **4d:** 48–49
    capitalization of, **4a:** 105–07
    collective, **6a:** 65–66
    compound, 12–13, 195
    defined and classified, 565
    functions of, 13
    plural forms of, **18d:** 187
    possessive forms of, **15a:** 153
nowhere near, 222
nowheres, 222
number
    abbreviation of, 122–23
    usage, 223

number, singular or plural
  agreement in, **6:** 61–62
  defined, 566
  indicated in conjugation, 74–76
  indicated in declension, 51–52
  shifts in, **27b:** 281–82
numbers. See also *figures*.
  as words or figures, **11f:** 121–23
  at beginning of sentences, 123
  hyphenated, **18f:** 196
  page, 94–122
  special usage of, 122–23

O

O, oh, **9d:** 109
object complements, **4b:** 44–45, 566
objective case
  after *than* or *as,* **5b:** 55–56
  in compound constructions, **5a:** 53–55
  uses of, **5:** 52–53
  whom, **5b:** 55; **5c:** 57
  with infinitives, **5e:** 59
objects
  defined and classified, 566
  of prepositions, 15
  of verbs, recognition of, 5–10
obsolete words, **19f:** 210
o'clock, **15b:** 154
of, 223
of which and *whose,* **5:** 52
off of, 223
oftentimes, 223
OK, O.K., okay, 223
Old English, 204–05
omission of necessary words, **22:** 248–52
  after *so, such, too,* **22d:** 252
  articles, conjunctions, **22a:** 248–49
  in comparisons, **22c:** 251
  in parallel elements, **26b:** 277
  prepositions, pronouns, **22a:** 248–49
  verbs and auxiliaries, **22b:** 250
omissions, indicated by
  apostrophe, **15b:** 154
  comma, **21d:** 246; **22a:** 249
  ellipsis points, **17i:** 175–77
one
  as antecedent, **6b:** 68
  as subject, **6a:** 65

only, position of, **25a:** 269
or
  antecedents joined by, **6b:** 69
  as coordinating conjunction, 16
  as transitional word, **32b:** 337
  linking main clauses, **12a:** 127–29
  parallel elements with, 274
  subjects joined by, **6a:** 63
organization. See *arrangement of ideas.*
organizations, names of, **9a:** 106
origin of the English language, 202–06
ornate style, **19h:** 211
other, in comparison, **4c:** 47
otherwise, **3b:** 39; **32b:** 337
outlines, 379–81
  indention and numbers in, 379–81
  sentence, 380–81
  topic, 380
overwriting, **19h:** 211

P

page numbers
  figures for, 122
  in APA style citations, 483
  of manuscript, **8b:** 93
pamphlets, in "Works Cited," 445
paperback, as reprint, 441
paradox, defined, 567
paragraphs, 567
  adequate development, **32c:** 341–43
  arrangement of ideas, **32b:** 329–35
    chronological order, 329
    general to specific, 331
    order of importance, 330–31
    problem and solution, 333
    question and answer, 332–33
    spatial order, 330
    specific to general, 331
  coherence in, **32b:** 329, 335–41
  concluding, 386–88
  development strategies
    analogy, 350
    analysis, 351–52
    cause and effect, 347–48
    classification and division, 350–52
    combined, 353–55
    comparison and contrast, 349–50
    definition, 352–53

Index

paragraphs, development strategies
    (*continued*)
    description, 345–46
    examples, 343
    narration, 344–45
    process, 347
    specific details, 342
    in dialogue, **16a:** 158–59
    indention of, **8b:** 82
    introductory, 383–85
    length of, 323
    topic sentences, **32a:** 325–28
    transitional, 340–41
    transitions between, **32b:** 339–40
    transitions within, 335–39
    unity in, **32a:** 324–25
parallelism, 567
    in balanced sentence, **29g:** 298
    in coherent paragraphs, **32b:** 337–38
    in topic outlines, **33f:** 379
    of clauses, sentences, **26a:** 276
    of words, phrases, **26a:** 275
    repetition in, **26b:** 277
    uses of, 274–75
    with correlatives, **26c:** 278
paraphrase, **34e:** 426–27
parentheses
    and emphasis, 172–73
    for enumerations, **17f:** 172
    for parenthetical matter, **17f:** 173
    question mark within, **17b:** 169
    replaced by brackets, **17g:** 173–74
    with other punctuation, **16e:** 163;
        17f: 173
    with repeated numbers, **11:** 123
parenthetical citations
    APA style, **34g:** 483–85
    MLA style, **34f:** 429–36
parenthetical element
    and emphasis, 173
    brackets with, **16g:** 173–74
    commas with, **12d:** 138, 173
    dashes with, **17e:** 170
    defined, 567
    parentheses with, **17f:** 172–73
participial phrase, 18, 20, 567
    dangling, **25b:** 272
    for variety, **30b:** 303

    introductory, **12b:** 130–31; **30b:** 303
    misused as sentence, **2a:** 30
    recognition of, 18–20
participle, 78–80, 567
    in verb phrase, **7a:** 78
    retention of -*d* or -*ed*, 45, **7a:** 78
    tense forms, 73–74, **7b:** 85
particle, in phrasal verbs, 4–5, 567
parts of speech, 10, 201, 567
    functions of, 10–17
    labeled in dictionary, 11
    recognition of, 10–17
passive voice, 568
    and emphasis, **29d:** 295
    tense forms, **7:** 74–76
    word order and, 7
past and past perfect tenses, **7:** 75–76,
    83
past participle, **7a:** 78. See also *participle*.
per, 223
percentages, figures for, **11:** 123
perfect infinitive or participle, use of, **7b:**
    84–85
perfect tenses, **7b:** 83–85, 568
period
    after abbreviations, **17a:** 166
    and ellipsis points, **17i:** 176
    at end of sentences, **17a:** 166
    in bibliography, 437
    in citations, 435
    with parentheses, 172–73, 466–67
    with quotation marks, **16e:** 163
periodic sentence, **29b:** 292–93
periodicals
    in APA "References," **34g:** 486–87
    in MLA "Works Cited," **34f:** 442–44
    indexes to, 412–14
    italics for titles of, **10a:** 112–13
person, as antecedent, **6b:** 68
person (1st, 2nd, or 3rd), 568
    agreement in, **6:** 61–63
    indicated in conjugation, 74
    indicated in declension, 51–52
    shift in, **27b:** 281
personal pronoun, **5:** 51–52, 568
personification, 568
perspective, shift in, **27e:** 283
perspectives, types of, **33c:** 370

persuasive writing, 361–62, 568
photocopies, annotated, 423–24
phrasal prepositions, list of, 15
phrasal verbs, 4–5, 568
phrases, 568–69
  absolute, **12d**: 138–39
  as modifiers, 20–21
  as nouns, 18–19
  dangling, **25b**: 272
  for variety, **30b**: 303–04; **30d**: 307–08
  introductory, **12b**: 130–31
  misplaced, **25a**: 270
  misused as sentences, **2a**: 30–31
  nonrestrictive, **12d**: 134–36
  recognition of, 17–21
  restrictive, **12d**: 134–36
  subordination with, **21a**: 262–63
  transitional, lists of, 39, 337
plagiarism, **34e**: 424–25, 569
planning, 569. See *composition.*
plays
  capitalized titles of, **9c**: 108
  citations of, **34f**: 434
  in "Works Cited," **34f**: 440
  italics for titles of, **10a**: 112–13
plot, 514, 530
plurals
  of figures, etc., **15c**: 155
  of nouns, **18d**: 187–88
plus, 223
poetry
  in citations, **34f**: 434
  quoting from, **16a**: 160–61
  writing about, 521
point of view, 515, 569
positive degree, 46. See also *comparison.*
possessive case
  before gerund, **5d**: 58–59
  misused apostrophe with, **15d**: 155–56
  of indefinite pronouns, **15a**: 152–53
  of nouns, **15a**: 153
  of personal pronouns, **5**: 51–52
postal abbreviations, **11b**: 118–19
post hoc fallacy, **31c**: 320
predicate, 569
predicate adjective, 14, **4b**: 44–45, 569
predicate noun, **6a**: 66, 569
predication, faulty. See *faulty predication.*

prefix, 569
  hyphen after, **18f**: 197
  in titles, **9c**: 108
  spelling of, with root, **18c**: 184
prejudice. See *bias, prejudice.*
premises in syllogism, **31b**: 314–15, 570
prepositional phrase, 15, 570
  as modifier, 20–21
  as noun, 18–19
  for variety, **30b**: 301; **30c**: 306–07
  introductory, **12b**: 130–31
  placement of, **25a**: 270
prepositions, 570
  at end of sentence, 15
  idiomatic use of, **20b**: 235–36
  in parallel structure, **26b**: 277
  in titles, **9c**: 108
  lists of, 15
  omission of, **22a**: 249
  phrasal, 15
  recognition of, 15
present and present perfect tenses, **7b**: 82–84
present participle, **7a**: 78. See also *participle.*
prewriting, 570
principal parts of verbs, 77–78, 570
  functions of, **7a**: 82–83
  lie, lay, sit, set, **7a**: 81
  lists of, 78–80
  spelling of, **7a**: 80
principal, principle, 223
process. See *writing process.*
process analysis, as strategy, 570
progressive verb, 74, 83, 570
pronouns, 570
  agreement of verb with, **6a**: 64–65
  agreement with antecedent, **6b**: 68–69
  and sexism in language, **6b**: 68–69
  as aid to coherence, **32b**: 335–36
  case of, **5**: 51–60
  omission of, 23, 57, **22a**: 248–49
  personal, 51–52
  recognition of, 13
  reference of, 28, 285–90
  referring to Deity, **9a**: 106
  referring to title, **28b**: 286–87

pronouns (*continued*)
  relative, 52
  use of, to avoid repetition, **21d:** 246
pronunciation
  and spelling, **18a–18b:** 181–84
  as shown in dictionary, 181
proofreading, 97–98, 392–93, 449–50. See
    also *revisions*.
proper adjective, **9a:** 107, 570
proper name (noun), **9a:** 105–07, 570–71
provincialisms, **19d:** 209
punctuation. See also *comma, period*.
  and manuscript form, **8b:** 94
  in citations, 435–36
  in "Works Cited," 437–38
purpose, of a composition, **33a:** 359–62,
    571

Q
qualifier, 571
question mark
  after direct question, **17b:** 167
  to show uncertainty, 167
  with quotation marks, **16e:** 164
questions
  direct, indirect, **17b:** 167
  for variety, **30e:** 308
  tag, comma before, 37
quotation marks
  double and single, **16a:** 157–58
  for dialogue, **16a:** 158–59
  for direct quotation, **16a:** 158
  for titles, **16b:** 161–62
  for word used in special sense, **16c:** 162
  misuse for title of paper, **8b:** 94
  overuse of, **16c:** 162–63
  single quotation marks, **16a:** 157–58
  with other punctuation marks, **16e:** 163
quotations
  capital for first word of, **9e:** 109
  citations of, **34f:** 424–25
  colon before, **17d:** 169
  direct and indirect, 157–61
  divided, **3c:** 40
  from poetry, **16a:** 158–59; **17h:** 174–75
  from prose, **16a:** 159–60
  indention of, **16a:** 158

  interpolations in, **17g:** 173–74
  omissions in, **17i:** 175–77
  within other quotations, **16a:** 157–58

R
radio programs
  in "Works Cited," 445
  italics for titles of, **10a:** 112–13
raise, rise, 223
rarely ever, 224
Readers' Guide, 412–14
real, really, **4a:** 43, 224
reciprocal pronouns, 571
record of revisions, 101
recordings, in "Works Cited," 446
redundancy, 571. See also *wordiness*.
reference books, list of, 415–17
reference of pronouns
  ambiguous, **28a:** 286
  awkward *you* or *it*, **28d:** 288–89
  broad, **28c:** 287–88
  to implied idea, **28c:** 287–88
  to modifier, **28b:** 286–87
  to remote antecedent, **28b:** 286–87
"References" (APA), **34g:** 485–87, 501–03
reflexive pronoun, 571
regional words, **19d:** 209
regular verb, 72, 571
relative clause, 571
relative perspective, **33c:** 370
relative pronouns, 571
  and subject-verb agreement, **6a:** 64
  case forms of, **5:** 52
  list of, 22
  omission of, 23, 57
remote reference, **28b:** 286–87
repetition
  as aid to coherence, **32b:** 336
  for emphasis, **29e:** 296–97
  in parallel elements, **26b:** 277
  needless, **21c:** 245
  ways to avoid, **21d:** 246
reports, business, **35b:** 549
reprint, in "Works Cited," 441
research paper, **34:** 405–505
  and library resources, 408–19
  APA style documentation, 485–87

audience of, 405–06
citations in APA style, 483–85
citations in MLA style, 431–36
endnote or footnote style, 480–82
MLA "Works Cited," 436–47
note-taking for, **34c:** 420–22
plan or outline for, **34d:** 423
purpose of, 405
quotations in, **16a:** 159–60, 425–26
samples of, 488–503 (APA); 452–81
     (MLA)
style books for, list of, 504–05
subject for, 406–07
title page of, sample, 489
working bibliography, **34b:** 418–19
writing and revising, 429, 458, 464,
     472–73
respective, respectful, 224
restrictive elements, 133, 571
   clauses, phrases, appositives, **12d:**
        134–36
   misused commas with, **13d:** 143
résumés, **35b:** 542–45
Reviser's Checklist, **33g:** 390–92
revisions, 572
   after marked by instructor, 97–100
   checklist for, 390–92
   during writing process, 393–400, 449
   record of, 101
   use of word processor, **8:** 101–03
rhetoric, 572
rhythm, 523
rise. See *raise, rise.*
root and prefix, in spelling, **18c:** 184
round numbers, **11:** 123
run-together sentences, **3:** 34–41

S

-s (or *-es*)
   and subject-verb agreement, 62
   for plural of nouns, **18d:** 187
salutation, business letter, 539
satellites, names of, **10c:** 114
says. See *go, goes.*
scarcely, **4e:** 49
schwa, in spelling, 181
seldom ever. See *hardly ever.*

self-, hyphen with, **18f:** 197
semicolon
   and emphasis, **29a:** 292
   between items in series, **14b:** 148–49
   between main clauses, **14a:** 146–48
   misuse of, **14c:** 149–50
   with *and, but,* etc., 128–47
   with quotation marks, **16e:** 163
   with *therefore,* etc., **3b:** 38–39; **14a:** 146
sensory details, 346
sensuous, sensual, 224
sentence fragment, **2:** 28–33. See also
        fragment.
sentence modifier, 572
sentence outline, 379–81
sentences, 24–26, 572. See also
        coordination; subordination.
   balanced, **29g:** 298
   choppy, **24a:** 262–64
   combining, **21b:** 243–45; **24a:** 262–63
   effective, **23–30:** 254–309
   expanded, 17
   fragmentary, **2:** 28–33
   fused or run-on, **3:** 34–41
   grammar of, **1:** 2–27
   loose, **29b:** 292–93
   parallel, **26a:** 276
   periodic, **29b:** 292–93
   recognition of types of, 24–26
   stringy, **30c:** 306–07
   topic, **32a:** 325–37
   unity in, **23:** 254–61
   variety in, **30:** 300–09
sequence of tenses, **7b:** 82–84
series
   colon before, **17d:** 169
   commas with, **12c:** 132–33
   dash after, **17e:** 172
   enumeration of items in, **17f:** 172
   figures in, **11:** 123
   parallel elements in, 274
   question mark with, **17b:** 167
   semicolon with, **14b:** 148–49
set, sit, **7a:** 81, 224
setting, 513–14
sexist language, 68–69, 572. See also
        inclusive language.
shall and *will,* 86–87

Index

shifts
  in discourse, **27c:** 282
  in number or person, **27b:** 281
  in perspective or viewpoint, **27e:** 283
  in tense or mood, **7d:** 88–89; **27a:** 280–81
  in tone or style, **27d:** 282–83
  in voice, **27a:** 280–81
ships, names of, **10c:** 114
should, would, **7c:** 86–87
sic, **17g:** 174
signature, business letter, 540
simile, 233–34, 522, 572
simple predicate, 2–3
simple sentence, 25
simple subject, 2
simple tenses, 572
single quotation marks, **16a:** 157–58
sit, set, **7a:** 81
slang, **19c:** 206–07, 572
slanted evidence, 313
slash, uses of, **17h:** 174
so
  as transitional word, **32b:** 337
  between main clauses, **12a:** 127
  versus *so that,* 224
  without completing clause, **22d:** 252
some, verb agreement with, **6a:** 65, 224
someone, some one. See *anyone, any one.*
somewheres, 225
sonnet, 73, 529
sort, sort of a. See *kind, kind of a.*
sound, **19b:** 211, 522
sources for research paper
  acknowledgment of, 423–28
  evaluation of, 418
  taking notes on, 420–22
spatial (space) order, 330, 572
spacecraft, names of, **10c:** 114
spacing
  for legibility, **8c:** 95
  in "References," 485
  in "Works Cited," 437
  of indented quotations, **6a:** 159–60
  on page, **8b:** 93–94
specialized audience, 362–63
specific words, **20a:** 230–32
spelling
  adding suffixes, **18d:** 185–88

and computer software, 180
British and American, 180–81
changing *y* to *i,* **18d:** 186
dictionary as authority for, 180–81
doubling final consonant, **18d:** 186
dropping final *e,* **18d:** 185
ei and *ie,* **18e:** 188–89
homonyms, 561
lists, 181–82, 189–94
mispronunciation and, **18a:** 181
of verb forms, **7a:** 80
of words confused, **18b:** 182–84
plurals, **18d:** 187
prefix and root, **18c:** 184
retaining final *l,* **18d:** 187
split infinitive, **25a:** 271
squinting modifier, **25a:** 271
static perspective, **33c:** 370
stationary, stationery, 225
statistics, figures for, **11:** 123
still, **3b:** 39; **32b:** 337
structure words, 11
style, 573
style books, list of, 504–05
style of documentation
  APA, 483–87
  endnote or footnote, 480–82
  list of style books, 504–05
  MLA, 429–47
subject, grammatical, 573
  agreement of verb with, **6a:** 62–67
  and predicate, 3–4
  case of, **5:** 52–53
  complete, 2
  compound, **6a:** 63
  double, **21a:** 241
  of infinitive, case of, **5e:** 59
  of verb, recognition of, 3–4
  simple, 2
  unstated or understood, 5
subject complement, 573
  adjective as, 13–14, **4b:** 44–45
  case of, **5:** 52–53; **5f:** 59–60
subject of composition
  exploring and focusing, **33c:** 367–73
  finding an appropriate, **33b:** 366–67
subjective case, 554
  after *than* or *as,* **5b:** 55–56
  for appositive, 54

for subject complement, 52–53, **5f:** 59–60
for subject of verb, 51
in compound constructions, **5a:** 53–54
who, in clause, **5b:** 55
subjunctive mood, **7c:** 86–88
after *demand, move,* etc., 86–87
alternatives for, 86
in *if* or *as if* clauses, 87
should, would, 87
to express wish or condition, 87
verb forms in, 86
would have for *had,* 87
subordinate clauses, 573
and subordination, **24a:** 262–64
as modifiers, 23–24
as nouns, 22–23
list of markers of, 22
misused as sentence, **2b:** 31–32
recognition of, 21–22
subordinating conjunctions, 22, 573
subordination, 573
and coordination, **24:** 261–68
faulty or excessive, **24c:** 266–67
in combined sentences, **24a:** 262–64
to avoid stringy main clauses, **24b:** 264–66
subordinators, 22, 573
"Subplot as Commentary in *King Lear,* The," 531–35
subsequently, 225
subtitle of book
colon before, **17d:** 168
in "Works Cited," 438
such, 225
such as, punctuation with, **17d:** 170
such, such . . . that, **22d:** 252
suffixes, 573. See also *inflection.*
adding, in spelling, **18d:** 185–88
adjective-forming, 14, 42–43
adverb-forming, 42–43
-d or *-ed,* 72–74, 78
-ics, agreement and, 66–67
noun forming, 12–13
-s, -es, 62, **18d:** 187
verb forming, 12
summary, 428
superfluous commas
between subject and verb, **13a:** 142

between verb and object, **13a:** 142
for nonparenthetical words, **13c:** 142
with coordinating conjunction, **13b:** 142
with items in a series, **13c:** 143
with restrictive elements, **13d:** 143
superlative degree, **4c:** 148–50. See also *comparison.*
suppose to, supposed to, 225
sure, surely, **4a:** 43, 225
syllabication
and word division, **8d:** 95–97
as shown in dictionary, 200
syllogism, **31b:** 314–15, 573
symbolism, 516
synonyms
awkward use of, **21d:** 246
in definition, **23e:** 258–60
in dictionary, thesaurus, 199, 200–02
synopsis of verb forms, 74–76
syntax, defined, 573

T

table of contents, for report, 549
tag question, 37
taking notes. See *note-taking.*
tautology, **21a:** 241
technical words, **19g:** 210–11
television programs
episodes of, **16b:** 161
in "Works Cited," 445
italics for titles of, **10a:** 112–13
tense, defined, 574
tense forms, 82–84, 574
and time, 74–76
classification, 74
in sequence, **7b:** 82–84
indicated in conjugation, 74–76
meaning of, **7b:** 82
shifts in, **27a:** 278–79; **7d:** 88
synopsis of, 74
term paper. See *research paper.*
tests, essay, 400–04
than
case of pronoun after, **5b:** 55–56
parallel elements with, 274
that, in restrictive clause, 135
that is, **32b:** 337
their, there, they're, 225

Index

theirself, theirselves, 225
them, 225
theme. See *composition.*
"Themes in *Frankenstein,*" 517–20
then, 225
  as conjunctive adverb, 16, 39
  as transitional word, **3b:** 39; **32b:** 337
there + verb + subject, **6a:** 64
therefore, **3b:** 39; **32b:** 337
thesaurus, use of, 202
these kind . . . those sort. See *kind, sort.*
thesis, **33d:** 373–77, 510, 574
this here . . . them there, 225
thus, **3b:** 39; **32b:** 337
thusly, 225
time, related to tense, 73–74, 82–83
time order, 329. See *chronological order.*
title of composition
  development of, **33f:** 388
  manuscript form for, **8b:** 92
  reference of pronoun to, **28b:** 286–87
title page, sample, 489
titles of books, articles
  capitalization of, **9c:** 108, 485
  in APA "References," 485–87
  in citations, 429, 432
  in MLA "Works Cited," 438–45
  italics for, **10a:** 112–13
  quotation marks for, **16b:** 161–62
  verb-agreement with, **6a:** 66–67
titles of person
  abbreviations of, **11a:** 117–18
  capitalization of, 107–08
  in business writing, **35b:** 540
  redundant use of, **11a:** 118
tone, 515, 574
  and audience, **33a:** 366
  shift in, **27d:** 282–83
to, too, 225
too, and completing phrase, **22d:** 252
topic outline, **33e:** 379–80
topic sentence, **32a:** 325–27, 574
Toulmin method, 315–17
trademarks, **9a:** 105; **10c:** 114
trains, names of, 114
transitional devices, use of, **32b:** 335–41
  conjunctions, 336–37
  parallel structure, 337–38

  pronouns, 335–36
  related words, 336
  repetition of key ideas, 336
  transitional expressions, 336–37
transitional expressions
  as aid to coherence, 335–41
  between main clauses, **3b:** 39; **14a:** 146–47
  for variety, **30b:** 303–04
  introductory, **12b:** 131
  lists of, 39, 336–37
  position of, 39
transitional paragraph, 339–40
transitions, 574
transitive verb, 76
translation, in "Works Cited," 441
triteness, **20c:** 236–37
try and, 226
"Tulips, The," 525–28
typed papers, form of, **8a:** 93
typing, legibility of, **8c:** 95

U

underlining. See *italics.*
understatement, 574
uninterested. See *disinterested, uninterested.*
unique, **4c:** 47
unity, 574
  in compositions, 374–75
  in paragraphs, **32a:** 324–29
  in sentences, **23:** 254–60
us/we students, **5a:** 54
usage. See also *words, choice of.*
  examples of, in dictionary, 199
  glossary of, **19i:** 212–26
  labels in dictionary, 207
  related to spelling, 180–81
used to could, 226
use to, used to, 226

V

validity, 318, 574
variety, sentence, **30:** 300–09
  in beginnings, **30b:** 303–05
  in length, **30a:** 301–02

in sentence types, **30c**: 306–07
in subject-verb sequence, **30d**: 307–08
use of a question, etc., **30c**: 308–09
verb phrase, recognition of, 3–4
verbals, 18, 575. See also *gerund;*
infinitive; participle.
dangling, **25b**: 272–73
for variety, **30b**: 303; **30c**: 306–07
in sentence fragments, **2a**: 30–31
parallel in form, 274–75
verb-forming suffixes, 12
verbs, 3–5, 574–75
active and passive, 7, 76–77
agreement with subject, **6a**: 62–67
auxiliary or helping, 4
conjugation of, sample, 74–76
intransitive and transitive, 76–77
irregular, 72–73
linking, 14, **4b**: 45
mood of, 76
phrasal, 4–5
principal parts of, **7a**: 77–82
progressive, 74, 83
recognition of, 3–5, 12–13
regular, 72
tenses of, 74–76, **7b**: 82–89
very, 226
viewpoint, shift in, **27e**: 283
vocabulary, 202–06
vocabulary (lexical) words, 12, 575
voice, in poetry, 521
voice of verbs, 575
and emphasis, **29d**: 295
shift in, **27a**: 280–81

W

ways, 226
we/us students, 54
what clause as subject, **6a**: 66
whenever, 226
where, 226
where . . . at, where . . . to, 226
whether . . . or, parallelism with, **26c**:
278
which, in restrictive clause, 135, 226
-wise, 226
who or *whom,* **5b**: 55

whose, for *of which,* **5**: 52
whose, who's, **15d**: 155
will and *shall,* 86–87
with regards to, 226
word classes, 11–12
word division, **8d**: 95–97
word order, 575
word processor
and legibility of printer, **8c**: 95
and spelling, 180
as revision tool, 101–03
wordiness
meaningless words as, **21a**: 241–42
revising to avoid, **21b**: 243–45
tautology, **21a**: 241
words, choice of
abstract and general, **20a**: 231–33
archaic and obsolete, **19f**: 210
clichés, **20c**: 236–37
concrete and specific, **20a**: 231–33
confused, list of, **18b**: 183–84
connotations, **20a**: 228–29
denotations, **20a**: 228–29
euphemisms, **20c**: 236–37
exact, **20**: 227–39
figurative language, **20a**: 233–35
formal usage, **19b**: 207–08, 210
Glossary of Usage, **19i**: 212–26
idiomatic, **20b**: 235–36
informal or colloquial, **19b**: 207–08
jargon, **19g**: 210–11
nonstandard, **19e**: 210
ornate or flowery, **19h**: 211
regional or dialectal, **19d**: 209–10
slang, **19c**: 208–09
technical, **19g**: 210–11
transitional, **32b**: 337
trite or worn-out, **20c**: 236–37
words referred to as words
agreement of verb with, **6a**: 66
italics for, **10d**: 114
plural forms of, **15c**: 155
working bibliography, 418–19
working plan, **33c**: 377–78
"Works Cited" (MLA), **34f**: 436–47,
477, 479
would of, 226
writing process, 576. See *composition.*

Index

Y

yes
    in indirect discourse, quotation marks
        with, 162
    introductory, **12b:** 131
yet
    as transitional word, **32b:** 337
    between main clauses, **12a:** 127

you, awkward use of, **28d:** 288–89
your, you're, 226
you was, 226

Z

zip code, 166

1
2
E 3
F 4
G 5
H 6
I 7
J 8

LISTS FREQUENTLY CONSULTED	OTHER CORRECTION SYMBOLS

Abbreviations

Permissible in ordinary writing, 120

Postal, 118–19

Used in bibliographies, etc., 447–49

Auxiliaries, 4

Case forms of pronouns, 52

Comparative and superlative forms, 46

Conjunctions and other transitional expressions, 22, 39, 339

Coordinating and correlative conjunctions, 16

Editing Checklist, 392–93

Grammatical and Rhetorical Terms, 551–76

Idiomatic phrases, 235

Linking verbs, 14

Personal pronouns, 51–52

Prepositions, 14–15

Relative pronouns, 22, 52

Reviser's Checklist, 390–92

Style sheet for capitalization, 110

Subordinating conjunctions, 22

Transitional phrases, 39

Trite expressions, 236

Usage Glossary, 212–26

Verb forms

Conjugation of *see*, 74–76

Principal parts, 78–80

Words frequently confused, 183–84

Words frequently misspelled, 189–94